Regulating Corporate Human Rights Violations

Despite the continuous addition of regulatory initiatives concerning corporate human rights responsibilities, what we witness more often than not is a situation of corporate impunity for human rights abuses. The Bhopal gas leak – examined as a site of human rights violations rather than as a mass tort or an environmental tragedy – illustrates that the regulatory challenges that the victims experienced in 1984 have not yet been overcome. This book grapples with and offers solutions to three major regulatory challenges to obligating companies to comply with human rights norms whilst doing business: *why* companies should adhere to human rights, *what* these responsibilities are, and *how* to ensure that companies comply with their responsibilities.

Building on literature in the fields of law, human rights, business ethics, management, regulation and philosophy, this book proposes a new 'integrated theory of regulation' to overcome inadequacies of the existing regulatory framework in order to humanize business.

This book will be of interest to scholars, students, researchers, policy makers and human rights activists working in the fields of law, business and human rights.

Surya Deva is Associate Professor at the School of Law of City University of Hong Kong. His primary research interests lie in corporate social responsibility, Indo-Chinese constitutional law, international human rights, globalization, and sustainable development.

Routledge Research in Human Rights Law

Available titles in this series include:

The Right to Development in International Law
The Case of Pakistan
Khurshid Iqbal

Global Health and Human Rights
Legal and Philosophical Perspectives
John Harrington and Maria Stuttaford

The Right to Religious Freedom in International Law
Between group rights and individual rights
Anat Scolnicov

Emerging Areas of Human Rights in the 21st Century
The role of the Universal Declaration of Human Rights
Marco Odello and Sofia Cavandoli

The Human Right to Water and its Application in the Occupied Palestinian Territories
Amanda Cahill

International Human Rights Law and Domestic Violence
The Effectiveness of International Human Rights Law
Ronagh McQuigg

Human Rights in the Asia-Pacific Region
Towards Institution Building
Hitoshi Nasu and Ben Saul

Human Rights Monitoring Mechanisms of the Council of Europe
Gauthier de Beco

The Positive Obligations of the State under the European Convention of Human Rights
Dimitris Xenos

Vindicating Socio-Economic Rights
International Standards and Comparative Experiences
Paul O'Connell

The EU as a 'Global Player' in Human Rights?
Jan Wetzel

Regulating Corporate Human Rights Violations
Humanizing Business
Surya Deva

Forthcoming titles in this series include:

The European Court of Human Rights in the Post-Cold War Era
Universality in Transition
James A. Sweeney

Children and International Human Rights Law
The Right of the Child to be Heard
Aisling Parkes

Ensuring and Enforcing Economic, Social and Cultural Rights
The Jurisprudence of the UN Committee on Economic, Social and Cultural Rights
Marco Odello and Francesco Seatzu

Jurisdiction, Immunity and Transnational Human Rights Litigation
Xiaodong Yang

Regulating Corporate Human Rights Violations
Humanizing Business

Surya Deva

LONDON AND NEW YORK

First published 2012
by Routledge
2 Park Square, Milton Park, Abingdon, Oxon, OX14 4RN

Simultaneously published in the USA and Canada
by Routledge
711 Third Avenue, New York, NY 10017

Routledge is an imprint of the Taylor & Francis Group, an informa business

© 2012 Surya Deva

The right of Surya Deva to be identified as author of this work has been asserted by him in accordance with sections 77 and 78 of the Copyright, Designs and Patents Act 1988.

All rights reserved. No part of this book may be reprinted or reproduced or utilized in any form or by any electronic, mechanical, or other means, now known or hereafter invented, including photocopying and recording, or in any information storage or retrieval system, without permission in writing from the publishers.

Trademark notice: Product or corporate names may be trademarks or registered trademarks, and are used only for identification and explanation without intent to infringe.

British Library Cataloguing in Publication Data
A catalogue record for this book is available from the British Library

Library of Congress Cataloging in Publication Data
Deva, Surya.
Regulating corporate human rights violations : humanizing business/ Surya Deva.
   p. cm.—(Routledge research in human rights law)
   ISBN 978-0-415-66821-7 (hardback)—ISBN 978-0-203-12561-8 (e-book) 1. Corporate governance—Law and legislation.   2. Human rights.   3. Corporations—Corrupt practices.   I. Title.
K1327.D48 2012
345'.0268—dc23
                                                                2011036412

ISBN 978–0–415–66821–7 (hbk)
ISBN 978–0–203–12561–8 (ebk)

Typeset in Garamond
by RefineCatch Limited, Bungay, Suffolk

Printed and bound in Great Britain by
CPI Antony Rowe, Chippenham, Wiltshire

*To my parents
for nurturing the value of
being human*

Contents

	Table of cases	x
	Table of statutes	xiii
	List of illustrations	xv
	List of abbreviations	xvi
	Preface	xix
1	Introduction	1
2	Understanding 'Bhopal' afresh	24
3	Evaluation of existing regulatory initiatives – An analytical framework	46
4	Existing regulatory initiatives – An evaluation of (in)adequacy	64
5	Just profit or *just* profit – Why should corporations have human rights obligations?	119
6	How to behave in 'Rome'? Determining standards applicable to MNCs	152
7	The integrated theory of regulation – A critical response to 'responsive regulation'	176
8	Vision of an integrated framework of corporate regulation	200
9	Conclusion	232
	Bibliography	241
	Index	265

Table of cases

Abdullahi v. Pfizer 2002 US Dist. LEXIS 17436 66
Adams v. Cape Industries plc. [1991] 1 All ER 929 50
Abrams v. Societe Nationale Des Chemins de fer Français 175 F.
  Supp. 2d 423 (2001) 66
Aguinda v. Texaco, Inc. 945 F. Supp. 625 (SDNY, 1996) 66, 69
Aguinda v. Texaco, Inc. 303 F. 3d 470 (2002)...........................70

Bano Bi v. Union Carbide Corporation 1992 US Dist. LEXIS 1909 42
Bano Bi v. Union Carbide Corporation 984 F. 2d 582 (1993) 42
BCE Inc. v. 1976 Debentureholders [2008] 3 SCR 560 197
Beanal v. Freeport-McMoRan, Inc. 969 F. Supp. 362 (ED La., 1997) 71
Beanal v. Freeport-McMoran, Inc. 197 F. 3d 161 (5th Cir., 1999)............67
Bodner v. Banque Paribas 114 F. Supp. 2d 117 (2000) 66

Cambridge Water Co. v. Eastern Counties Leather [1994] 2 AC 264 35
Charan Lal Sahu v. Union of India AIR 1990 SC 1480 38

Dann v. Hamilton [1939] 1 KB 509.....................................174
Doe v. Exxon Mobil Corporation WL 2652384 (DC Cir., 2011)...........69, 74
Doe v. Unocal 963 F. Supp. 880 (CD Cal., 1997) 67, 69
Doe v. Unocal 110 F. Supp. 2d 1294 (CD Cal., 2000).....................71
Doe v. Unocal 248 F. 3d 915 (9th Cir., 2001).........................50, 68
Doe v. Unocal 2002 US App. LEXIS 19263 69
Donoghue v. Stevenson [1932] AC 562 ....34, 147

Estate of Himoud Saed Atban et al. v. Blackwater 611 F. Supp.
  2d 1 (DDC 2009) 67
Esther Kiobel v. Royal Dutch Petroleum Co. 621 F. 3d 111
  (2010)...6, 72, 73
Esther Kiobel v. Royal Dutch Petroleum Co. 2011 WL 338048...............74

Flores v. Southern Peru Copper 253 F. Supp. 2d 510 (SDNY, 2002) 66
Forti v. Suarez-Mason 672 F. Supp. 1531 (ND Cal., 1987) 71

Gabriel Ashanga Jota v. Texaco, Inc. 303 F. 3d 470 (2001)..................70
Guerra v. Italy (1998) 26 EHRR 357......................................149
Gulf Oil Corp. v. Gilbert 330 US 501 (1947)................................39

Hanoch Tel-Oren v. Libyan Arab Republic 726 F. 2d 774 (1984).............66
Haider Muhsin Saleh v. Titan Corp. 436 F. Supp. 2d 55
  (DDC 2006)...67
Hilao v. Estate of Marcos 25 F. 3d 1467 (9th Cir., 1994)..................71
Holocaust Victims of Bank Theft v. Magyar Nemzeti Bank
  2011 WL 1900340..74

Indian Council for Enviro-Legal Action v. Union of India (1996)
  3 SCC 212..32, 136
In re Holocaust Victim Assets Litigation 105 F. Supp. 2d 139
  (EDNY, 2000)...66
In re South African Apartheid Litigation 2004 US Dist.
  LEXIS 23944..66
In re Union Carbide Corporation Gas Plant Disaster at Bhopal,
  India in December 1984 634 F. Supp. 842 (1986).....................28, 39
In re Union Carbide Corporation Gas Plant Disaster at Bhopal,
  India in December 1984 809 F. 2d 195 (1987)............................39
In re Xe Services Alien Tort Litigation 665 F. Supp. 2d 569 (2009).....67, 70

Janki Bai Sahu v. UCC 418 F. Supp. 2d 407 (2005)......................43, 67
Janki Bai Sahu v. UCC 2006 US Dist. LEXIS 714.............................43
Janki Bai Sahu v. UCC 2006 US Dist. LEXIS 944.............................43
Janki Bai Sahu v. UCC 2006 US Dist. LEXIS 84475...........................43
Janki Bai Sahu v. UCC 548 F. 3d 59 (2d Cir., 2008)........................43
Janki Bai Sahu v. UCC 262 F.R.D. 308 (SDNY, 2009).........................43
Janki Bai Sahu v. UCC 746 F. Supp. 2d 609 (2010)..........................43
Janki Bai Sahu v. UCC 2010 WL 532307 (SDNY, 2010).........................43
Jose Francisco Sosa v. Humberto Alvarez-Machain 124 S. Ct. 2739
  (2004)...67, 71, 72
Jota/Ecuador v. Texaco 157 F. 3d 153 (1998)...............................70

Kadic v. Karadzic 70 F. 3d 232 (2d Cir., 1995)............................69
Kasky v. Nike, Inc. 79 Cal. App. 4th 165 (2000).......................60, 207
Kasky v. Nike, Inc. 27 Cal. 4th 939 (2002)............................60, 207
Keshub Mahindra v. State of Madhya Pradesh (1996) 6 SCC 129...............43
Khulumani v. Barclay National Bank Ltd 504 F. 3d 254 (2007)...............66

M. C. Mehta v. Union of India AIR 1987 SC 1086..................32, 35, 226

Nike, Inc. v. Kasky 539 US 654 (2003).................................60, 207

Owusu v. Jackson [2005] 2 WLR 942..117

Peoples Department Stores Inc. (Trustee of) v. Wise [2004] 3 SCR 461 197
Piper Aircraft Co. v. Reyno 454 US 235 (1981) 39
Presbyterian Church of Sudan v. Talisman Energy 244 F. Supp. 2d
 289 (SDNY, 2003). 66
Presbyterian Church of Sudan v. Talisman Energy 582 F. 3d 244 (2009). 69

Reparation of Injuries Suffered in the Services of the UN (1949)
 ICJ Rep. 174. 17
Rickards v. Lothian [1913] AC 263 35
Romero v. Drummond Co. 552 F.3d 1303 (11th Cir., 2008). 67, 74
Rylands v. Fletcher (1866) LR 1 Exch. 265. 35

Sajida Bano v. Union Carbide Corporation 2000 US Dist.
 LEXIS 12326. . . . . .43, 67
Sajida Bano v. Union Carbide Corporation 273 F. 3d 120 (2d Cir.
 NY, 2001) 43
Sajida Bano v. Union Carbide Corporation 2003 US Dist.
 LEXIS 4097. 43
Sajida Bano v. Union Carbide Corporation 361 F. 3d 696 (2d
 Cir. NY, 2004). 43
Sajida Bano v. Union Carbide Corporation 2005 US Dist. LEXIS
 32595 43
Sajida Bano v. Union Carbide Corporation 2005 US Dist. LEXIS
 22871 43
Sajida Bano v. Union Carbide Corporation 2006 US App. LEXIS
 21022 43
Sinaltrainal v. Coca-Cola 578 F. 3d 1252 (11th Cir., 2009). 74

Union Carbide Corporation v. Union of India (1989) 3 SCC 38 41
Union Carbide Corporation v. Union of India AIR 1990 SC 273 . . . . . . .40, 41, 43
Union Carbide Corporation v. Union of India AIR 1992 SC 248 . . . . .41, 43
United States v. Carroll Towing Co. 159 F. 2d 169 (2d Cir., 1947). 35

Visakha v. State of Rajasthan AIR 1997 SC 3011 149

Wal-Mart Stores Inc. v. Betty Dukes 131 S. Ct. 2541 (2011) 76
Wang Xiaoning v. Yahoo! 2007 US Dist. LEXIS 97566 (ND Cal.). 67
Wiwa v. Royal Dutch Petroleum Co. 1998 US Dist. LEXIS 23064. . . . . .66, 69–70
Wiwa v. Royal Dutch Petroleum Co. 226 F. 3d 88 (2000) 68, 70
Wooldridge v. Sumner [1963] 2 QB 43 174

Table of statutes

AUSTRALIA

Corporate Code of Conduct Bill 2000. . . . . .51, 58, 62, 65
Corporations Act 2001 . . . . .196, 197, 212

INDIA

Air (Prevention and Control of Pollution) Act 1981 . . . . .32, 168
Bhopal Gas Leak Disaster (Processing of Claims) Act 1985. . . . . .37, 38
Companies Bill 2009 . . . . .197, 212
Constitution of India 1950. . . . . .32, 150
Environment (Protection) Act 1986 . . . . .32, 168
Factories Act 1948 . . . . .32, 168
Foreign Exchange Management Act 1999. 27
Foreign Exchange Regulation Act 1973 27
Indian Penal Code 1860 . . . . .43, 44
Industrial Development and Regulation Act 1951 27
Insecticides Act 1968. 168
Maternity Benefit Act 1961 32
Minimum Wages Act 1948 32
Public Liability Insurance Act 1991 32
Trade Unions Act 1926 32

INDONESIA

Limited Liability Companies Law 2007 . . . . .197, 212

SOUTH AFRICA

Companies Act 2008 . . . . .197, 212
Constitution of the Republic of South Africa 1996. 149

UNITED KINGDOM

Companies Act 2006 . . . . .96, 212
Corporate Responsibility Bill 2003 . . . . .51, 58, 62, 65

UNITED STATES

Alien Tort Claims Act 1789 . . . . .6, 12, 37, 42, 49, 51, 56, 60–62, 64–7, 115, 234
Civil Rights Act 1964 76
Corporate Code of Conduct Bill 2000. . . . . .51, 58, 62, 65
Torture Victim Protection Act 1991. . . . . .68, 70, 74

List of illustrations

Tables

2.1	Victims' quest for justice and the five phases of litigation	37
3.1	The basis and the objective for classifying existing regulatory regimes	52
4.1	Tabular taxonomy of existing regulatory initiatives	65
8.1	Integrated employment of implementation strategies and sanctions at three regulatory levels	221

Figure

7.1	Example of an enforcement pyramid of sanctions	178

List of abbreviations

AC	Appeal Cases
AIR	All India Reports
All ER	All England Reports
ATCA	Alien Tort Claims Act
BBC	British Broadcasting Corporation
BHP	Broken Hill Proprietary
BLIHR	Business Leaders Initiative on Human Rights
CBI	Central Bureau of Investigation
CD Cal.	Central District of California
CEO	Chief executive officer
COP	Communication on Progress
CSR	Corporate Social Responsibility
Cir.	Circuit
Cong.	Congress
EDNY	Eastern District of New York
ED La.	Eastern District of Louisiana
ED Pa.	Eastern District of Pennsylvania
EHRR	European Human Rights Reports
EU	European Union
Exch.	Exchequer
F. Supp.	Federal Supplement
GA Res.	General Assembly Resolution
HL	House of Lords
HRW	Human Rights Watch
ICC	International Criminal Court
ICC	International Chamber of Commerce
ICCPR	International Covenant on Civil and Political Rights
ICESCR	International Covenant on Economic, Social and Cultural Rights
ICHRP	International Council on Human Rights Policy
ILM	International Legal Materials
ILO	International Labour Organization
IMF	International Monetary Fund

IOE	International Organisation of Employers
IPC	Indian Penal Code
ISO	International Organization for Standardization
KB	King's Bench
LR	Law Reports
MIC	Methyl Isocyanate
MNCs	Multinational Corporations
MNEs	Multinational Enterprises
NCPs	National Contact Points
ND Cal.	Northern District of California
NGOs	Non-Governmental Organizations
OECD	Organization for Economic Cooperation and Development
PDE	Principle of Double Effect
PIG	Public Interest Groups
plc.	Public Limited Company
Pub L	Public Law
Pvt.	Private
QB	Queen's Bench
Rs	Rupees
SA	Social Accountability
SC	Supreme Court
SCC	Supreme Court Cases
SCR	Supreme Court Reports
SDNY	Southern District of New York
SLP	Special leave petition
SNEs	Supranational entities
SRSG	United Nations Secretary-General's Special Representative on human rights and transnational corporations and other business enterprises
S. Ct.	Supreme Court Reporter
Sess.	Session
Suppl.	Supplement
TFT	Tit-for-Tat
TNCs	Transnational Corporations
TVPA	Torture Victim Protection Act
UCC	Union Carbide Corporation
UCIL	Union Carbide India Limited
UDHR	Universal Declaration of Human Rights
UN	United Nations
UNCITRAL	United Nations Commission on International Trade Law
UNCTAD	United Nations Conference on Trade and Development
UN Doc.	United Nations Document
UNDP	United Nations Development Programme
UN ESCOR	United Nations Economic and Social Council Official Records

USC	United States Code
USD	US Dollars
US App.	United States Appeals Court
US Dist.	United States District Court
WTO	World Trade Organization
WWH	Why, What and How

Preface

The roots of this book go back to the year 2000, when I joined the National Law Institute University in Bhopal. Living in Bhopal and teaching the law of torts meant that I could not have escaped from noticing the negative facet of business in the form of 'Bhopal' as a global symbol of corporate impunity for human rights abuses. Two issues struck me most: that it was not the government but a company that was *directly* responsible for human rights violations and that the involvement of a foreign multinational company undermined the capacity or political will of the Indian government to bring to justice both natural and legal persons responsible for Bhopal. That was good enough to trigger my research interest towards the intersection of business and human rights. I ended up at the Sydney Law School to do a PhD in this area and this book is based on my doctoral thesis submitted in 2007.

Lawyers are not often accredited with inventions. But the corporation is arguably one of those inventions that has changed the face of humanity. At this point of time, it is almost impossible to imagine life without companies. This book is a good example. I could not have published this book without the assistance of companies at every step – from typing the manuscript on a computer to 'googling' the web for updated information, flying around the world to test my ideas at conferences, and drinking gallons of water supplied by companies to keep me going. Companies are behind almost everything we do. But who are behind the companies? More than anything else, I think companies consist of people and companies depend on people as much as people depend on them. This *mutual dependency* means that companies should not do anything to harm the interests of a diverse range of people – from corporate executives to shareholders, employees, consumers, people working in supply chains, and the unborn future generations. Human rights reflect a common language to denote the interests of all these people. Therefore, rather than profiting from human rights abuses, human rights should run into the veins of business alongside the desire to maximize profit.

This book is a humble attempt to grapple with the challenges in accomplishing the goal of humanizing business. I deal with three such challenges here: *why* companies should have human rights, *what* these responsibilities are, and *how* to ensure that companies comply with their responsibilities. Although corporations may be 'specialized institutions' of society, this is no argument to deny their human rights obligations, otherwise other specialized institutions (e.g. 'family', 'church' and 'university') can operate with a license to infringe the human rights of people within their respective spheres. The scope and nature of corporate human rights responsibilities should not be identical to that of states, but, at the same time, it should be commensurate with their current power and functions. Companies should not be allowed to trample on human rights by exploiting regulatory loopholes or states' incapacity or unwillingness to promote human rights. It is critical that regulatory initiatives at various levels employ a range of incentives and disincentives to encourage companies to internalize human rights norms within their business operations.

Many people have helped me in diverse ways in accomplishing this project. To begin with, my two PhD supervisors, Fleur Johns and Rosemary Lyster, offered critical insights and all the support that any researcher could ask for. I am grateful to Fleur and Rosemary in assisting me to lay a solid foundation for this book. Over the years, I have benefited from discussions with numerous people as well as participants at different conferences where I presented papers on diverse aspects of humanizing business. In particular, I would like to thank David Bilchitz, Danwood Chirwa, Mark Kilesgard, David Kinley, Carlos Lopez, Radu Mares, Justine Nolan, Gabriela Quijano, Anita Ramasastry, Paul Redmond, Beate Sjåfjell, M. P. Singh, Parmanand Singh, Shelly Wright and Yogesh Tyagi. I should also express my gratitude to the examiners of my doctoral thesis and the anonymous reviewers, whose comments benefited me in revising the manuscript. The students who took my elective course on Corporate Social Responsibility at the School of Law of City University of Hong Kong participated in stimulating discussions and allowed me to test ideas. I am thankful to all those students.

Some of the ideas developed in this book have been canvassed before and published in various journals. I would like to thank the following journals for granting me permission to use in this book some materials from articles published previously: *George Washington International Law Review, Syracuse Journal of International Law and Commerce, Georgetown International Environmental Law Review, Buffalo Human Rights Law Review, Newcastle Law Review, Melbourne Journal of International Law*, and *Connecticut Journal of International Law*.

I am also grateful to the City University Law School for granting me sabbatical leave to revise the manuscript and to my research assistants, Prabhjyot Kaur, Calvin Ho and Keith Tam, for helping me in a range of editorial tasks promptly and efficiently. I would like to thank the entire editorial and production team at Routledge, especially Katie Carpenter, Stephen Gutierrez, Holly Davis and Paula Devine, who made this book possible. It was Katie's email that forced me to find time to substantially revise and update the doctoral thesis. Thank you very much Katie for being a trigger for this book.

My entire family has been a constant source of encouragement, motivation and inspiration. Each one of them deserves special gratitude for believing in, and being with, me in this journey unfolding outside India. In particular, I would like to express special thanks to my parents, my guru and mentor Professor M. P. Singh, M. S. Arya and my two sisters – I could not have done this without your support! Finally, I would like to thank my wife Swati, who found time to read all the chapters and gave some useful suggestions. More importantly, she – along with our two sons, Vyom and Varun – provided me an environment to work on this book without having to worry too much about anything but the business of corporations. I am indebted to Swati, Vyom and Varun and I hope that they will excuse me for spending more time on corporations than with them.

1 Introduction

This book is about humanizing business by effectively regulating the human rights violative activities of corporations. 'Humanizing' is used here in the sense of injecting business with human rights. Humanizing business implies that companies/corporations – the two terms that I will use interchangeably to represent business – ought to comply with their human rights responsibilities while conducting business. This claim raises three sets of fundamental questions, the answers to which are far from settled. First of all, *why* should companies have such a responsibility? Is it not the responsibility of companies to focus merely on creating wealth and maximizing shareholders' profits? Are states not the primary custodians of peoples' rights? If so, what useful purpose will be served by placing independent human rights responsibilities on companies? Are companies suited to carry out these responsibilities? Will this not result in states abdicating or transferring their human rights responsibilities to companies?

Second, *what* is the exact nature and scope of corporate human rights responsibilities? Are the human rights responsibilities of companies similar to, and as extensive as, those of states? What standards of human rights should apply to companies that operate at a transnational level in vastly diverse political, social, economic and cultural environments? Moreover, do companies violate human rights when they merely benefit from the violations of others, provide support to violators, or remain silent about violations as a business strategy? What about those situations where violations are carried out by their subsidiaries, business partners or suppliers?

Third, *how* can companies, especially multinational corporations (MNCs), be made accountable for human rights violations? Companies differ from states in several distinct ways. Do these differences pose unique obstacles in enforcing human rights norms against companies? How can those obstacles be overcome? Would this require fundamental changes in the current regulatory paradigms?

These three sets of questions represent the three broad challenges to the goal of humanizing business: *why, what* and *how* (the WWH challenges). This book is an attempt to grapple with these three challenges in an 'integrated' manner. The existing scholarship as well as regulatory initiatives in this area have not paid adequate attention to the interrelationship between the WWH challenges identified here. This, in my view, partly explains why we still do not have an effective regulatory regime in place to hold companies accountable for human rights violations.

As a remedial response, this book canvasses an 'integrated theory of regulation' that should help in overcoming the regulatory obstacles currently experienced in humanizing business. The integrated theory of regulation is developed and defended in Chapters 7 and 8. But at the outset, let me outline the central idea that underpins this theory. The central idea is to seek integration between different variables to either take cognizance of their dynamic relationship or to complement the weaknesses of one strategy with the strength of another. The theory emphasizes the necessity of establishing a balance between the often-conflicting human rights issues and business issues, as both human rights and business are important for the development of individuals as well as society as a whole. It also posits that the WWH challenges should be met in an integrated manner, because one influences the nature of the other. Moreover, since no single regulatory strategy, implementation technique, or sanction is adequate to deal effectively with difficult regulatory targets such as MNCs, there is a need to employ different available levels of regulation, strategies of implementation, and types of sanctions in an integrated manner.

I use 'Bhopal' – an Indian city where thousands of people died on the night of 2–3 December 1984 due to a leak of methyl isocyanate (MIC) and other toxic gases from a chemical plant run by Union Carbide India Ltd. (UCIL), a subsidiary of Union Carbide Corporation (UCC)[1] – as a symbol of *inhumane business*. Bhopal is employed to investigate how MNCs are able to violate human rights and then evade accountability by exploiting the loopholes in existing regulatory initiatives. Although other case studies will be referred to when necessary, Bhopal is the principal case study employed in this book, not only to expose the inadequacy of existing regulatory initiatives but also to explore, test, support, or illustrate various arguments advanced in this book to stress the need to humanize business. The justifications for choosing Bhopal as a representative case study are offered in the next chapter.

Backdrop of globalization

I conceive globalization in terms of interconnectedness and interdependence leading to reciprocal influences as well as changes. This interconnectedness and interdependence is brought by movement – of ideas, goods, services, people and so on – that is taking place now in a relatively easy, speedy and

---

1 See, for details, Chapter 2.

inexpensive manner. Among others, this is what differentiates the globalization of today from the globalization of yesterday.[2]

Globalization provides two useful contexts to the present work. It has had a significant impact on the changing dynamics of human rights. Globalization has also influenced the WWH challenges to the corporate human rights responsibility discourse. Let me begin by mapping the changing dynamics of human rights. In contemporary times, the debate about human rights is no longer confined to the matrix of individuals and states. Individuals are not the sole beneficiaries of human rights,[3] as was once thought[4] and states are not the only institutions under an obligation to respect, protect and promote human rights.[5] Globalization of the world economy and trade, especially under the umbrella of the World Trade Organization (WTO), has played its part in changing the dynamics of human rights and also posed new challenges for their realization.[6] The shift in paradigms is not, however, limited to the changing relationship of 'right-duty bearers': there is a change not only in the content, prioritization, and enforcement of human rights but also in the nature of human rights violators.[7] The growing role, power and influence of companies in public spheres have afforded them more opportunities to violate human rights. Companies, acting alone or in complicity with states, pose a real threat of violating a wide range of civil, political, social, economic and cultural human rights in diverse ways. In short, the impact of day-to-day (and apparently innocuous business) decisions taken by companies is not limited to shareholders alone; it rather affects a larger community.

Let us now consider how globalization has influenced the WWH challenges. An important facet of globalization is the liberalization of economies under which companies enjoy a significant space to operate – from offering public services to running prisons, providing security (including in war zones), controlling tremendous amounts of personal data and impacting on

---

2 See J. Bhagwati, *In Defense of Globalization*, New York: Oxford University Press, 2004, pp. 10–13.
3 M. Addo, 'The Corporation as a Victim of Human rights Violations' in M. Addo (ed.) *Human Rights Standards and the Responsibility of Transnational Corporations*, The Hague: Kluwer Law International, 1999, p. 190. See also J. Ohlin, 'Is the Concept of the Person Necessary for Human Rights?' *Columbia Law Review*, 2005, vol. 105, 209.
4 'If human rights are the rights that one has simply as a human being, then only human beings have human rights; if one is not a human being, then by definition one cannot have a human right.' J. Donnelly, *Universal Human Rights: In Theory and Practice*, Ithaca: Cornell University Press, 1989, p. 20.
5 See, e.g. A. Clapham, *Human Rights Obligations of Non-State Actors*, Oxford: Oxford University Press, 2006.
6 D. Shelton, 'Protecting Human Rights in a Globalising World' in C. Ku and P. Diehl (eds.), *International Law: Classic and Contemporary Readings*, 2nd edn., Boulder, Colorado: Rienner Publishers, 2003, p. 333, at 335.
7 S. Deva, 'Human Rights Realisation in an Era of Globalisation: The Indian Experience', *Buffalo Human Rights Law Review*, 2006, vol. 12, 93, at 112–15.

access to basic needs like water and food. This wide spectrum of corporate activities depicts a change in the traditional role and place of companies in society. Historically, companies were instruments to serve public purposes and were tightly controlled by the state.[8] In contrast, modern companies are widely regarded as wealth-generating entities with no specific mandate to accomplish a given public purpose. Against this background, it is natural to ask *why* companies should not be responsible for human rights abuses contributed by, or linked to, their business activities.

Globalization has also affected the nature of corporate responsibilities, the *what* challenge. Unlike overseas operations of chartered companies of the sixteenth and seventeenth centuries,[9] companies today operate across the globe through a complex web of subsidiaries and affiliate concerns. Companies now also frequently resort to outsourcing key stages of their operations. In these circumstances, various questions are naturally raised about the nature and extent of the human rights responsibilities of companies. For instance, what standards of human rights should a company from a developed country apply when operating in a developing country with vastly different cultural and religious values? For that matter, should a company be responsible for the conduct of its subsidiaries or suppliers?

Similarly, *how* companies are made accountable has been influenced by globalization in both positive and negative ways. Since companies now operate at a transnational level and can move their operations from one jurisdiction to another, holding them accountable has become more difficult under municipal law, thus indicating the need for supplementing municipal regulation with extraterritorial and/or supra-state regulatory initiatives. At the same time, globalization has enabled the employment of informal means of regulation against companies. Civil society activism is a case in point.

The history of corporate abuses and regulatory attempts

The involvement of corporations in human rights abuses is not a new phenomenon. The British East India Company – a company that was chartered by Queen Elizabeth I to trade into the East Indies on 31 December 1600 – was linked to slave trade, famine deaths and drug trafficking activities as early as in the seventeenth and eighteenth centuries,[10] a time when even the notion of

---

8 P. Blumberg, *The Multinational Challenge to Corporation Law: The Search for a New Corporate Personality*, New York: Oxford University Press, 1993, pp. 5–8; J. Bakan, *The Corporation: The Pathological Pursuit of Profit and Power*, New York: Free Press, 2004, p. 153.
9 J. Micklethwait and A. Wooldridge, *The Company: A Short History of a Revolutionary Idea*, New York: Modern Library, 2003, pp. 17–28.
10 See J. Keay, *The Honourable Company: A History of the English East India Company*, London: Harper Collins Publishers, 1991, pp. 430–1, 454–5; O. Prakash, *European Commercial Enterprise in Pre-colonial India*, Cambridge: Cambridge University Press, 1998, pp. 328–35.

human rights in its present form was unknown. However, both modern corporations and their role in human rights violations differ significantly from their ancestors.[11] As noted before, today's corporations operate at a transnational level as part of a corporate group and are considered indispensable to the development process of nation states. More importantly, in the era of neo-colonization, corporations act more as independent entities or in partnership with states rather than as the agents of colonial powers.[12] There is a qualitative difference even in terms of the nature of the human rights violated, the *modus operandi* of such violations and the places where such violations are occurring: a wide range of human rights are violated; the violations are occurring not only by direct actions of companies but also by providing assistance to states;[13] and serious violations are taking place mostly in developing countries.[14]

How did law and regulatory regimes react to the growing instances of human rights violations by companies, acting alone or in complicity with states? Over a period of time, a plethora of regulatory responses incrementally came onto the scene so much so that it is not possible to mention all of them here. Apart from voluntary initiatives launched by public figures, business leaders, corporations, manufacturers, industry associations and Non-Governmental Organizations (NGOs), national governments also had general laws that had human rights implications for local corporations.[15] However, there was hardly any municipal law which 'specifically' elaborated the human rights responsibilities of companies. States not only doubted their capacity to effectively regulate the activities of MNCs, but also showed a degree of unwillingness to act tough against even local subsidiaries of MNCs, primarily because of the fear that this might impair their competitiveness to attract much needed foreign investment for development.[16]

An attempt by some countries to enact a specific extraterritorial law to deal with human rights violations by overseas subsidiaries of their companies did

---

11 S. Ratner, 'Corporations and Human Rights: A Theory of Legal Responsibility', *Yale Law Journal*, 2001, vol. 111, 443, at 446; P. Muchlinski, 'Human Rights and Multinationals: Is There a Problem?' *International Affairs*, 2001, vol. 77, 31.
12 In fact, it is arguable that now many states are more than willing to act as agents of MNCs (e.g. when states enact laws to suit corporate interests, or when states file complaints before the WTO's dispute settlement body). S. Deva, 'From 3/12 to 9/11: Future of Human Rights?' *Economic and Political Weekly*, 2004, vol. 39, 5198, at 5200.
13 See, e.g. Human Rights Watch, '*Race to the Bottom': Corporate Complicity in Chinese Internet Censorship*, New York: HRW, 2006.
14 Commission on Human Rights, 'Interim Report of the Special Representative of the Secretary General on the Issue of Human Rights and Transnational Corporations and Other Business Enterprises', E/CN.4/2006/97 (22 February 2006), para. 30.
15 One could find scattered provisions related to corporate (human rights) responsibilities in municipal laws in areas such as constitution, tort, contract, consumer protection, advertising, anti-discrimination, labour disputes, occupational health and safety, and the environment.
16 Clapham, above n. 5, p. 238.

not materialize.[17] The innovative use of the Alien Tort Claims Act (ATCA) provided an avenue in the United States (US) courts to make companies accountable for human rights abuses committed abroad.[18] However, litigation under the ATCA has faced serious problems.[19] Apart from a few instances in which an out-of-court settlement has been reached,[20] hardly any case has been decided finally against a company on the merits. More critically, in *Kiobel* v. *Royal Dutch Petroleum Co*, the Second Circuit Court of Appeals, by majority, has ruled that companies cannot be sued under the ATCA because corporate criminal liability does not exist under customary international law.[21]

At international level, on the other hand, there was no real push for regulating MNCs' activities until the mid-1970s, despite the involvement of companies in perpetuating human rights abuses during the Second World War[22] and other concerns generated by their activities since the 1960s.[23] Before that period, the primary concern of international human rights law was securing human rights against state action.[24] Apart from a limited number of *jus cogens* or customary human rights,[25] the predominantly state-centric international human rights did not, at least in the beginning, envisage imposing

---

17 Such an attempt was made in the US, Australia and the UK. See J. Zerk, *Multinationals and Corporate Social Responsibility: Limitations and Opportunities in International Law*, Cambridge: Cambridge University Press, 2006, pp. 165–70; A. McBeth, 'A Look at Corporate Code of Conduct Legislation', *Common Law World Review*, 2004, vol. 33, 222.
18 28 USC § 1350 (2003). See S. Joseph, *Corporations and Transnational Human Rights Litigation*, Oxford: Hart Publishing, 2004, pp. 21–54.
19 See Joseph, above n. 18, pp. 87–99, 129–43.
20 'Energy Giant Agrees Settlement with Burmese Villagers', *The Guardian*, 15 December 2004. Available at: www.guardian.co.uk/world/2004/dec/15/burma.duncancampbell (accessed 20 May 2011). 'Yahoo Settles Its China Lawsuit', *BBC News*, 13 November 2007. Available at: http://news.bbc.co.uk/2/hi/7093564.stm (accessed 20 May 2011). 'Shell Settlement With Ogoni People Stops Short of Full Justice', *The Guardian*, 10 June 2009. Available at: www.guardian.co.uk/environment/cif-green/2009/jun/09/saro-wiwa-shell (accessed 20 May 2011).
21 621 F.3d 111 (2010). Several international human rights organizations have filed an amicus brief in the US Supreme Court to reverse the *Kiobel* ruling.
22 See, e.g. E. Black, *IBM and the Holocaust: The Strategic Alliance between Nazi Germany and America's Most Powerful Corporation*, New York: Crown Publishers, 2001.
23 P. Muchlinski, *Multinational Enterprises and the Law*, 2nd edn, Oxford: Oxford University Press, 2007, pp. 3–4; Zerk, above n. 17, pp. 8–10; N. Jägers, *Corporate Human Rights Obligations: In Search of Accountability*, Antwerpen: Intersentia, 2002, pp. 100–1.
24 S. Fitzgerald, 'Corporate Accountability for Human Rights Violations in Australian Domestic Law', (2005) 11 *Australian Journal of Human Rights*, 2005, vol. 11, 33; D. Weissbrodt, 'Business and Human Rights', *University of Cincinnati Law Review*, 2005, vol. 74, 55, at 59.
25 International Council on Human Rights Policy (ICHRP), *Beyond Voluntarism: Human Rights and the Developing International Legal Obligations of Companies*, Versoix: ICHRP, 2002, pp. 62–4.

specific human rights obligations on corporations.²⁶ Nor is reliance on a reference to the responsibilities of 'every individual and every organ of society' in the UDHR sufficient to make explicit the human rights responsibilities of corporations.²⁷

Rather than generating confusion between what corporate responsibilities international human rights law *actually* envisaged and *ought* to have envisaged, it is more appropriate to concede that during its early years international human rights law at best adopted an 'indirect' approach to imposing and enforcing human rights obligations against MNCs.²⁸ The rationale was that states' legal obligation to respect and promote human rights also implied a derivative obligation to ensure that all natural or legal actors, including corporations, operating within their respective territories respected human rights.²⁹ This early 'blankness' or the 'indirect' approach of international human rights law regarding MNCs' human rights obligations – though remarkable – was consistent with how human rights have historically evolved in the context of individuals versus states.

However, both the 'blankness' and 'indirect' approach of international human rights law concerning corporate human rights responsibilities slowly began to change from the early 1970s. The first sign of this change came when the UN decided to research the impact of MNCs' activities on development; the UN Commission on Transnational Corporations then proceeded to draft a code of conduct specifying the responsibilities of MNCs.³⁰ Although this attempt to draft a code at international level failed to materialize,³¹ it at least emphasized the need for international regulation of MNCs' activities. The Organization for Economic Cooperation and Development (OECD) Guidelines

---

26 This remains the case despite persuasive argument made by Clapham that the provisions of several regional and international human rights conventions do extend, or could be interpreted to extend, to cover 'private' human rights violations. A. Clapham, *Human Rights in the Private Sphere*, New York: Oxford University Press, 1993, pp. 91–101.
27 Commenting on the scope of the Preamble to the UDHR, Henkin famously argued: '*Every individual* includes juridical persons. *Every individual and every organ of society* excludes no one, no company, no market, no cyberspace. The Universal Declaration applies to them all.' L. Henkin, 'Universal Declaration at 50 and the Challenge of Global Markets', *Brooklyn Journal of International Law*, 1999, vol. 25, 17, at 25 (emphasis in original).
28 Weissbrodt, above n. 24, pp. 60–2; Zerk, above n. 17, pp. 83–4.
29 See A. Reinisch, 'The Changing International Legal Framework for Dealing with Non-State Actors' in P. Alston (ed.), *Non-State Actors and Human Rights*, Oxford: Oxford University Press, 2005, p. 37, at 79–82; Zerk, above n 17, pp. 83–91. Complaints to the UN Human Rights Committee had been lodged against states parties for human rights violations done by non-state entities within their jurisdiction. Y. Tyagi, *The UN Human Rights Committee: Practice and Procedure*, Cambridge: Cambridge University Press, 2011, pp. 413–15.
30 Jägers, above n. 23, pp. 119–24.
31 Muchlinski, above n. 23, pp. 660–2.

of 1976 and the International Labour Organization (ILO) Tripartite Declaration of 1977 for the first time sought to prescribe *directly* and *specifically* the human rights responsibilities of MNCs in limited areas.[32] Arguably, these initiatives were evidence of the fact that in order to achieve a fuller and wider realization of human rights, the spectrum of human rights obligations should directly cover even companies. However, as far as the compliance with human rights responsibilities was concerned, both these regulatory initiatives, though admittedly voluntary in nature, continued to rely primarily, though not exclusively, on the 'indirect' approach.

Although the limitations of the OECD Guidelines and the ILO Declaration are highlighted in more detail in Chapter 4, one point may be noted here. The predominant reliance of both these regulatory initiatives on states for enforcement is problematic, as states sometimes may be *unable* and/or *unwilling* to vigorously enforce human rights responsibilities against MNCs. It is, therefore, critical that, in order to be effective, any international regulatory initiative also invokes mechanisms that do not exclusively rely on states to make companies accountable for breaches of human rights obligations. A few relatively recent international regulatory initiatives seemed to move in this direction in distinct ways. The UN Global Compact, though still a totally voluntary initiative, conceives a role for multiple stakeholders to promote responsible corporate citizenship. The Norms on the Responsibilities of Transnational Corporations and other Business Enterprises with regard to Human Rights (UN Norms) proposed to implement corporate human rights responsibilities through a range of measures and institutions instead of relying solely on states.[33] The UN Norms thus marked a clear departure from the erstwhile indirect approach of international law in specifying and enforcing corporate human rights responsibilities.[34] More recently, the Guiding Principles proposed by the UN Secretary-General's Special Representative on human rights and transnational corporations and other business enterprises (SRSG) acknowledge the usefulness of non-state

---

32 OECD Declaration and Decisions on International Investment and Multinational Enterprises (21 June 1976), reprinted in *ILM*, 1976, vol. 15, 967. The OECD Guidelines were revised in 2002 (*ILM*, 2001, vol. 40, 237) and updated in May 2011. ILO Tripartite Declaration of Principles Concerning Multinational Enterprises and Social Policy (16 November 1977), reprinted in *ILM*, 1978, vol. 17, 422. The ILO Declaration was revised in 2000 (*ILM*, 2001, vol. 41, 186) and 2006.
33 Norms on the Responsibilities of Transnational Corporations and other Business Enterprises with regard to Human Rights, E/CN.4/Sub.2/2003/12/Rev.2 (13 August 2003), paras 15–19.
34 S. Deva, 'UN's Human Rights Norms for Transnational Corporations and Other Business Enterprises: An Imperfect Step in the Right Direction?' *ILSA Journal of International and Comparative Law*, 2004, vol. 10, 493, at 499–500.

mechanisms,³⁵ though they do not go as far as favouring direct regulation of companies by international law.

This brief mapping of the major existing regulatory initiatives that seek to impose and enforce human rights obligations on companies was intended to indicate that there has not been any dearth of regulatory initiatives. Regulatory mechanisms have flowed, and more could flow in the future, from an internal or an external source,³⁶ or in some cases from a partnership between internal and external sources.³⁷ These regulatory regimes operate at various levels – from (corporate) institutional to national, regional and international levels. Despite the plethora of regulatory regimes directed towards fixing responsibility on companies for human rights violations, more often than not, what we witness is a widely documented situation of impunity. Companies continue to remain unaccountable for human rights violations by exploiting gaps or loopholes in the existing regulatory mechanisms. They are also able to employ various legal tools to resist, delay or escape liability for human rights abuses.³⁸

As examined in detail in Chapter 4, the situation of impunity arises, in my view, not because of any perceived vacuum of regulatory responses but because of the *inadequacy* of existing regulatory regimes.³⁹ Against this background, this book confronts the current state of corporate impunity for human rights violations and an inadequate regulatory response to such conduct.

The WWH challenges: Nature and interrelationship

It will be useful at this stage to understand the nature and interrelationship of the WWH challenges to humanizing business. The first and foremost challenge pertaining to *why* questions the very basis of, and need for, any relation between business and human rights that results in business actors attracting human rights obligations. In view of business and human rights being perceived as different pursuits having conflicting interests as well as

---

35 Human Rights Council, 'Guiding Principles on Business and Human Rights: Implementing the United Nations "Protect, Respect and Remedy" Framework', A/HRC/17/31 (21 March 2011), Principles 28–30.
36 By an 'internal' regulatory mechanism I mean an initiative that is introduced by possible violators themselves, individually or collectively. An 'external' regulatory regime, on the other hand, is developed and implemented by those organs of society which aim to protect human rights.
37 The UN Global Compact provides a good example of this. See S. Deva, 'Global Compact: A Critique of UN's "Public-Private" Partnership for Promoting Corporate Citizenship', *Syracuse Journal of International Law and Commerce*, 2006, vol. 34, 107.
38 Corporate reliance on the principle of separate legal personality and the doctrine of *forum non conveniens* is a case in point.
39 A regulatory regime is considered 'adequate' if it can prevent or pre-empt human rights violations by companies – at least in some cases – and can also offer adequate relief to victims in cases of violations. See Chapter 3 for further elaboration.

theoretical underpinnings,[40] why should it be the business of business to respect and promote human rights, especially when compliance with human rights obligations might impede their primary objective of profit maximization? Although the vigour of this challenge has diminished in recent years in view of scholars making a strong case for corporate human rights responsibility,[41] and many corporations accepting that they have some responsibilities,[42] a few dissenting voices can still be heard.[43] In view of this, I critique in Chapter 5 the thesis of two prominent scholars – Milton Friedman and Elaine Sternberg – who argued that the only responsibility of business is to maximize shareholders' profits or value. It is contended that such a view is narrow, unsound and outdated in the current economic climate.

Advancing strong justifications for corporate human rights responsibility is critical so as to provide an overall sound base to the integrated theory of regulation proposed in this book, for the requisite 'what' and 'how' could hardly be rooted on a fragile response to 'why'.[44] An investigation into 'why' tells us about the role and place of corporations in society. Their given role and place in society has a direct bearing on the question of 'what', that is, the extent of human rights responsibilities of corporations. 'Why' also informs us of the reasons for corporations hesitating to take on board human rights responsibilities. For instance, if we know that the prisoner's dilemma[45] discourages corporations from assuming their human rights responsibilities, it is rational to think that something should be done as to 'how' we regulate companies.

Once we overcome the why challenge and agree that companies do have human rights responsibilities, the next challenge is in ascertaining the nature and scope of these responsibilities. Several issues arise here. I will confront one of these issues: *what* human rights standards should be applied by companies operating in many states that differ drastically from each other in material particulars? These differences often create a business dilemma for MNCs:

---

40 Garcia, for instance, examines the normative conflict between trade law and human rights law. F. Garcia, 'The Global Market and Human Rights: Trading Away the Human Rights Principle', *Brooklyn Journal of International Law*, 1999, vol. 25, 51, at 64–76.
41 See, for example, Ratner, above n. 11; B. Stephens, 'The Amorality of Profit: Transnational Corporations and Human Rights', *Berkeley Journal of International Law*, 2002, vol. 20, 45; Muchlinski, above n. 11.
42 Zerk, above n. 17, p. 42.
43 See, e.g. E. Sternberg, *Just Business: Business Ethics in Action*, 2nd edn, Oxford: Oxford University Press, 2000.
44 '[I]f MNEs are to be subjected to direct and legally enforceable obligations to observe fundamental human rights, the grounds for doing so must be strong and conceptually unassailable.' Muchlinski, above n. 11, p. 32.
45 The prisoner's dilemma is a situation in which two (or more) persons have to take decision on a given issue. Each person has an option to 'cooperate' or 'defect', but each of them may decide to defect in order to maximize their own advantage, even if that harms the other party. See S. Hargreaves Heap and Y. Varoufakis, *Game Theory: A Critical Text*, 2nd edn, London: Routledge, 2004, pp. 172–4.

should they apply the standards of the host country, the standards of the home country, or adopt international standards irrespective of where they operate? The determination of precise human rights standards for MNCs should be a priori to their accountability for human rights violations. However, the existing regulatory initiatives, howsoever paradoxical it may sound, do not resolve this dilemma of varying standards.

This book intends to fill this gap by exploring both the approach that does generally guide (the *business* approach) and the approach that should guide (the *human* approach) MNCs in resolving the dilemma concerning varying standards of human rights. As the titles itself indicate, 'business' and 'human' respectively are central to these two approaches, which represent contrasting positions as to the place and role of corporations in society. The *business* approach perceives corporations primarily as economic entities, and logically puts profit as reflected in the financial statements first and foremost. As stockholders' profit maximization guides the business approach, the protection and promotion of stakeholders' human rights is not, in itself, considered a part of 'profits' quantified in dollars. For this reason, the business approach does not take a principled stand *vis-à-vis* human rights: it is profits that will determine whether human rights are to be respected and if so, then which standards are to be followed.

In comparison to the business approach, the *human* approach would require MNCs to resolve their dilemma as to varying standards with reference to the impact of their decisions on the realization of human rights of their stakeholders. The human approach takes a more holistic view of the role of corporations in society. It considers corporations an integral part of society; the role of corporations, according to this view, is multi-faceted rather than being limited to efficient wealth creation.[46] In other words, the goal of profit maximization is not to be pursued at the expense of other equally important social objectives (e.g. human rights realization).

What is the relationship of 'what' to the other two challenges 'why' and 'how'? If the human rights standards are vague and imprecise or if companies would have to spend a considerable amount of time in ascertaining their precise responsibilities, they may either decide not to comply with applicable standards or their compliance may be symbolic. Conversely, clarity of applicable human rights standards is likely to enhance both the chances and quality of compliance. In either case, this would have resource and policing implications for the 'how' challenge.

That brings us to the third challenge to the goal of humanizing business: *how* to implement and enforce effectively human rights obligations against

---

46 'Profit for owners and directors remain one consideration, and a very important one, essential as an index and for survival. But it is one among others, not a unique guiding light.' M. Fogarty, *Company and Corporation – One Law?* London: Geoffrey Chapman, 1965, p. 9.

companies? The regulatory framework should not only be able to encourage companies to take on board their human rights responsibilities but should also be capable of dealing robustly with those companies which are not so encouraged. Issues related to this challenge are again many and quite diverse. For example, what should be the nature and form of such an enforcement mechanism? At which level, or levels, should regulatory initiatives be put in place to ensure an effective enforcement framework? Should (and could) international law impose and enforce human rights obligations upon companies directly? What types of implementation strategies and sanctions could prove effective against MNCs? How should the obstacles arising from corporate reliance on the principle of separate legal personality and the doctrine of *forum non conveniens* be overcome? Each of these issues has the potential to be treated in a book on its own and therefore, it is not possible to deal with them in detail here. Nevertheless, most of these issues will receive a varying level of treatment as part of a regulatory framework based on the integrated theory of regulation. The book will identify how the obstacles identified concerning *how* could be overcome to a significant extent by the proposed regulatory framework.

In terms of the relationship of 'how' with the other two challenges, it can be said that if the enforcement mechanism (how) is robust and effective, then companies would have more incentive to comply with their human rights responsibilities, rather than asking the question why they should follow. Similarly, if we know that 'corporate actors are deterred not only by economic losses but also by reputational losses, then consideration can be given to adverse publicity sanctions for regulatory offenders'[47] – demonstrating further a relationship between the 'why' and the 'how'.

Major claims

This book makes two major claims, one 'prerequisite' and the other 'central'. The *prerequisite claim* is that existing regulatory initiatives that seek to make companies (and MNCs in particular) accountable for human rights abuses are seriously inadequate. It is not feasible to evaluate all, or even a majority of, current regulatory initiatives which differ significantly from each other in terms of their nature, content, form, scope, source, and level of operation. Therefore, seven representative initiatives have been chosen for a critical assessment: the ATCA, corporate codes of conduct, the OECD Guidelines, the ILO Declaration, the Global Compact, the UN Norms and the Guiding Principles. On the basis of the evaluation of these specific regulatory initiatives, a general claim about the inadequacy of existing regulatory initiatives relating to companies is supported.

---

47 I. Ayres and J. Braithwaite, *Responsive Regulation: Transcending the Deregulation Debate*, New York: Oxford University Press, 1992, p. 22.

Although all types of companies can violate human rights and/or resist attempts to make them accountable, MNCs are more likely not only to violate a wider range of human rights in diverse settings but also to resist, delay or evade accountability for such violations in view of their power and influence.[48] It is, therefore, sensible to explore the issue of the inadequacy of existing regulatory regimes with reference to MNCs and not just uni-national corporations. For the same reason, it will be pertinent to assess the strengths of the regulatory framework proposed in this book with reference to MNCs.

The *central claim* that this book advances is that the integrated theory of regulation can anchor a regulatory framework that could overcome, to a great extent, the inadequacies of existing regulatory regimes and in turn, redress the current state of corporate impunity for human rights violations. In addition to tackling the WWH challenges to humanizing business together, the integrated theory proposes 'integration' on two more counts: between human rights and business; and between different available levels of regulation, strategies of implementation, and types of sanctions.

The arguments related to these two claims are presented in a logical order. After demonstrating the limitations of existing regulatory initiatives on the basis of a review of seven representative regimes, the three limbs of the integrated theory (i.e. *why, what* and *how*) are dealt with individually. The book is divided into nine chapters, including this introductory chapter. A brief overview of the chapters that will follow the present introductory chapter is given below.

Since Bhopal is a common thread that runs through the whole book, the next chapter aims to offer an understanding not only of the background and circumstances under which UCC established its chemical plant at Bhopal but also of the litigation that unfolded both in the US and India after the gas leakage. A fresh perspective on Bhopal is provided by analyzing it as an instance of human rights violation. Bhopal is used to show how pre-entry negotiations between MNCs and host states could prepare the groundwork for MNCs to violate human rights in developing countries by adopting inferior human rights standards or otherwise.

Chapter 3 conceptualizes what 'adequacy' entails for a regulatory framework and develops an analytical framework for the critical evaluation of regulatory initiatives concerning corporate human rights responsibilities. The chapter suggests five factors that could be used to understand the taxonomy of existing regulatory regimes: the *source* from which they flow; the *content* of obligations; the *strategy* that they adopt to reach companies; their *level* of operation; and their *nature* in terms of compliance strategy. These factors are then used to select a representative sample of regulatory initiatives to be evaluated

---

48 'C. Grossman and D. Bradlow, 'Are We Being Propelled towards a People-Centered Transnational Legal Order?' *American University Journal of International Law and Policy*, 1993, vol. 9, 1, at 8.

critically to ascertain their adequacy in controlling human rights abuses by companies.

Applying the analytical framework developed in Chapter 3, Chapter 4 reviews seven representative regulatory initiatives that seek to render corporations accountable for human rights violations. I argue that the existing regulatory framework suffers from a three-fold inadequacy: it offers insufficient or contestable rationales for compliance, does not prescribe sufficiently clear human rights standards, and is supported by deficient or undeveloped implementation and enforcement mechanisms. These inadequacies should be taken into account when reforming existing regulatory initiatives or introducing new initiatives.

Chapter 5 aims to overcome the 'why' challenge faced by a theory of corporate human rights responsibility. It questions the thesis of both Friedman and Sternberg, who argued that the only social responsibility of business is to maximize shareholders' profits. This chapter also highlights why it is problematic to rely too much on the 'business case' for human rights as a compliance rationale. As an alternative justification for corporate human rights responsibilities, I argue that all corporations should have human rights responsibilities because of their *relationship to* and *position in* society.

Chapter 6 deals with one question concerning the 'what' challenge: which standards – out of the home, host and international standards – should an MNC adopt while operating in different countries? I illustrate with the help of the Bhopal case that the business approach will often fail to protect human rights of people in developing countries, as this approach encourages MNCs to adopt host standards which most of the time are inadequate. MNCs' decisions should, therefore, be guided by the human approach: requiring them to apply in host countries the home or international standards modified in view of morally relevant local differences. Local differences are morally relevant only if they facilitate a better realization of human rights.

Chapters 7 and 8 together relate to the final limb of the integrated theory of regulation: 'how' to make companies accountable for human rights violations in an effective manner? While Chapter 7 elaborates the integrated theory, Chapter 8 outlines how a regulatory framework based on this theory could be put in place. Chapter 7 begins with a critique of the model of responsive regulation proposed by Ayres and Braithwaite,[49] with a view to ascertaining if this model could support a framework for corporate accountability for human rights abuses. Ayres and Braithwaite develop an enforcement pyramid that allows regulators to employ a hierarchy of sanctions and regulatory strategies. I highlight the limitations of the enforcement pyramid – which progressively introduces more punitive sanctions or regulatory techniques upon the failure of softer techniques adopted earlier – and the

---

49 Ayres and Braithwaite, above n. 47.

model of enforced self-regulation in controlling and redressing corporate human rights violations. As an alternative, the integrated theory proposes that regulatory techniques should be integrated (i.e. employed in 'tandem to complement one another')[50] rather than being invoked only when the techniques situated lower on the regulatory pyramid fail to deliver.

Chapter 8 maps how the conduct of companies should be regulated, in an integrated manner, at an institutional level through voluntary codes, at a national level by the laws enacted by governments of home and host countries of MNCs, and at international level by a declaration or convention delineating corporate human rights responsibilities. It is also proposed that a Model Law on Business and Human Rights should be drafted to offer guidance to states in dealing with the privatization of human rights. Regulatory initiatives at all three levels should invoke, as far as possible, twin implementation strategies (incentives and coercion) and triple sanctions (civil, criminal and social) simultaneously, so as to result in a robust enforcement of corporate human rights responsibilities.

One aspect stressed under the proposed framework is that, in view of inherent limitations of law and states in regulating MNCs, it is imperative for regulatory initiatives to employ non-legal regulatory initiatives, techniques and sanctions that do not primarily rely on state agencies, processes, or mechanisms. This approach is in consonance with contemporary regulatory ideas that do not see and/or link regulation exclusively to formal law, state and legal institutions.[51] Since both the state and law suffer from inherent limitations in regulating the conduct of corporations[52] and it is doubtful if law alone could bring about the required change in the behaviour of corporations,[53] *informality* is a key methodical aspect of the integrated theory of regulation canvassed here.

Chapter 9 presents an overview of the key ideas mooted in this book. In particular, it highlights how and why current regulatory initiatives which aim to promote corporate human rights responsibilities should be informed by the integrated theory of regulation. This concluding chapter also outlines

---

50 F. Haines, *Corporate Regulation: Beyond 'Punish' or 'Persuade'*, Oxford: Clarendon Press, 1997, p. 221.
51 P. Grabosky, N. Gunningham and D. Sinclair, 'Parties, Roles, and Interactions' in N. Gunningham, P. Grabosky and D. Sinclair, *Smart Regulation: Designing Environmental Policy*, Oxford: Clarendon Press, 1998 p. 93; Haines, above n. 50, pp. 229–33.
52 'The capacity of law to regulate corporations is limited by the opacity and complexity of corporate structures, the desire to avoid over-regulation, and the fact that corporate management has such a great capacity to control employee workplace behaviour.' C. Parker, *The Open Corporation: Effective Self-regulation and Democracy*, Cambridge: Cambridge University Press, 2002, p. viii. See also P. Yeager, *The Limits of Law: The Public Regulation of Private Pollution*, Cambridge: Cambridge University Press, 1991, pp. 29–47.
53 See C. Stone, *Where the Law Ends: The Social Control of Corporate Behaviour*, Prospect Heights, Illinois: Waveland Press, 1991.

16 *Introduction*

the future direction that should be taken to achieve the goal of humanizing business rather than be misled by the SRSG's rhetoric of consensus.

Conceptual signposts

Definitions of some key terms used in this book are presented below. The terms defined are configured in relation to an 'identified problem' and a 'suggested response'. The identified problem is human rights violations by companies and the suggested response is an integrated theory of legal responsibility.

Human rights

Defining 'human rights' is vital because the obligations/duties/responsibilities – the terms being used interchangeably in this book – of companies will be framed with reference to what these rights are. The term 'human rights' is taken to include *all internationally recognized* civil, political, social, economic, environmental, and cultural rights which companies could *possibly* violate. This definition of human rights signifies two things. First, at international level, there is a general consensus on what these human rights are. I take the International Bill of Rights[54] and other international instruments[55] as an example of this consensus despite some states not ratifying all these conventions, or not implementing the obligations undertaken. This conceptualization of human rights is wider in scope than how the term is defined by the Guiding Principles to mean at a minimum those rights 'expressed in the International Bill of Human Rights and the principles concerning fundamental rights set out in the International Labour Organization's Declaration on Fundamental Principles and Rights at Work'.[56]

Second, I think that there is no need to reformulate human *rights* that could be claimed exclusively against corporations. Rights do change and new rights may be created, but no new list of rights needs to be drawn afresh to regulate corporate activities. Therefore, what needs to be done is to formulate *duties* specific to companies with reference to the rights enumerated in the Bill of Rights and other instruments. Instead of adopting the approach advanced by the Guiding Principles, it is important to undertake this process because most of the international human rights instruments were framed primarily with

---

54 The expression 'International Bill of Rights' is used for the UDHR, GA Res. 217A (III), UN Doc. A/810 (1948); ICCPR, GA Res. 2200A (XXI), UN Doc. A/6316 (1966); and the International Covenant on Economic, Social and Cultural Rights (ICESCR), GA Res. 2200A (XXI), UN Doc. A/6316 (1966), all taken together.

55 Such instruments, mostly adopted by the UN and its specialized agencies, may be issue-specific (such as the environment and labour rights) or people-specific (like those related to children, women and indigenous people).

56 Guiding Principles, above n. 35, Principle 12.

states in mind. I treat the OECD Guidelines, the ILO Declaration, the Global Compact and the UN Norms as an attempt, albeit an imperfect one, to catalogue the human rights obligations of companies.

States were and are treated as primary duty-holders under the International Bill of Rights. But this does not mean that other duty-holders did not or could not co-exist with states.[57] The international conventions imposed obligations primarily on states because at that point only states were regarded as subjects of international law. However, over a period of time many non-state actors have been accepted as subjects of international law.[58] It is also forcefully contended that the classification between subjects and objects of international law does not serve any useful purpose[59] and that even MNCs should be accepted as (at least limited) subjects of international law[60] to keep international law alive to changing circumstances. There is, therefore, no legal bar to invoke state-centric international human rights law to deduce responsibilities of companies. Nor is there any obstacle from a jurisprudential point of view. Joseph Raz argues that an 'ability' to impose new duties is a special feature of rights:

> [T]here is no closed list of duties which correspond to the right. . . . A *change of circumstances may lead to the creation of new duties based on the old right.* . . . This dynamic aspect of rights, *their ability to create new duties*, is fundamental to any understanding of their nature and function in practical thought.[61]

It is plausible to argue that the shift of powers and functions from states to companies signifies a sufficient change in circumstances to justify the creation of new duties for companies. Therefore, in order to develop a theory of corporate human rights responsibility, the need is not to redefine human

---

57 C. Jochnick, 'Confronting the Impunity of Non-State Actors: New Fields for the Promotion of Human Rights', *Human Rights Quarterly*, 1999, vol. 21, 56, at 61.
58 See *Reparation of Injuries Suffered in the Services of the UN* (1949) ICJ Rep 174, at 179–80 and 185; S. Skogly, *The Human Rights Obligations of the World Bank and the International Monetary Fund*, London: Cavendish Publishing, 2001, pp. 63–71; I. Brownlie, *Principles of Public International Law*, 6th edn, Oxford: Oxford University Press, 2003, pp. 57–66, 648–50.
59 R. Higgins, *Problems and Process: International Law and How We Use It*, Oxford: Clarendon Press, 1994, pp. 49–50.
60 Jägers, above n. 23, pp. 19–23; Clapham, above n. 5, pp. 76–82; D. Kinley and J. Tadaki, 'From Talk to Walk: The Emergence of Human Rights Responsibilities for Corporations at International Law', *Virginia Journal of International Law*, 2004, vol. 44, 931, at 944–7; Zerk, above n. 17, pp. 73–6; S. Deva, 'Human Rights Violations by Multinational Corporations and International Law: Where from Here?' *Connecticut Journal of International Law*, 2003, vol. 19, 1, at 48–56. See also D. Ijalaye, *The Extension of Corporate Personality in International Law*, New York: Oceana Publications, 1978.
61 J. Raz, *The Morality of Freedom*, Oxford: Clarendon Press, 1986, p. 171 (emphasis added).

18 *Introduction*

rights, but to reconceptualize and extend the existing obligations to include companies (and such other entities) as new duty-holders together with states.[62]

Violation

When can a company be said to have violated human rights? The question can arise in three different situations: first, when a company itself is violating human rights directly; second, when a company assists or contributes to human rights violations done by state agencies or other business entities; and third, when independent entities with which the company in question has a business relationship (i.e. the subsidiaries and suppliers) violate human rights.[63] In each of these situations, the question of 'violation' necessarily arises in the context of breaching an obligation. Therefore, the meaning of violation could properly be understood with reference to the nature and scope of human rights obligations of companies.

Should the nature and scope of corporate obligations be similar to those of states (i.e. to respect, protect and fulfil human rights)? In relation to the first situation described above, it is generally accepted that companies have an obligation to respect human rights, though the Guiding Principles seem to challenge that position by choosing the term 'responsibility' over 'duty'. But the legal position is far from settled when it comes to corporate obligation to protect and fulfil human rights. Many companies would resist any attempt to frame positive duties in terms of protect and fulfil. Some scholars are also likely to support this position. Thomas Donaldson, for example, contends that the duties of corporations do not extend to protecting from deprivation or aiding the deprived, because such duties are within the province of governments.[64]

I argue, however, that the human rights obligations of companies cannot be limited to merely 'respecting' human rights. Although the scope of their 'protect' and 'fulfil' component of duties cannot be as extensive as that of states, companies should still have three-fold duties. It is notable that even the Guiding Principles contemplate corporate responsibilities on the lines of 'protect' and 'fulfil',[65] though erroneously include them under the rubric of 'respect'. This conflating of duties is one of the flaws of the approach adopted

---

62 Ratner, above n. 11, p. 469.
63 Mares discusses some of these questions concerning the scope of corporate human rights responsibilities. R. Mares, 'Transnational Corporate Responsibility for the 21st Century: Defining the Limits of Corporate Responsibilities against the Concept of Legal Positive Obligations', *George Washington International Law Review*, 2009, vol. 40, 1157.
64 T. Donaldson, *The Ethics of International Business*, New York: Oxford University Press, 1989, pp. 83–4.
65 Guiding Principle 11 states that 'Business enterprises . . . should address adverse human rights impact with which they are involved.' See also Principles 13 and 17, above n. 35.

by the Guiding Principles. As Henry Shue points out, although the distinction between positive and negative rights may be illusory and misguided, a 'useful distinction' among duties correlative to rights does exist.[66]

As analyzed below, the 'protect' and 'fulfil' components of corporate human rights responsibilities would be critical in those situations in which human rights are violated by the business partners of a company or where the company is accused of being complicit with state agencies.[67] There are a number of reasons why duties of companies should include these positive elements. First, human rights cannot be fully realized unless 'multiple kinds of duties' are imposed on all those actors which could abridge these rights.[68] In a situation where states are no longer the sole duty bearers, it is desirable that even non-state actors such as companies are subjected to positive obligations. Second, the scope of the duties should be coterminous with possible ways in which rights could be breached, that is, both by diverse actions as well as omissions. Companies could violate human rights in a wide range of scenarios and unless they are subjected to positive obligations, all kinds of human rights abuses cannot be addressed. Third, in view of how companies conduct their business, it will not be sufficient if the loop of human rights obligations is limited to their own activities. Companies should not be allowed to contract out human rights abuses to their business partners and supply chain participants over which they often exercise effective control.[69]

The positive obligations of companies should not, however, be identical or as extensive as those of states. To illustrate, the 'fulfil' obligations should be limited by the economic capacity of companies and arise in relation to those human rights which are relevant to their business operations.[70] So, a company manufacturing life-saving medicines should have an obligation to make available such medicines at a reasonably affordable price (not free or at a nominal price as the obligation on the government might be) as failure to do so would violate the right to life and health.[71] Nevertheless, such a company should not be expected to help small shop owners whose business is threatened by the

---

66 H. Shue, *Basic Rights: Subsistence, Affluence, and US Foreign Policy*, 2nd edn, Princeton: Princeton University Press, 1996, pp. 35–46, 52. Three duties are: (1) duties to *avoid* depriving, (2) duties to *protect* from deprivation and (3) duties to *aid* the deprived. Ibid., 52.
67 Clapham, above n. 5, pp. 230–1; Jägers, above n. 23, pp. 92–5.
68 'The complete fulfilment of each kind of rights involves the performance of multiple kinds of duties.' Shue, above n. 66, p. 52.
69 See Zerk, above n. 17, pp. 265–7.
70 D. Wood, 'Corporate Social Performance Revisited', *Academy of Management Review*, 1991, vol. 16, 691, at 697; M. Porter and M. Kramer, 'The Link between Competitive Advantage and Corporate Social Responsibility', *Harvard Business Review*, 2006, vol. 84:12, 78, at 84–91.
71 See S. Joseph, 'Pharmaceutical Corporations and Access to Drugs: The "Fourth Wave" of Corporate Human Rights Scrutiny', *Human Rights Quarterly*, 2003, vol. 25, 425, at 430.

opening of Wal-Mart-style shopping malls. The 'protect' obligations of companies should be limited to their subsidiaries and business partners over which they exercise some control or influence.

Dealing specifically with the second situation identified above, can a company violate human rights by merely providing aid or assistance to state agencies involved in violations? This scenario is often analyzed in relevant literature as a situation of complicity.[72] Although this issue is not dealt with in detail in this book, in my view, if a company directly and knowingly contributes to human rights abuses by state agencies, it should be held accountable. As long as there is a direct contribution, the level of contribution should be relevant to determine only the extent of liability (e.g. the quantum of compensation) rather than the question of liability. On the other hand, the knowledge requirement can be satisfied when the company has actual knowledge, or it should have reasonably known, of the violations committed by state agencies.

Finally, can a company be considered to violate human rights when actual violations are caused by independent entities with which the company in question has a business relationship? Ordinarily, a person is not liable for the actions or omissions of an independent entity. There are, however, certain well-recognized exceptions to this rule (e.g. the principle of vicarious liability). The duty of states to protect against human rights abuses by third parties within its territory is another instance in which an entity can be held in breach of its human rights obligations for merely failing to prevent and redress abuse by independent third parties within its jurisdiction.

Considering the current business practices, a company should be held to have violated human rights also if violations are done in certain circumstances by a 'related' independent entity. This corporate responsibility is analogous to states' duty to protect against human rights abuses, but with one key difference: unlike states, we cannot apply the territorial or jurisdictional yardstick to companies in relation to third parties. The notion of 'related' is, therefore, an alternative jurisprudential basis to ground as well as limit the extent of liability. An entity can be considered 'related' in two ways. First, when the company in question controls – *de jure* or *de facto* – either the management of the independent entity or the manner in which such entity is performing its tasks or functions. Accordingly, a parent company should be responsible for human rights violations by its subsidiaries, unless it has taken appropriate due diligence steps. Similarly, a company that engages an independent recruitment agency and advises it to hire non-pregnant women personnel should be responsible for any discriminatory hiring practices (e.g. mandatory pregnancy tests) adopted by such recruitment agency.

---

72 See, e.g. A. Clapham and S. Jerbi, 'Categories of Corporate Complicity in Human Rights Abuses', *Hastings International and Comparative Law Review*, 2001, vol. 24, 339.

Second, an independent entity is related to the company in question if they have a business relation and the latter is aware of the human rights violations by the former as part of their business transactions but takes no steps to remedy the situation so as to continue reaping the benefits of such violations. For example, a company that specifies design/material and sets deadlines for its independent contractor manufacturing footwear should be liable for the use of forced child labour in the contractor's factories if it was aware of this practice but remained silent.

The above formulation of violation is admittedly wide. This is justified to avoid the potential mischief of companies outsourcing human rights violations. This approach creates incentives for companies to be proactive in monitoring the behaviour of their business partners. By way of caution and clarity, it should be noted that the expansive conception of corporate human rights responsibilities mooted here should not be taken as diminishing the human rights obligations of states. Corporate responsibilities only supplement, and do not supplant, states' responsibility to respect, protect and fulfil human rights.

MNCs

The term 'MNCs' is used to refer to all similar terminologies such as transnational corporations (TNCs), multinational enterprises (MNEs), transnational enterprises (TNEs) and supranational entities (SNEs). The task of defining an MNC is a complex one.[73] However, some of the definitional difficulties could be overcome, to a great extent, if we were to identify two considerations: the type of corporations needed to be covered and the policy objective sought to be achieved by including them in the definition. Regarding the first consideration, it could be said that the need is to target those corporations which operate in more than one country, including by owning, managing or controlling other corporations as well as acting, in part, through suppliers and contractors. The objective is to subject such corporate actors to a regulatory mechanism that does not suffer from the weaknesses of municipal regimes.

In view of these parameters, an MNC, for the purposes of this book, is an economic entity (whether called a company, corporation or enterprise) that owns, controls, or manages operations, either alone or in conjunction with other entities, in two or more countries. The central element of this definition is the *control* exercised by a corporation over operations outside the country in which it is established. This control could be exercised in various ways, including by ownership of shares, control over the board of directors, or through management of operations and affairs.

---

73 See C. Baez *et al.*, 'Multinational Enterprises and Human Rights', *University of Miami International & Comparative Law Review*, 1999–2000, vol. 8, 183, at 187–9; Muchlinski, above n. 23, pp. 5–8.

Integrated theory of regulation

The integrated theory of regulation mooted in this book is a response to the inadequacy of prevailing regulatory strategies and theories that underpin existing regulatory initiatives concerning corporate human rights responsibilities. In particular, the theory is a critical response to the model of responsive regulation put forward by Ayres and Braithwaite in that it seeks not only to plug the gaps in responsive regulation but also extends the scope of integration. As outlined in more detail in Chapter 7, it is argued that attempts should be made to achieve a three-fold integration.

First of all, the integrated theory emphasizes the necessity of striking a balance to resolve conflicts between human rights issues and business issues. I will argue that corporate law is one of the sites where such integration should take place: corporate law should try to create an environment in which companies do not pursue profit maximization at the cost of harming the interests of their stakeholders. In many cases it should be possible to arrive at such a balance, satisfactory for both human rights and business constituencies. However, if the conflict between human rights and business interests persists at an irreconcilable level, the former should prevail over the latter. Recognition of such a hierarchy in the case of unavoidable conflict is essential because businesses could still survive if subordinated to human rights, though the reverse may not be true.[74]

Second, in order for any theory of corporate human rights responsibility to be viable, it should overcome the WWH challenges. The integrated theory seeks to confront all three challenges together rather than focusing only on one or two of these. I have already noted before that a cumulative treatment of the three challenges is necessary because of the dynamics between them.

Third, the theory posits that as no single regulatory strategy, implementation technique, or sanction is adequate to deal with difficult regulatory targets such as MNCs, we need to invoke more than one strategy and sanction in an integrated fashion to remove the gaps in the regulatory framework. This integration rationale applies to the levels at which regulatory initiatives should be put in place, the implementation strategies to be adopted, and the types of sanctions to be invoked in case of non-compliance.

Responsibility and/or accountability

It is possible to draw a distinction between corporate responsibility and corporate accountability.[75] Generally speaking, 'responsibility' implies duties – which are by and large voluntary in nature – rooted in morality and ethics, rather than

---

74 The idea of human rights as 'trumps' could be used to support this hierarchy. R. Dworkin, *Taking Rights Seriously*, London: Duckworth, 1977, p. xi.
75 See J. Nolan, 'The United Nations' Compact With Business: Hindering or Helping the Protection of Human Rights?' *University of Queensland Law Journal*, 2005, vol. 24, 445, at 448; Clapham, above n. 5, pp. 195–8.

in law. 'Accountability', on the other hand, tends to suggest mandatory obligations, flowing mostly from law, which are enforced by sanctions.

Despite such differences between these terms, responsibility and accountability are used in this book interchangeably. The distinction between the two is not as clear as is often canvassed. The responsibility and accountability approaches are not mutually exclusive because a given corporate human rights obligation could be underpinned by both morality and law. It is also possible that performing what is merely a moral duty today may take the character of a legal obligation in the future. Moreover, the distinction between the two might disappear in practice. Responsibility (e.g. in the form of a voluntary code of conduct) may acquire a non-voluntary character in view of 'naming and shaming' and/or boycotts by market forces. On the other hand, legally binding obligations (accountability on paper) may not mean much in practice because of conceptual, legal or practical obstacles in holding companies accountable through the judicial process.

It should also be considered that neither of these two approaches is self-sufficient; in fact, the voluntary approach of responsibility and the mandatory approach of accountability could complement each other.[76] Since what is required is a combination of both, the distinction between responsibility and accountability is not consciously adhered to.

Summary

The interaction of human rights and business is manifold and there are many questions that might be broached under this rubric. Even the issues arising out of corporate human rights abuses are too diverse and too complex to be effectively dealt with in one book. This book does not claim to do the seemingly impossible task of dealing exhaustively with all issues relevant to this much-debated topic. Rather, it limits itself to identifying and confronting the three major challenges to humanizing business, a goal that is likely to remain central to human civilization in years to come.

Against the backdrop of the changing dynamics of human rights and the continued impunity of companies for human rights violations, the book seeks to make and defend two major claims. First, that because of a three-fold deficit, existing regulatory initiatives are inadequate to make companies accountable for human rights abuses. Second, that an integrated theory of regulation can redress the many loopholes present in existing regulatory regimes that seek to ensure that companies comply with their human rights responsibilities. Of various case studies of corporate human rights violations, I have selected Bhopal to demonstrate the need to humanize business, explain the dynamics of the WWH challenges and illustrate how the proposals mooted here might respond to human rights abuses by MNCs more effectively. I begin in the next chapter by unpacking the Bhopal narrative.

76 Zerk, above n. 17, pp. 32–6.

2 Understanding 'Bhopal' afresh

Since Bhopal is the principal case study used in this book, it is vital to understand not only the background and circumstances under which UCC established its chemical plant at Bhopal but also the litigation that unfolded after the gas leakage. The chapter begins with advancing justifications for choosing Bhopal as a case study. It is argued that although 27 years have passed since the gas leakage, the relevance of Bhopal in illustrating corporate impunity for human rights violations has not diminished. The chapter then moves on to capture the central features of the Bhopal narrative, from UCC's entry into India to the five phases of litigation directed at securing justice for the victims.

What value will this analysis add to the existing rich literature on Bhopal? Whereas the existing literature has treated Bhopal typically as an example of mass tort or an environmental tragedy and not as a human rights issue,[1] the present analysis is refreshing in that it focuses on the human rights implications of Bhopal – from UCC's entry into India to the long litigation that unfolded after the gas leak. With the help of Bhopal, I argue that the roots of corporate human rights abuses could be traced to the circumstances and conditions under which MNCs enter and continue to operate in emerging markets.

Why 'Bhopal'?

Bhopal is selected because it is representative of a typical scenario of human rights violations occurring in a developing country. Although no country is completely immune from instances of corporate human rights abuses, there is a noticeable bias: a great majority of human rights violations by MNCs take place in developing or underdeveloped countries.[2] Considering where most of

---

1 B. Rajagopal, *International Law from Below: Development, Social Movements and Third World Resistance*, Cambridge: Cambridge University Press, 2003, p. 196.
2 Commission on Human Rights, 'Interim Report of the Special Representative of the Secretary General on the Issue of Human Rights and Transnational Corporations and Other Business Enterprises', E/CN.4/2006/97 (22 February 2006), paras 27 and 30.

the MNCs are based, it is not surprising that a significant number of companies involved in such violations are from developed countries, though this scenario might change in future as MNCs from developing countries like China, Brazil and India are emerging on the world stage.[3] There are two more components of this typical scenario: the reluctance of host states to actively pursue MNCs involved in human rights abuses and a large pool of generally poor and/or largely ignorant victims.

Further, in making UCC account for Bhopal, the victims encountered almost all the major obstacles that, over the years, have impeded the process of bringing MNCs to justice for infringing human rights. Consider, in particular, the following:

(i) lack of specific human rights obligations for corporations
(ii) inadequate or fragile regulatory frameworks
(iii) unwillingness or incapacity of states to vigorously pursue MNCs
(iv) economic leverage that MNCs enjoy to influence regulatory initiatives
(v) (non)liability of a parent corporation for human rights abuses by its subsidiaries
(vi) corporate misuse of the doctrine of *forum non conveniens*
(vii) use of litigation delay as a defence by MNCs
(viii) large number of victims, many of whom could be poor and/or illiterate
(ix) absence of, or difficulties in imposing, effective sanctions against MNCs and
(x) inherent hurdles in criminal prosecution of MNCs and their executives.

It has been 27 years since the gas leak in December 1984, but still most of these obstacles have not been overcome. Bhopal thus remains a challenge to the project of humanizing business. Over the years, although some progress has been made, no effective legal regulatory framework has yet been put in place. It is difficult to conceive how the legal process would be able to respond more effectively and swiftly if Bhopal was to occur today. For example, even after almost a decade of litigation pursued in a developed legal system (the US), no *legal* liability could be imposed on anyone for grave human rights violations in a more recent case concerning Unocal's operations in Myanmar. The victims had to be content with an opaque settlement.

Before proceeding further, a brief note on the terminology used here. There is no consensus on how to label the Bhopal gas leakage. Many different terms have been used to describe what happened in Bhopal on the night of 2 December 1984: incident, accident, disaster, tragedy, catastrophe, crisis,

---

3 Whereas more than 90 per cent of all MNCs were located in developed countries in the early 1990s, this figure came down to about 72 per cent by 2008. United Nations Conference on Trade and Development, *World Investment Report 2010: Investing in a Low-Carbon Economy*, New York: UN, 2010, p. 17.

industrial genocide, sabotage, and massacre.⁴ It is thus clear that labels of Bhopal are loaded with what a particular stakeholder would like that label to convey. In order to avoid any such bias, I prefer to simply refer it as 'Bhopal'. Arguably, 'Bhopal' has acquired a secondary meaning and therefore, it no longer requires any other adjective to describe what it symbolizes, that is, the impunity of MNCs for human rights violations, the timid response of a government to such impunity, and the continuing misery of the victims.⁵

Context of UCC's entry and operations in India

Understanding the circumstances and conditions under which MNCs enter and operate in the markets of developing countries is as important as an investigation of their actual conduct or operations. In fact, pre-entry negotiations between MNCs and host developing countries are fundamental to whether or not MNCs operate as responsible corporate citizens. Although such negotiations generally determine the conditions under which foreign investment and/or transfer of technology will take place, they could also prepare the groundwork for MNCs to violate human rights in developing countries by adopting inferior human rights standards.⁶

The core issues related to foreign investment – which country gets *how much* foreign investment *from where* and on *what terms* – are the subject matter of bargaining and negotiations between potential investors and countries seeking foreign investment.⁷ At the pre-entry stage, rules of operation regarding several aspects such as technology transfer, tax treatment/concessions, competition policy, property expropriation, employment of foreign personnel and compliance with national safety, labour and environmental laws are negotiated, often in the context of a foreign investment agreement. MNCs, because of their stronger bargaining position *vis-à-vis* developing countries,⁸ are often able to set favourable terms for their post-entry operations. This hypothesis is

---

4 W. Bogard, *The Bhopal Tragedy: Language, Logic, and Politics in the Production of a Hazard*, Boulder, Colorado: Westview Press, 1989, p. viii; P. Shrivastava, *Bhopal: Anatomy of a Crisis*, Massachusetts: Ballinger Publishing Co., 1987, p. 85.
5 S. Deva, 'From 3/12 to 9/11: Future of Human Rights?' *Economic and Political Weekly*, 2004, vol. 39, 5198, at 5200.
6 The memorandum of understanding between the government of the state of Orissa and POSCO to establish an integrated steel plant in Orissa illustrates this again. 'Memorandum of Understanding between the Government of Orissa and M/s POSCO for Establishment of an Integrated Steel Plant at Paradeep', 22 June 2005. Available at: www.orissa.gov.in/posco/POSCO-MoU.htm (accessed 3 June 2011).
7 S. Deva, 'The *Sangam* of Foreign Investment, Multinational Corporations and Human Rights: An Indian Perspective for a Developing Asia', *Singapore Journal of Legal Studies*, 2004, 305, at 320.
8 P. Redmond, 'Transnational Enterprise and Human Rights: Options for Standard Setting and Compliance', *International Lawyer*, 2003, vol. 37, 69, at 72–3.

affirmed by the circumstances and conditions under which UCC entered and expanded into the Indian market. UCC – 'with 130 subsidiaries in some 40 countries, approximately 500 production sites, and 120,000 employees'[9] – was clearly the more influential party in its negotiations with the Indian government. It will be clear from the analysis below that apart from gaining access to the huge Indian market for pesticides, UCC basically got whatever an MNC could ask for in a developing country during that period.

There were a number of ways in which UCC exerted influence in its negotiations with the Indian government. The first example of UCC's influence relates to the very circumstances in which it came to establish the chemical plant at Bhopal. The Industrial Development and Regulation Act 1951 had reserved the pesticide formulation activity (i.e. the process of mixing concentrate with sand) for small firms of Indian nationality, but UCC was able to convince the Indian government to waive this requirement.[10] The government arguably sanctioned the project under pressure to industrialize, even though the appropriate industrial infrastructure and support systems were missing.[11] In short, as William argues, the genesis of the Bhopal gas leakage lies in the 'political economy of development in the Third World'.[12]

The second instance of UCC's influence in decision making is evident in how it overcame (so as to maintain control over UCIL) the limitation on foreign investment imposed by Indian law at that time. Apart from the general policy of the Indian government to push for indigenous ownership,[13] the Foreign Exchange Regulation Act of 1973 specifically limited foreign investment in Indian companies to 40 per cent.[14] Faced with this restriction, UCC reduced its holding in UCIL from 60 per cent to 50.90 per cent, but no further.[15] It rather successfully persuaded the Indian government to grant an exemption from the 40 per cent rule in view of 'significant export volume and the technological sophistication of its operations'.[16] This exemption from foreign control again 'attests to the power' of UCC *vis-à-vis* the Indian government.[17] UCC was holding 50.90 per cent shares of UCIL and, as Jones reminds

---

9 D. Lapierre and J. Moro, *It Was Five Past Midnight in Bhopal*, New Delhi: Full Circle Publishing, 2001, p. 29.
10 Ibid., pp. 54–65, 72, 77.
11 Shrivastava, above n. 4, p. 4.
12 Bogard, above n. 4, p. xi.
13 J. Cassels, 'Outlaws: Multinational Corporations and Catastrophic Law', *Cumberland Law Review*, 2000–2001, vol. 31, 311, at 314.
14 Act No. 46 of 1973, s. 29. In view of increasing liberalization, this law has now been replaced with the Foreign Exchange Management Act 1999 (No. 42 of 1999).
15 U. Baxi and A. Dhanda (eds), *Valiant Victims and Lethal Litigation: The Bhopal Case*, Bombay: N M Tripathi Pvt. Ltd, 1990, p. 37.
16 T. Jones, *Corporate Killing: Bhopals will Happen*, London: Free Association Books, 1988, pp. 38–9.
17 J. Cassels, *The Uncertain Promise of Law: Lessons from Bhopal*, Toronto: University of Toronto Press, 1993, p. 41.

us, 'UCIL was one of the few firms in India in which the parent company was allowed to maintain a majority interest.'[18] It is apparent that for UCC, control over UCIL was critical. This control enabled UCC to take all critical decisions for UCIL, including those which led to the gas leakage. But at the same time it maintained a safe distance by design from UCIL as part of its 'arm's-length' corporate policy[19] and relied on the separate entity status of UCIL when it came to the question of legal liability for Bhopal.[20]

Third, closely related to the control exercised by parent MNCs like UCC over their subsidiaries are two other factors: centralized policy-making and its effect on communications within the group, and a conflict of interest between the parent MNC and the host government. These interrelated factors in some way contributed to Bhopal. Consistent with how many MNCs are organized and structured, UCC practised centralized policy-making and controlled the functioning of its subsidiary UCIL.[21] The control that UCC exercised over the UCIL-run Bhopal plant was not limited to share ownership or representation on the board of directors,[22] but extended to the taking of key decisions regarding issues such as technology, plant design, safety, storage and handling of MIC, training of employees, and the financial viability of the plant.[23] This excessive centralization not only resulted in a rift between the formulation of 'global' policies and their 'local' implementation, but also contributed to a communication and management gap between UCC and UCIL.[24] Cassels gives a concrete example of how this rift played its part in the occurrence of Bhopal: 'Safety information was not properly communicated from the head office, and what information was communicated was ignored.'[25]

There was also a mismatch between what the parent corporation (UCC) would have liked its subsidiary (UCIL) to achieve and the expectations of the host state (India) from that particular subsidiary.[26] Given that the 'Bhopal

---

18 Jones, above n. 16, pp. 38–9.
19 Judge Keenan in his judgment noted that the design Transfer Agreement and the Technical Service Agreement between UCC and UCIL 'were negotiated at "arm's-length" pursuant to Union Carbide corporate policy.' *In Re: Union Carbide Corporation Gas Plant Disaster at Bhopal, India in December 1984*, 634 F. Supp. 842, at 856 (1986).
20 Jones, above n. 16, pp. 33–7; D. Kurzman, *A Killing Wind: Inside Union Carbide and the Bhopal Catastrophe*, New York: McGraw-Hill, 1987, pp. 181–5.
21 UCC's Corporate Policy Manual, for example, clearly provided that '[e]xcept for certain special situations, it is the general policy of the Corporation to secure and maintain effective management control of an affiliate.' As quoted in Amnesty International, *Clouds of Injustice: Bhopal Disaster 20 Years On*, London: Amnesty International, 2004, p. 46.
22 UCC held 50.90 per cent shares of UCIL and controlled the appointment of five out of 11 directors. Kurzman, above n. 20, p. 182.
23 See Amnesty International, above n. 21, pp. 39–49; K. Fortun, *Advocacy after Bhopal: Environmentalism, Disaster, New Global Orders*, Chicago: University of Chicago Press, 2001, pp. 26, 115–17.
24 Cassels, above n. 17, p. 21.
25 Ibid., p. 20.
26 Ibid., pp. 33–5.

plant was an unprofitable unit in an unimportant division of the corporation',[27] UCC was no longer interested in the proper management or successful running of the plant. The Indian government, on the other hand, would have preferred the Bhopal plant to continue operating safely, because it manufactured pesticides locally and provided much-needed employment. In this disjunction of priorities of UCC and the Indian government regarding the Bhopal plant, the issue of safety took a back seat: at the critical time, safety was not the priority of UCC, while the Indian government was seemingly not serious about safety, or considered safety the sole business of UCC.

Fourth, the location of the chemical plant in close proximity to the Bhopal railway station was inappropriate and somewhat suspicious.[28] While allotting the land, the state government did not adequately consider 'the population pressure and the growing needs of the town',[29] or the human rights-cum-environmental implications of the project. Nor did it consider the consequences of any escape of harmful gases to people living in adjoining places or who might be using the Bhopal railway station especially when it was a busy station. Moreover, the objection of the Bhopal municipal authorities to the site of the plant – in that it was meant only for commercial or light industrial use – was overruled by the central and state governments.[30] The state government also quelled any attempts to relocate the plant.[31] It is, therefore, logical to conclude that the central and state governments – in permitting UCC-UCIL to operate in violation of relevant rules and regulations – were either swayed by the development rhetoric or must have acted for reasons other than merit and objectivity. In either case, this again verifies that MNCs like UCC can exert so much influence on the governments of developing countries that they may not be able to decide and act for the benefit of their own people.

In view of the above analysis, Bhopal was predictable, and to some extent this predictability was rooted in the context in which UCC-UCIL was allowed to enter and continue to do business in India. Bhopal only surfaced in the year 1984 – a year in which Freeman presented his stakeholder model[32] – but its roots go back to the early 1960s when UCC was expanding its business in India.

The factual matrix surrounding the gas leakage

On the night of 2 December 1984, there was a massive leakage of toxic gases from the MIC storage tank of the Bhopal chemical plant. The immediate

---

27 Shrivastava, above n. 4, p. 51.
28 L. Shastri, *Bhopal Disaster: An Eye Witness Account*, New Delhi: Criterion Publications, 1985, p. 12.
29 Ibid. The lack of proper town planning regulations also played their part. T. Kletz, *Learning from Accidents*, 2nd edn, Oxford: Butterworth-Heinemann, 1994, p. 97.
30 Kurzman, above n. 20, pp. 22–3.
31 Cassels, above n. 17, pp. 15–16.
32 R. Freeman, *Strategic Management: A Stakeholder Approach*, Boston: Pitman, 1984.

cause of the reaction and the consequent leakage of gases was the introduction of water into the MIC storage tank.[33] However, there is no consensus on how water entered the tank.[34] UCC tried to explain this using a sabotage theory, while the Indian government suggested that water might have entered the tank during the routine washing of pipes on that night.[35] Although there are 'gaps and anomalies' in the two conflicting explanations of how water might have entered the tank,[36] it seems more plausible that UCC invoked the sabotage theory as a line of defence, or at best as a 'convenient conclusion'.[37]

A number of factors jointly contributed to the gas leakage.[38] This issue is dealt with in more detail in Chapter 6 with special reference to those causal factors that establish how the application of inferior standards by MNCs such as UCC could infringe the human rights of many people. Here it should suffice to note that Bhopal was inevitable in view of several decisions taken (or not taken) by UCC-UCIL over a period of time. After the gas leak, in a plant that was presented as a symbol of 'state of the art technology',[39] UCC started shifting all the blame for Bhopal to its subsidiary UCIL.[40]

In this blame game, some blame was rightly attributed to the central and state governments in India which at their levels facilitated the occurrence of Bhopal (e.g. by granting regulatory exemptions, improper planning permission, not fully appreciating the hazardous nature of the process in the chemical plant, the lax enforcement of safety laws, and allowing slums to develop in the immediate vicinity of the plant).[41] I will show later in this chapter how the Indian government allowed UCC to escape easily and lightly from its legal liability for Bhopal. All this demonstrates how even a democratic state eager to appease, or acting in concert with, MNCs can actually harm the interests of its poor populace while purportedly seeking to do the opposite.

In terms of the consequences of the gas leakage, no one knows with certainty the precise number of dead and injured.[42] According to the official government figure, about 3,000 people died immediately after the tragedy.[43] This

---

33 Cassels, above n. 17, p. 4.
34 Amnesty International, above n. 21, p. 40; Kletz, above n. 29, pp. 98–9; Kurzman, above n. 20, pp. 185–9.
35 Cassels, above n. 17, pp. 8–11.
36 Ibid., p. 11.
37 Cassels, above n.13, p. 315.
38 Shrivastava, above n. 4, pp. 42, 48–54; Cassels, above n. 17, pp. 12–25.
39 Bogard, above n. 4, p. 21.
40 Kurzman, above n. 20, p. 181; Fortun, above n. 23, p. 115.
41 Cassels, above n. 17, pp. 15–16, 23–4; Shastri, above n. 28, pp. 29–30, 77–8.
42 Amnesty International, above n. 21, pp. 10–12; M. Galanter, 'Legal Torpor: Why so Little has Happened in India After the Bhopal Tragedy?' *Texas International Law Journal*, 1985, vol. 20, 273, at 282–3.
43 Bhopal Gas Tragedy Relief and Rehabilitation Department, Bhopal, State of Madhya Pradesh, 'Profile'. Available at: www.mp.nic.in/bgtrrdmp/profile.htm (accessed 13 June 2006).

figure was revised to 15,248 in the 2003 report of the Bhopal Gas Tragedy Relief and Rehabilitation Department, State of Madhya Pradesh.[44] However, according to Amnesty International's estimate 'between 7,000 and 10,000 people died within three days of the gas leak' and over 20,000 to date.[45] Perhaps more tragic is the plight of survivors of Bhopal and their post-Bhopal children. It is estimated that about two-thirds of the total population of Bhopal was affected by the gas leakage.[46] Many survivors still suffer from a range of (and in some cases multiple) medical conditions – from respiratory illness to eye disease, immunity impairment, neurological damage, neuromuscular damage, cancers, gynaecological disorders, miscarriages and compromised mental health.[47] Bhopal also led to environmental pollution in the vicinity of the plant, including contamination of the ground water.[48]

The human rights implications of Bhopal

How does this loss of life, the continued misery of survivors and environmental contamination in Bhopal translate in terms of the human rights discourse? Amnesty International's *Clouds of Injustice: Bhopal Disaster 20 Years On* was perhaps the first major work that tried to analyze Bhopal 'through a human rights lens'.[49]

The reason why the existing literature on Bhopal did not generally invoke the analytical framework of human rights is not too difficult to find. At the time of Bhopal in December 1984, the entity that arguably violated human rights (UCC-UCIL) was under no clear human rights obligations under international or Indian law. With the exception of the ILO Declaration,[50] international law instruments in the early 1980s hardly imposed direct human rights duties on MNCs in areas that could have been relevant to the case of Bhopal. Bhopal thus exposed a dichotomy in the international human rights framework in that it imposed human rights obligations on *perceived* violators (states) but not on other *potential* violators (non-state actors).

The possibility of UCC-UCIL being subject to human rights responsibilities flowing from municipal Indian laws was not encouraging either. At the time of Bhopal, India did not have any 'specific' law that imposed human

---

44 Amnesty International, above n. 21, 12.
45 Ibid., 10, 12.
46 Above n. 43, 'Facts and Figures'. Available at: www.mp.nic.in/bgtrrdmp/facts.htm (accessed 13 June 2006).
47 Kurzman, above n. 20, pp. 145–7; B. Dinham and S. Sarangi, 'The Bhopal Gas Tragedy of 1984 to? The Evasion of Corporate Responsibility', *Environment and Urbanization*, 2002, vol. 14, 89, at 92–6.
48 Amnesty International, above n. 21, pp. 22–6.
49 Ibid, p. 2.
50 ILO, Tripartite Declaration of Principles Concerning Multinational Enterprises and Social Policy (16 November 1977), reprinted in *ILM*, 1978, vol. 17, 422.

rights obligations on corporations.⁵¹ In fact, Bhopal triggered the enactment or amendment of laws in several areas (e.g. the enactment of the Environment (Protection) Act 1986 and the Public Liability Insurance Act 1991, and the amendment of the Factories Act in 1987 to insert special provisions dealing with 'hazardous processes').⁵² Thus, with the possible exception of the Air (Prevention and Control of Pollution) Act 1981, there was hardly any positive legal human rights obligation that UCC-UCIL could have breached by doing what it did in Bhopal.⁵³ Similarly, although the protection of certain fundamental rights under the Indian Constitution does extend beyond the state action,⁵⁴ most of the developments *vis-à-vis* the human rights obligations of non-state actors such as corporations have taken place after Bhopal.⁵⁵

Amnesty International's human rights lens for Bhopal: A critique

It is not straightforward to analyze Bhopal as a site for human rights violations. However, Amnesty's *Clouds of Injustice* fails to acknowledge, confront and overcome these challenges. It seeks to use a 'human rights framework to examine . . . what obligations under international law have been breached and what protective standards failed'.⁵⁶ *Clouds of Injustice* refers to various regional or international treaties, conventions, declarations, standards and judicial decisions to make a case for Bhopal resulting in the violation of several human rights such as the right to life, the right to the highest attainable standard of health, the right to remedy and the right to a safe environment.⁵⁷

Amnesty International's human rights analysis of Bhopal has some flaws. For obvious reasons, Amnesty's report investigates Bhopal as a human rights tragedy primarily from the perspective of states: it was the government of India and/or the state of Madhya Pradesh that violated human rights by

---

51 There were scattered provisions in some laws such as the Trade Unions Act (No. 16 of 1926), the Minimum Wages Act (No. 11 of 1948), the Factories Act (No. 63 of 1948), the Maternity Benefit Act (No. 53 of 1961), and the Air (Prevention and Control of Pollution) Act (No. 14 of 1981).
52 Factories Act (No. 63 of 1948). The Amendment Act No. 20 of 1987 inserted Chapter IV-A in the Factories Act.
53 It is arguable that discharging emissions in air beyond the permissible limits – as stipulated by Section 20 of the Air (Prevention and Control of Pollution) Act – will violate, at least, the right to life and the right to health.
54 Constitution of India, arts. 15(2), 17, 23(1) and 24. The concept of 'state action' has also been liberally interpreted by the Indian Supreme Court. See M. P. Singh, *Shukla's Constitution of India*, 11th edn, Lucknow: Eastern Book Co., 2008, pp. 23–31.
55 The Supreme Court, for example, developed the absolute liability principle in *M. C. Mehta* v. *Union of India* (1987) 1 SCC 393 and the 'polluter pays' principle in *Indian Council for Enviro-Legal Action* v. *Union of India* (1996) 3 SCC 212.
56 Amnesty International, above n. 21, p. 27.
57 Ibid., pp. 28–38. Arguably, a glaring omission from this list is the right to information.

allowing UCC-UCIL to indulge in hazardous activities. Although the report admits that 'human rights responsibilities extend beyond states',[58] how the conduct of UCC-UCIL itself could have violated human rights is given a superficial and vague treatment.[59] Nowhere does the report mention how and which specific human rights responsibilities UCC-UCIL breached in relation to their Bhopal plant.

Moreover, instead of grounding its case in legal provisions as they stood in December 1984, Amnesty's *Clouds of Injustice* on many occasions refers to post-1984 legal developments to support its position.[60] How could one reasonably expect the Indian government or UCC to follow legal standards that did not exist at the time of the gas leak in December 1984? Therefore, unless one assumes that human rights were violated not merely by the gas leakage but also continuously since then, such a position is plainly untenable.

An alternative human rights analysis of Bhopal

Considering these loopholes in the analysis of Amnesty's *Clouds of Injustice*, how could one then pursue a human rights analysis of Bhopal? Without being exhaustive, I offer here two potentially more convincing lines of argument to posit that UCC and UCIL breached certain human rights with reference to their Bhopal plant operations. The first argument relies on the ILO Declaration of 1977, which was applicable to the operation of the chemical plant run by a subsidiary of UCC, because UCC as an MNC was expected to observe the principles contained therein.[61] Some of the provisions of the ILO Declaration had direct relevance to the factual matrix of Bhopal. UCC, for example, was 'commended' to observe the UDHR,[62] to 'ensure that relevant training is provided for all levels of their employees in the host country, as appropriate, to meet the needs of the enterprise,'[63] and to 'maintain the *highest standards* of safety and health . . . bearing in mind their *relevant experience within the enterprise as a whole*, including any *knowledge of special hazards*'.[64] It should also have made available, *inter alia*, to workers' representatives the 'information on the *safety and health standards* relevant to their local operations, *which they observe in other countries*'.[65] As we have briefly seen above and will see in more detail in Chapter 6, UCC was clearly in breach of these and several other principles. Breach of these standards directly resulted in violation, for example, of the rights to life, health, information, and a clean environment.

58 Ibid., p. 28.
59 Ibid., pp. 35–8.
60 Ibid., pp. 29, 31, 32, 36–8.
61 ILO Declaration of 1977, above n. 50, pp. 423 (Preamble) and 424 (para. 4).
62 Ibid., p. 424 (para. 8).
63 Ibid., p. 426 (para. 30).
64 Ibid., p. 427 (para. 37) (emphasis added).
65 Ibid. (emphasis added).

The second, and an indirect, way to deduce the human rights obligations of UCC-UCIL is through the law of torts. Human rights, or at least the underlying interests, could be protected through non-human rights laws too, namely, constitutional law, criminal law, and tort law.[66] Out of these legal fields, the suitability of tort law in protecting and promoting human rights is widely acknowledged.[67] The law of torts is apt to assume this role because it has the required 'fertility and flexibility to protect' almost all basic human rights,[68] could be invoked to sue even non-state actors, and in the past victims have used it to 'secure accountability' of decision makers.[69] This is not to suggest that the resort to tort law to protect human rights does not have its limitations, or that there are no conceptual differences between tort law and human rights law. Rather the objective is to highlight that human rights could be secured additionally by recourse to tort law.

I contend that it is possible to invoke Indian tort law to deduce human rights duties applicable to UCC-UCIL at the time of Bhopal. One could explore how the tortious principles relating, for example, to negligence, nuisance, strict liability and product liability might be used to enforce obligations to protect the human rights of life, health and environment. Let us consider and test the conduct of UCC-UCIL on the touchstone of the tort of negligence and the strict liability principle.

The tort of negligence requires a duty of care, breach of that duty and such breach causing harm to the plaintiff(s).[70] UCC-UCIL undoubtedly owed a duty under the neighbour principle,[71] not only to its workers, but also to those who lived in the vicinity of the plant. UCC-UCIL breached this duty because it did not exercise a reasonable standard of care in its maintenance and operation of the plant and consequently the MIC gas leaked out of the chemical plant. A person breaches the duty of care by 'behaviour that creates

---

66 Lord Bingham of Cornhill, 'Tort and Human Rights' in P. Cane and J. Stapleton (eds), *The Law of Obligations: Essays in Celebration of John Fleming*, Oxford: Clarendon Press, 1998, p. 1, at 2.
67 See J. Wright, *Tort Law and Human Rights*, Oxford, Portland Oregon: Hart Publishing, 2001; J. Stapleton, 'The Golden Thread at the Heart of Tort Law: Protection of the Vulnerable', *Australian Bar Review*, 2003, vol. 24, 1.
68 Lord Bingham in Cane and Stapleton (eds), above n. 66, p. 12.
69 C. Harlow, *State Liability: Tort Law and Beyond*, Oxford: Oxford University Press, 2004, p. 49. See also C. Scott (ed.), *Torture as Tort: Comparative Perspectives on the Development of Transnational Human Rights Litigation*, Oxford: Hart Publishing, 2001.
70 J. Murphy, *Street on Torts*, 1st Indian reprint, New Delhi: Oxford University Press, 2006, pp. 177–8; G. P. Singh, *Ratanlal and Dhirajlal's The Law of Torts*, 23rd edn, Nagpur: Wadhwa & Co., 1997, p. 412; J. Zerk, *Multinational and Corporate Social Responsibility: Limitations and Opportunities in International Law*, Cambridge: Cambridge University Press, 2006, pp. 216–23.
71 *Donoghue v. Stevenson* [1932] AC 562. Even the parent company (UCC) was arguably under a duty of care as it could foresee the possibility of harm to victims and there was a proximity (which need not be physical) between the MNC and the victims.

unreasonable foreseeable risk of injury'.[72] The risk was unreasonable because even the known safety precautions were not complied with; it was unreasonable even by Judge Hand's famous 'B < PL' test,[73] based on a cost–benefit analysis that corporations often do. The risk of injury as well as the magnitude of injury should have been foreseeable given that MIC was an in-house invention of UCC and the company was very much aware of its chemical composition, reactive nature and health risks associated with its contact.[74] UCC-UCIL also failed in their duty to adequately caution the public about the dangers of MIC before, during and after the gas leakage – thus causing serious harm to thousands of victims.

The principle of strict liability laid down in *Rylands* v. *Fletcher*[75] provides an additional tool to hold UCC-UCIL accountable.[76] Strict liability does not require fault, but still demands 'foreseeability' of harm arising from the activity undertaken.[77] Given that the Indian courts have applied the strict liability principle,[78] one could have invoked this principle against UCC-UCIL because a dangerous substance did escape from the Bhopal plant and caused harm.[79] There was arguably a 'non-natural use' of land by UCC-UCIL if we apply the test laid down by *Rickards* v. *Lothian* that there 'must be some special use bringing with it increased dangers to others'.[80] Even the precondition of foreseeability should stand satisfied in the Bhopal case – both as to the escape of MIC and the significant harm that it might cause upon escape.[81] Finally, none of the exceptions to the *Rylands* v. *Fletcher* principle (e.g. acts of a stranger, consent, contributory negligence and statutory authority) seem to have been attracted in the case of Bhopal.

---

72 R. Wright, 'The Standards of Care in Negligence Law' in D. Owen (ed.), *Philosophical Foundations of Tort Law*, Oxford: Clarendon Press, 1995, p. 249, at 249–50.
73 *United States* v. *Carroll Towing Co.* 159 F. 2d 169 (2d Cir., 1947). In the B < PL formula, B is the burden (cost) of taking precautions, P is the probability of loss, and L is the gravity of loss. The product of P x L must be a greater amount than B to create a duty of due care for the defendant.
74 UCC's Reactive and Hazardous Chemicals Manual stated clearly that MIC is 'a hazardous material by all means of contact' and 'a recognised poison by inhalation'. UCC, *Bhopal Methyl Isocyanate Incident Investigation Team Report*, March 1985, 24, as quoted in Amnesty International, above n. 21, p. 11.
75 *Rylands* v. *Fletcher* (1866) LR 1 Exch. 265.
76 In December 1986, the Indian Supreme Court enunciated the principle of absolute liability (which recognizes no defences) in *M. C. Mehta* v. *Union of India* AIR 1987 SC 1086. I am consciously not relying on that principle because it was a post-gas leakage development.
77 *Cambridge Water Co.* v. *Eastern Counties Leather* [1994] 2 AC 264 (HL).
78 Singh, above n. 70, pp. 437, 439–40, 447–9.
79 P. Muchlinski, 'The Bhopal Case: Controlling Ultrahazardous Activities Undertaken by Foreign Investors', *Modern Law Review*, 1987, vol. 50, 545, at 566.
80 [1913] AC 263, at 280.
81 Muchlinski, above n. 79, p. 581.

In view of the above analysis, it is logical to contend that in addition to negligence, UCC-UCIL could have been held liable for Bhopal under the strict liability principle as well. The failure of UCC-UCIL to comply with their duties – whether under the tort of negligence or the principle of strict liability – resulted in the loss of lives, infliction of injuries, and environmental pollution. Conversely, the right to life, the right to health, and the right to a clean environment could have been protected had UCC-UCIL complied with these tortious obligations. The basic objective of the thought experiment undertaken here was to illustrate that even if national and international human rights laws do not impose any specific and direct obligation on MNCs, one could still find comparable corporate human rights responsibilities under tort law or some other law.

Victims' quest for justice and the five phases of litigation

The victims' quest to seek justice against UCC-UCIL, Dow Chemical (which took over UCC in 2001) and the Indian government has turned out to be another catastrophe for the Bhopal victims.[82] The report of Amnesty International, *Clouds of Injustice*, aptly points out that what happened in Bhopal 'was not just a tragedy of the past; it has continued to be a tragedy ever since'.[83] Attempts to seek justice for the victims of Bhopal through judicial as well as non-judicial means (such as students' protests, public campaigns, marches, or shareholders' resolutions) have continued unabated in both the US and India. This section will focus primarily on the struggle inside the courts which, as Table 2.1 shows, could broadly be divided into five phases of litigation. Whereas the place of struggle in each of these five phases has been the Indian and/or the US courts, the time span and the objective of struggle have been different.

How and where to litigate?

In terms of the administration of justice, Bhopal presented multiple challenges as to compensating victims and fixing liability for the massive gas leakage. Some of the challenges arose because of the large number of victims (a majority of whom were poor and/or ignorant of their rights), evidentiary problems (including those related to causation and attribution), undeveloped Indian law dealing with such disasters, the economic incapacity of the Indian subsidiary (UCIL) to fully compensate victims, corporate law principles of limited liability and separate legal personality, and other difficulties inherent in any transnational litigation (e.g. choice of law). Various judicial as well as non-judicial alternatives were mooted and debated to overcome these challenges.[84] But ultimately the choice narrowed down to a judicial recourse. At least the

---

82 Cassels, above n. 13, p. 311.
83 Amnesty International, above n. 21, p. 10.
84 Cassels, above n. 17, pp. 110–12.

Table 2.1 Victims' quest for justice and the five phases of litigation

	Place of Struggle	Objective and Time Span
Phase I	India	*How and where to litigate?* (December 1984 to March 1985)
Phase II	US Courts	*Going after the 'parent' in the US* (April 1985 to January 1987)
Phase III	Indian Courts	*Struggle to fix responsibility in India* (September 1986 to December 1989)
Phase IV	Both US and Indian Courts	*Trying to overturn the settlement* (1990–1993)
	Indian Courts	Seeking compensation and medical care (1993–2004)
Phase V	US Courts	*Resort to the ATCA & common law* (2000–)
	Indian Courts	*Quest for criminal liability* (1992–)

following four issues were contentious: *who* should file the case (individuals, government, or a consolidated class action); *against whom* (out of UCC, UCIL and the Indian government); *where* (in the US or Indian courts); and *under what law* (e.g. product liability, tort law, breach of contract, and/or criminal law).

These issues attained an element of urgency because, just a few days after the gas leak, American lawyers started reaching Bhopal with a promise of securing millions of dollars in compensation.[85] To counter the possible exploitation of mostly poor-illiterate victims by these US lawyers and in conformity with its eagerness to file the case in the US courts, the Indian government as *parens patriae* acted swiftly and enacted the Bhopal Gas Leak Disaster (Processing of Claims) Act (Act/Bhopal Act) in March 1985.[86] The Act vested in the central government of India an 'exclusive right to represent, and act in place of (whether within or outside India) every person who has made, or is entitled to make, a claim' arising out of the Bhopal disaster.[87] This extraordinary power was conferred on the central government to deal with Bhopal claims 'speedily, effectively, equitably and to the best advantage of the claimants'.[88] In order to balance this exceptional provision, the Act preserved the victims' limited right to have their views taken into account by the Indian government and be represented by a lawyer of their choice in the suits or proceedings initiated by the government.[89]

---

85 Kurzman, above n. 20, pp. 111, 127–30, 133–5; Muchlinski, above n. 79, pp. 546–7.
86 Bhopal Gas Leak Disaster (Processing of Claims) Act 1985 (No. 21 of 1985).
87 Ibid., s. 3.
88 Ibid., Preamble.
89 Ibid., s. 4.

The Bhopal Act, although an innovative piece of legislation, received a great deal of criticism[90] and also faced a constitutional challenge to its validity.[91] The Act, however, settled the first two issues (*who* will file a case and *against whom*): the vesting of exclusive standing to deal with all claims arising out of Bhopal in the central government virtually meant that the government could not be sued for its contribution in the occurrence of Bhopal. The Bhopal Act also indicated *where* such cases could be filed in that it expressly contemplated the possibility of the Indian government representing victims' claims abroad. The principles of liability (i.e. *under what law*) were to be made explicit soon by the complaint filed by the government before the US District Court.

Going after the 'parent' in the US

The Indian government considered it a better strategy to sue the parent corporation UCC in the US courts.[92] On the other hand, UCC's legal strategy was to project and push for an early settlement as being in the interest of victims, while maintaining that if a trial had to take place, it should happen in India.[93] These strategies underpinned the respective positions of UCC and the Indian government in the years to come.

Exercising its power under the Bhopal Act, on 8 April 1985, the Indian government filed a complaint in the Southern District Court presided over by Judge Keenan. In order to overcome the key legal challenges pointed out before, the complaint was grounded in two notable principles: absolute and/or strict liability for ultrahazardous and inherently dangerous activity, and enterprise liability for MNCs.[94] Both of these principles as well as their application to Bhopal were strongly rebutted by UCC both inside and outside the courts. Whereas the Indian government tried to impress upon Judge Keenan the general incompetence of Indian courts and the legal system to handle effectively a case of this magnitude, UCC defended the soundness of the Indian legal system and made a robust plea for dismissing the suit on the ground of *forum non conveniens*.[95]

---

90 L. Hawkes, '*Parens Patriae* and the Union Carbide Case: The Disaster at Bhopal Continues', *Cornell International Law Journal*, 1988, vol. 21, 181, at 186–96.
91 The Indian Supreme Court upheld the constitutional validity of the Bhopal Act in *Charan Lal Sahu* v. *Union of India* AIR 1990 SC 1480.
92 Kurzman, above n. 20, pp. 195–6; S. Chopra, 'Multinational Corporations in the Aftermath of Bhopal: The Need for a New Comprehensive Global Regime for Transnational Corporate Activity', *Valparaiso University Law Review*, 1994, vol. 29, 235, at 247–8.
93 R. Trotter et al, 'Bhopal, India and Union Carbide: The Second Tragedy', *Journal of Business Ethics*, 1989, vol. 8, 439, at 443; Kurzman, above n. 20, pp. 196–204, 229.
94 'Complaint Filed by the Union of India in the US District Court, New York', as reproduced in N.R.M. Menon (ed.), *Documents and Court Opinions on Bhopal Gas Leak Disaster Case*, Bangalore: National Law School of India University, 1991, p. 1, at 3–4.
95 Ibid., pp. 32–5; Muchlinski, above n. 79, pp. 552–60.

When the parties failed to reach a settlement, on 12 May 1986, Judge Keenan dismissed the suit on the ground of *forum non conveniens*. As all private and public interest factors favoured the dismissal of the suit,[96] he was 'firmly convinced that the Indian legal system is in a far better position than the American courts to determine the cause of the tragic event and thereby fix liability.'[97] The dismissal was nevertheless subject to the following three conditions: (i) UCC shall consent to submit to the jurisdiction of the courts of India; (ii) UCC shall agree to satisfy any judgment rendered by an Indian court provided that it conforms with the minimal requirements of due process; and (iii) UCC shall be subject to discovery under the model of the US Federal Rules of Civil Procedure.[98]

On appeal, the US Court of Appeals affirmed the order of dismissal on the ground of *forum non conveniens*, but removed the last two conditions.[99] The dismissal of the suit from the US courts was seen as a victory for UCC, which did prefer to litigate, if at all, in India. The Indian government and victims, on the other hand, sought consolation in the fact that UCC – the parent corporation with deep pockets – had agreed to submit to the jurisdiction of the Indian courts.[100]

Struggle to fix responsibility in India

In its struggle to fix responsibility for Bhopal, the Indian government had its own 'settlement versus litigation' dilemma. A settlement was likely to result in swift compensation for victims, but any resultant settlement also risked lacking legitimacy and public support if the government was seen to be negotiating with the culprit foreign company. On the other hand, the government neither wanted its role exposed and subjected to international scrutiny in a lengthy litigation,[101] nor did it want the Bhopal litigation to discourage other MNCs from investing in India.[102]

---

96 Whereas 'private interest' factors concern the interests of the specific litigants to an action, 'public interest' factors affect not merely given litigants but the society generally. On this issue, the US Supreme Court decisions in *Gulf Oil Corp.* v. *Gilbert* 330 US 501 (1947) and *Piper Aircraft Co.* v. *Reyno* 454 US 235 (1981) are considered authoritative and were relied on by Judge Keenan to reason why India was a more convenient forum to adjudicate the Bhopal case.
97 *In Re: Union Carbide Corporation Gas Plant Disaster at Bhopal, India in December 1984*, above n. 19, p. 866.
98 Ibid., p. 867.
99 *In Re: Union Carbide Corporation Gas Plant Disaster at Bhopal, India in December 1984*, 809 F. 2d 195 (1987).
100 Chopra, above n. 92, p. 250.
101 Kurzman, above n. 20, p. 191; Galanter, above n. 42, p. 285.
102 Cassels, above n. 13, p. 321; Kurzman, above n. 20, pp. 191, 213.

Amidst this dilemma, on 5 September 1986, the Indian government filed a suit against UCC in the Bhopal district court.[103] The Indian government by and large persisted with the principles of liability invoked originally before Judge Keenan: it maintained that UCC exercised effective control over UCIL and was, therefore, strictly and/or absolutely liable for indulging in an ultrahazardous and inherently dangerous activity. UCC resolutely refuted all the contentions based on what Baxi terms a recourse to 'massive negation' – denying everything from the very existence of the concept of 'multinational corporation' to the fact that it controlled UCIL, that MIC was an ultrahazardous and dangerous substance, and that it was liable for Bhopal in any way.[104] UCC also challenged the power of Indian courts to award interim compensation in tort cases,[105] assailed the application of the absolute liability principle to the Bhopal case,[106] and opposed any attempt to pierce the corporate veil to reach UCC.[107]

The litigation before the Bhopal district court (or even before the High Court and the Supreme Court) never proceeded to an assessment of the merits of the case. Throughout the time that the Indian courts were adjudicating on the matter, UCC played its cards skilfully (e.g. delaying proceedings, increasing the complexity of the case, asserting the separate existence of its subsidiary UCIL, filing cross-appeals, challenging the powers and jurisdiction of the Indian courts, and even conveying a veiled threat about the non-enforceability of an Indian judgment against UCC in the US) to coerce the government to enter into a settlement.[108] After years of futile litigation, the Indian Supreme Court approved a settlement between UCC and the central government by its two orders dated 14 and 15 February 1989.[109] The settlement order, *inter alia*, read: 'The aforesaid payments [US$470 million] shall be made to the Union of India as claimant and *for the benefit of all victims* of the Bhopal gas disaster . . . and *not as fines, penalties, or punitive damage*.'[110] So, UCC agreed to award compensation not in pursuance of any legal liability but as a token of mercy shown to the Bhopal victims.[111] Moreover, as the settlement

---

103 'Union of India's Plaint in Regular Suit No. 1113/86', as reproduced in Baxi and Dhanda, above n. 15, pp. 3–12.
104 Baxi, 'An Introduction' in Baxi and Dhanda, above n. 15, p. xiv, and generally pp. xiv–xix, 31–107, 198–222.
105 Ibid., pp. xxvii–xxxii, 243, 254–8, 306–31, 405–42.
106 Cassels, above n. 13, p. 328.
107 Baxi, 'An Introduction' in Baxi and Dhanda, above n. 15, pp. xxxii–xxxiii, 306–31, 415, 436–9.
108 Baxi and Dhanda, above n. 15, pp. xix–xxi, xxxv–xxxvi; Amnesty International, above n. 21, pp. 52–4.
109 *Union Carbide Corporation* v. *Union of India* AIR 1990 SC 273.
110 Ibid., p. 275 (emphasis added).
111 Fortun, above n. 23, pp. 98–101.

settled all civil proceedings, quashed pending criminal proceedings, and directed the central and state governments to take necessary steps to defend UCC-UCIL and their personnel against future proceedings, it also, in effect, conferred immunity on UCC-UCIL and their personnel against any future civil or criminal liability.[112]

It is notable that the two settlement orders were as brief as a few paragraphs. Beyond putting on record that such a settlement was considered 'just, equitable and reasonable' in view of 'the enormity of human suffering occasioned by the Bhopal gas disaster and the pressing urgency to provide immediate and substantial relief to victims of the disaster',[113] the orders, for example, contained no explanation as to how the magical figure of US$470 million was reached. The settlement orders provoked public outrage and fierce criticism, which forced the Supreme Court to provide reasons for its approval of the settlement later on.[114]

In the given circumstances of the case, a court-approved settlement was arguably the best result that the Indian government (or even the victims) could have asked for. In the end, the government got what it wanted. This settlement did not do much harm to UCC either: indeed it 'escaped a corporate catastrophe'.[115] As far as the victims were concerned, they were never a party, or even privy, to intricate details of the litigation-cum-settlement. Although both UCC and the Indian government supposedly acted for the benefit and in the best interest of victims, the victims were totally at the mercy of their twin custodians.

Trying to overturn the settlement, seeking compensation and medical care

Dismayed at what the victims considered an inadequate and non-transparent settlement, victims' groups sought to overturn the settlement order by challenging its constitutional and legal validity before the US and Indian courts. The Indian Supreme Court, rejecting the multiple arguments advanced by victims' lawyers, upheld the settlement award, but agreed to reinstate criminal charges against UCC-UCIL and their personnel.[116] Parallel to the challenge mounted before the Indian Supreme Court, some victims also knocked on the doors of US courts to assail the validity of the settlement contending that the Indian government had a conflict of interest position, that most of the

---

112 The Supreme Court, however, later restored criminal proceedings in *Union Carbide Corporation* v. *Union of India* AIR 1992 SC 248.
113 *Union Carbide Corporation* v. *Union of India* AIR 1990 SC 273.
114 *Union Carbide Corporation* v. *Union of India* (1989) 3 SCC 38.
115 C. Carr, 'Carbide Escape: Why India's Awkward Strategy Forced the Settlement?' *The American Lawyer*, 1989, vol. 11: 4, 99, at 105.
116 *Union Carbide Corporation* v. *Union of India* AIR 1992 SC 248.

victims opposed the settlement as grossly inadequate, and that their due process rights were violated.[117] As expected, the US courts dismissed these suits on procedural grounds.[118]

When it became apparent that the efforts to set aside the settlement might not bring the desired result, the victims' groups focused their attention on the disbursement of compensation and access to medical care. Time and again victims' groups or socially active lawyers had to approach the Supreme Court to ensure that interim relief was provided, compensation reached rightful victims swiftly and efficiently, and that the settlement money lying with the government was distributed to all victims on a pro rata basis.[119] This recourse to the judiciary was necessitated because the government's efforts to provide compensation, medical care and rehabilitation to victims were hampered by the sheer number of victims, bad planning, corruption, a cumbersome claims process, difficulty in medical categorization, inefficient administration, and an opportunistic cartel of doctors, lawyers and aid disbursement agencies.[120]

Resort to the ATCA and the continuing quest for criminal liability

As pointed out before, Bhopal also led to environmental pollution in the vicinity of the plant, including contamination of the ground water.[121] Greenpeace reports of 1999 and 2002 amply document the level of contamination of soil and water on and around the plant site.[122] The plant site has not been cleaned at the time of writing this book, so toxins continue to seep through and contaminate community water sources.

Being disappointed by the lack of will shown by the Indian government to respond effectively to the miseries of the Bhopal victims generally and to the contamination of the plant site specifically, victims' groups once again approached the US courts in November 1999 under the ATCA and/or

---

117 *Bano Bi* v. *Union Carbide Corporation* 1992 US Dist. LEXIS 1909; *Bano Bi* v. *Union Carbide Corporation* 984 F. 2d 582 (1993).
118 *Bano Bi* v. *Union Carbide Corporation* 1992 US Dist. LEXIS 1909, at 7.
119 See, for some of the early orders regarding interim relief, Baxi and Dhanda, above n. 15, pp. 667–79. In July 2004, the Supreme Court ordered the settlement amount lying with the government to be distributed among all the victims on a pro rata basis. J. Venkatesan, 'Court Orders Relief to Bhopal Gas Victims', *The Hindu*, 20 July 2004. Available at: www.hindu.com/2004/07/20/stories/2004072008760100.htm (accessed 14 June 2011).
120 Amnesty International, above n. 21, pp. 63–7; S. Muralidharan, 'Bhopal: Continuing Institutional Crisis', *Economic and Political Weekly*, 2004, vol. 39, 5196.
121 Amnesty International, above n. 21, pp. 22–6.
122 I. Labunska *et al.*, *The Bhopal Legacy: Toxic Contaminants at the Former Union Carbide Factory Site, Bhopal, India – 15 Years after the Bhopal Accident*, Greenpeace, November 1999; R. Stringer *et al.*, *Chemical Stockpiles at Union Carbide India Limited in Bhopal: An Investigation*, Greenpeace, November 2002.

common law. This time, specific claims were also made for environmental contamination including that of land and water wells, before as well as after the gas leak. A review of numerous judgments and orders passed by the US courts – dealing with diverse pleas (e.g. veil piercing, discovery of documents and assignment of the case to another judge) – reveals that so far this litigation also failed to deliver any significant victory for the victims.[123]

The outcome of efforts to fix criminal liability on UCC-UCIL has not been much different from what we have seen regarding the struggle for civil responsibility. Although the Indian Central Bureau of Investigation (CBI) did file a charge sheet against UCC-UCIL and their personnel in December 1987, nothing much happened and the Supreme Court's settlement order then quashed all pending criminal proceedings in February 1989.[124] The quest for criminal liability gained some momentum again after the Court reinstated the criminal proceedings in October 1991.[125] But even after this, the criminal proceedings moved at a snail's pace and had many twists and turns. To begin with, Warren Anderson, the chief executive officer of UCC – who was arrested soon after landing in India and then released on bail on the same day – did not appear before the court and was declared a proclaimed offender.[126] Later, the Indian Attorney General advised the government that the proceedings in the US for extradition of Anderson 'are not likely to succeed and, therefore, the same may not be pursued against'.[127] The Indian Supreme Court, by reversing the judgment of the High Court, diluted the charges levelled at UCIL and its Indian officers (but not against Anderson) from 'culpable homicide not amounting to murder' under Section 304 Part II of the Indian Penal Code (IPC) to causing death by a 'rash or negligent act' under Section 304A.[128]

---

123 *Sajida Bano* v. *UCC* 2000 US Dist. 12326; *Sajida Bano* v. *UCC* 273 F. 3d 120 (2d Cir. NY, 2001); *Sajida Bano* v. *UCC* 2003 US Dist. LEXIS 4097; *Sajida Bano* v. *UCC* 361 F. 3d 696 (2d Cir. NY, 2004); *Sajida Bano* v. *UCC* 2005 US Dist. LEXIS 32595; *Sajida Bano* v. *UCC* 2005 US Dist. LEXIS 22871; *Janki Bai Sahu* v. *UCC* 418 F. Supp. 2d 407 (2005); *Janki Bai Sahu* v. *UCC* 2006 US Dist. LEXIS 714; *Janki Bai Sahu* v. *UCC* 2006 US Dist. LEXIS 944; *Sajida Bano* v. *UCC* 2006 US App. LEXIS 21022; *Janki Bai Sahu* v. *UCC* 2006 US Dist. LEXIS 84475; *Janki Bai Sahu* v. *UCC* 548 F. 3d 59 (2d Cir.2008); *Janki Bai Sahu* v. *UCC* 262 F.R.D. 308 (SDNY, 2009); *Janki Bai Sahu* v. *UCC* 746 F. Supp. 2d 609 (2010); *Janki Bai Sahu* v. *UCC* 2010 WL 532307 (SDNY).
124 *Union Carbide Corporation* v. *Union of India* AIR 1990 SC 273.
125 *Union Carbide Corporation* v. *Union of India* AIR 1992 SC 248.
126 S. Murlidhar, 'Unsettling Truths, Untold Tales: The Bhopal Gas Tragedy Victims' "Twenty Years" of Courtroom Struggles for Justice', *IELRC Working Paper 2004/5*, pp. 36–9. Available at: www.ielrc.org/content/w0405.pdf (accessed 28 May 2011). The courts can declare a person who faces criminal charges but neither appears before it nor responds to its summons a 'proclaimed offender'.
127 'Litigation: Opinion of the Attorney General', *Frontline*, vol. 19:1, 5–18 January 2002. Available at: www.hinduonnet.com/fline/fl1901/19011020.htm (accessed 28 May 2011).
128 *Keshub Mahindra* v. *State of Madhya Pradesh* (1996) 6 SCC 129.

More than 25 years after the gas leak, on 7 June 2010, a criminal court convicted eight persons (UCIL and seven of its officials) for causing death by negligence under Section 304A of the IPC.[129] Whereas the court directed UCIL to pay Rs 5 lakh (about USD11,000) in fines, others were sentenced to two years in prison and a fine of about Rs one lakh (about USD2,200) each. In response to the public outrage that the verdict attracted, the central government proposed several steps to pacify public sentiment.[130] The government filed a special leave petition (SLP) in the Supreme Court seeking review of the 1996 judgment that had diluted the criminal charge from 'culpable homicide not amounting to murder' to 'death by negligence'.[131] Although the Court rejected this SLP, it allowed – in an unprecedented move – a curative petition to revisit the 1996 judgment.[132] But this ray of hope did not last long, as the Court subsequently rejected this curative petition on account of a long delay of 14 years in filing the petition.[133]

Arguably, the Indian government failed to live up to the expectations of victims on this front too. It did not vigorously pursue the extradition of Anderson and in fact supported the dilution of the criminal charge against the Bhopal defendants. It was only in July 2010 that the government initiated the process of decontaminating and remedying the Bhopal plant site.[134] This overall inability and unwillingness of the Indian government to bring UCC and others to justice seem to indicate that the Indian government has considered the creation of an MNC-friendly environment to be more important than safeguarding the rights of its own populace.

129 S. Gupta, 'Bhopal Gas Case Verdict: Justice Delayed, Denied', *The Times of India*, 8 June 2010. Available at: http://timesofindia.indiatimes.com/india/Bhopal-gas-case-verdict-Justice-delayed-denied/articleshow/6021821.cms (accessed 28 May 2011).
130 'GoM for Hike in Payout, Review of Verdicts', *The Times of India*, 22 June 2010. Available at: http://timesofindia.indiatimes.com/india/GoM-for-hike-in-payout-review-of-verdicts/articleshow/6076562.cms (accessed 28 May 2011).
131 'Supreme Court Sore Over Delay in Bhopal Gas Tragedy Case', *The Hindu*, 8 August 2010. Available at: www.hindu.com/2010/08/08/stories/2010080859750400.htm (accessed 28 May 2011).
132 D. Mahapatra, 'SC Reopens Bhopal Case, Notices to Accused on Homicide Charge', *The Times of India*, 1 September 2010. Available at: http://articles.timesofindia.indiatimes.com/2010-09-01/india/28217038_1_s-b-majmudar-curative-petition-devadatt-kamat (accessed 28 May 2011).
133 'SC Dismisses CBI petition, Rejects Harsher Punishment for Bhopal Gas Tragedy Accused', *The Times of India*, 11 May 2011. Available at: http://articles.timesofindia.indiatimes.com/2011-05-11/india/29531515_1_bhopal-gas-tragedy-deadly-methyl-isocyanate-gas-review-petition (accessed 28 May 2011).
134 Ministry of Environment and Forests, 'Press Release: Bhopal Environmental Remediation Oversight Committee Constituted', 7 July 2010. Available at: http://moef.nic.in/downloads/public-information/PM_Bhopal.pdf (accessed 28 May 2011).

Summary

This chapter has tried to offer a basic understanding of Bhopal to the readers – Bhopal as a site of victims' struggle for justice against UCC-UCIL and, at a general level, Bhopal as a symbol of corporate impunity for human rights violations. An understanding of Bhopal is essential because, throughout the book, Bhopal will be invoked to investigate various issues related to corporate human rights abuses and in turn test, support, illustrate, or demonstrate various arguments advanced herein. Understanding Bhopal is critical for another reason too: as no one consensual narrative of the Bhopal story is readily available or even possible, readers should know how I prefer to read Bhopal and why.

Although it was a Herculean task to elucidate fully the multiple dimensions of Bhopal in one chapter, I have attempted to capture the central features of Bhopal. I have explained why Bhopal could be considered a representative case study to understand the dynamics of modern corporate human rights abuses. The analysis of Bhopal undertaken here was refreshing in that I tried to see Bhopal through the prism of human rights, a prism that has the potential to humanize business. Through this analysis, I also tried to show that pre-entry negotiations between MNCs and host states often prepare the groundwork for MNCs to violate human rights in developing countries by adopting inferior human rights standards.[135]

A brief examination of the five phases of Bhopal litigation highlights the absence and/or inadequacy of legal mechanisms to effectively deal with instances of human rights abuses by MNCs. The next two chapters highlight this inadequacy in more detail.

---

135 The ten principles proposed by the SRSG offer useful guidance – at least on paper – to identify, avoid and mitigate human rights risks during contract negotiations. Human Rights Council, 'Principles for Responsible Contracts: Integrating the Management of Human Rights Risks into State-Investor Contract Negotiations – Guidance for Negotiators', A/HRC/17/31/Add.3 (25 May 2011).

3 Evaluation of existing regulatory initiatives
An analytical framework

This chapter and the next elaborate upon the claim that existing regulatory initiatives are inadequate to make companies accountable for human rights abuses. Both these chapters should, therefore, be read in conjunction with each other. Whereas this chapter develops an analytical framework for evaluating existing regulatory initiatives that seek to make companies accountable for human rights violations, Chapter 4 evaluates selective representative initiatives according to the framework developed herein.

Developing such an analytical framework serves two objectives: it provides a yardstick to judge the adequacy of regulatory frameworks and also helps in selecting a representative sample out of a wide spectrum of regulatory initiatives concerning corporate human rights responsibilities. I propose that the adequacy of regulatory initiatives should be judged with reference to the objective of regulation, that is, the expected effect on the conduct of regulatees. A regulatory initiative that aims to ensure that companies respect their human rights obligations should be labelled as adequate if it is effective in both preventing and redressing corporate human rights abuses.

It is argued that the following five 'differentiating variables' could be used to understand the taxonomy of regulatory initiatives: the *source* from which regulatory initiatives flow; the *content* of obligations; the *targeting approach*; the *level of operation*; and the *nature* in terms of compliance strategy. The five differentiating variables identified here correspond to five 'regulatory dilemmas' that in my view make MNCs a difficult regulatory target: *who* should regulate *what* activities of *which* corporation, *where*, and *how*. These differentiating variables can help us to classify existing regulatory initiatives under different heads. One can then select, as I do in Chapter 4, certain representative initiatives from these heads and make a general claim about the inadequacy of the existing regulatory framework by evaluating the working of chosen specific initiatives.

This chapter begins with a brief explanation of the two levels of efficacy and their interrelation. It then explores the five regulatory dilemmas that make MNCs difficult regulatory targets. Finally, an attempt is made to understand the taxonomy of existing regulatory initiatives with the help of five differentiating variables.

The 'twin efficacy' test

The adequacy of existing regulatory initiatives that seek to impose and enforce human rights obligations on companies should be judged with reference to their efficacy. The efficacy of a norm can be tested by inquiring about the extent to which it has achieved its objectives, that is, by comparing the 'actual' effect of a given norm with its 'intended' effect.[1] Regulatory initiatives, for the present purpose, can secure their intended effects if they are able to: (a) encourage companies to comply with their human rights responsibilities, and (b) bring to justice those companies that are not so encouraged. Hence, a regulatory initiative related to corporate human rights responsibilities should be considered 'effective' if it can prevent or pre-empt human rights violations by companies – at least in some cases – *and* could offer adequate relief to victims in cases of violations.[2] I will label these as 'preventive' and 'redressive' levels of efficacy, respectively.

Two levels of efficacy

At the preventive level, a regulatory regime will be effective if it is able to encourage, persuade or convince not all, but a sizable number of companies to take on board human rights responsibilities and take steps to avoid, as far as possible, contributing to human rights violations. By doing so, a regulatory initiative might achieve a degree of preventive efficacy by pre-empting human rights abuses. Each regulatory initiative would have to make a case, in its own way, that committing or participating in human rights violations is not a viable option for business. Let me offer one illustration how this may happen. Assuming that a majority of companies (or at least the people who run them) behave rationally most of the time,[3] a regulatory regime may enhance the potential cost of violating human rights in comparison to the cost of complying with them and convey this message to potential violators. It is important, however, that regulatory regimes – in order to achieve this preventive efficacy – are able to convey such a message before companies take decisions that result in human rights violations.

However, as it is likely that some companies will not be persuaded to respect human rights norms, or may defy the assumption of being rational economic actors, a regulatory initiative should also have a redressive element in order to be effective. I suggest that to achieve efficacy at the redressive level,

---

1 F. Tulkens, 'Human Rights, Rhetoric or Reality?', *European Review*, 2001, vol. 9, 125, at 129.
2 This meaning of 'efficacy' is quite different from the effectiveness criteria for non-judicial grievance mechanisms proposed by the SRSG. Human Rights Council, 'Guiding Principles on Business and Human Rights: Implementing the United Nations "Protect, Respect and Remedy" Framework', A/HRC/17/31 (21 March 2011), Principle 31.
3 R. Posner, *Economic Analysis of Law*, 5th edn, New York: Aspen, 1998, pp. 3–4.

a regulatory regime should exhibit several characteristics. It should be able to respond with a range of sanctions or adverse consequences in a high percentage of cases involving corporate human rights violations. A reasonable certainty about an adverse penalty is *sine qua non* for efficacy, because too much uncertainty or unpredictability might induce potential violators to take chances with regulation. Sanctions or adverse consequences need not always come from formal judicial institutions, but may also flow from market forces and stakeholders. This idea of 'social sanctions' is developed in Chapter 8.

A regulatory regime should also be able to deal with instances of alleged human rights violations by companies in a swift manner, as companies have been able to use 'litigation delay' as a defence in the past. For those regulatory initiatives which rely on formal judicial mechanisms to make companies accountable for human rights abuses, achieving this objective will necessarily involve overcoming delays caused by the corporate misuse of the doctrine of *forum non conveniens* and the principle of separate legal personality.[4]

Another indicator of a regime's efficacy is the cost of enforcement it places on the victims of human rights violations. In a majority of the cases of large-scale human rights abuses involving MNCs, the victims are from a poor or disadvantaged section of the society.[5] It will be unreasonable for regulators to expect that such victims will be able to fight for justice at any cost against an opponent possessing far greater economic and legal power. An effective regulatory regime should, therefore, have provisions for legal aid (or at least for a scheme that encourages lawyers to take cases on 'no win, no fee' basis) and a liberal *locus standi* requirement so as to balance the position of litigating parties.

Moreover, redressive efficacy would require that a given regulatory initiative can deliver adequate relief to the victims of human rights violations. Relief can take the form of compensation, injunction, public apology or restitution. But companies should not be able to claim immunity from liability by paying a pittance. Nor should settlements under which the compensation to the victims is paid as a matter of charity or mercy rather than in pursuance of the legal liability for a wrong be regarded as a sign of an effective regulatory framework.[6]

---

4 P. Blumberg, 'Asserting Human Rights against Multinational Corporations under the United States Law: Conceptual and Procedural Problems', *American Journal of Comparative Law*, 2002, vol. 50, 493; P. Muchlinski, 'Holding Multinationals to Account: Recent Developments in English Litigation and the Company Law Review', *Company Lawyer*, 2002, vol. 23:6, 168.

5 Consider, for example, the victims of Bhopal gas tragedy (labourers and slum dwellers), Shell's operations in Nigeria (indigenous Ogoni community), Unocal's operations in Myanmar (poor and illiterate villagers), or the workers in factories of Nike and Apple in Asia (women, children or rural migrants).

6 A prominent characteristic of 'rights' is that the bearers of rights could make a demand from others about a particular conduct. H. Shue, *Basic Rights: Subsistence, Affluence, and US Foreign Policy*, 2nd edn, Princeton, NJ: Princeton University Press, 1996, pp. 13–15. This element of demand should not be lost when a remedy is sought for the violation of rights.

The settlement between UCC and the Indian government in the Bhopal case (discussed in Chapter 2) illustrates this well. The Bhopal settlement should not be dismissed as an aberration. In September 2003, Nike did not admit any liability, but agreed to pay US$1.5 million to the Fair Labour Association to settle a case which alleged it of making false and misleading statements about its labour practices.[7] Similarly, James Hardie agreed to fund a compensation scheme for asbestos victims, again without admitting its legal liability for violating the right to life and the right to health of thousands of people.[8] Any regulatory regime which allows companies to secure immunity from potential liability for public wrongs (as opposed to private wrongs) is anything but effective, for the wrongdoer accepts no responsibility for the wrong committed.[9]

Interrelation between the two levels of efficacy

The two levels of efficacy are interrelated and complementary to each other in the sense that the efficacy of a regulatory regime at one level will enhance its efficacy at the other level. Companies, on a balance of probabilities, might decide not to violate human rights if they are convinced that violation will result in a penalty or adverse consequences which are *significant* and are *certain* to follow in a *swift* manner. On the other hand, if a regulatory initiative is effective in preventing or pre-empting human rights abuses, this should significantly reduce the enforcement costs or burden and in turn increase the redressive efficacy of the given regulatory initiative.

Nevertheless, it should be noted that not all regulatory initiatives will focus on, or aim to achieve, both levels of efficacy equally. For example, the ATCA – or any similar legislation at the municipal level – is directed more towards the redressive rather than the preventive level of efficacy. Conversely, an initiative like the Global Compact pays attention primarily to the preventive level by encouraging corporations to respect and promote human rights. It is a different matter that in view of an interrelation between the two levels of efficacy, the regulatory initiatives in both these examples are likely to contribute indirectly to the other level of efficacy as well. So, the requirement of twin efficacy is satisfied as long as a regulatory initiative incorporates components of both preventive and redressive levels of efficacy.

Regulatory initiatives are likely to employ different strategies to achieve these two levels of efficacy. To illustrate: whereas regulatory initiatives flowing from states could offer tax incentives to encourage corporations to respect

---

7 S. Joseph, *Corporations and Transnational Human Rights Litigation*, Oxford: Hart Publishing, 2004, pp. 104–5.
8 James Hardie, 'Asbestos Compensation'. Available at: www.ir.jameshardie.com.au/jh/asbestos_compensation.jsp (accessed 29 May 2011).
9 See X. Han, 'The Wiwa Cases', *Chinese Journal of International Law*, 2010, vol. 9, 433, pp. 447–8.

human rights, corporate codes of conduct could put in place an internal mechanism by which human rights issues are integrated into day-to-day business decisions. Conversely, whereas state initiatives could redress corporate human rights abuses by introducing a range of coercive measures, codes of conduct could contribute to redressing grievances by laying down a complaints procedure and prescribing the range of compensation to be provided to those affected by corporate activities.

MNCs and regulatory dilemmas

Several factors make MNCs difficult regulatory targets. The regulation of conduct is a difficult task, more so when one has to regulate a fictitious legal person. Not only do individuals tend to lose 'some of the ordinary internalized restraints' when placed in an organizational structure, but some major sanctions that can be invoked to control human beings are also unavailable against corporations.[10] Furthermore, as we are dealing with the regulation of not mere corporations but MNCs, such a fiction becomes multi-layered and could be called 'fiction infinite' because by and large there are no limits on how an MNC can structure its operations through a web of parent, subsidiary and affiliate sister concerns. This legal leeway *ipso facto* makes MNCs difficult regulatory targets.

Another related reason is provided by the twin vintage principles of corporate law: the principles of separate legal personality and limited liability. Although these principles evolved at a time when the notion of an MNC or a corporate group was unknown,[11] modern MNCs take full advantage of them to escape the clutches of regulatory initiatives. Of course, in principle it is permissible to pierce the corporate veil in certain given situations,[12] but the associated evidentiary burden has not proved to be easy to discharge, because parent corporations keep 'distance by design' from their subsidiaries and courts generally demand a high level of proof regarding the control exercised by the parent over its subsidiaries.[13]

MNCs also become difficult regulatory targets because they operate at a transnational level and can move their operations from one jurisdiction to

---

10 C. Stone, *Where the Law Ends: The Social Control of Corporate Behaviour*, Prospect Heights, Illinois: Waveland Press, 1991, pp. 35–6.
11 In fact, historically corporations even lacked the power to acquire and hold shares of other corporations unless expressly granted by special statute or charter provisions. P. Blumberg, *The Multinational Challenge to Corporation Law: The Search for a New Corporate Personality*, Oxford: Oxford University Press, 1993, p. 52.
12 Courts can lift the veil and disrobe the separate legal personality of a corporation when it is a sham, or used as a 'cloak' for fraud or illegality, or when the corporation is a 'puppet' of the owner. See P. Davies, *Gower and Davies's Principles of Modern Company Law*, 7th edn, London: Sweet & Maxwell, 2003, pp. 176–90.
13 See, e.g. *Adams v. Cape Industries plc.* [1991] 1 All ER 929; *Doe v. Unocal Corporation* 248 F. 3d 915 (2001).

another, especially if they apprehend that legal proceedings against them could be instituted in a particular jurisdiction.[14] In fact, in the course of moving their operations, MNCs may legally become invisible, disappear totally, or take a new form and name. If victims try to sue the overseas parent company, it is most likely to frustrate victims' strategy by invoking the doctrine of *forum non conveniens*. All this makes the regulation of MNCs' human rights violative activities extremely difficult, especially by municipal law mechanisms.

The primary objective and ideology that guides the establishment as well as running of corporations provide another reason for MNCs being considered difficult regulatory targets. In an environment of free markets and globalized economies, states – both developed and developing – face different pressures and dilemmas when it comes to regulating the activities of powerful and influential MNCs.[15] Although MNCs are not operating in a regulatory vacuum, there is a general lack of a strong political will to effectively regulate their human rights violative activities. Out of numerous examples, a few illustrative ones should suffice to support this point. The US government has opposed the use of the ATCA to make companies accountable for human rights abuses abroad.[16] Attempts to enact an extraterritorial law to regulate the overseas activities of corporations registered in their respective jurisdictions have failed in the US, Australia, and the UK.[17] The government of Papua New Guinea went out of its way to legislate to limit the liability of an MNC for causing environmental degradation and violating human rights.[18] We have already seen in Chapter 2 how the Indian government handled the issue of Warren Anderson's extradition to face criminal charges for Bhopal.

The above summary account may give the impression that dilemmas in the regulation of MNCs' activities arise because MNCs are difficult regulatory targets. In other words, regulatory dilemmas are the 'consequence' of MNCs

---

14 The investigation into the shifting of location from Australia to The Netherlands by James Hardie Industries provides a good example of this. 'The Special Commission of Inquiry into Medical Research and Compensation Foundation'. Available at: www.dpc.nsw.gov.au/publications/publications/publication_list_-_new#11330 (accessed 31 May 2011).
15 Dine explains this as a 'willing capture' of governments. J. Dine, *Companies, International Trade and Human Rights*, Cambridge: Cambridge University Press, 2005, pp. 27–30.
16 Joseph, above n. 7, pp. 55–60.
17 Corporate Code of Conduct Bill 2000 (US), HR 4596, 106th Cong. (2d Sess. 2000). Available at: http://thomas.loc.gov/cgi-bin/query/z?c106:H.R.4596: (accessed 31 May 2011). Corporate Code of Conduct Bill 2000 (Aus). Available at: www.comlaw.gov.au/Details/C2004B01333 (accessed 31 May 2011) (hereinafter the Australian Bill). Corporate Responsibility Bill 2003 (UK) (hereinafter the UK Bill). Available at: www.publications.parliament.uk/pa/cm200203/cmbills/129/2003129.pdf (accessed 31 May 2011).
18 B. Burton, 'The Big Ugly at Ok Tedi', *Multinational Monitor*, January/February 2002, vol. 23. Available at: http://multinationalmonitor.org/mm2002/02jan-feb/jan-feb02front.html (accessed 31 May 2011).

being difficult regulatory targets. However, I tend to think that regulatory dilemmas are the 'cause' of MNCs being difficult regulatory targets. Various reasons identified here relate to one or the other of the following regulatory dilemmas concerning the regulation of MNCs or their operations: *who* should regulate *what* activities of *which* corporation, *where*, and *how*? These five dilemmas have made MNCs difficult regulatory targets, and consequently regulatory initiatives have so far not been able to match the power and transnational structure, operations and *modus operandi* of MNCs.

The taxonomy of existing regulatory initiatives

The five regulatory dilemmas could also help us to understand the taxonomy of current regulatory initiatives, as they correspond to five differentiating variables (noted at the beginning of this chapter) that can be used to classify regulatory initiatives concerning corporate human rights obligations into different categories. This classification may then be used to select a representative sample of the existing initiatives.

The relationship between differentiating variables and regulatory dilemmas is illustrated in Table 3.1. As one may note, the first variable *source* is a response

Table 3.1 The basis and the objective for classifying existing regulatory regimes

	Regulatory dilemmas	*Differentiating variables*	*Analytical objective served*
1	*Who* should regulate?	Source	Measuring the gap between corporate commitments and the expectations of stakeholders; judging the integrity of regulatory actors.
2	*What* should be regulated?	Content	Evaluating the amplitude and strength of human rights protection afforded by a regulatory initiative.
3	*Which* corporation of a corporate group is to be regulated?	Targeting approach	Analyzing the efficacy of relying on the entity versus enterprise principles; assessing the limits of state-centred enforcement.
4	*Where* should regulation occur?	Level of operation	Identifying the limitations and advantages of regulatory initiatives at different levels.
5	*How* should regulation be supported?	Nature	Understanding the relative viability and efficacy of compliance strategies as well as various types of sanctions.

to the first regulatory dilemma of 'who' should regulate MNCs' activities. The second dilemma – 'what' should be regulated – translates into the *content* of human rights obligations. 'Which' corporation of a corporate group should be regulated, the third regulatory dilemma, corresponds to the third variable, namely, the *targeting approach* adopted by different regulatory initiatives. Similarly, the fourth differentiating variable (the *level of operation*) is a direct response to 'where' regulation should occur. Lastly, the fifth variable (*nature*) is a reflection of the fifth regulatory dilemma (i.e. 'how' regulation should be supported).

Table 3.1 also throws some light on the analytical objective served by differentiating one regulatory regime from another on the basis of five variables chosen here. Due to space constraint, I will not be able to explain in detail how these objectives could be served. Nevertheless, let me illustrate this point with reference to internal versus external sources of regulation. By making this distinction on the basis of the source of regulation, one can measure the gap between corporate acceptance of their human rights responsibilities through internal codes and the expectations of their stakeholders reflected in external regulatory initiatives. It will also be particularly useful to contrast and impeach the actual conduct of companies with reference to the codes of conduct drawn and adopted by them rather than *vis-à-vis* external regulatory initiatives. Additionally, we can judge, by reference to the distinction between internal and external initiatives, the level of commitment, integrity and seriousness of the regulatory actors behind a given initiative in ensuring that companies respect their human rights obligations. For instance, drawing on the research on the pitfalls involved in private rule writing,[19] one may investigate if the vagueness in specifying human rights responsibilities and the lack of enforcement provisions in a given internal code of conduct is evidence of window dressing.[20] Similar factors in an external regulatory initiative may point towards lack of a political will and/or an attempt for public appeasement.

'Who' should regulate? – The source of regulatory initiatives

The first dilemma concerns *who* should regulate the activities of MNCs in order to ensure that they respect their human rights obligations? Should regulatory initiatives flow from MNCs, states, international organizations, civil society organs, or all of the above? This kind of regulatory dilemma points towards the 'source' of regulatory initiatives: *internal* and *external*. As noted in

---

19 B. Hutter, 'Is Enforced Self-regulation a Form of Risk Taking? The Case of Railway Health and Safety', *International Journal of the Sociology of Law*, 2001, vol. 29, 379.
20 See P. Simons, 'Corporate Voluntarism and Human Rights: The Adequacy and Effectiveness of Voluntary Self-Regulation Regimes', *Relations Industrielles*, 2004, vol. 59, 101, at 106–8.

Chapter 1, a regulatory initiative is internal when it owes its origin to the potential violators of human rights (MNCs in the present case), while it is external if it flows from those organs of society that aim to promote human rights (such as states, international institutions and NGOs). Voluntary codes of conduct or principles formulated and adopted by MNCs are an example of internal regulatory initiatives. Although internal regulatory initiatives would seem to be the most efficient way of ensuring that MNCs respect human rights,[21] they have proved to be an inadequate mechanism of regulation for reasons discussed in the next chapter.[22]

The visible inadequacy of internal regulatory measures has led to the demands and search for more effective methods of external regulation. Numerous regulatory initiatives at municipal and international levels fall in this category. The Sullivan Principles,[23] the Clean Clothes Campaign,[24] the Sustainability Guidelines of the Global Reporting Initiative,[25] and the codes of conduct or labelling techniques framed by NGOs like Amnesty International[26] and Social Accountability International[27] are also examples of external regulatory initiatives. However, external regulatory initiatives too have limitations. States may be unwilling to regulate MNCs, or even if they are willing, may find themselves incapable of regulating effectively the activities of MNCs. The regulatory initiatives at international level, though desirable, lay down vague guidelines and generally lack effective implementation tools. In short, regulatory initiatives flowing from both internal and external sources have their own limitations, and the debate about a judicious mix of internal and external regulatory initiatives has so far not provided any concrete answers.

Despite the distinction drawn here between internal and external regulatory initiatives, one should not lose sight of the fact that the distinction may not always be very clear, especially when more and more emphasis is being

---

21 S. Picciotto, 'Rights, Responsibilities and Regulation of International Business', *Columbia Journal of Transnational Law*, 2003, vol. 42, 131, at 144–9.
22 M. Baker, 'Tightening the Toothless Vice: Codes of Conduct and the American Multinational Enterprise', *Wisconsin International Law Journal*, 2001. vol. 20, 89, at 137–40; P. Redmond, 'Transnational Enterprise and Human Rights: Options for Standard Setting and Compliance', *International Lawyer*, 2003, vol. 37, 69, at 91–5.
23 The Global Sullivan Principles of Social Responsibility. Available at: www.thesullivanfoundation.org/about/global_sullivan_principles (accessed 31 May 2011).
24 Clean Clothes Campaign Code of Labour Practices for the Apparel Industry. Available at: www.cleanclothes.org/resources/ccc/corporate-accountability/full-package-approach-to-labour-codes-of-conduct/485 (accessed 31 May 2011).
25 The Global Reporting Initiative, The 2002 Sustainability Reporting Guidelines. Available at: www.uneptie.org/scp/gri/pdf/gri_2002_guidelines.pdf (accessed 31 May 2011).
26 Amnesty International, Human Rights Principles for Companies (1998), AI Index: ACT 70/01/98.
27 Social Accountability (SA) 8000. Available at: www.sa-intl.org/_data/n_0001/resources/live/2008StdEnglishFinal.pdf (accessed 31 May 2011).

put on developing cooperative regulatory partnerships[28] and on the participation of affected groups in the decision-making process. For example, a company may formulate a code of conduct after extensive consultations with consumers, human rights activists, NGOs and labour unions. Similarly, the Guiding Principles combine both internal and external regulatory mechanisms, while external agencies such as the OECD, the ILO and the UN often consult with companies (or at least their representative bodies) before finalizing what has been designated here as an external code. A similar overlap also exists in relation to the implementation and enforcement mechanism under internal and external regulatory initiatives. Whereas an internally formulated regulatory code could be enforced both internally as well as externally,[29] an external regulatory initiative also involves a process of internalization.

'What' should be regulated? – The content of regulatory initiatives

The next regulatory dilemma could be framed in terms of *what*: what are the exact areas or activities of companies that need to be regulated? Should labour rights or environmental rights be dealt with separately (and by separate institutions) from human rights? In Chapter 1, I alluded to disagreements about the scope and extent of the human rights obligations of companies. In view of a significant divergence between the regulatory expectations of companies and their representative bodies on the one hand and human rights activists on the other, states – either acting individually or collectively – struggle to balance these contradictions. Companies generally prefer and often demand all-pervasive deregulation, except in those areas where deregulation hampers their capacity to maximize profit (e.g. intellectual property rights or law and order). Civil society organizations, on the other hand, demand extensive regulation in matters affecting the public interest, including human rights. They expect states to provide a level playing field for the otherwise unequal bargaining positions of MNCs and the general public, whether as employees, consumers or otherwise.

A lack of consensus about the precise content of corporate human rights obligations makes it very difficult to put in place a regulatory framework that comprehensively deals with all human rights obligations. A comparison of current regulatory initiatives reveals that the content of the human rights obligations of companies differs primarily in two respects: the 'breadth' of

---

28 The Global Compact is a very good example of such partnership. UN Global Compact. Available at: www.unglobalcompact.org (accessed 2 June 2011). See also P. Utting, 'Regulating Business via Multistakeholder Initiatives: A Preliminary Assessment' in R. Jenkins *et al.*, *Voluntary Approaches to Corporate Responsibility: Readings and a Resource Guide*, Geneva: UN-NGLS, 2002, 61.

29 The model of 'enforced self-regulation' proposed by Ayres and Braithwaite encompasses, for example, the involvement of corporations, public interest groups and regulatory agencies in enforcing rules. I. Ayres and J. Braithwaite, *Responsive Regulation: Transcending the Deregulation Debate*, New York: Oxford University Press, 1992, pp. 106–7.

obligations (i.e. the subject areas covered) and the 'depth' of obligations (i.e. whether corporate obligations extend beyond respecting human rights and include the duty to protect and fulfil human rights).

In terms of the *breadth* of human rights obligations, the UN Norms,[30] coupled with the Commentary appended to them,[31] had provided the most comprehensive and detailed statement of the human rights (including labour and environmental rights) obligations of companies. The ATCA, on the other hand, is probably an example of the other extreme in that it provides a cause of action only for torts committed against non-US nationals in violation of the law of nations or a treaty of the US.[32] In between these two extremes, one could place various other regulatory regimes such as the OECD Guidelines,[33] the ILO Declaration,[34] the Global Compact[35] and various types of codes of conduct. The Guiding Principles deserve a special mention here, because instead of cataloguing the human rights responsibilities of companies, they stipulate that business enterprises should respect all 'internationally recognized human rights'.[36] The use of this term may *prima facie* suggest an extensive breadth of responsibilities. However, this might not be the case in actual practice, as environmental rights or the special rights of certain vulnerable sections of society are not included in what internationally recognized human rights mean 'at a minimum'. This aspect is dealt with in more detail in Chapter 4.

As far as the *depth* of corporate human rights obligations is concerned, the UN Norms were again at the forefront of canvassing positive human rights obligations.[37] The positive content of corporate obligations is less clear under the Global Compact,[38] the ILO Declaration,[39] and the OECD

---

30 Norms on the Responsibilities of Transnational Corporations and Other Business Enterprises with Regard to Human Rights, E/CN.4/Sub.2/2003/12/Rev.2 (13 August 2003), paras 1–14.
31 Commentary on the Norms on the Responsibilities of Transnational Corporations and other Business Enterprises with Regard to Human Rights, E/CN.4/Sub.2/2003/38/Rev.2.
32 The phrase 'law of nations' has received restrictive judicial interpretation and even the violation of a treaty of the US has been interpreted to refer to only self-executing treaties. See further discussion in Chapter 4.
33 OECD Guidelines for Multinational Enterprises, 27 June 2000, reprinted in *ILM*, 2001, vol. 40, 237. See Chapter 4 for an analysis of the updated Guidelines of 2011.
34 ILO Tripartite Declaration of Principles Concerning Multinational Enterprises and Social Policy, 17 November 2000, reprinted in *ILM*, 2002, vol. 41, 186.
35 UN Global Compact, above n. 28.
36 Guiding Principles, above n. 2, Principle 12.
37 UN Norms, above n. 30, paras 1 and 12. See also the Commentary on the Norms, above n. 31, Commentary (b) to para. 1.
38 Principle 2, for example, provides that businesses should 'make sure that they are not complicit in human rights abuses.' Similarly, under Principle 8 businesses agree to 'undertake initiatives to promote greater environmental responsibility'. UN Global Compact, 'The Ten Principles'. Available at: www.unglobalcompact.org/AboutTheGC/TheTenPrinciples/index.html (accessed 2 June 2011).
39 ILO Declaration, above n. 34, pp. 188–91 (e.g. paras 2, 5, 8, 16, and 22).

Guidelines.[40] The Guiding Principles, on the other hand, canvass the corporate responsibility to 'respect' human rights and envisage companies adopting a 'due diligence' approach to identify, prevent, mitigate and address the adverse human rights impacts of their operations.[41] Although this conceptualization of corporate responsibilities includes taking positive actions, these primarily relate to the 'respect' component of the duty typology with a partial mix of duties concerning 'protect' and 'fulfil'. As examined further in Chapter 4, this approach is not only inadequate, but also theoretically unsound.

'Which' corporation of a corporate group should be regulated? – The targeting approach of regulatory initiatives

As MNCs, by definition, consist of several integrated corporations – structured in pyramidal order or otherwise[42] – their structure *per se* poses another regulatory dilemma. *Which* corporation of a given corporate group should be targeted by a regulatory initiative? Should the parent company be held accountable for the conduct of all its corporations so as to treat the whole group as one 'enterprise', or should each and every corporation of a group be treated as a separate 'entity'?[43] This dilemma reaches its zenith when the ultimate or immediate parent of an apparent corporate violator is located outside the territorial boundaries of the state in which the human rights violations occur.

Questions arise as to how states should and could overcome this regulatory dilemma. States have responded in diverse ways such as supporting the evolution of an international regulatory regime, attempting to reach overseas subsidiaries through extraterritorial laws, or approaching the courts of the country where the parent company is based to plead for either the piercing of the corporate veil or recognition of the enterprise principle. Similarly, existing regulatory initiatives have adopted different approaches to overcome this dilemma. Regulatory initiatives could be classified into different heads on the basis of whether they have adopted the entity principle or the enterprise

---

40 One can infer this from the use of the terms 'contribute', 'provide' and 'promote' in the OECD Guidelines at several places. OECD Guidelines, above n. 33, pp. 240–4 (paras II.1, II.8, IV.1/2/3, and V.7/8).
41 Guiding Principles, above n. 2, Principles 11–19.
42 P. Muchlinski, *Multinational Enterprises and the Law*, 2nd edn, Oxford: Oxford University Press, 2007, pp. 56–66; M. Eroglu, *Multinational Enterprises and Tort Liabilities: An Interdisciplinary and Comparative Examination*, Gloucester: Edward Elgar Publishing, 2008, pp. 42–69.
43 The 'enterprise principle' and 'entity principle' provide opposing justifications for the appropriate reach of a regulatory regime. Whereas the traditional 'entity principle' treats each corporation as a separate person, the 'enterprise principle' treats all the constituent corporations of a group as one legal person for a particular purpose, provided they are part of an integral business group. Blumberg, above n. 11, pp. viii–ix.

principle for the purpose of imposing and enforcing human rights obligations against MNCs.

The Global Compact and the internal corporate codes of conduct are seemingly wedded to the principle of separate legal personality and therefore treat every corporation of a corporate group as a separate entity for the purpose of imposing obligations.[44] The OECD Guidelines[45] and the ILO Declaration[46] – though do not adopt the enterprise principle – expect various entities of a corporate group to cooperate and provide assistance to each other to facilitate the observance of the listed responsibilities. The UN Norms, however, tried to overcome this entity versus enterprise dilemma by extending responsibilities not only to MNCs but also to other business enterprises.[47] The Guiding Principles follow this approach and contemplate human rights responsibilities for all business enterprises. This is the correct approach, as all types of business entities should have human rights responsibilities. But even adopting this approach does not solve the problem of attributing responsibility within a corporate group. Both the UN Norms and the Guiding Principles unfortunately failed to offer any guidance on the issue of the liability of a parent company for human rights abuses committed by its subsidiaries.

The clearest adoption of the enterprise principle to impose human rights obligations on MNCs was seen in the unsuccessful legislative initiatives in the US, Australia and the UK.[48] Of these three Bills, the UK Bill was by far the most radical: the Bill invoked the enterprise principle to enforce human rights obligations in that it clearly proposed the liability of a parent corporation for wrongs committed by its subsidiaries.[49]

One issue concerning the 'targeting approach' that is relevant only in the context of international regulatory initiatives is if they impose and implement obligations against MNCs through states – an *indirect* approach – or try to

---

44 It is, however, possible that some business participants of the Compact may treat themselves as a single enterprise, thus not requiring their subsidiaries to join the initiative. UN Global Compact, 'Subsidiary Participation and Communication on Progress'. Available at: www.unglobalcompact.org/HowToParticipate/Business_Participation/Subsidiary_Engagement.html (accessed 8 June 2011).
45 'The Guidelines are addressed to all the entities within the multinational enterprise (parent companies, and/or local entities). According to the actual distribution of responsibilities among them, the different entities are expected to 'co-operate and assist one another to facilitate observance of the Guidelines'. OECD Guidelines, above n. 33, p. 239 (para. I.3). This principle is retained in the updated OECD Guidelines of 2011. OECD Guidelines for Multinational Enterprises: Recommendations for Responsible Business Conduct in a Global Context, 25 May 2011, pp. 15–16 (para. I.4). Available at: www.oecd.org/dataoecd/43/29/48004323.pdf (accessed 10 June 2011).
46 It is expected that various entities of a multinational enterprise 'will cooperate and provide assistance to one another as necessary to facilitate observance of the principles laid down in the Declaration'. ILO Declaration, above n. 34, p. 189 (para. 6).
47 UN Norms, above n. 30, paras 20 and 21.
48 Above n. 17.
49 UK Bill, above n. 17, s. 6(1)/(3).

reach them *directly*. All major international regulatory initiatives – such as the UN Norms, ILO Declaration, OECD Guidelines and the Global Compact – contemplate direct human rights responsibilities of MNCs. The Guiding Principles are no exception in that in addition to indirect responsibilities, they conceive direct corporate responsibility to respect internationally recognized human rights. Differences exist, though, regarding the enforcement of obligations. Whereas the UN Norms envisaged invoking both state-based (direct) and non-state (indirect) implementation techniques,[50] the Global Compact relies on a wide variety of formal or informal dialogues, partnerships and networking amongst all relevant parties including participating companies to ensure observance of its principles.[51] Both these initiatives thus show a departure from the exclusively state-centred enforcement mechanism. The Guiding Principles rightly carry forward this approach and contemplate various non-state-based grievance mechanisms.[52] In comparison, the ILO Declaration[53] and the OECD Guidelines[54] principally rely on states to ensure that companies comply with human rights obligations.

'Where' should regulation occur? – The level *of regulation*

There is another dilemma which confronts the architects of regulatory regimes: *where* should the regulation take place in order to be effective? Should the activities of companies be regulated at an institutional, municipal, regional or international level, or at all of these levels? In the absence of any consensus as to the most appropriate level of regulation, regulatory initiatives, flowing both from internal and external sources, have mushroomed at all four levels. The 'level of operation' can thus provide another criterion to classify different regulatory initiatives that impose and enforce human rights obligations against companies. Whereas at the institutional level there are varied kinds of codes of conduct, labelling schemes and principles formulated and adopted by companies or industry associations, one can see the evolution of regional initiatives in terms of the European Commission's Green Paper.[55]

---

50 UN Norms, above n. 30, paras 15–17.
51 UN Global Compact, 'Integrity Measures'. Available at: www.unglobalcompact.org/ AboutTheGC/IntegrityMeasures/index.html (accessed 16 May 2011).
52 Guiding Principles, above n. 2, Principles 28–30.
53 The ILO Declaration repeatedly urges states to take measures or adopt policies to implement the labour obligations. ILO Declaration, above n. 34, pp. 190–3 (paras 9, 12–14, 21, 29 and 39).
54 OECD Guidelines rely on National Contact Points to ensure implementation of its provisions. OECD Guidelines, above n. 33, p. 239 (para. I.10).
55 European Commission's Green Paper on Promoting a European Framework for Corporate Social Responsibility, COM(2001) 366 Final. Available at: http://eur-lex.europa.eu/Lex UriServ/site/en/com/2001/com2001_0366en01.pdf (accessed 2 June 2011). See also 'Implementing the Partnership for Growth and Jobs: Making Europe a Pole of Excellence on Corporate Social Responsibility', COM(2006) 136 Final. Available at: http://eur-lex.europa.eu/ LexUriServ/LexUriServ.do?uri=COM:2006:0136:FIN:en:PDF (accessed 2 June 2011).

60 *Evaluation of existing regulatory initiatives*

At the municipal level, several regulatory experiments are under way which seek either to employ or reinvent the existing mechanisms. In addition to general legislative instruments which deal with different aspects of human rights norms and could be used against companies,[56] in some jurisdictions the victims have tried to make companies accountable under tort law principles.[57] The ATCA has undoubtedly proved to be the most fertile ground for instituting legal actions against companies for human rights violations. An attempt was also made to impeach the conduct of an MNC for false advertising and unfair competition laws with reference to its codes of conduct.[58]

For several reasons, these experiments at the municipal level have not proved very successful. MNCs are able to move from one place to another quite easily. To evade national regulation, they can also disappear from one jurisdiction,[59] or become 'invisible' by taking new forms.[60] In view of this general dichotomy between the *modus operandi*-cum-structure of MNCs and the regulatory structure of national initiatives regulating their activities,[61] increasingly people are looking towards international law for a solution. However, international law, as Zerk shows, is no panacea:[62] several conceptual, theoretical and political hurdles will have to be overcome before it is able to deal with MNCs effectively. For example, the issue of the 'invisibility' of MNCs under international law would have to be addressed.[63] Despite such inherent hurdles, several international regulatory initiatives have been put in place.

'How' should regulation be supported? – The nature *of regulatory initiatives*

The fifth and final regulatory dilemma concerning the regulation of MNCs is: *how* should regulatory initiatives against MNCs be enforced? In order to be

---

56 See, for example, the laws dealing with minimum wages, health and safety, advertising, anti-discrimination, environment, consumer protection, and workers' rights. See S. Fitzgerald, 'Corporate Accountability for Human Rights Violations in Australian Domestic Law', *Australian Journal of Human Rights*, 2005, vol. 11, 33, at 39–52.
57 Joseph, above n. 7, pp. 65–77.
58 *Kasky* v. *Nike, Inc.* 79 Cal. App. 4th 165 (2000); *Kasky* v. *Nike, Inc.* 27 Cal. 4th 939 (2002); *Nike, Inc.* v. *Kasky* 539 US 654 (2003).
59 H. Ward, 'Securing Transnational Corporate Accountability through National Courts: Implications and Policy Options', *Hastings International and Comparative Law Review*, 2001, vol. 24, 451, at 463.
60 One common possibility is that one MNC may be taken over by another MNC, or there may be a merger between two MNCs. For example, after the merger of Unocal with Chevron, one cannot even locate the website of Unocal through a Google search.
61 B. Stephens, 'The Amorality of Profit: Transnational Corporations and Human Rights', *Berkeley Journal of International Law*, 2002, vol. 20, 45, at 54.
62 J. Zerk, *Multinational and Corporate Social Responsibility: Limitations and Opportunities in International Law*, Cambridge: Cambridge University Press, 2006, p. 103.
63 F. Johns, 'The Invisibility of the Transnational Corporation: An Analysis of International Law and Legal Theory', *Melbourne University Law Review*, 1994, vol. 19, 893.

effective and efficient, should the compliance strategy be voluntary, mandatory or a combination of the two? Furthermore, what type of sanctions could be invoked against companies that fail to respect their human rights responsibilities? Resolving this regulatory dilemma is critical because the implementation and enforcement of human rights obligations remains the common weakest link of all the existing regulatory initiatives that aim to ensure that companies comply with their human rights obligations.

Traditionally, the debate about the appropriate compliance strategy used to be cast in terms of 'voluntary versus mandatory'[64] – in which corporations generally preferred the former, whereas stakeholders emphasized the need for the latter. However, this 'either or' approach is not only misguided[65] but also inappropriate because it is desirable to develop a synergy between the two approaches. It is also rightly contended that even the voluntary initiatives are not totally voluntary in that stakeholders can use them to move shareholders' resolutions, impeach the conduct of MNCs before the courts, or run a 'naming and shaming' campaign.[66]

As far as the compliance strategies and sanctions are concerned, many measures such as government incentives,[67] civil liability,[68] pressure flowing from consumers and investors,[69] 'naming and shaming',[70] and criminal sanctions[71] could be employed to make companies comply with their human rights responsibilities. It is still a moot point which one (or a combination) of these measures are most suitable to bring about corporate compliance with human rights obligations.

In view of the above diversity in enforcement strategies and sanctions, the 'nature' of regulatory initiatives in terms of the implementation and enforcement strategies that they adopt becomes a natural choice for investigation and a basis for classification of such initiatives. Such classification could arguably be done at two levels: primary and secondary. At the primary level, one could

---

64 International Council on Human Rights Policy, *Beyond Voluntarism: Human Rights and the Developing International Legal Obligations of Companies*, Versoix: ICHRP, 2002, pp. 7–11.
65 Zerk, above n. 62, pp. 34–6.
66 M. Kielsgard, 'Unocal and the Demise of Corporate Neutrality', *California Western International Law Journal*, 2005, vol. 36, 185; A. Simaika, 'The Value of Information: Alternatives to Liability in Influencing Corporate Behaviour Overseas', *Columbia Journal of Law and Social Problems*, 2005, vol. 38, 321.
67 Zerk, above n. 62, pp. 188–94.
68 See, for example, the cases filed under the ATCA or the law of torts.
69 E. Macek, 'Scratching the Corporate Back: Why Corporations Have No Incentive to Define Human Rights', *Minnesota Journal of Global Trade*, 2002, vol. 11, 101, at 110–18.
70 J. Braithwaite and P. Drahos, 'Zero Tolerance, Naming and Shaming: Is there a Case for it with Crimes of the Powerful?' *The Australian and New Zealand Journal of Criminology*, 2002, vol. 35, 269.
71 A. Ramasastry and R. Thompson (FAFO), *Commerce, Crime and Conflict: Legal Remedies for Private Sector Liability for Grave Breaches of International Law – A Survey of Sixteen Countries*, Oslo: FAFO, 2006.

ask whether an initiative is voluntary or mandatory. If a regulatory initiative is found to be mandatory in nature, a secondary query could be raised, namely, which coercive techniques are employed to ensure compliance with the mandate.

At the primary level, the current regulatory initiatives related to companies could normally be placed in either the voluntary or mandatory category. With the exception of general national laws (including the tortious principle of duty of care) and the ATCA, all other regulatory initiatives are by and large voluntary in that non-compliance with human rights obligations is not met with any formal sanction or penalty. The UN Norms, however, muddied the water in that they were labelled as neither voluntary nor mandatory but *non-voluntary*.[72] The evolution of this middle 'non-voluntary' category can be interpreted as evidence of a need for mandatory standards.

The regulatory initiatives that are mandatory in nature can be classified further on the basis of the type of techniques and sanctions they employ to bring about compliance with human rights obligations. The US courts hearing cases under the ATCA have the power to use all the civil remedies that are generally available in tort cases such as awarding damages and issuing injunctions. The three lapsed extraterritorial Bills differed from each other in terms of the compliance and enforcement strategy that they adopted: the US Bill relied on incentives, investigations and civil damages;[73] the Australian Bill on annual reporting, civil penalties and civil action;[74] and the UK Bill on reporting, consultation, disclosure, auditing civil actions and criminal penalties.[75] The UN Norms provided for several techniques – such as internalization, self-evaluation, monitoring and verification by national and international mechanisms and regulation by states – to ensure that companies comply with their human rights obligations.[76] The UN Norms also made provision for prompt, effective and adequate reparation to those who are adversely affected by failure to comply with the human rights responsibilities.[77]

The Guiding Principles stipulate that companies should provide for remediation of the adverse human rights impacts that they have caused or to which they have contributed.[78] But not many details are provided as to what such remediation entails. The Guiding Principles also envisage state-based (judicial as well as non-judicial) and non-state-based (non-judicial) grievance

---

72 D. Weissbrodt and M. Kruger, 'Norms of the Responsibilities of Transnational Corporations and Other Business Enterprises with Regard to Human Rights', *American Journal of International Law*, 2003, vol. 97, 901, at 913.
73 US Bill, above n. 17, ss. 4–8.
74 Australian Bill, above n. 17, ss. 14, 16 and 17.
75 UK Bill, above n. 17, ss. 3–11.
76 UN Norms, above n. 30, paras 15–17.
77 Ibid., para. 18.
78 Guiding Principles, above n. 2, Principle 22.

mechanisms to secure access to remedy.[79] These grievance mechanisms may invoke a range of remedies (e.g. apology, restitution, rehabilitation, compensation, punitive sanctions and injunctions).[80]

Summary

This chapter has developed an analytical framework to evaluate the adequacy of existing regulatory initiatives that aim to impose and enforce human rights obligations on companies. Developing such a framework was essential to accomplish two objectives: to ascertain the meaning of 'adequacy' and to understand the taxonomy of current regulatory regimes. It is proposed that a regulatory initiative is adequate if it is effective at both the *preventive* level and the *redressive* level. The efficacy of a regulatory initiative ought to be judged with reference to its ability to prevent/pre-empt, at least in some cases, human rights violations by companies and to redress such violations adequately if they do occur.

I also tried to explain why MNCs are considered difficult regulatory targets. It was contended that MNCs are difficult regulatory targets because of five regulatory dilemmas – *who* should regulate *what* activities of *which* corporation, *where*, and *how* – that their regulation poses. But these regulatory dilemmas have not, surprisingly, stifled the growth of regulatory initiatives related to MNCs. Such multiplicity *per se* is not problematic in the context of the regulation of MNCs; in fact, multiple regulatory initiatives may be essential to regulate the activities of MNCs in an effective manner. However, an un-coordinated proliferation of regulatory initiatives might have had a negative impact on the efficacy and efficiency of the overall regulatory framework. Multiple regulatory initiatives clearly make the task of companies to identify and implement their human rights obligations quite challenging. This situation also leaves companies prone to multiple (and sometimes also vexatious) legal proceedings.

Finally, this chapter suggested five differentiating variables, which correspond to the five regulatory dilemmas, to understand the taxonomy of existing regulatory initiatives related to MNCs. I argued that one could classify the current regulatory initiatives into different categories on the basis of the following five variables: the *source* from which they flow; the *content* of obligations; the *targeting approach*; the *level of operation*; and the *nature* in terms of compliance strategy. Such classification not only serves important analytical objectives but can also help in selecting a representative sample of the multiple, diverse regulatory initiatives for the purpose of evaluating their (in)adequacy. In the light of the analytical framework developed in this chapter, I will now proceed to evaluate the adequacy of seven selected regulatory initiatives that seek to ensure that companies respect their human rights obligations.

79 Ibid., Principles 25–30.
80 Ibid., Commentary on Principle 25.

4 Existing regulatory initiatives
An evaluation of (in)adequacy

[handwritten margin note: can only be developed in case law]

The central argument advanced in this chapter is that the existing regulatory initiatives are inadequate to ensure that companies comply with their human rights obligations, for they fail to satisfy the twin test of efficacy laid down in Chapter 3. The inadequacy arises because of three broad deficiencies: insufficient or contestable rationales for compliance with human rights obligations; the lack of precise, measurable human rights standards; and deficient or undeveloped implementation and enforcement mechanisms.

I intend to support this claim of inadequacy by surveying the following seven regulatory initiatives (shown in bold font in Table 4.1): the ATCA, corporate codes of conduct, the OECD Guidelines, the ILO Declaration, the Global Compact, the UN Norms, and the Guiding Principles. These initiatives are representative of existing mechanisms that seek to regulate human rights violative activities of companies. The selection is representative because these regimes represent both types of sources (internal and external); all degrees of content (narrow, limited, wide and extensive); divergent targeting approaches (the entity principle as well as its variation, and both direct as well as indirect implementation techniques); different levels of operation (from institutional to municipal and international); and are different in terms of their nature (voluntary, non-voluntary and mandatory).

Table 4.1 depicts the taxonomy of major existing regulatory regimes concerning corporate human rights responsibilities. In this table, the qualitative values assigned to each regulatory initiative *vis-à-vis* five differentiating variables signify the response of that particular initiative to the corresponding regulatory dilemma. For example, the corporate codes of conduct flow from an internal source (*who*), are narrow in content (*what*), recognize the entity principle (*which*), operate at the institutional level (*where*), and are voluntary in nature (*how*). The UN Norms, on the other hand, owed their origin to an external source (*who*), were extensive in scope (*what*), applied to almost all business enterprises and relied on direct-cum-indirect implementation techniques (*which*), operated at international level (*where*), and were non-voluntary in nature (*how*).

Table 4.1 Tabular taxonomy of existing regulatory initiatives

	Source (Who)	Content (What)	Targeting approach (Which)	Level of operation (Where)	Nature (How)
Alien Tort Claims Act	External	Narrow	Entity Principle	Municipal, but extraterritorial	Mandatory
Codes of Conduct, Principles or Labels by Non-State Entities[a]	External	Limited	Entity Principle; Direct	International	Voluntary
Corporate Codes of Conduct	Internal	Narrow	Entity Principle	Institutional	Voluntary
Duty of Care Principle	External	Narrow	Entity Principle	Municipal	Mandatory
General					
Municipal Laws	External	Narrow	Entity Principle	Municipal	Mandatory
Global Compact	External	Wide	Entity Principle; Direct	International	Voluntary
Guiding Principles	External	Wide	Entity Principle; Direct/Indirect	Primarily Institutional and Municipal	Both Voluntary and Mandatory
ILO Declaration	External	Wide	Entity Principle;[b] Direct/Indirect	International	Voluntary
International Bill of Rights	External	Limited[c]	Entity Principle; Indirect	International	Mandatory[d]
OECD Guidelines	External	Extensive	Entity Principle;[b] Direct	International	Voluntary
Specific					
Municipal Bills (US, UK & Australia)	External	Limited	Enterprise Principle	Municipal, but extraterritorial	Mandatory
UN Human Rights Norms	External	Extensive	Entity Principle;[b] Direct/Indirect	International	Non-voluntary

a One may refer to regulatory initiatives such as the Global Sullivan Principles of Social Responsibility; the Equator Principles; the Sustainability Reporting Guidelines of the Global Reporting Initiative; Amnesty International's Human Rights Principles for Companies; Clean Clothes Campaign Code of Labour Practices for the Apparel Industry; Social Accountability 8000; and ISO 26000.

b As explained in Chapter 3, one may though notice measures encompassed to overcome, in diverse ways, the hurdles posed by the entity principle.

c It is limited primarily because most of its provisions are not directed at companies.

d Certainly the provisions of the ICCPR and ICESCR are binding on state parties to these conventions under the principle of *pacta sunt servanda*; arguably all human rights are mandatory for all states and other international legal subjects to the extent that they embody customary norms, but at least this is the case for those rights which have acquired the status of *jus cogens* or *erga omnes* norms.

The Alien Tort Claims Act

The ATCA provides that 'the district courts shall have original jurisdiction of any civil action by an alien for a tort only, committed in violation of the law of nations or a treaty of the United States.'[1] There is an unusual degree of uncertainty about the origin, exact scope, and the legislative intent behind the enactment of the ATCA.[2] Yet it is relatively non-contentious that in its current form the jurisdiction of district courts to entertain civil actions is limited by three factors: only an *alien* can invoke this provision; there should be an allegation of the commission of a *tort*; and the alleged tort should have been committed either in violation of the *law of nations* or a *treaty* of the US.

Despite these limitations (the seriousness of which is examined in some detail below), victims of corporate human rights abuses have pursued several corporations in the US courts under the ATCA.[3] Such cases have been quite frequent since the mid-1990s, so much so that this has been labelled as a 'second wave' of human rights litigation.[4] Companies have been sued under the ATCA for a wide range of issues such as environmental pollution;[5] beating, arbitrary arrest and detention, torture, and execution;[6] drug experimentation without informed consent;[7] breach of the rights to life, health and sustainable development;[8] extra-judicial killing, forcible displacement and aiding/abetting genocide;[9] Holocaust war crimes;[10] participation in, or abetting, the regime of apartheid;[11] personal injury and property damage due to chemical

---

1 28 U.S.C. 1350 (2004).
2 Justice Bork observed:

> I have discovered no direct evidence of what Congress had in mind when enacting the provision. The debates over the Judiciary Act in the House – the Senate debates were not recorded – nowhere mention the provision, not even, so far as we are aware, indirectly. . . . Historical research has not yet disclosed what section 1350 was intended to accomplish.

Hanoch Tel-Oren v. *Libyan Arab Republic* 726 F. 2d 774, at 812 (1984).
3 J. Paust, 'Human Rights Responsibilities of Private Corporations', *Vanderbilt Journal of Transnational Law*, 2002, vol. 35, 801, at 804–8, 817–19; S. Joseph, *Corporations and Transnational Human Rights Litigation*, Oxford: Hart Publishing, 2004, pp. 21–54.
4 C. Bradley, 'Customary International Law and Private Rights of Action', *Chicago Journal of International Law*, 2000, vol. 1, 421.
5 *Aguinda* v. *Texaco, Inc.* 945 F. Supp. 625 (SDNY 1996).
6 *Wiwa* v. *Royal Dutch Petroleum Co.* 1998 US Dist. LEXIS 23064.
7 *Abdullahi* v. *Pfizer* 2002 US Dist. LEXIS 17436 (SDNY, 2002).
8 *Flores* v. *Southern Peru Copper* 253 F. Supp. 2d 510 (SDNY, 2002).
9 *The Presbyterian Church of Sudan* v. *Talisman Energy* 244 F. Supp. 2d 289 (SDNY, 2003).
10 *Abrams* v. *Societe Nationale Des Chemins de fer Français* 175 F. Supp. 2d 423 (EDNY, 2001); *Bodner* v. *Banque Paribas* 114 F. Supp. 2d 117 (2000); *In re Holocaust Victim Assets Litigation* 105 F. Supp. 2d 139 (EDNY, 2000).
11 *In re South African Apartheid Litigation* 2004 US Dist. LEXIS 23944; *Khulumani* v. *Barclay National Bank Ltd.* 504 F. 3d 254 (2007).

pollution;[12] forced dislocation, torture, forced labour, murder and rape;[13] knowingly and wilfully aiding and abetting the commission of torture for exercising the right to freedom of speech and expression;[14] detention-cum-interrogation at the Abu Ghraib prison as well as unlawful killing and beating;[15] extra-judicial killings and war crimes;[16] and cultural genocide.[17]

Although the recourse to the ATCA for redressing corporate human rights abuses did raise high hopes initially, the final results to date have not been very encouraging. Out of several dozens of cases filed against companies so far under the ATCA, rarely a case has been decided on merits,[18] as most of the cases have been dismissed on procedural or technical grounds. An out-of-court settlement has been reached in a few cases such as Unocal, Shell, Yahoo!, and Blackwater.[19] Perhaps this dismal outcome is partly because of the fact that this one-section statute hardly offers any guidance on relevant substantive or procedural issues. Since this leaves almost everything for argumentation, courts as well as academic commentators differ widely about the exact contours of this legislation. Until the US Supreme Court ruling in *Jose Francisco Sosa* v. *Humberto Alvarez-Machain*,[20] there was no consensus even on the basic issue whether this legislation is about a 'right', a 'remedy' or both.[21]

---

12 *Sajida Bano* v. *UCC* 2000 US Dist. LEXIS 12326; *Janki Bai Sahu* v. *UCC* 418 F. Supp. 2d 407 (2005).
13 *Doe* v. *Unocal* 963 F. Supp. 880 (CD Cal., 1997).
14 *Wang Xiaoning* v. *Yahoo!* 2007 U.S. Dist. LEXIS 97566 (ND Cal.).
15 *Haider Muhsin Saleh* v. *Titan Corp.* 436 F. Supp. 2d 55 (DDC, 2006).
16 *Estate of Himoud Saed Atban et al.* v *Blackwater* 611 F. Supp. 2d 1 (DDC, 2009); *In re Xe Services Alien Tort Litigation* 665 F. Supp. 2d 569 (2009).
17 *Tom Beanal* v. *Freeport-McMoran, Inc.* 197 F 3d 161 (5th Cir., 1999).
18 The jury verdict reached in *Romero* v. *Drummond Co.* 552 F. 3d 1303, at 1313 (11th Cir. 2008) is one exception.
19 'Energy Giant Agrees Settlement with Burmese Villagers', *The Guardian*, 15 December 2004. Available at: www.guardian.co.uk/world/2004/dec/15/burma.duncancampbell (accessed 6 June 2011). 'Yahoo Settles Its China Lawsuit', *BBC News*, 13 November 2007. Available at: http://news.bbc.co.uk/2/hi/7093564.stm (accessed 6 June 2011). 'Shell Settlement With Ogoni People Stops Short of Full Justice', *The Guardian*, 10 June 2009. Available at: www.guardian.co.uk/environment/cif-green/2009/jun/09/saro-wiwa-shell (accessed 6 June 2011). 'Blackwater Settles Series of Civil Lawsuits', *The Guardian*, 7 January 2010. Available at: www.guardian.co.uk/world/feedarticle/8888224 (accessed 6 June 2011).
20 The Court held that 'the statute was intended as jurisdictional in the sense of addressing the power of the courts to entertain cases concerned with a certain subject'. *Jose Francisco Sosa* v. *Humberto Alvarez-Machain* 124 S. Ct. 2739, at 2755 (2004).
21 W. Casto, 'The Federal Court's Protective Jurisdiction over Torts Committed in Violation of the Law of Nations', *Connecticut Law Review*, 1986, vol. 18, 467, at 479–80; C. Bradley and J. Goldsmith, 'The Current Illegitimacy of International Human Rights Litigation', *Fordham Law Review*, 1997, vol. 66, 319, at 357–63; A. D'Amato, 'What Does Tel-Oren Tell Lawyers? Judge Bork's Concept of the Law of Nations is Seriously Mistaken', *American Journal of International Law*, 1985, vol. 79, 92, at 100–4.

Limitations of the ATCA

Despite the dismal record of the ATCA in making companies accountable for human rights violations, this statute is undoubtedly the most frequently used initiative to grill companies. The ATCA has proved to be an attractive option because not many better alternatives seem to be available to sue companies in courts and because ATCA litigation enhances the bargaining position of victims, so as to compel powerful companies to settle cases outside the court. Nevertheless, a review of the ATCA jurisprudence reveals that the statute suffers from several serious limitations – some of which stem from the fact that the ATCA was never designed to redress contemporary human rights violations by companies.[22]

The first limitation stems from the fact that only an 'alien' can rely upon the ATCA to sue a corporation for human rights violations. So, even if a US corporation abridges the human rights of US citizens in the US or abroad, they are barred at the outset from basing their claim on this statute. This is a serious limitation, for it denies US citizens an avenue to seek justice for human rights violations even in a situation where other alternatives such as the Torture Victim Protection Act (TVPA) do not cover their cases.[23] Nor can the US government rely on the ATCA to rein in its own corporations from indulging in human rights abuses abroad.[24]

Moreover, the suits under this statute are subject to the general requirement that the US district courts must have personal jurisdiction over the alleged wrongdoer company. In other words, the ATCA, in effect, enables victims of human rights violations to approach the US courts for relief not against *any* company but only those companies which have some jurisdictional connection with the US. This jurisdictional hurdle is quite serious in view of the principles of corporate law which normally 'restrict legal action against individual members of a corporate group'.[25] Needless to say that in the absence of sufficient jurisdiction over the company which is sued, the victims' suit will be dismissed at the outset.[26]

---

22 M. Ramsey, 'Multinational Corporate Liability under the Alien Tort Claims Act: Some Structural Concerns', *Hastings International and Comparative Law Review*, 2001 vol. 24, 361, at 362–3.
23 Pub. L. No. 102–256, 106 Stat. 73 (1992).
24 E. Borg, 'Sharing the Blame for September Eleventh: The Case for New Law to Regulate the Activities of American Corporations Abroad', *Arizona Journal of International and Comparative Law*, 2003, vol. 20, 607, at 622–3.
25 P. Redmond, 'Transnational Enterprise and Human Rights: Options for Standard Setting and Compliance', *International Lawyer*, 2003, vol. 37, 69, at 84.
26 For example, the Court of Appeals for the Ninth Circuit in the *Unocal* case did not admit a suit against Total SA, the French parent of the Total Group, merely because of its interrelation with California based subsidiaries of the Total Group. *Doe v. Unocal Corporation* 248 F. 3d 915 (2001). The court held that the mere existence of a relationship between the parent and subsidiary is not sufficient to attract jurisdiction. Ibid., p. 926. But see *Wiwa v. Royal Dutch Petroleum Co.* 226 F. 3d 88 (2000).

Considering that a tort to be actionable under the ATCA should be committed in *violation* of the law *of* nations or a treaty of the US, this brings two additional, related limitations. Should the alleged misconduct, in order to be actionable, satisfy the 'state action' requirement? Another issue is when a company should be taken to have 'violated' human rights: only when it directly indulges in human rights abuses, or also when it merely assists, encourages, supports, abets, acquiesces in, or tolerates human rights violations. Regarding the first issue, the courts have insisted on state action as a prerequisite for a successful cause of action,[27] except in those cases which involved the violation of *jus cogens* norms such as torture, genocide, crimes against humanity, war crimes, forced labour, and slavery.[28] As far as the question of construing 'violation' is concerned, the US courts have sent mixed signals. In the *Unocal* case, the Court of Appeals for the Ninth Circuit ruled that the appropriate standard in determining the liability of Unocal was whether it provided 'knowingly practical assistance or encouragement that has a substantial effect on the perpetration of the crime' which 'requires actual or constructive knowledge'.[29] However, in the *Talisman Energy* case, the Court of Appeals for the Second Circuit proposed a more stringent test by holding that 'the *mens rea* standard for aiding and abetting liability in ATS [Alien Tort Statute] actions is purpose rather than knowledge alone' and that no liability can be imposed 'on individuals who *knowingly* (but not purposefully) aid and abet a violation of international law.'[30] Therefore, the state action doctrine and the rigid complicity test do pose serious hardships in making companies accountable for the violation of human rights norms.

The doctrine of *forum non conveniens* operates as another obstacle in victims' pursuit of justice under the ATCA. This common law doctrine allows courts to dismiss cases on the ground that the balance of relevant public and private interest factors favours that the trial takes place in a foreign forum. Out of many, two decisions can illustrate this point. First is the case of *Aguinda* v. *Texaco, Inc.*, involving environmental pollution caused by Texaco in Ecuador, where the district court dismissed the plaintiffs' claim by invoking this doctrine.[31] Similarly, in *Wiwa* v. *Royal Dutch Petroleum Co.*, the US district

---

27 Joseph, above n. 3, pp. 33–9; Redmond, above n. 25, pp. 82–3.
28 *Kadic* v. *Karadzic* 70 F 3d 232 (2nd Cir., 1995); *Doe* v. *Unocal Corp* 963 F Supp. 880 (CD Cal., 1997).
29 *Doe* v. *Unocal* 2002 US App LEXIS 19263, *35–*36 (9th Cir., 2002). Technically speaking, this ruling has no force, because the court had decided to vacate the decision and re-hear the case.
30 *The Presbyterian Church of Sudan* v. *Talisman Energy* 582 F. 3d 244, 259 (2009) (emphasis in original). However, the US Court of Appeals for the District of Columbia Circuit in *Doe* v. *Exxon*, by majority of 2:1, rejected the 'purpose' requirement to impute liability for aiding and abetting. *Doe* v. *Exxon Mobil Corporation* WL 2652384, *19 (DC Cir., decided 8 July 2011).
31 *Aguinda* v. *Texaco, Inc.* 945 F. Supp. 625 (SDNY, 1996).

court dismissed on *forum non conveniens* grounds a case in which the plaintiffs alleged human rights abuses at the hands of Nigerian authorities with direct/indirect participation of the defendant Dutch and British oil companies.[32]

One could, however, point out that the US Court of Appeals has subsequently overruled the district court's decisions in both *Aguinda*[33] and *Wiwa*[34] and that the position is changing after the Court of Appeals' decision in the *Wiwa* case.[35] But still it should be noted that on neither of these occasions did the Court of Appeals rule that the doctrine of *forum non conveniens* has no role to play in cases filed under the ATCA. In fact, the Court of Appeals, while overruling the district court's ruling in *Wiwa*, noted that even the TVPA has not 'nullified, or even significantly diminished, the doctrine of *forum non conveniens*'.[36] So the ghost of *forum non conveniens* will still haunt the victims relying on the ATCA.[37]

In terms of remedies too, the ATCA offers inadequate remedies, because a court hearing an action under this statute could only award relief similar to that for a tort action.[38] So, criminal sanctions will be out of the question even in cases where egregious human rights abuses are proved. This is a serious limitation, though not exposed yet since no company has been ordered to pay compensation by the court under the ATCA at the time of writing this book.

The meaning of 'law of nations' after Sosa

The most serious limitation of the ATCA stems from the narrow interpretation of the phrase 'law of nations' given by the courts. The phrase 'law of nations' seemingly looks quite wide in its ambit, but the US courts have not

---

32 *Wiwa* v. *Royal Dutch Petroleum Co. and Shell Transport & Trading Co.* 1998 US Dist. LEXIS 23064.
33 *Jota/Ecuador* v. *Texaco, Inc.* 157 F. 3d 153, at 159 (1998). It is noteworthy that on reconsideration the district court again dismissed the suit on the *forum non conveniens* ground – *Maria Aguinda* v. *Texaco, Inc.; Gabriel Ashanga Jota* v. *Texaco, Inc.* 303 F. 3d 470 (2001) – and this time the Court of Appeals did affirm that decision: *Aguinda* v. *Texaco, Inc.* 303 F. 3d 470 (2002).
34 *Wiwa* v. *Royal Dutch Petroleum Co. and Shell Transport & Trading Co.* 226 F. 3d 88 (2000).
35 Joseph, above n. 3, pp. 90–8; M. Skolnik, 'The *Forum non Conveniens* Doctrine in Alien Tort Claims Act Cases: A Shell of its Former Self after Wiwa', *Emory International Law Review*, 2002, vol. 16, 187.
36 *Wiwa* v. *Royal Dutch Petroleum Co. and Shell Transport & Trading Co.* 226 F. 3d 88, at 106 (2000).
37 An argument based on the doctrine of *forum non conveniens* did not succeed because no alternative forum was available to hear the case. *In re Xe Services Alien Tort Litigation* 665 F. Supp. 2d 569, at 602 (2009).
38 In tort cases, the two most common remedies are damages (including punitive damages in appropriate cases) and injunctions. J. Slawotsky, 'Doing Business around the World: Corporate Liability under the Alien Tort Claims Act', *Michigan State Law Review*, 2005, 1065, at 1099–1101.

consistently adopted a broad yardstick to judge the scope of the ATCA.[39] The decision of the US Supreme Court in *Sosa* further limits the scope of the ATCA by its narrower interpretation of this term.[40] The majority in *Sosa* held that the ATCA provides a 'limited, implicit sanction to entertain the handful of international law *cum* common law claims understood in 1789'.[41] The Court observed that the 'federal courts should not recognize private claims under federal common law for violations of any international law norm with less *definite content* and *acceptance* among civilized nations than the historical paradigms familiar when' the statute was enacted.[42] The requirement that today's norms should have acquired a comparable degree of acceptance to the small number of international legal causes of action recognized in the eighteenth century – that is, violations of safe conduct, offences against ambassadors, and piracy – places a heavy burden on the shoulders of victims of corporate human rights abuses.[43]

However, the US Supreme Court in *Sosa* did not stop there. In addition to satisfying the stringent restrictions in terms of the content and acceptability of a norm by states, the determination of the question whether a norm is sufficiently definite or not 'should (and, indeed, inevitably must) involve an element of judgment about *the practical consequences of making that cause available to litigants* in the federal courts'.[44] This leeway would satisfy those who argue that a wide use of the ATCA for making US corporations accountable for human rights violations abroad might interfere with US foreign policy, adversely affect the economy of US allies, discourage foreign investment in developing countries, and/or hamper the war on terrorism.[45] Furthermore, and quite importantly, the Supreme Court in *Sosa* left open the question of imposing additional limiting requirements such as the exhaustion of domestic law remedies in the litigant's home jurisdiction and 'a policy of case-specific deference to the political branches'.[46]

Thus, in view of a narrower interpretation of the term 'law of nations' adopted in *Sosa*, the scope of the ATCA to remedy corporate human rights

---

39 See *Forti* v. *Suarez-Mason* 672 F Supp. 1531 (ND Cal., 1987); *Hilao* v. *Estate of Marcos* 25 F. 3d 1467 (9th Cir., 1994); *Beanal* v. *Freeport-McMoRan, Inc.* 969 F. Supp. 362 (ED La., 1997); *Doe* v. *Unocal* 110 F. Supp. 2d 1294 (CD Cal., 2000).
40 C. Bradley, J. Goldsmith and D. Moore, 'Sosa, Customary International Law, and the Continuing Relevance of Erie', *Harvard Law Review*, 2007, vol. 120, 869, at 896–901, 924–9.
41 *Sosa* v. *Alvarez-Machain*, above n. 20, p. 2754.
42 Ibid., 2765 (emphasis added).
43 V. Gomez, 'The Sosa Standard: What Does it Mean for Future ATS Litigation?' *Pepperdine Law Review*, 2006, vol. 33, 469, at 485.
44 *Sosa* v. *Alvarez-Machain*, above n. 20, p. 2766 (emphasis added).
45 See Ramsey, above n. 22; C. Bradley, 'The Costs of International Human Rights Litigation', *Chicago Journal of International Law*, 2001, vol. 2, 457.
46 *Sosa* v. *Alvarez-Machain*, above n. 20, p. 2766.

abuses is more restricted now than ever before.[47] Although in principle the court could have interpreted the 'law of nations' more liberally,[48] it preferred not to do so. The US Supreme Court rather considered it a constitutional imperative to perform 'vigilant door-keeping' as far as the judicial recognition of new actionable international norms for ATCA purposes was concerned.[49]

The Kiobel challenge

It is well-known that the US government as well as various other states – in addition to several international law scholars[50] – have not been supportive of an expansive application of the ATCA so as to make it an umbrella legislation to redress all types of corporate human rights abuses occurring anywhere. The US government along with the governments of the UK, Australia and Switzerland had filed *amici curiae* briefs before the US Supreme Court in *Sosa* to oppose the wholesale use of the ATCA for redressing human rights violations by US-based MNCs.[51]

The ATCA survived these threats. However, a more serious challenge to the capability of the ATCA to redress corporate human rights abuses is posed by the ruling of the Court of Appeals for the Second Circuit in *Esther Kiobel* v. *Royal Dutch Petroleum Co.*[52] In the case, the plaintiff alleged that Dutch, British, and Nigerian corporations engaged in oil exploration and production aided and abetted the Nigerian government in committing human rights abuses in violation of the law of nations.[53] Justice Cabranes, writing the majority judgment, considered the question whether corporations could be sued under the ATCA to be an open and unresolved one.[54] The majority went on to answer the

---

47 James Boeving, 'Half Full . . . or Completely Empty?: Environmental Alien Tort Claims Post *Sosa v Alvarez-Machain*', *Georgetown International Environmental Law Review*, 2005, vol. 18, 109; Bradley *et al*, above n. 40.
48 Dodge, for example, canvasses four alternative standards – from the most expansive to the most restricted – that might be utilized to determine what constitutes a tort in violation of the law of nations. W. Dodge, 'Which Torts in Violation of the Law of Nations?', *Hastings International and Comparative Law Review*, 2001, vol. 24, 351, at 352–3. D'Amato also explains the wide ambit of the phrase 'law of nations' by contrasting it with 'international law'. D'Amato, above n. 21, p. 103.
49 *Sosa* v. *Alvarez-Machain*, above n. 20, p. 2764.
50 See, for example, J. Ku, 'The Curious Case of Corporate Liability under the Alien Tort Statute: A Flawed System of Judicial Lawmaking', *Virginia Journal of International Law*, 2011, vol. 51, 353; Bradley, above n. 45; D. Kochan, 'Constitutional Structure as a Limitation on the Scope of the "Law of Nations" in the Alien Tort Claims Act', *Cornell International Law Journal*, 1998, vol. 31, 153.
51 Joseph, above n. 3, pp. 55–60.
52 621 F. 3d 111 (2010).
53 Ibid., p. 117.
54 Ibid.

question in the negative. It reasoned that customary international law is the substantive law that determines the court's jurisdiction and that the ATCA requires federal courts 'to examine the specific and universally accepted rules that the nations of the world treat as binding *in their dealings with one another*'.[55] Applying this test, the majority held that companies cannot be sued under the ATCA because 'imposing liability on corporations for violations of customary international law has not attained a discernible, much less universal, acceptance among nations of the world in their relations *inter se*' and that '[n]o corporation has ever been subject to *any* form of liability (whether civil, criminal, or otherwise) under the customary international law of human rights'.[56]

On the other hand, Justice Leval – who concurred with the majority on dismissal of the complaint but disagreed with the reasoning of the majority – noted that the 'majority opinion deals a substantial blow to international law and its undertaking to protect fundamental human rights'.[57] He highlighted the pitfalls of the majority judgment as follows:

> The new rule offers to unscrupulous businesses advantages of incorporation never before dreamed of. So long as they incorporate . . ., businesses will now be free to trade in or exploit slaves, employ mercenary armies to do dirty work for despots, perform genocides or operate torture prisons for a despot's political opponents, or engage in piracy – all without civil liability to victims.[58]

Justice Leval finds fault in the reasoning of the majority by pointing out that the 'fact that international tribunals do not impose *criminal punishment* on corporations in no way supports the inference that corporations are outside the scope of international law and therefore can incur no *civil compensatory liability* to victims when they engage in conduct prohibited by the norms of international law'.[59] In his view, since international law leaves it to individual states to determine if civil liability should be imposed on companies for violation of its norms and the US has enacted the ATCA to impose civil liability, companies can be held liable under it.[60]

One can mount arguments against the majority judgment in *Kiobel*.[61] However, my objective here is different. Against the backdrop of the *Kiobel*

---

55 Ibid., p. 118 (emphasis in original) and pp. 126–31 generally.
56 Ibid., pp. 145, 148 (emphasis in original).
57 Ibid., p. 149.
58 Ibid., p. 150.
59 Ibid., p. 152 (emphasis in original).
60 Ibid., pp. 152–3.
61 O. Murray, D Kinley and C. Pitts, 'Exaggerated Rumours of the Death of an Alien Tort? Corporations, Human Rights and the Remarkable Case of *Kiobel*', *Melbourne Journal of International Law*, 2011, vol. 12, 57; J. Paust, 'Nonstate Actor Participation in International Law and the Pretence of Exclusion', *Virginia Journal of International Law*, 2011, vol. 51, 977.

ruling putting a question mark, at least for the time being, on the future of ATCA in making juridical persons like companies liable for human rights violations,[62] I argue that even if *Kiobel* is overruled on this point by the Supreme Court in the future (the best case scenario),[63] the ATCA only offers a limited potential in holding companies accountable for human rights abuses. As I have tried to show, this innovative experiment has not proved very successful to date and it offers little hope for a better outcome in future for the several reasons pointed out above. The ATCA litigation has had two major indirect positive effects: it has brought the issue of corporate human rights accountability to the fore (the *limelight effect*) and enhanced the bargaining position of victims *vis-à-vis* companies leading to several out-of-court settlements (the *leverage effect*). But apart from these positive effects, it is arguable that the ATCA fails the twin test of efficacy proposed in Chapter 3. Although the ATCA might have encouraged some companies to pay greater attention to human rights norms, it is clear that this regulatory initiative has not provided adequate relief to the victims of corporate human rights abuses. The ATCA litigation has resulted in out-of-court settlements in some cases, but it is problematic to cite these positive by-products as clinching evidence of the redressive efficacy of this statute.[64]

Corporate codes of conduct

A number of companies, especially the bigger or more prominent ones, are increasingly formulating and adopting some kind of voluntary corporate code of conduct.[65] Such codes can take various forms in terms of their nature, scope, objective, label, applicability, and implementation.[66] The adoption of codes of conduct is driven by several considerations (e.g. a 'right' or 'just' way of doing business,[67] a response to pressure emanating from market forces and

---

62 On 4 February 2011, the majority rejected a petition to rehear the case. *Esther Kiobel* v. *Royal Dutch Petroleum Co.* 2011 WL 338048.
63 The Court of Appeals for the Eleventh Circuit has taken a contrary stand in a few decisions. *Sinaltrainal* v. *Coca-Cola* 578 F. 3d 1252, at 1263 (11th Cir., 2009); *Romero* v. *Drummond Co., Inc.* 552 F. 3d 1303, at 1315 (11th Cir., 2008). See also *Holocaust Victims of Bank Theft* v. *Magyar Nemzeti Bank*, 2011 WL 1900340 and *Doe* v. *Exxon Mobil Corporation*, WL 2652384 (DC Cir.). On 17 October 2011, the US Supreme Court agreed to hear whether corporations can be sued under the ATCA and the TVPA.
64 See B. Fishman, 'Binding Corporations to Human Rights Norms through Public Law Settlement', *New York University Law Review*, 2006, vol. 81, 1433.
65 Business and Human Rights Resource Centre, 'Company Policy Statements on Human Rights'. Available at: www.business-humanrights.org/Documents/Policies (accessed 18 June 2011).
66 Redmond, above n. 25, pp. 88–9; B. Frey, 'The Legal and Ethical Responsibilities of Transnational Corporations in the Protection of International Human Rights', *Minnesota Journal of Global Trade*, 1997, vol. 6, 153, at 177–80.
67 D. Cassel, 'Corporate Initiatives: A Second Human Rights Revolution?' *Fordham International Law Journal*, 1996, vol. 19, 1963, at 1978–80.

stakeholders,[68] a way of gaining competitive advantage over one's business rivals,[69] and as a smokescreen[70] or a 'window dressing' device, a human face for inhuman business activities). My objective here is not to examine these and similar other motivating factors, but first to highlight the advantages that corporate codes of conduct present *vis-à-vis* other external regulatory initiatives and then outline their limitations for both preventing and redressing human rights violations by companies.

Advantages of corporate codes of conduct

Unlike general regulatory initiatives, voluntary codes offer flexibility, thus allowing each corporation to tailor a code of conduct to its specific business needs, corporate structure and/or local operating circumstances.[71] Codes can be especially useful to deal with a situation in which a corporation, say, doing business in the mining industry faces some human rights issues that will be different from a corporation that manufactures medicines or is engaged in investment business.

Corporate codes of conduct also seem to be a more efficient way of regulating corporate conduct and ensuring that companies respect human rights. Apart from the efficiency that results from the specificity and particularity of the content of codes designed for a given company or industry,[72] codes contribute to compliance-cum-enforcement efficiency by cutting the cost of employing investigators, regulators, prosecutors and judges. Codes contribute to efficient regulation in another way – they provide an opportunity for corporations to work together with their stockholders as well as stakeholders to chart a commonly accepted course of conducting business in a humane way. Such a cooperative enterprise is likely to develop a feeling of trust, thus reducing frictions and disputes between companies and parties affected by their operations.

In addition, by creating 'a web of transnational obligation',[73] codes of conduct can prove immensely useful in guiding the conduct of companies and

---

68 R. Liubicic, 'Corporate Codes of Conduct and Product Labelling Schemes: The Limits and Possibilities of Promoting International Labour Rights through Private Initiatives', *Law and Policy in International Business*, 1998, vol. 39, 111, at 114–16; S. Picciotto, 'Rights, Responsibilities and Regulation of International Business', *Columbia Journal of Transnational Law*, 2003, vol. 42, 131, at 139–41.
69 OECD, *Codes of Corporate Conduct: An Expanded Review of their Content*, TD/TC/WP(99)56/FINAL, June 2000, pp. 20–2.
70 E. Engle, 'Corporate Social Responsibility: Market-Based Remedies for International Human Rights Violations?' *Willamette Law Review*, 2004, vol. 40, 103, at 120.
71 This flexibility, however, brings its own problem of 'self-selection' and 'patchy and uneven content'. Picciotto, above n. 68, p. 147.
72 OECD, *Corporate Responsibility: Private Initiatives and Public Goals*, Paris: OECD, 2001, p. 23.
73 Redmond, above n. 25, p. 90.

their suppliers in an environment where state-based regulatory initiatives are non-existent due to weak governance, economic incapacity, conflict or corruption.[74] Codes can also secure cooperation of companies in the promotion of human rights when states themselves are indulging in, or tolerating, human rights violations. Consider, for instance, the role played by the Sullivan Principles in fighting the apartheid in South Africa.[75]

Codes could also work as a stepping-stone for the evolution of legally binding human rights obligations flowing from external sources. States – either acting individually at a municipal level or collectively at a regional or international level – might rely on codes formulated and adopted by various companies to develop generally agreeable human rights standards.[76]

The US Supreme Court decision in *Wal-Mart Stores Inc.* v. *Betty Dukes*[77] provides another (perhaps unintentional) advantage of codes for companies; they can plead codes as a shield against allegations of human rights abuses being committed as part of a 'corporate culture'. In this case, about 1.5 million current/former women employees of Wal-Mart filed a class action suit alleging that the company discriminated against them on the basis of their sex by denying them equal pay or promotions in violation of Title VII of the Civil Rights Act 1964. The Supreme Court reversed the decision of the Court of Appeals certifying this as a class action – showing again the procedural obstacles that victims face when bringing class suits against companies. But more importantly, Justice Scalia observed that the allegation that Wal-Mart operated under a general policy of discrimination cannot be accepted because Wal-Mart's 'announced policy forbids sex discrimination'.[78] It is questionable if an express corporate policy should be taken as a conclusive evidence of the concerned company's practice for, as we will see below, divergence between policy on paper and actual practice is quite common.

Limitations of corporate codes of conduct

Corporate codes of conduct suffer from serious inherent limitations which directly limit their value in promoting corporate human rights responsibilities.[79]

---

74 See N. Jaffe and J. Weiss, 'The Self-Regulating Corporation: How Corporate Codes can Save Our Children', *Fordham Journal of Corporate and Financial Law*, 2006, vol. 11, 893.
75 S.P. Lu, 'Corporate Codes of Conduct and the FTC: Advancing Human Rights through Deceptive Advertising Law', *Columbia Journal of Transnational Law*, 2000, vol. 38, 603, at 612–13; E. Westfield, 'Globalisation, Governance, and Multinational Enterprise Responsibility: Corporate Codes of Conduct in the 21st Century', *Virginia Journal of International Law*, 2002, vol. 42, 1075, at 1092–5.
76 D. Kinley and J. Tadaki, 'From Talk to Walk: The Emergence of Human Rights Responsibilities for Corporations at International Law', *Virginia Journal of International Law*, 2004, vol. 44, 931, at 957–60.
77 131 S. Ct. 2541 (2011).
78 Ibid., p. 2553.
79 Redmond, above n. 25, pp. 91–5.

Codes usually use general, vague language and are selective in their content – thus hardly providing sufficiently clear human rights standards to guide the conduct of corporate employees, who are expected to implement them. Besides, there is a tendency in codes to maintain lower standards rather than agreeing to work towards achieving higher standards step-by-step. Two studies by the ILO and the OECD, based on a survey of hundreds of codes, have found that a majority of codes used 'self-defined' standards, often referred to national standards as compared to international standards, and did not attach adequate significance to important rights such as freedom of expression or collective bargaining.[80] Liubicic identifies yet another limitation related to the scope of corporate codes of conduct: a vast majority of these codes do not apply to overseas workers employed on a contract basis, or to those that work in the informal, unorganized sector.[81]

A similar concern arises in relation to the applicability of codes to corporate supply chains. If codes adopt a 'hands off' approach and are not geared to regulate the conduct of the suppliers and contractors of companies adopting such codes, they would prove ineffective in controlling and redressing human rights abuses committed by business partners. In fact, even when a code is specifically designed to apply to suppliers,[82] serious implementation challenges surface. The 2011 Supplier Responsibility Report of Apple Inc. – which 'monitors compliance with the Code through a rigorous program of onsite factory audits, followed by corrective action plans and verification measures' – illustrates this difficulty.[83] The Report reveals that out of 127 supplier facilities audited by Apple in 2010, the maximum 60 hours per week stipulation was exceeded in 76 facilities, 30 facilities conducted pregnancy tests, workers were not wearing appropriate personal protective equipment in 54 facilities, and 80 facilities were not storing or handling hazardous chemicals properly.[84] On a positive note, one can say that this kind of proactive monitoring of the conduct of business partners shows that certain MNCs are now becoming more transparent about their supply chain and are willing to share information with various stakeholders.

Another major limitation is that a great majority of codes of conduct do not provide for external independent assessment, verification or monitoring of corporate conduct *vis-à-vis* the obligations undertaken under such codes.[85] Codes are either silent about the implementation and enforcement aspects of

---

80 Picciotto, above n. 68, pp. 142–3; OECD, above n. 69, pp. 12–14.
81 Liubicic, above n. 68, pp. 139–40.
82 See e.g. Apple Supplier Code of Conduct (Version 3.1, 2009). Available at: http://images.apple.com/supplierresponsibility/pdf/Supplier_Code_of_Conduct_V3_1.pdf (accessed 10 June 2011).
83 Apple Inc., 'Apple Supplier Responsibility: 2011 Progress Report', February 2011, p. 3.
84 Ibid., pp. 23–4.
85 Of the 246 codes surveyed by the OECD, only 26 (less than 11 per cent) contained a provision for independent, external monitoring. OECD, above n. 69, p. 35.

obligations contained therein, or at best provide for internal follow-up action.[86] Even in those select codes that contain a provision for external monitoring and/or verification,[87] scholars and human rights activists often doubt the independence, resourcefulness or competence of the external agencies so appointed.[88] Although scholars have canvassed some means by which voluntary codes may be 'clothed in legal garb' and thus enforced,[89] these options too are very limited in scope. Voluntary codes, therefore, face a serious legitimacy crisis[90] and 'have no meaning unless they are translated into action and unless that action is monitored and audited'.[91]

In the absence of any external monitoring, the extent of codes' *actual* influence on corporate conduct largely depends on the response (often in the form of pressure) of corporate stakeholders such as consumers, investors, the media and NGOs. However, in the face of codes lacking any coherence or credibility, it would be unrealistic to assume that these stakeholders might exert their influence over the involved companies adequately and regularly.[92] I develop this argument further in Chapter 5 in relation to limitations of the business case for human rights.

A sincere commitment to the adoption and observance of codes of conduct on the part of companies also faces several practical challenges. In the absence of a clear, positive relation of codes of conduct to business profits, several corporations may be hesitant to adopt and/or implement such codes;[93] 'corporations will not regulate themselves into competitive disadvantage'.[94] In fact, the prisoner's dilemma might discourage corporations from observing (if not adopting) these voluntary codes both in their letter and spirit.[95] Moreover, those companies which do not have or need an image to protect, or produce 'intermediate-use goods' are also less inclined to adopt and observe such codes.[96] Conversely, codes are not always able to bring a material change in

---

86 Liubicic, above n. 68, p. 134.
87 J. Anderson, 'Respecting Human Rights: Multinational Corporations Strike Out', *University of Pennsylvania Journal of Labour and Employment Law*, 2000, vol. 2, 463, at 486–8.
88 Lu, above n. 75, p. 615; Picciotto, above n. 68, p. 143.
89 Kinley and Tadaki, above n. 76, pp. 956–8.
90 S. Cleveland, 'Global Labour Rights and the Alien Tort Claims Act', *Texas Law Review*, 1998, vol. 76, 1533, at 1553.
91 Sir G. Chandler, 'Keynote Address: Crafting a Human Rights Agenda for Business' in Michael K. Addo (ed.), *Human Rights Standards and the Responsibility of Transnational Corporations*, The Hague: Kluwer Law International, 1999, p. 39, at 41.
92 Liubicic, above n. 68, p. 119 and generally pp. 131–9.
93 E. Macek, 'Scratching the Corporate Back: Why Corporations Have No Incentive to Define Human Rights', *Minnesota Journal of Global Trade*, 2002, vol. 11, 101, at 113–18.
94 Engle, above n. 70, p. 113.
95 S. Scalet, 'Prisoner's Dilemma, Cooperative Norms, and Codes of Business Ethics', *Journal of Business Ethics*, 2006, vol. 65, 309, at 316.
96 Liubicic, above n. 68, pp. 116, 141–2.

the conduct of those companies that adopt them. There is some empirical evidence to support this claim: many of the companies that were sued or publicly chastized for violating human rights obligations had some sort of internal code of conduct in force at the time when the alleged violations took place.[97]

One may, therefore, conclude that while corporate codes have some value, they suffer from serious limitations which undermine their viability as a robust mechanism for making companies accountable for human rights violations. Unless these limitations are addressed and codes of conduct are taken to 'the next level' by an ambitious course charted for governments by Murphy,[98] they will continue to offer limited regulatory benefit. Thus, the twin efficacy of corporate codes of conduct is suspect: at best they may have encouraged a small number of companies to internalize human rights norms in their business operations, but most of the codes perform miserably at the redressive level by not even providing for any remedy or relief to the victims of human rights abuses. However, at this stage it remains an open question, as Liubicic puts it, 'whether today's private initiatives will gradually evolve into this complete and effective system of self-regulation, or whether they will remain public relations tools that fail to achieve meaningful results'.[99]

It is worth noting here that the Guiding Principles (discussed later in this chapter) propose some measures that, if sincerely adopted by companies, should enhance the efficacy of codes of conduct by overcoming some of the limitations highlighted above. In order to meet their responsibility to respect human rights, companies should, among others, adopt a policy statement, which should be approved at the most senior level of a given company, stipulate the company's expectations of its business partners, and be publicly available as well as communicated both internally and externally.[100] Moreover, companies should establish effective 'operational-level' grievance mechanisms to address early and remedy directly any possible grievances of individuals or communities.[101]

---

97 R. Steinhardt, 'Corporate Responsibility and the International Law of Human Rights: The New *Lex Mercatoria*' in P. Alston (ed.), *Non-State Actors and Human Rights*, New York: Oxford University Press, 2005, p. 177, at 186; M. Kielsgard, 'Unocal and the Demise of Corporate Neutrality', *California Western International Law Journal*, 2005, vol. 36, 185, at 208–9.
98 S. Murphy, 'Taking Multinational Corporate Codes of Conduct to the Next Level', *Columbia Journal of Transnational Law*, 2005, vol. 43, 389, at 396, 423–32.
99 Liubicic, above n. 68, p. 158.
100 Human Rights Council, 'Guiding Principles on Business and Human Rights: Implementing the United Nations "Protect, Respect and Remedy" Framework', A/HRC/17/31 (21 March 2011), Principle 16.
101 Ibid., Principle 29.

80 *Existing regulatory initiatives*

OECD Guidelines

The OECD Guidelines, which are part of the Declaration on International Investment and Multinational Enterprises, came into effect on 21 June 1976.[102] The Guidelines were revised in June 2000[103] and updated in May 2011.[104] The Guidelines, which are recommendations jointly addressed by governments to MNCs,[105] encourage MNCs to observe the principles and standards laid down in the Guidelines in areas such as human rights, disclosure, employment and industrial relations, environment, combating bribery, consumer interests, science and technology, competition and taxation.[106]

Positives out of the 2000 review of the Guidelines

The 2000 review of the Guidelines resulted in a significant improvement over the original Guidelines of 1976 in terms of widening their scope, improving the process of implementation, and including a specific recommendation on human rights.[107] Some of these improvements are worth noting.

First, as compared to the 1976 Guidelines – which were limited to MNCs 'operating in' the territories of member states[108] – the revised Guidelines were made applicable to MNCs '*operating* in or *from*' the territories of member states.[109] The Guidelines not only asked MNCs to observe the provisions 'wherever they operate',[110] but also expected them to encourage their 'business partners, including suppliers and sub-contractors, to apply principles of corporate conduct compatible with the Guidelines'.[111]

Second, the post-2000 review Guidelines specifically provided that MNCs should 'respect the human rights of those affected by their activities consistent with the host government's international obligations and commitments'.[112]

---

102 OECD Declaration on International Investment and Multinational Enterprises, 21 June 1976, reprinted in 1976, *ILM*, vol. 15, 967 (hereinafter OECD Guidelines of 1976).
103 OECD Declaration on International Investment and Multinational Enterprises 2000, reprinted in 2001, *ILM*, vol. 40, 237 (hereinafter OECD Guidelines of 2000).
104 OECD Guidelines for Multinational Enterprises: Recommendations for Responsible Business Conduct in a Global Context, 25 May 2011. Available at: www.oecd.org/dataoecd/43/29/48004323.pdf (accessed 10 June 2011) (hereinafter OECD Guidelines of 2011).
105 OECD Guidelines of 2000, above n. 103, pp. 237 (Preface, para. 1) and 239 (para. I.1).
106 Ibid., pp. 240–6 (para. II–X).
107 N. Jägers, *Corporate Human Rights Obligations: In Search of Accountability*, Antwerpen: Intersentia, 2002, pp. 102–6.
108 OECD Guidelines of 1976, above n. 102, pp. 968 (para. I) and 970 (para. 6).
109 The OECD Declaration and Decisions on International Investment and Multinational Enterprises: Basic Texts, DAFE/IME (2000) 20, 8 November 2000, p. 5 (para. I) (hereinafter Decisions of the OECD Council).
110 OECD Guidelines of 2000, above n. 103, p. 239 (para. I.2).
111 Ibid., p. 240 (para. II.10).
112 Ibid., p. 240 (para. II.2).

On the face of it, the term 'affected by their activities' is wide enough to include stakeholders of MNCs, meaning thereby that MNCs ought not to violate stakeholders' human rights enshrined in the international obligations of the host country.

Third, the revised Guidelines encouraged MNCs to disclose publicly 'information on the social, ethical and environmental policies of the enterprise and other codes of conduct to which the company subscribes'.[113] Since the flow of information is critical for stakeholders acting as informal checks on the conduct of corporations, this provision is important, especially because the 'information should be disclosed *for the enterprise as a whole* and, where appropriate, along business lines or geographic areas'.[114]

Fourth, the revised Guidelines formulated special obligations of MNCs regarding environmental protection, combating bribery and protecting consumers' interests – something that was totally missing in the Guidelines of 1976. In addition, as compared to the original Guidelines of 1976, the provisions related to employment and industrial relations under the Guidelines of 2000 were much stronger and wider. For example, MNCs should not only contribute to 'the effective abolition of child labour' as well as 'the elimination of all forms of forced or compulsory labour,'[115] but should also 'take adequate steps to ensure occupational health and safety in their operations.'[116] On the other hand, a provision that MNCs should observe 'standards of employment and industrial relations *not less favourable than* those observed by comparable employers *in the host country*' did not go far enough because in many cases the standards applied in host states may not be adequate.[117]

Fifth, the 2000 Guidelines also provided that MNCs should 'refrain from seeking or accepting exemptions not contemplated in the statutory or regulatory framework related to environment, health, safety, taxation, financial incentives or other issues'.[118] This provision should discourage MNCs from seeking special exemptions – which in some cases may (in)directly contribute to human rights violations – from the regulatory framework in force in host states. It is, however, doubtful if this could counter the problem of a 'race to the bottom' which forces host countries to lower their human rights standards in order to attract investment by MNCs.

Sixth, the 2000 review of the Guidelines improved the compliance process too. The revised Guidelines stipulated that the governments adhering to them *will* promote and encourage their use, including by establishing National Contact Points (NCPs) and participating in 'review and consultation

---

113 Ibid., p. 241 (para. III.5.a).
114 Ibid., p. 240 (para. III.1) (emphasis added).
115 Ibid., pp. 241–2 (para. IV.1.b/c).
116 Ibid., p. 242 (para. IV.4.b).
117 Ibid., p. 242 (para. IV.4.a) (emphasis added).
118 Ibid., p. 240 (para. II.5).

82 *Existing regulatory initiatives*

procedures to address issues concerning interpretation of the Guidelines'.[119] A 'special instances' procedure was introduced under which the NCPs can entertain complaints relating to alleged violations of the OECD Guidelines by MNCs.[120] Should a complaint merit an examination, the concerned NCP offers its good offices to help the parties resolve the dispute.[121] If the parties did not reach an agreement on the issue raised, the relevant NCP can issue a statement and may also make appropriate recommendations on the implementation of the Guidelines.[122] The efficacy of NCPs in ensuring compliance with the Guidelines is analyzed below.

Drawbacks of the OECD Guidelines

Despite the improvements brought about by the 2000 review, the real impact of these Guidelines in terms of making MNCs accountable for human rights violations remained rather limited.[123] One could come to this conclusion by looking at the provisions of the Guidelines that dealt with the formulation and implementation of human rights standards as well as their operation. At the outset, it was surprising that the Guidelines did not consider it necessary to offer 'a precise definition' of MNEs,[124] something that was fundamental to their scope. Besides, the Guidelines (pre-2011 update) were very general and vague in formulating human rights standards. The recommendation on human rights found its place only in a section on General Policies and, unlike for other matters, the Guidelines contained no specific section on human rights. Even where a specific human rights obligation was construed, the language was very weak. For example, instead of the Guidelines totally prohibiting MNCs from practising either child labour or forced/compulsory labour, they laid down that MNCs '*should contribute*' towards the said goals, and that too 'within the framework of applicable law, regulations and *prevailing labour relations and employment practices*'.[125]

---

119 Ibid., p. 239 (para. I.5/10).
120 Decisions of the OECD Council, above n. 109, p. 28; OECD, *OECD Guidelines for Multinational Enterprises: 2005 Annual Meeting of the National Contact Points – Report by the Chair*, June 2005, p. 13. Available at: www.oecd.org/dataoecd/20/13/35387363.pdf (accessed 20 January 2007).
121 Decisions of the OECD Council, above n. 109, p. 28.
122 Ibid., p. 28.
123 See, for example, Christian Aid, Amnesty International and Friends of the Earth, *Flagship or Failure? The UK's Implementation of the OECD Guidelines and Approach to Corporate Accountability*, November 2005, pp. 13–20. Available at: www.christianaid.org.uk/images/F1167PDF.pdf (accessed 10 June 2011).
124 OECD Guidelines of 2000, above n. 103, p. 239 (para. I.3).
125 Ibid., pp. 241–2 (para. IV.1.b/c) (emphasis added).

There was also a problem in the Guidelines' inclination to rely too much on the policies, practices, regulations, obligations or standards of the 'host' countries of MNCs on any given issue.[126] As many such enterprises operate in developing countries – where the above guidance variables are less stringent and also suffer from lax enforcement – compliance with merely the standards of host countries might not prove to be sufficient. One wonders whether the Guidelines should not have provided that MNCs should apply the higher of the standards emanating from their 'home' and 'host' countries.

Another fundamental lacuna of the Guidelines lies in the lack of a strong enforcement system if MNCs do not follow these principles. The Guidelines clearly state that 'observance of the Guidelines by enterprises is voluntary and not legally enforceable'.[127] The efficacy of their implementation depends upon the mandate and working of NCPs and the Committee on International Investment and Multinational Enterprises (Investment Committee).[128] All member countries are expected to set up NCPs so that they can promote the OECD Guidelines, hold discussions with relevant parties, handle enquiries, and deal with 'specific instances' related to the implementation of the Guidelines.[129] The Investment Committee – which is 'comprised of representatives from all OECD member countries and observers'[130] – is responsible for 'clarification' of the Guidelines, but cannot 'reach conclusions on the conduct of individual enterprises'.[131]

It is thus clear that these two-tier institutions have, in principle, some potential to promote the observance of the Guidelines by MNCs, for they provide a forum for the exchange of views and perform advisory, consultative, recommendatory and clarificatory functions.[132] In particular, the mandate of NCPs to resolve issues related to the alleged non-implementation of the OECD Guidelines by MNCs in specific instances is crucial. Since the special instances procedure was put in place in June 2000, the NCPs have received 106 requests for special instances.[133] The NCPs have taken up and pursued further 72 instances, out of which 44 have been 'concluded' and the rest are 'ongoing'.[134] In some cases the NCPs could resolve the matter to the

---

126 Ibid., pp. 240 (para. II.2), 242 (para. IV.4.a) and 243 (para. V).
127 Ibid., p. 239 (para. I.1).
128 See International Council on Human Rights Policy (ICHRP), *Beyond Voluntarism: Human Rights and the Developing International Legal Obligations of Companies*, Versoix: ICHRP, 2002, pp. 99–102; J. Karl, 'The OECD Guidelines for Multinational Enterprises' in Addo (ed.), above n. 91, p. 89, at 93–5.
129 Decisions of the OECD Council, above n. 109, pp. 25, 27–8.
130 Christian Aid *et al*, above n. 123, p. 12.
131 Decisions of the OECD Council, above n. 109, p. 26.
132 Ibid., pp. 25–9.
133 OECD, above n. 120, p. 14.
134 Ibid. It is notable that out of 72 instances that were further investigated by NCPs, 44 concerned activities in non-OECD member states. Ibid.

84 *Existing regulatory initiatives*

satisfaction of the concerned parties.[135] For example, in a complaint against GSL Australia for breaching the Guidelines and other international human rights instruments in operating the immigration detention centres, the Australian NCP was able to secure a mediated settlement under which GSL agreed to take a number of remedial steps.[136] Similarly, in relation to a complaint against Bayer, the German company accepted responsibility for child labour in its supply chain and agreed to improve the situation.[137]

However, the mediation process did not work in many instances because, for example, the activities did not have the necessary investment character, or the particular enterprise was not truly multinational.[138] Even where the mediation process resulted in a settlement, the situation on the ground might not change on the promised lines. The complaint against Vedanta is a case in point: it was alleged that that Vedanta did not engage with the affected tribal community in the Indian state of Orissa and resorted to physical threats to stop the complainant from monitoring the follow-up steps taken by the company.[139] Vedanta denied these allegations, but the UK NCP did not do anything further to verify the facts; rather it merely summarized the contrary position of the two parties in its follow-up report.[140] It is against this background that the OECD Watch concludes that 'the vast majority of OECD Guidelines cases have unfortunately not led to any significant improvement in the respective company's behaviour or the situation that led to the complaint'.[141]

On the face of it, the 'special instances' complaint procedure should have ensured that MNCs operating *in* and *from* the OECD member states comply with the Guidelines. However, this has not happened for a number of reasons.[142] Although the NCPs try to resolve issues arising out of the Guidelines through consensual and non-adversarial means, they have no power to enforce their recommendations.[143] The OECD's procedure and usual practice of maintaining confidentiality of proceedings and the resulting reluctance to reveal the identity of an enterprise involved in a dispute make the

---

135 OECD Watch, *10 Years On: Assessing the Contribution of the OECD Guidelines for Multinational Enterprises to Responsible Business Conduct*, June 2010, pp. 21–7.
136 Statement by the Australian National Contact Point, 'GSL Australia Specific Instance'. Available at: www.ausncp.gov.au/content/reports_newsletters/downloads/reports/GSL_Statement.pdf (accessed 10 June 2011).
137 OECD Watch, above n. 135, p. 22.
138 Ibid., p. 11; OECD, above n. 120, pp. 14–16, 44–56;.
139 'UK NCP Follow-up Statement: Complaint from Survival International against Vedanta Resources plc' (March 2010). Available at: www.bis.gov.uk/assets/biscore/business-sectors/docs/10-778-survival-international-against-vedanta-resources.pdf (accessed 10 June 2011).
140 Ibid.
141 OECD Watch, above n. 135, p. 23.
142 Christian Aid *et al.*, above n. 123; A. Clapham, *Human Rights Obligations of Non-State Actors*, Oxford: Oxford University Press, 2006, pp. 208–10.
143 Decisions of the OECD Council, above n. 109, p. 28.

matter worse,[144] as there remains no scope for invoking 'social sanctions' against an MNC that infringes the Guidelines.[145] In addition, the follow-up process is taken up only in 42 adhering countries,[146] and not throughout the world. Even in countries where follow up has taken place, NGOs have sometimes assailed the working of NCPs.[147]

Improvements made by the 2011 update

The May 2011 update introduced several improvements in the OECD Guidelines, some of which directly address the drawback highlighted above. The purpose of the update was to ensure that the Guidelines continue to be 'a leading international instrument for the promotion of responsible business conduct'.[148] The terms of reference for the update had set an ambitious agenda to strengthen various components of the Guidelines.[149] Given the close liaison between the OECD and the SRSG at the consultation stage,[150] it comes as no surprise that the update of the Guidelines has a significant imprint of the SRSG's 'protect, respect and remedy' framework. Due to space constraints, I will only focus on the key improvements relating to the elaboration of human rights standards and their implementation process through the NCPs.

The Guidelines remain voluntary, but now they acknowledge that adhering states (if not MNCs) are obliged to implement them and that some matters covered in the Guidelines may be binding under national or international laws.[151] Equally important is the recommendation that if domestic laws conflict with the Guidelines, companies 'should seek ways to honour such principles and standards to the fullest extent which does not place them in violation of domestic law'.[152] This is an improvement from an earlier position in which inferior standards in host countries often prevailed over the Guidelines as a routine.

As noted above, the OECD Guidelines of 2000 only contained one short recommendation about human rights in the chapter on General Policies. Even

---

144 Christian Aid *et al.*, above n. 123, pp. 10, 22–3.
145 Kinley and Tadaki, above n. 76, p. 950.
146 In addition to 34 OECD member states, Argentina, Brazil, Egypt, Latvia, Lithuania, Morocco, Peru and Romania have also decided to adhere to the Guidelines. OECD Guidelines of 2011, above n. 104, p. 5.
147 Christian Aid *et al.*, above n. 123, pp. 13–20.
148 OECD, 'Terms of Reference for an Update of the OECD Guidelines for Multinational Enterprises' (May 2010), p. 2. Available at: www.oecd.org/dataoecd/61/41/45124171.pdf (accessed 18 June 2011).
149 Ibid., pp. 3–6.
150 OECD, 'Consultation on the Guidelines for Multinational Enterprises and the UN "Protect, Respect and Remedy" Framework'. Available at: www.oecd.org/document/36/0,3746,en_2649_34889_46078244_1_1_1_1,00.html> (accessed 18 June 2011).
151 OECD Guidelines of 2011, above n. 104, pp. 11 (Preface, para. 1) and 15 (para. I.1).
152 Ibid., p. 15 (para. I.2).

that recommendation to respect human rights was qualified with 'the host government's international obligations and commitments'. The 2011 update has revised this to 'internationally recognized human rights'.[153] Moreover, it is provided now that companies should carry out 'risk-based due diligence' to avoid causing contributing to adverse human rights impacts and engage with relevant stakeholders in relation to the planning of projects that may significantly impact local communities.[154] The due diligence provisions, which are borrowed from the SRSG's framework, are laudable, but they are likely to encounter practical difficulties in relation to supply chains – something that is acknowledged by the commentary on the Guidelines itself.[155] Concerns about a lack of implementation also remain. What if a company does not conduct due diligence, or does not share its findings with relevant stakeholders, or there are disputes between a company and the local community about the nature of business linkage with human rights abuses?

The May 2011 update has also added a specific chapter on human rights, which provides that companies should respect human rights, have a policy commitment to this effect, carry out due diligence, and provide for legitimate processes for remediation of adverse human rights impacts.[156] Since these recommendations as well as the commentary appended to them again draw upon the SRSG's framework and the Guiding Principles, they offer the same potential and face the same hazards as the Guiding Principles discussed later in this chapter. But a related point about improvements made in relation to labour rights may be noted here. The chapeau to the chapter on Employment and Industrial Relations refers to 'international labour standards' – rather than being limited to the applicable standards of host countries – as a reference point for deducing the labour responsibilities of companies.[157] Moreover, the updated OECD Guidelines do not stop at asking companies to contribute to the effective abolition to child labour; they also expect companies to 'take immediate and effective measures to secure the prohibition and elimination of the worst forms of child labour as a matter of urgency.'[158] Companies should also 'take adequate steps to ensure that forced or compulsory labour does not exist in their operations'.[159]

The 2011 update of the OECD Guidelines thus introduced considerable improvements in setting standards for companies. It would be useful here to review the proposals aimed at strengthening the potential of NCPs in implementing the Guidelines. Although the adhering countries have flexibility in organizing their NCPs, they must ensure that the NCPs are able to operate in

---

153 Ibid., p. 17 (para. II.2).
154 Ibid., p. 18 (paras II.10–12 and 13).
155 Ibid., p. 22.
156 Ibid., p. 29 (para. IV.1–6).
157 Ibid., p. 33.
158 Ibid., p. 33 (para. V.1.c).
159 Ibid., p. 33 (para. V.1.d).

an impartial manner.¹⁶⁰ This should address concerns raised by NGOs that some NCPs act more like business arms of the government. The governments may make the composition of NCPs diverse by including representatives of the business community, worker organizations and NGOs.¹⁶¹ It is worth considering if the inclusion of business and civil society representatives should be made obligatory so as to provide NCPs more legitimacy.

The NCPs should respond to enquiries from other NCPs, companies, NGOs, and the government of non-adhering countries.¹⁶² But more importantly, the NCPs should try to resolve issues relating to the implementation of the Guidelines in specific instances in an 'impartial, predictable, equitable and compatible' manner.¹⁶³ If an NCP, after an initial assessment, concludes that the issues raised in a specific instance merit further examination, it should offer 'good offices' to help the parties resolve the issues and take several steps, including facilitating conciliation or mediation.¹⁶⁴ Once this process is completed, the NCP should make the results publicly available, for example, by issuing a statement outlining the issues raised and the procedures undertaken to resolve the issues.¹⁶⁵ While the good office processes are on, confidentiality of the proceedings is to be maintained.¹⁶⁶

To handle multi-jurisdictional disputes more efficiently, the updated Guidelines provide that the concerned NCPs 'should consult with a view to agreeing on which NCP will take the lead in assisting the parties.'¹⁶⁷ The NCPs should not decline to consider a specific instance solely because parallel proceedings have been conducted, are under way or available to the parties considered.¹⁶⁸ The NCPs should strive to conclude procedures within 12 months from receipt of the specific instance.¹⁶⁹

Despite several improvements introduced by the 2011 update of the OECD Guidelines, some concerns remain. Confidentiality of proceedings and outcomes has been an issue that limits the social enforceability of the Guidelines. One can understand the need to maintain confidentiality during the proceedings, but it is difficult to comprehend why even the content of the agreement reached between the parties has to be kept secret unless the parties wish to make it public.¹⁷⁰ When it comes to confidentiality, conciliation/mediation in commercial or private disputes should be differentiated from

---

160 Ibid., p. 68 (para. A.1).
161 Ibid., p. 68 (para. A.2).
162 Ibid., p. 69 (para. B.3).
163 Ibid., p. 69 (para. C).
164 Ibid., pp. 69–70 (para. C.1–2).
165 Ibid., p. 70 (para. C.3).
166 Ibid., p. 70 (para. C.4).
167 Ibid., p. 78.
168 Ibid., p. 79.
169 Ibid., pp. 82–3.
170 Ibid., p. 70 (para. C.3.b).

conciliation/mediation in human rights issues in which the society as a whole has an interest.

A great majority of specific instances filed with the NCPs so far related to non-adhering countries.[171] So, one would expect that a robust process will be put in place to deal with such cases by the home NCPs. However, the updated Guidelines offer very weak guidance on this critical issue by stating that the NCPs will 'take steps to develop an understanding of the issues involved' and may 'pursue enquiries and engage in other fact finding activities'.[172] The OCED Guidelines could and should have overcome this problem by providing that the NCP of a country where the parent company is incorporated will entertain the specific instance and help resolve issues in such cases. Moreover, the 2011 update of the Guidelines has not endowed the NCPs with any 'teeth'; they remain almost helpless if their recommendations are not complied with or a given company manifestly breaches the Guidelines. Nor have the NCPs been obliged to make a determination, if the mediation fails, as to the merits of the complaint in relation to the alleged breach of the Guidelines. This is the minimum that the NCPs should do if they lack enforcement powers, so that social sanctions can come into play.

On the basis of the preceding analysis, it is reasonable to conclude that although the OECD Guidelines offer some potential (especially after the 2011 update) they are hardly adequate – on account of offering very limited preventive and redressive efficacy – to ensure that MNCs respect their human rights responsibilities wherever they operate.

ILO Declaration

Soon after the OECD issued its Guidelines in 1976, the ILO released the ILO Declaration in 1977.[173] This Declaration, too, was revised in 2000.[174] The ILO Declaration was an attempt to reach an *'agreed solution in a highly complex and controversial area of social policy* through dialogue and negotiations between governments, employers and workers'.[175] Keeping in mind its 'tripartite' character, the ILO Declaration invited 'governments of state members of the ILO, the employers' and workers' organisations concerned and the multinational enterprises operating in their territories to observe the principles

---

171 OECD Watch, above n. 135, p. 10.
172 OECD Guidelines of 2011, above n. 104, pp. 71, 82.
173 Tripartite Declaration of Principles Concerning Multinational Enterprises and Social Policy, ILO, 204th Sess., 16 November 1977, reprinted in 1978, *ILM*, vol. 17, 422 (hereinafter ILO Declaration of 1977).
174 ILO Tripartite Declaration of Principles Concerning Multinational Enterprises and Social Policy 2000, reprinted in 2002, *ILM*, vol. 41, 186 (hereinafter ILO Declaration). In March 2006, the ILO Declaration was revised again to include references to relevant ILO instruments that have been adopted since the 2000 revision.
175 ILO Declaration of 1977, above n. 173, p. 422 (emphasis added).

embodied therein'.[176] It was hoped that the Declaration would facilitate the positive contribution that MNCs can make to economic and social progress.[177]

Scope of the ILO Declaration

The ILO Declaration lays down principles for organizations of employers and workers, governments and MNCs which they are 'recommended to observe on a voluntary basis'.[178] Most of the guidelines in the Declaration deal with labour rights in four areas:

(i) *employment* (promotion, equality of opportunity and treatment, and security of employment)
(ii) *training*
(iii) *conditions of work and life* (wages, benefits and conditions of work, minimum age, and safety and health) and
(iv) *industrial relations* (freedom of association and the right to organize, collective bargaining, consultation, examination of grievances, and the settlement of industrial disputes).

However, paragraph 8 – which is part of General Policies – has a specific human rights mandate. It provides that all the concerned parties 'should respect the Universal Declaration of Human Rights and the corresponding International Covenants adopted by the General Assembly'.[179] The ILO envisages that 'adherence to the Declaration by all concerned would contribute to a climate more conducive to economic growth and social development'.[180]

The ILO Declaration also contains some rhetorical statements, which still enshrine important principles. Paragraph 10, for example, reads:

> Multinational enterprises should *take fully into account established general policy objectives* of the countries in which they operate. Their activities should be in *harmony with the development priorities and social aims* and structure of the country in which they operate. To this effect, *consultations should be held* between multinational enterprises, the government and, wherever appropriate, the national employers' and workers' organizations concerned.[181]

It is really doubtful if MNCs can, or should, fully appreciate and take into account the 'policy objectives' of countries in which they seek to operate. The

---

176 Ibid., p. 423.
177 Ibid., p. 422.
178 ILO Declaration, above n. 174, p. 189 (para. 7).
179 Ibid., p. 189 (para. 8).
180 Ibid., p. 187 (Introduction).
181 Ibid., p. 190 (para. 10) (emphasis added).

same could be said of MNCs conducting their activities in harmony with the development priorities and social aims of concerned states. The issue of 'consultation' with stakeholders is, however, an important one and should go a long way towards ensuring that the activities and policies of MNCs do not abridge the provisions of the ILO Declaration. However, in order to be effective, such consultation should be held before the proposed activities.

The 2000 revision of the ILO Declaration made two important positive changes. First, a newly inserted paragraph provides that MNCs, as well as national enterprises, 'should respect the minimum age for admission to employment or work in order to secure the effective abolition of child labour'.[182] Second, the Declaration lays down that MNCs 'should *contribute* to the realisation of the ILO Declaration on Fundamental Principles and Rights at Work and its Follow-up, adopted in 1998'.[183] The addition and application of this new principle to MNCs is significant because the 1998 ILO Declaration commits member states to respect, promote and realize – irrespective of whether they ratified the relevant Conventions or not – the following four rights:

(i) freedom of association and the effective recognition of the right to collective bargaining
(ii) the elimination of forced or compulsory labour
(iii) the abolition of child labour and
(iv) the elimination of discrimination in respect of employment and occupation.[184]

Limitations of the ILO Declaration

The limitations of the ILO Declaration again lie in its limited scope, directory nature, the absence of any monitoring process and the lack of any implementation mechanism. Although the ILO Declaration – like the OECD Guidelines – declares that '[t]o serve its purpose this Declaration does not require a precise definition of multinational enterprises', it goes on to detail certain indicia of MNEs.[185] This approach only creates avoidable doubts as to which enterprises this Declaration does *not* apply to, because the Declaration reflects good practice even for national enterprises. Another issue relating to the scope of the Declaration is that despite the fact that the Declaration makes a reference to the UDHR and the relevant international covenants adopted by the General Assembly, its scope is apparently limited to labour rights. It does not,

---

182 Ibid., p. 193 (para. 36).
183 Ibid., p. 189 (para. 8).
184 ILO Declaration on Fundamental Principles and Rights at Work, 86th Session, June 1998, para. 2. Available at: www.ilo.org/declaration/thedeclaration/textdeclaration/lang-en/index.htm (accessed 26 January 2011).
185 ILO Declaration, above n. 174, p. 189 (para. 6).

therefore, deal with several other important facets of human rights such as the right to life and security of person, cultural rights, or the right to a clean environment.[186]

It also seems that some provisions of the Declaration have not kept pace with the changed dynamics of the global economy and have thus become redundant in practice. Paragraph 20 of the ILO Declaration provides that in order to promote employment in developing countries, MNCs 'should give consideration to the conclusion of contracts with national enterprises for the manufacture of parts and equipment, to the use of local raw materials and to the progressive promotion of the local processing of raw materials.' Such a provision might have made sense in the 1970s, but it is almost impossible to comply with this aspiration today when supply chains are not constrained by territorial boundaries and outsourcing is the norm. Like the OECD Guidelines, the Declaration needs a comprehensive revision to remain relevant.

Furthermore, all the principles of the ILO Declaration, without any exception, are drafted in terms of 'should', and are 'recommendatory' except for convention provisions that are binding on the member states.[187] For this reason, the Declaration neither provides for a robust implementation mechanism nor makes any effort whatsoever to institutionalize external monitoring of the conduct of MNCs *vis-à-vis* the principles laid down therein. No doubt, a Committee on Multinational Enterprises has been constituted, but its role is limited to interpreting the provisions of the Declaration when disagreement arises over their meaning.[188] Even the right to approach the Committee to interpret a provision in case of disagreement over its meaning is severely restricted. As a *rule* only the governments of member states – and not even organizations of employers or workers – are allowed to approach the Committee on Multinational Enterprises with such a request.[189]

Another limitation stems from the fact that the ILO Declaration, similar to the OECD Guidelines, undermines the value of its provisions by asking MNCs to follow the labour standards prevalent in host countries.[190] To illustrate, paragraph 33 provides that 'Wages, benefits and conditions of work offered by multinational enterprises should be *not less favourable* to the workers

---

186 Although the right to a clean environment is not explicitly recognized in the International Bill of Rights, it could be deduced from certain rights mentioned therein, e.g. Article 12 the ICESCR (the right to health) and Article 6 of the ICCPR (the right to life). See M. Anderson, 'An Overview' in A. Boyle and M. Anderson (eds), *Human Rights Approaches to Environmental Protection*, New York: Oxford University Press, 1996, p. 1, at 4.
187 ILO Declaration, above n. 174, p. 198.
188 Ibid., pp. 200–1.
189 Ibid., p. 201. See also L. Compa, 'Exceptions and Conditions: The Multilateral Agreement on Investment and International Labor Rights: A Failed Connection', *Cornell International Law Journal*, 1998, vol. 31, 683, at 706–7.
190 P. Muchlinski, *Multinational Enterprises and the Law*, 2nd edn., Oxford: Oxford University Press, 2007, p. 477.

than those offered by comparable employers in the country concerned.'[191] Such a yardstick, even if complied with, can hardly ensure that the workers in developing countries are treated humanely and paid decent wages, for the problem in such countries relates to the lack of adequate labour standards and/or their lax enforcement.

To conclude, barring some core labour rights, the ILO Declaration ends up being a merely aspirational declaration without any legal enforceability, or even the possibility of market coercion in the absence of any process for publicly 'naming and shaming' delinquent companies. Apart from lacking the teeth to implement the provisions of the Declaration, it also fails to offer any sound basis, rationale or strategy to encourage MNCs to observe best labour practices wherever they operate. The ILO Declaration thus fails the twin test of efficacy and could not be relied upon to promote labour rights against MNCs' continued drive for access to cheap labour in developing countries.

Global Compact

On 31 January 1999, while speaking at the World Economic Forum in Davos, the former UN Secretary General Kofi Annan tried to revive the role and relevance of the UN in regulating corporate human rights abuses by proposing the Global Compact.[192] The Compact originally comprised nine principles in the areas of human rights, labour and the environment. In June 2004, a tenth principle relating to anti-corruption was added. It is claimed that the ten principles enjoy 'universal consensus' and are 'derived' from the UDHR, the ILO Declaration of Fundamental Principles and Rights at Work, the Rio Declaration on Environment and Development, and the UN Convention against Corruption.[193]

The Global Compact is a multi-stakeholder initiative involving diverse actors such as governments, corporations, labour and civil society organizations, and the UN.[194] It calls upon business enterprises to 'embrace, support and enact, within their sphere of influence, a set of core values' in the four covered areas.[195] The ten principles of the Global Compact are very short but are quite ambitious in their scope and try to 'fill a void between regulatory regimes, at one end of the spectrum, and voluntary codes of industry conduct,

---

191 ILO Declaration, above n. 174, p. 192 (emphasis added).
192 S. Deva, 'Global Compact: A Critique of UN's "Public-Private" Partnership for Promoting Corporate Citizenship', *Syracuse Journal of International Law and Commerce*, 2006, vol. 34, 107, at 107–14.
193 UN Global Compact, 'The Ten Principles'. Available at: www.unglobalcompact.org/AboutTheGC/TheTenPrinciples/index.html (accessed 2 June 2011).
194 G. Kell, 'The Global Compact: Origins, Operations, Progress, Challenges', *Journal of Corporate Citizenship*, 2003, vol. 11, 35, at 37–9.
195 UN Global Compact, above n. 193.

at the other'.[196] To participate in the Compact, the Chief Executive Officer of the company must send a letter to the UN Secretary General expressing support for the Global Compact and its principles.[197] The participants are also expected to set in motion changes to its business operations, publicly advocate the Compact and its principles and annually communicate the progress made in implementing the principles by publishing a public report.[198]

The Global Compact 'in its simple form is the dissemination of and adherence to good business practices'.[199] At a wider level, the vision of the Compact is to promote responsible corporate citizenship so that business can be part of the solution to the challenges of globalization.[200] It pursues two 'complementary goals': first, to make efforts to internalize the Compact principles as part of business strategy and operations and second, to facilitate 'co-operation and collective problem-solving between different stakeholders'.[201] The Compact seeks to achieve these goals through the following four engagement mechanisms:

(i) *leadership* (promoting initiatives supporting the Global Compact at all levels)
(ii) *dialogues* (engaging in policy dialogues with all concerned stakeholders)
(iii) *learning* (enabling dissemination of best business practices through sharing of 'examples' and 'case studies') and
(iv) *outreach or networking* (providing action platforms, including promotion of public-private partnership projects).[202]

The Global Compact is not a regulatory but a voluntary instrument – it 'is not designed, nor does it have the mandate or resources, to monitor or measure participants' performance'.[203] It is not even a 'benchmarking system that

---

196 Global Compact Office, 'Global Compact: Report on Progress and Activities' (July 2002, Draft), p. 4. Available at: www.iccwbo.org/home/global_compact/ProgressReport%20July%203.pdf (accessed 15 June 2011).
197 UN Global Compact, 'How to Participate: Business Organizations'. Available at: www.unglobalcompact.org/HowToParticipate/How_to_Apply_Business.html> (accessed 10 June 2011).
198 Ibid.
199 B. King, 'The UN Global Compact: Responsibility for Human Rights, Labour Relations, and the Environment in Developing Nations', *Cornell International Law Journal*, 2001, vol. 34, 481, at 482; J. Ruggie, ' "Trade, Sustainability and Global Governance": Keynote Address', *Columbia Journal of Environmental Law*, 2002, vol. 27, 297, at 301.
200 UN Global Compact, 'Overview of the UN Global Compact'. Available at: www.unglobalcompact.org/AboutTheGC/index.html> (accessed 10 June 2011).
201 Kell, above n. 194, p. 36.
202 Ibid., pp. 36–7, 39–40; Global Compact Office, above n. 196, pp. 4–6.
203 UN Global Compact, 'Integrity Measures'. Available at: www.unglobalcompact.org/AboutTheGC/IntegrityMeasures/index.html (accessed 10 June 2011).

measures good and bad'.[204] Since the Compact is a 'learning dialogue and a platform of action',[205] it relies on a range of unconventional means and strategies to promote respect for its principles. These include principle-based change, risk management, public accountability, the enlightened self-interest of companies, sharing good practices, and partnerships.[206]

Global Compact's evolution

Since the inception of the idea in 1999, the Global Compact has constantly evolved and grown, so much so that today it is acclaimed as 'the largest voluntary corporate responsibility initiative in the world.'[207] To understand better the evolution of the Compact, some important milestones in its journey are revisited here, because it has undergone 'intense experimentation'.[208] Doubts were expressed by some about this 'public–private' partnership between the UN and business,[209] but several General Assembly resolutions have quelled those doubts and conferred legitimacy on this initiative.[210]

As the Global Compact Office is concerned about the 'brand management' of its initiative,[211] in recent years it has taken a few integrity measures to ensure that participants do not misuse the name or goodwill of the Compact.[212] Apart from formulating a Logo Policy that specifies permissible

---

204 PriceWaterhouseCoopers, 'The UN Global Compact: Moving to the Business Mainstream, An Interview with Georg Kell', *Corporate Responsibility Report*, Winter 2005, vol. 2. Available at: www.unglobalcompact.org/docs/news_events/9.5/pwc_int_2005.pdf (accessed 10 June 2011).
205 Ibid.
206 Ibid.
207 UN Global Compact, above n. 200. See, for an overview of evolution, A. Rasche and G. Kell (eds.), *The United Nations Global Compact: Achievements, Trends and Challenges*, Cambridge: Cambridge University Press, 2010.
208 Kell, above n. 194, p. 36. Even the original language of its principles has been changed. For example, Principle 1 initially provided that world business should 'support and respect the protection of international human rights within their sphere of influence'. It now reads: 'Businesses should support and respect the protection of internationally proclaimed human rights'.
209 I. Bunn, 'Global Advocacy for Corporate Accountability: Transatlantic Perspectives from the NGO Community', *American University International Law Review*, 2004, vol. 19, 1265, at 1283.
210 'Towards Global Partnerships', GA Res. 56/76, UN Doc. A/RES/56/76 (24 January 2002); 'Towards Global Partnerships', GA Res. 58/129, UN Doc. A/RES/58/129 (19 February 2004); 'Towards Global Partnerships', GA Res. 60/215, UN Doc. A/RES/60/215.
211 Global Compact Office, 'Final Report: Inaugural Meeting of the Global Compact Board', 28 June 2006, pp. 8–10. Available at: www.unglobalcompact.org/docs/about_the_gc/final_rep_board030806.pdf (accessed 20 May 2011).
212 UN Global Compact, above n. 203.

and non-permissible uses of the logo,[213] the Compact Office has developed a Policy for the Communication on Progress (COP).[214] Every Compact participant is expected to communicate annually to stakeholders the efforts it has made to implement the Global Compact principles. The COP Policy, which was originally introduced in 2003, has been adjusted and refined several times since then.[215] For example, earlier a company was declared 'inactive' if it failed to submit its COP for two consecutive years.[216] This 'inactive' category has now been phased out: under the revised policy, any business participant that has been 'non-communicating' for more than one year is delisted.[217] In February 2011, the Compact Office started differentiating participating companies into Active Level and Advanced Level, 'based on their level of disclosure on progress made in integrating the Global Compact principles and contributing to broader UN goals'.[218]

More importantly, the Global Compact Office has introduced a mechanism to address credible allegations of systematic or egregious abuses of the Compact's principles. This process is basically a 'dialogue facilitation mechanism' between the concerned company and the party raising the allegation.[219] If the Compact Office concludes, exercising its own judgement, that an allegation is *prima facie* frivolous, it informs the party raising the matters and then no further action is taken. The Compact Office also does not get involved in disputes that could more appropriately be handled by other institutions.[220] However, if the matter is not found to be frivolous, it will forward the matter to the concerned participating company with a request to provide written comments directly to the party raising the matter, with a copy to the Compact

---

213 UN Global Compact, 'Policy on the Use of the Global Compact Name and Logos'. Available at: www.unglobalcompact.org/AboutTheGC/Global_Compact_Logo/GC_Logo_Policy.html (accessed 10 June 2011).
214 UN Global Compact, 'Policy for the Communication on Progress'. Available at: www.unglobalcompact.org/docs/communication_on_progress/COP_Policy.pdf (accessed 10 June 2011).
215 U. Hamid and O. Johner, 'The United Nations Global Compact Communication on Progress Policy: Origins, Trends and Challenges' in Rasche and Kell (eds.), above n. 207, p. 265, at 265–71.
216 S. Deva, 'Corporate Complicity in Internet Censorship in China: Who Cares for the Global Compact or the Global Online Freedom Act?', *George Washington International Law Review*, 2007, vol. 39, 255, at 298.
217 Hamid and Johner, above n. 215, p. 271. The Global Compact also reserves the right to publish the names of companies that have been so delisted for failing to communicate on their progress. UN Global Compact, above n. 203.
218 UN Global Compact, 'Differentiation Programme'. Available at: www.unglobalcompact.org/COP/differentiation_programme.html (accessed 10 June 2011).
219 U. Wynhoven and M. Stausberg, 'The United Nations Global Compact's Governance Framework and Integrity Measures' in Rasche and Kell (eds.), above n. 207, p. 251, at 262.
220 Ibid., p. 263.

Office.²²¹ In addition, the participating company is requested to keep the Global Compact Office informed of any actions taken by it to address the allegation. It may also take several other steps (e.g. use its own good offices to encourage resolution of the matter, ask the relevant local Compact network to assist with the resolution of the matter, or refer the matter to one or more of the UN entities that are the guardians of the Global Compact principles for advice, assistance or action). Moreover, in appropriate cases, the Compact Office may advise the parties to avail the specific instance procedure of the OECD Guidelines.²²²

In order to strengthen the quality, integrity and governance components of the Global Compact, the first Global Compact Board was constituted in 2006. The Board provides ongoing strategic and policy advice for the initiative, makes recommendations to the Global Compact Office and is expected to play a role in implementing the integrity measures.²²³ The Global Compact Board consists of 20 members from four constituency groups: business, civil society, labour and the UN.²²⁴ Since 11 out of 20 members come from the business sector, the dominance of corporations on the Board – which will provide 'ongoing strategic and policy advice' to the corporate citizenship initiative – is apparent.²²⁵

Deficiencies in the Global Compact

The Global Compact has received mixed reactions from companies, labour organizations, NGOs and member countries.²²⁶ Nonetheless, the Compact has been continuously attracting new participants – from fewer than 50 participants in July 2000, numbers increased to 2,735 by December 2005 and had increased to 9,036 by June 2011.²²⁷ Despite this success in attracting new participants, I will show that the Global Compact suffers from several deficiencies that seriously limit its efficacy both in terms of preventing and

---

221 UN Global Compact, above n. 203.
222 Ibid.
223 'The UN Global Compact Board'. Available at: www.unglobalcompact.org/About-TheGC/The_Global_Compact_Board.html (accessed 10 June 2011).
224 Ibid.
225 J. Nolan, 'The United Nations' Compact with Business: Hindering or Helping the Protection of Human Rights?' *University of Queensland Law Journal*, 2005, vol. 24, 445, at 465.
226 W. Meyer and B. Stefanova, 'Human Rights, the UN Global Compact, and the Global Governance', *Cornell International Law Journal*, 2001, vol. 34, 501, at 503–4; A. Taylor, 'The UN and the Global Compact', *New York Law School Journal of Human Rights*, 2001, vol. 17, 975, at 980–2; A. Blackett, 'Global Governance, Legal Pluralism and the Decentred State: A Labour Law Critique of Codes of Corporate Conduct', *Indiana Journal of Global Legal Studies*, 2001, vol. 8, 401, at 442; Global Compact Office, above n. 196, pp. 10, 25–30.
227 Based on a search of all participants conducted on 26 June 2011. Available at: www.unglobalcompact.org/participants/search (accessed 26 June 2011).

redressing corporate human rights abuses. First of all, it seems that the Compact is built on a theoretical contradiction in terms of its true nature. It is expressly asserted that the Compact is not a regulatory framework, but in effect it does try to regulate, using the disguise of voluntary self-regulation. After the introduction of the annual COP requirement coupled with a delisting threat and the mechanism to address credible allegations of systematic or egregious abuses of the Compact's principles, the Global Compact can hardly be considered a purely voluntary initiative. The Compact management has arguably adopted a very narrow and outdated 'command and control' model of regulation where regulation is seen in terms of legally binding rules that carry sanctions for non-compliance. At this point in time, regulation is seen in a much more broad sense and the Compact does, in fact, regulate the behaviour of companies by asking them to adopt and embrace the ten principles in the conduct of their business.

Second, the language of the Global Compact principles is so general and vague that companies can easily circumvent or comply with them without doing anything to promote human rights.[228] The ten principles of the Compact are basically 'one-liners',[229] at best an example of a 'minimalist code' of corporate conduct.[230] They hardly provide adequate and concrete guidance to corporations about the conduct expected from them.[231] A certain level of generality or flexibility in the guiding principles of any international initiative is desirable, but not if it can be taken to include or exclude anything according to individual corporate convenience. Let me illustrate this with reference to the stand taken by BHP (now BHP Billiton) regarding the obligation flowing from Principle 3 of the Compact, which lays down that 'businesses should uphold ... the effective recognition of the right to collective bargaining'. Even though the plain text of this principle should *prima facie* require BHP (or any participating corporation) to institutionalize 'collective bargaining', it continued to require its *new* employees to sign individual contracts and disputed that Principle 3 directed that employment be based on collective bargaining.[232] What is more troublesome is that even the Global Compact Office seemingly agreed with this misinterpretation.[233]

---

228 Deva, above n. 192, pp. 129–33.
229 D. Weissbrodt, 'Business and Human Rights', *University of Cincinnati Law Review*, 2005, vol. 74, 55, at 66.
230 Murphy, above n. 98, p. 425.
231 Nolan, above n. 225, p. 460.
232 Deva, above n. 192, p. 131–2. BHP, in fact, claimed that it offers a 'choice' even to its new employees: 'But new employees have a choice. If they want to join BHP Billiton, they can apply to join but we do require them to sign the individual contract.' Ibid., p. 131.
233 The Compact Office in its letter dated 1 December 2003 to BHP clarified: 'The Global Compact does not prescribe any particular form of workplace arrangements. Hence, we do not expect participants to change their industrial relations framework as a result of signing on to the Global Compact.' Ibid., p. 132.

98 Existing regulatory initiatives

The Compact Office is, however, aware of this limitation of its principles and it has taken some steps to provide more guidance to companies (e.g. by offering a detailed commentary on each principle,[234] providing specific guidance on implementing the Compact Principles,[235] and initiating a forum to discuss business dilemmas in relation to human rights).[236] The usefulness of these measures in changing corporate behaviour would require further research.

Third, the Global Compact hardly provides for any recourse if the participating companies ignore the 'moral compass' of embracing its principles.[237] Dialogue with businesses and learning forums are central tools of the Global Compact in ensuring respect for human rights, which have their limitations in promoting responsible corporate citizenship.[238] Even without abandoning this strategy, the Compact Office can take steps to enhance the credibility of this framework. Considering that it lacks both the capacity and the resources to monitor the behaviour of thousands of participating companies, the Compact Office should consider engaging with civil society, academic institutions and labour organizations to perform this quality control task. It can also be more differentiating when admitting companies and continuing their membership based on the level of performance shown in implementing the Compact principles.

The fourth deficiency of the Global Compact lies in its progress reporting mechanism. The Compact participants are required to submit an annual COP; failure to do so may result in companies being labelled as 'non-communicating' or even 'delisted'. Although it is hazardous to generalize, it seems that this exercise may have proved to be a mere ritual or a public relations exercise in the absence of any proper and independent monitoring of the conduct of corporations.[239] The requirement to submitting an annual COP is not very onerous. Nevertheless, a survey conducted in 2006 showed that 24.88 per cent of the total participants (mostly corporations) did not satisfy even this requirement,[240] thus casting serious doubts about their sincerity in

---

234 UN Global Compact, above n. 193.
235 UN Global Compact, 'Issue Specific Guidance'. Available at: www.unglobalcompact.org/COP/making_progress/issue_specific_guidance.html> (accessed 10 June 2011).
236 UN Global Compact, 'Human Rights and Business Dilemmas Forum'. Available at: http://human-rights.unglobalcompact.org/ (accessed 10 June 2011).
237 'At its core, the Compact is nothing more than a moral compass.' Kell, above n. 194, p. 47.
238 P. Alston, 'Resisting the Merger and Acquisition of Human Rights by Trade Law: A Reply to Petersmann', *European Journal of International Law*, 2002, vol. 13, 815, at 837; E. Oshionebo, 'The UN Global Compact and Accountability of Transnational Corporations: Separating Myth from Realities', *Florida Journal of International Law*, 2007, vol. 17, 1, pp. 20–2.
239 See C. Hillemanns, 'UN Norms of the Responsibilities of Transnational Corporations and Other Business Enterprises With Regard to Human Rights', *German Law Journal*, 2003, vol. 4, 1065, at 1069.
240 Deva, above n. 192, pp. 137–41.

following the Compact principles. A search conducted on the Global Compact's website on 26 June 2011 revealed that out of 6,230 business participants, 1,564 (about 25.10 per cent) were non-communicating.[241] The situation has therefore not improved between 2006 and 2011, despite the heightened focus on integrity measures during this period.

While the mechanism to deal with serious allegations of non-compliance with the Compact principles is praiseworthy, the working of the mechanism so far shows that the Compact Office takes a very conservative and cautious approach in dealing with documented abuses of the Compact's aim and principles. The June 2009 complaint by Baby Milk Action against Nestlé is a case in point.[242] The Compact Office declined to review the submitted evidence and delist Nestlé, claiming that 'abuses of the 10 Principles do occur; however we believe that such abuses only indicate that it is important for the company to remain in the Compact and learn from its mistakes'.[243]

Similarly, the complaint against the alleged complicity of PetroChina and China National Petroleum Corporation in the human rights abuses by the government of Sudan provides another instance where the Compact Office could have taken, had it wished, a more pro-active role.[244] But again, it refrained from doing much. What is more puzzling is one of the rationales behind its decision. The Compact Office reasoned: 'The matters you raised in your correspondence could equally apply to a number of companies operating in conflict prone countries. . . . PetroChina has been singled out largely because it . . . has recently taken the step of joining the Global Compact. Since we are a learning initiative, this is a step that should be welcomed instead of criticized.'[245] The Compact Office could have decided not to follow up on the complaint for a number of reasons. However, declining to act on the ground that PetroChina is not the only company indulging in such behaviour defies logic, for it would have made no sense to complain to the Office against a non-participant company. Equally irrelevant was the fact no such complaint was made against the other Compact participants.

In short, although the Global Compact Office has taken some steps to reduce the chances of the Compact being used by companies as a marketing tool or to 'bluewash' their reputation/image, progress so far is far from satisfactory. Further measures are required to ensure that the Compact principles contribute to

---

241 See above n. 227.
242 Baby Milk Action, 'Nestle, the UN Global Compact and OECD Guidelines'. Available at: http://info.babymilkaction.org/news/policyblog210510 (accessed 9 February 2011).
243 Ibid.
244 'Letter to Mr Georg Kell, Executive Director of the Global Compact', 15 December 2008. Available at: http://investorsagainstgenocide.net/2008-1215%20UNGC%20 complaint%20against%20PetroChina.pdf (accessed 9 February 2011).
245 UN Global Compact, 'UN Global Compact Office Responds to NGO Letter (Update: 9 February 2009)'. Available at: www.unglobalcompact.org/NewsAndEvents/news_archives/2009_01_12b.html (accessed 9 February 2011).

100 *Existing regulatory initiatives*

humanizing business: companies should be encouraged to respect human rights (preventive efficacy) and victims should start to look towards the Global Compact when seeking justice for irresponsible corporate conduct (redressive efficacy).

The UN Norms[246]

The UN Norms[247] were drafted by the five-member UN Working Group on the Working Methods and Activities of TNCs over a period of four years.[248] The UN Norms, coupled with the commentary appended to them,[249] provided a comprehensive statement of corporate human rights obligations and also outlined the procedure for their implementation.[250] Although the Sub-commission on the Promotion and Protection of Human Rights approved the Norms in August 2003,[251] the Commission on Human Rights declared that they lack any 'legal standing'.[252] In the light of stiff opposition from the business sector and an antagonistic position adopted by the SRSG,[253] their journey was cut short prematurely. Nevertheless, as I will show below, the Norms made significant progress in moving the business and human rights agenda forward.

Contribution of the UN Norms

The UN Norms presented a promising framework to establish the accountability of companies for human rights violations.[254] The Preamble to the Norms

---

246 This section draws on my previously published article: S. Deva, 'UN's Human Rights Norms for Transnational Corporations and Other Business Enterprises: An Imperfect Step in the Right Direction?' *ILSA Journal of International and Comparative Law*, 2004, vol. 10, 493.
247 UN Norms on the Responsibilities of Transnational Corporations and Other Business Enterprises with Regard to Human Rights, UN Doc E/CN.4/Sub.2/2003/12/Rev.2 (13 August 2003).
248 D. Weissbrodt and M. Kruger, 'Norms of the Responsibilities of Transnational Corporations and Other Business Enterprises with Regard to Human Rights', *American Journal of International Law*, 2003, vol. 97, 901, at 903–7.
249 Commentary on the Norms on the Responsibilities of Transnational Corporations and other Business Enterprises with Regard to Human Rights, E/CN.4/Sub.2/2003/38/Rev.2.
250 D. Kinley and R. Chambers, 'The UN Human Rights Norms for Corporations: The Private Implications of Public International Law', *Human Rights Law Review*, 2006, vol. 6, 447; Deva, above n. 246.
251 Sub-commission on the Promotion and Protection of Human Rights, Resolution 2003/16 (13 August 2003), E/CN.4/Sub.2/2003/L.11, pp. 52–5.
252 Commission on Human Rights, 60th Session, Agenda Item 16, E/CN.4/2004/L.73/Rev.1 (16 April 2004), para. (c).
253 Commission on Human Rights, 'Interim Report of the Special Representative of the Secretary General on the Issue of Human Rights and Transnational Corporations and Other Business Enterprises', E/CN.4/2006/97 (22 February 2006), paras 56–69.
254 T. Rule, 'Using "Norms" to Change International Law: UN Human Rights Laws Sneaking in through the Back Door?' *Chicago Journal of International Law*, 2004, vol. 5, 326; Kinley and Chambers, above n. 250, p. 493.

referred to the UN Charter, the UDHR and other international treaties as the bases to deduce the obligations of companies. Whether the UN Norms *restated* existing international human rights law[255] or *extended* it,[256] they rightly sought to deduce obligations of companies with reference to the International Bill of Rights. The Norms indicated the change required in the character of international law in view of the inadequacy of the prevailing state-centric framework in fully realizing human rights.

Instead of being limited to labour and/or environmental rights, the UN Norms presented a comprehensive list of human rights obligations. Besides a general obligation 'to respect, ensure respect for, prevent abuse of, and promote human rights recognised in international as well as national law',[257] there were specific obligations relating to:

(i) the right to equal opportunity and non-discriminatory treatment
(ii) the right to security of person
(iii) the rights of workers
(iv) respect for national sovereignty and human rights and
(v) consumer and environmental protection.

The general obligation to respect 'international human rights' was a potent provision in view of paragraph 23, which provided that a reference to 'international human rights' in the UN Norms includes all civil, cultural, economic, political and social rights. Paragraph 12 provided further specificity to these obligations.

In terms of the depth of human rights obligations as well, the Norms clearly made progress over other regulatory initiatives. As companies could violate human rights in several ways, it is insufficient to frame obligations in predominantly conventional 'negative' terms (i.e. that companies should respect or should not violate human rights). The UN Norms imposed 'positive' obligations on companies[258] who were obligated to not only refrain from directly or indirectly contributing to, and benefiting from, human rights violations, but also 'use their influence in order to promote and ensure respect for human rights'.[259]

Quite crucially, the UN Norms substituted the conventional approach of 'should' with 'shall' in terms of the standard for compliance with the

---

255 Hillemanns, above n. 239, p. 1070; J. Nolan, 'With Power Comes Responsibility: Human Rights and Corporate Accountability', *University of New South Wales Law Journal*, 2005, vol. 28, 581, at 586.
256 Commission on Human Rights, above n. 253, paras 60–5.
257 UN Norms, above n. 247, para. 1.
258 This was clear from the use of terms obligation to 'promote' and 'protect' human rights in paragraph 1. See also paragraph 12 where an obligation was constructed in terms of not only respecting but also contributing to the realization of human rights.
259 Commentary on the Norms, above n. 249, Commentary (b) to para. 1.

obligations.[260] This change of terminology coupled with provisions for implementation of the norms embodied tacit acceptance of the fact that the voluntary compliance approach alone was not proving to be adequate.[261] As a corollary to the Norms opting for a non-voluntary approach to compliance, they proposed specific provisions for the implementation of human rights norms.[262] In addition to asking corporations to adopt, disseminate and internally implement the obligations laid down therein,[263] the UN Norms urged states to 'establish and reinforce the necessary legal and administrative framework for ensuring that the Norms' are implemented by companies.[264] The Norms also proposed independent and transparent periodic monitoring as well as verification by national and international (including UN) mechanisms.[265] This again was a departure from the existing *indirect* mode of implementation in which the responsibility of enforcing corporate human rights responsibilities lay almost exclusively with states. Note must be taken of another significant provision of the UN Norms which provided for prompt, adequate and effective reparation to persons and communities adversely affected by the failure of companies to comply with their responsibilities thereunder.[266]

In addition to MNCs, the Norms also brought 'other business enterprises' – such as partnerships, contractors, suppliers, licensees or distributors[267] – within their ambit and thus deviated from the approach adopted by the OECD Guidelines and the ILO Declaration. The Norms placed a direct obligation on MNCs to show that their business partners respected human rights and implemented the Norms.[268] This was a much-needed approach because in many situations the actual violator might not be an MNC, but rather a business partner or subsidiary over which it exercised considerable control or influence.

---

260 It is worth noting that paragraph 14 of the final draft of the UN Code of Conduct on Transnational Corporations had chosen 'shall' in place of 'should'. It read: 'Transnational corporations shall respect human rights and fundamental freedoms in the countries in which they operate.' Draft of the UN Code of Conduct on Transnational Corporations, UN ESCOR, Doc. E/1990/94 (1990).
261 M. Monshipouri, C. Welch, Jr and E. Kennedy, 'Multinational Corporations and the Ethics of Global Responsibility: Problems and Possibilities', *Human Rights Quarterly*, 2003, vol. 25, 965, at 979–82.
262 UN Norms, above n. 247, paras 15–19. See Weissbrodt and Kruger, above n. 248, pp. 915–21.
263 UN Norms, above n. 247, para. 15.
264 Ibid., para. 17.
265 Ibid., para. 16. One of the suggestions was that the existing human rights treaty bodies could take the responsibility of monitoring the compliance with the UN Norms. Commentary on the Norms, above n. 249, Commentary (b) to para. 16. Trade unions were also encouraged to use the UN Norms as a basis of negotiating agreements with MNCs. Ibid., Commentary (c) to para. 16.
266 UN Norms, above n. 247, para. 18.
267 Ibid., para. 21.
268 Ibid., paras 1 and 15.

Shortcomings of the UN Norms

The UN Norms broke new grounds in terms of formulating and implementing corporate human rights obligations. Nevertheless, they had some serious operational shortcomings. The Norms made frequent reference to numerous international treaties negotiated/signed by and directed at states.[269] This approach was problematic for several reasons.[270] For instance, some of these instruments have not even been ratified by a majority of the states. Nor would it be reasonable to expect corporate executives to go through all the listed human rights instruments to ascertain their specific human rights responsibilities. Moreover, the UN Norms seemingly provided an 'overly inclusive' list of human rights for corporations,[271] probably driven by a desire to maximize the scope of corporate human rights responsibilities. Paragraph 12 of the Norms illustrates this. It stated that companies shall, among others, *contribute* to the realization of economic, social and cultural rights as well as civil and political rights, 'in particular the rights to development, adequate food and drinking water, the highest attainable standard of physical and mental health, adequate housing, privacy, education, freedom of thought, conscience, and religion and freedom of opinion and expression'. Such an extensive formulation of corporate human rights responsibilities, both in terms of breadth and depth, was quite ambitious and resulted in a strong backlash from the business community. The SRSG also rightly questioned the appropriateness of the 'spheres of influence' tool adopted by the Norms in allocating responsibilities between states and companies.[272]

A related issue was that the Norms did not adequately address the issue of translating the universality of human rights into precise standards for an MNC operating in different countries. The issue of *localization of universality* – or the question of which local differences MNCs should take into account or disregard while operating in countries that differ from each other in material particulars – is an important one.[273] However, the UN Norms apparently failed to address this aspect. Of course the Norms were not expected to detail industry-wide or state-wide human rights obligations, but they should have

---

269 'On a very rough count, . . . the text of the Norms refers to at least 56 instruments'. U. Baxi, 'Market Fundamentalisms: Business Ethics at the Altar of Human Rights', *Human Rights Law Review*, 2005, vol. 5, 1, at 5.
270 Deva, above n. 246, pp. 510–11; Baxi, above n. 269, pp. 3–6.
271 Nolan, above n. 255, p. 593, and generally pp. 593–9.
272 Commission on Human Rights, above n. 253, paras 66–8; Human Rights Council, 'Protect, Respect and Remedy: A Framework for Business and Human Rights – Report of the Special Representative of the Secretary-General on the Issue of Human Rights and Transnational Corporations and other Business Enterprises', A/HRC/8/5 (7 April 2008), paras 66–71.
273 The precise content, say, of the right to safe and healthy working environment, adequate remuneration, the right to health or the freedom of speech and expression will vary from one place to another.

at least provided guidelines with reference to which obligations at the municipal level could be formulated.

There was also uncertainty about the precise nature of the Norms, which were presented as neither voluntary nor mandatory, but 'non-voluntary'. Although the addition of this new category might be explained as a logical progressive step from 'soft' to 'hard' obligations,[274] this complicated the whole issue of compliance strategy. Not only was the distinction between 'mandatory' and 'non-voluntary' nonsensical, it also undermined the usefulness of the implementation provisions contained in the UN Norms. Moreover, barring a provision dealing with reparation,[275] the Norms failed to canvass other possible sanctions that might be employed against companies who fail to observe the obligations stipulated therein. The idea of establishing an enforcement mechanism, especially at international level, was also not clearly developed.[276] Nor did the UN Norms offer any insights on how to overcome the challenges posed by the corporate misuse of the doctrine of *forum non conveniens* and the principle of separate legal personality to delay or avoid their liability for human rights abuses.

In summary, the UN Norms moved forward the agenda of clarifying and elaborating corporate human rights responsibilities, underlined the need for moving beyond state-centric regulation and emphasized the importance of an implementation mechanism. Nevertheless, they fell short of what is required for establishing a robust international regulatory regime of corporate human rights responsibilities. In view of the shortcomings explained above, the Norms too are unlikely to satisfy the twin test of efficacy, though they come closest to doing so as compared to several other regulatory initiatives examined in this chapter. The UN Norms also proved to be a non-starter in view of the vocal opposition that they faced from MNCs, business organizations, some states and the SRSG. As analyzed below, although the SRSG has sought to make a departure from the UN Norms, the 'protect, respect and remedy' framework as well as the Guiding Principles are informed by the Norms in some vital respects.

Guiding Principles

On 16 June 2011, the Human Rights Council endorsed the Guiding Principles,[277] drafted by the SRSG after extensive consultation with various stakeholders. Since the Guiding Principles are rooted in the 'protect, respect and

---

274 Weissbrodt and Kruger, above n. 248, pp. 914–15.
275 UN Norms, above n. 247, para. 18.
276 Deva, above n. 246, p. 520; Rule, above n. 254, pp. 330–1, 333.
277 Human Rights Council, 'New Guiding Principles on Business and Human Rights endorsed by the UN Human Rights Council' (16 June 2011), www.ohchr.org/en/News-Events/Pages/DisplayNews.aspx?NewsID=11164&LangID=E (accessed 17 June 2011).

remedy' framework proposed by the SRSG, I will explain and critique both the Guiding Principles and the framework. But before I do so, I offer a brief preview of the SRSG's mandate. In its 2005 session, the Commission on Human Rights requested the UN Secretary General to appoint a Special Representative on the issue of human rights and transnational corporations.[278] In July 2005, Kofi Annan appointed Professor John Ruggie as the SRSG for an initial period of two years. This term was later extended for one more year and in June 2008, the Human Rights Council further extended the mandate for another three years.[279]

The original mandate of the SRSG was quite wide: among others, the SRSG was requested to 'identify and clarify standards of corporate responsibility and accountability' for MNCs with regard to human rights and also elaborate on the role of states in effectively regulating them.[280] The focus of the extended mandate was on operationalization of the 'protect, respect and remedy' framework canvassed by the SRSG in the 2008 Report. Acknowledging that MNCs' activities might affect vulnerable groups such as women and children more, the new mandate invited the SRSG to pay 'special attention' to persons of such groups. Another notable aspect of the extended mandate was that it requested the SRSG to 'explore options and make recommendations, at the national, regional and international level, for enhancing access to effective remedies available to those whose human rights are impacted by corporate activities'.[281]

From UN Norms to the 'protect, respect and remedy' framework and the Guiding Principles

The SRSG considered his mandate to be 'highly politicised' in that it was 'devised as a means to move beyond the stalemated debate' over the UN Norms.[282] To his credit, the SRSG was able to break the stalemate and forge a broad consensus around his proposals rooted in 'principled pragmatism'. However, this focus on consensus-building has arguably resulted in dilution of the framework's robustness in promoting corporate human rights responsibilities.

---

278 Commission on Human Rights, 'Promotion and Protection of Human Rights', E/CN.4/2005/L.87 (15 April 2005).
279 Human Rights Council, 'Mandate of the Special Representative of the Secretary General on the issue of Human Rights and Transnational Corporations and Other Business Enterprises', Resolution 8/7 (18 June 2008), para. 4.
280 Commission on Human Rights, above n. 278.
281 Human Rights Council, above n. 279.
282 SRSG for Business and Human Rights, 'Opening Statement to United Nations Human Rights Council' (25 September 2006). Available at: http://198.170.85.29/Ruggie-statement-to-UN-Human-Rights-Council-25-Sep-2006.pdf> (accessed 11 June 2011).

106 *Existing regulatory initiatives*

The 'protect, respect and remedy' framework is based on the notion of 'differentiated but complementary responsibilities'. The framework has three limbs: 'the State duty to protect against human rights abuses by third parties, including business; the corporate responsibility to respect human rights; and the need for more effective access to remedies'.[283] As the SRSG had found the nature of duties proposed by the UN Norms to be too wide, he selected only the 'protect' (with reference to states) and 'respect' (with reference to companies) elements from the well-established duty typology (i.e. the duty to respect, protect and fulfil human rights). Similarly, the choice of the term 'responsibility', rather than the 'duty', to respect human rights was deliberate, so as to denote that a breach of these duties might not entail legal consequences for companies.[284] These two aspects might have helped in earning corporate support for the framework, while the access to effective remedies limb might have swayed the civil society, without the realization that these remedies were tied to narrow corporate responsibilities.

Instead of cataloguing the responsibilities of companies (something that the Norms tried to do), the framework as well as the Guiding Principles adopted an approach in which companies have a responsibility to respect all 'internationally recognized human rights'. 'Due diligence' – implying taking steps 'to become aware of, prevent and address adverse human rights impacts' – is the central tool proposed to enable companies to meet their responsibility to respect human rights.[285] Companies should adopt a human rights policy, conduct impact assessments, integrate human rights policies throughout a company's operations and track their performance.[286] Access to remedies, part of both states' duty to protect and corporate responsibility to respect, is a crucial component of the framework. People aggrieved by corporate activities should be able to seek redress through a range of judicial, non-judicial and company-level grievance mechanisms.[287]

The Guiding Principles and the commentary appended to them seek to implement the 'protect, respect and remedy' framework. Principle 1 stipulates that states *must* 'protect against human rights abuse within their territory and/or jurisdiction by third parties, including business enterprises'. They *should* set out, including by adopting appropriate extraterritorial measures, 'the expectation that all business enterprises domiciled in their territory and/or jurisdiction respect human rights throughout their operations'.[288] In

---

283 Human Rights Council, above n. 272, para. 9.
284 'Failure to meet this responsibility can subject companies to the courts of public opinion – comprising employees, communities, consumers, civil society, as well as investors – and occasionally to charges in actual courts.' Human Rights Council, above n. 272, para. 54.
285 Ibid., para. 56.
286 Ibid., paras 60–4.
287 Ibid., paras 83–101.
288 Guiding Principles, above n. 100, Principle 2.

addition, states should enact and enforce laws that require, promote or guide companies to respect their human rights responsibilities.[289] Principle 7 further provides that states should take several steps – from offering assistance to denying access to public support – to help ensure that companies operating in conflict-affected areas are not involved in human rights abuses. Quite importantly, the Guiding Principles remind states to 'maintain adequate domestic policy space to meet their human rights obligations when pursuing business-related policy objectives with other states or business enterprises' and encourage multilateral institutions dealing with business-related issues to promote business respect for human rights within their respective mandates.[290]

Concurrent with states' duty to protect human rights, companies have a responsibility to respect human rights, meaning thereby that 'they should avoid infringing on the human rights of others and should address adverse human rights impacts with which they are involved.'[291] Principle 13 specifies a two-fold requirement to satisfy this responsibility: first, to avoid causing or contributing to adverse *human rights impacts through their own activities*, and to address such impacts when they occur; and second, to seek to prevent or mitigate adverse human rights impacts that are *directly linked to their operations, products or services* by their business relationships, even if they have not contributed to those impacts. The responsibility relates, at a minimum, to rights enumerated in the International Bill of Rights and the principles concerning fundamental rights set out in the ILO's Declaration on Fundamental Rights and Rights at Work.[292] Principle 15 provides that companies should adopt a policy commitment to meet their responsibility to respect human rights, conduct due diligence to identify, prevent, mitigate and account for how they address their impacts on human rights, and have processes in place to enable remediation of any adverse impact they cause or contribute to.[293] When faced with conflicting requirements, companies should seek ways to honour the principles of internationally recognized human rights.[294]

As part of their duty to protect against business-related human rights abuse, states must take appropriate judicial, administrative or legislative steps to ensure that affected people within their territory or jurisdiction have access to effective remedies.[295] The Guiding Principles contemplate that in addition to state-based judicial mechanisms, various types of state-based non-judicial mechanisms, non-state-based mechanisms and company-level grievance mechanisms should be used to provide the access to remedy.[296] In order

---

289 Ibid., Principle 3.
290 Ibid., Principles 9 and 10.
291 Ibid., Principle 11.
292 Ibid., Principle 12.
293 Guiding Principles 16 to 24 further elaborate these policies and processes. Ibid.
294 Ibid., Principle 24.
295 Ibid., Principles 25.
296 Ibid., Principles 26–30.

to satisfy the effectiveness criteria, non-judicial mechanisms should be legitimate, accessible, predictable, equitable, transparent, right-compatible and a source of continuous learning.[297]

Although Ruggie's critique of the Norms may give the impression that his framework and the Guiding Principles made a complete departure from the Norms and began with a clean slate, this does not seem to be the case. There are of course many important differences between the UN Norms and the approach adopted by the SRSG. But I will show how the SRSG also built on and refined some key ideas put forward by the Norms. Although framed differently, paragraph 1 of the Norms contemplated both states' duty to protect human rights and a corporate duty to respect human rights. The SRSG rightly clarified that the duties of states and companies should not be identical, but the first two limbs of his framework are not unique in any way. Unlike the suggestion and misconception that the Norms prescribed 'a limited list of rights',[298] paragraph 1 of the Norms stated at the outset that corporate duties relate to all 'human rights recognized in international as well as national law, including the rights and interests of indigenous peoples and other vulnerable groups'. The SRSG was perhaps misled by the specific elaboration of some corporate human rights duties in subsequent paragraphs of the Norms. If anything, the breadth of human rights obligations under the UN Norms was wider than the Guiding Principles, for the latter construe the term 'internationally recognized human rights' more narrowly as compared to the Norms.

The SRSG rejected the Norms' usage of 'sphere of influence' for being an imprecise concept and mooted 'due diligence' as an alternative.[299] However, due diligence is merely an approach already well-known to companies; it does not settle the question of the scope or territory of responsibilities. A business entity is expected to conduct due diligence not in wilderness, but only in relation to its operations or entities connected to it. The commentary on the Guiding Principles, in effect, implies that due diligence will be relevant in the context of the sphere of influence of a company.

In terms of the implementation of human rights responsibilities, the Norms had provided that companies shall 'adopt, disseminate and implement internal rules of operation in compliance with the Norms', periodically report on the implementation of the Norms, apply and incorporate these Norms in their contracts with business partners, conduct a periodic human rights impact assessment of their activities, and take remedial measures such as reparation, restitution and rehabilitation.[300] The imprint, albeit limited, of these proposals on what the Guiding Principles have proposed (e.g. assessing

---

297 Ibid., Principle 31.
298 Human Rights Council, above n. 272, para. 51.
299 Guiding Principles, above n. 100, Principles 15–21.
300 UN Norms, above n. 247, paras 15, 16 and 18.

adverse impacts, communicating how these impact are addressed, remediation through legitimate processes, and company-level grievance mechanisms) is clear. A similar connection can be seen between the UN Norms' push for invoking international enforcement mechanisms and the non-state-based grievance mechanisms mooted by the Guiding Principles.

One step forward, two steps back in the name of consensus?

The SRSG's framework and the Guiding Principles made progress in pushing the business and human rights agenda forward on several counts. The SRSG deserves credit for pointing out that extraterritorial regulation of MNCs' activities could be a legitimate option for states to set out the expectations that companies should respect human rights 'throughout their operations'[301] and that states should invoke laws (including corporate law) and policies to foster business respect for human rights.[302] Equally crucial is the reminder that states do not relinquish their human rights obligations when they contract out public services to private companies or when they negotiate trade and investment-related agreements or contracts.[303] The SRSG also deserves praise for outlining various practical due diligence steps that should help companies comply with their human rights responsibilities.[304] Moreover, the Guiding Principles rightly give due importance to the access to effective remedy (though not framed as a right) and map various types of redress mechanisms.[305]

However, at the same time, the Guiding Principles and framework embody some regressive steps that may not promote the goal of humanizing business. Let me begin by highlighting that the framework and the Guiding Principles offer no, or at best a weak, normative basis for why companies should have human rights responsibilities. In Chapter 1, I pointed out the importance of having a sound normative grounding of corporate human rights responsibilities. It seems that the SRSG posits that companies should have a responsibility to respect human rights because 'it is the basic expectation society has of business'.[306] This is, however, hardly a normative basis. We need to ask and answer why does society have this expectation from companies? Even if we are

---

301 Human Rights Council, above n. 272, para 19; Guiding Principles, above n. 100, Principle 2. See also Human Rights Council, 'Report of the SRSG – Corporate Responsibility under International Law and Issues in Extraterritorial Regulation: Summary and Legal Workshops', A/HRC/4/35/Add.2 (15 February 2007).
302 Human Rights Council, above n. 272, paras 29–32; Guiding Principles, above n. 100, Principle 3.
303 Guiding Principles, above n. 100, Principles 5 and 9.
304 Ibid., Principles 16–24.
305 Ibid., Principles 25–30.
306 Human Rights Council, above n. 272, para. 9; Guiding Principles, above n. 100, p. 4 (para. 6).

able to determine what constitutes and who represents the 'society', how do we measure what society wants? Could we ever gather a consensual view from society on this issue?

In human rights discourse, the duty typology is by and large settled.[307] States have a duty to respect, protect and fulfil human rights. While the human rights obligations of companies need not be identical to that of states, their obligations should also not be illusory or incommensurate to their current position, role and power in society. Under the UN Norms, corporate obligation mirrored the duties of states (though only within their spheres of influence, i.e. they had the obligation 'to promote, secure the fulfilment of, respect, ensure respect of and protect' human rights). This formulation of corporate duties represented one end of the spectrum. However, with the Guiding Principles, the pendulum has swung to the other extreme. Out of the three-fold duty typology, the SRSG has selected only one type of duty each for states and companies: whereas states have a duty to protect, companies have a responsibility to respect. This compartmentalized approach has several adverse implications for human rights. For one, it ignores the crucial link between states' duty to 'protect' human rights and corporate responsibility to 'respect' human rights. How can states enforce human rights obligations against corporations when the latter merely have a responsibility (not duty) to respect human rights in the first place? Moreover, this approach has shifted the focus of debate from the human rights obligations *of companies* to the obligations *of states*. The real issue is: should companies have independent 'obligations' along with states? The SRSG has responded by moving corporate obligations to the background and framing them in terms of 'responsibility'. Apart from putting an artificial limit on states' human rights obligations (and thus excluding the duties to protect and fulfil human rights), this approach has also unduly narrowed down the scope of corporate obligations. There are good reasons to contend that companies should have the 'protect' and 'fulfil' types of duties in certain situations.[308]

This pragmatic choosing of duties by the SRSG has also created a *conceptual anarchy*, because the Guiding Principles have ended up conflating the concepts of 'protect' and 'respect' with duties belonging to other categories. If a company is controlled by the state, the government would be complying with

---

307 H. Shue, *Basic Rights: Subsistence, Affluence, and US Foreign Policy*, 2nd edn, Princeton: Princeton University Press, 1996, pp. 52–3; ICHRP, above n. 128, pp. 46–54.
308 S. Deva, ' "Protect, Respect and Remedy": A Critique of the SRSG's Framework for Business and Human Rights' in K. Buhmann, L. Roseberry and M. Morsing (eds.), *Corporate Social and Human Rights Responsibilities: Global Legal and Management Perspectives*, Hampshire: Palgrave Macmillan, 2011, p. 108, at 122–4; D. Bilchitz, 'The Ruggie Framework: An Adequate Rubric for Corporate Human Rights Obligations?', *Sur – International Journal of Human Rights*, 2010, vol. 7:12, 199, at 204–15; F. Wettstein, *Multinational Corporations and Global Justice: Human Rights Obligations of a Quasi-governmental Institution*, Stanford: Stanford Business Books, 2009, pp. 305–16.

its 'respect' obligation (and not the 'protect' obligation) in ensuring that the said company does not violate human rights. Similarly, what the Guiding Principles expect from states in relation to ensuring effective judicial and non-judicial mechanisms of redress perhaps belong to the 'fulfil' type of duties. Some due diligence recommendations prescribed by the Guiding Principles for companies in relation to their business partners truly belong to the 'protect' category of duties rather than the 'respect' category. It is also arguable that Principle 22 concerning remediation fits better with the fulfil type of duties. In short, the SRSG's framework and the Guiding Principles have ignored the dynamics between three sets of duties.

The first limb of the framework – states' duty to protect against human rights abuse – is non-controversial. This approach can be useful in protecting human rights, but not in all cases,[309] something that has been acknowledged even by the SRSG. Past experience has shown that states are unable or unwilling to act against powerful companies. In such situations, the first limb would not offer much hope in either preventing or redressing corporate human rights abuses. Let us consider one concrete example. Principle 7 provides that states should engage, provide assistance or deny access to public support and services to companies operating in conflict-affected zones (depending on their cooperation or lack of it).[310] However, these recommendations are based on an erroneous assumption – that the concerned 'host' and/or 'home' states have both capacity and the willingness to act – which often does not exist in situations of state-business complicity in conflict zones. The Guiding Principles should have learned a lesson from history and complemented states' duty to protect with a supra-state institutional framework, at least in selected cases of egregious human rights violations. The Rome Statute of the International Criminal Court illustrates why the obligation to protect human rights cannot always be tied to states exclusively, because some states might lack the capacity and/or political will to hold people accountable for even most the serious wrongs (e.g. genocide and crimes against humanity).

In relation to the second limb, the use of word 'responsibility' rather than 'duty' to denote corporate human rights responsibilities is questionable. It is not only erroneous but also misleading to suggest that all human rights responsibilities of companies are without any legal consequences. It is equally unsound to say that the responsibility 'to respect human rights is distinct from issues of legal liability and enforcement, which remain defined largely by

---

309 See S. Pillay, 'Absence of Justice: Lessons from the Bhopal Union Carbide Disaster for Latin America', *Michigan State Journal of International Law*, vol. 14, 2006, 479, at 512–14.
310 See also Human Rights Council, 'Business and Human Rights in Conflict-Affected Regions: Challenges and Options towards State Response', A/HRC/17/32 (27 May 2011).

national law provisions in relevant jurisdictions'.[311] There is a much more dynamic interrelationship between international law and municipal laws, as opposed to the compartmentalized division suggested by the SRSG. While national courts rely on international law to interpret laws, municipal laws contribute to the evolution of international norms.

Moreover, instead of cataloguing the human rights responsibilities of companies, the Guiding Principles adopt an easier option of ascertaining responsibilities with reference to the International Bill of Rights. This approach is likely to bring its own set of problems, because these instruments were not drafted with companies in mind.[312] Consider, for instance, Article 9 of the ICESCR, which provides that the 'States Parties to the present Covenant recognize the right of everyone to social security, including social insurance'. What would be the responsibility of a company respecting the right to social security? Should it start offering social security to all its employees? Let us consider one more example. Article 12 of the ICESCR states that the 'States Parties to the present Covenant recognize the right of everyone to the enjoyment of the highest attainable standard of physical and mental health'. How can this right be translated into responsibilities of the business? Would a company breach this right by not providing medical insurance to its employees or by not paying them an adequate salary to obtain decent medical treatment? Such examples can be multiplied, but the point remains: it will not be easy or straightforward for companies (or their officers untrained in this exercise) to deduce their human rights responsibilities with reference to the state-centric International Bill of Rights. An attempt has to be made distil these corporate responsibilities, as the OECD Guidelines, the ILO Declaration and the UN Norms have done – albeit imperfectly.

One related issue is about the extent of corporate human rights responsibilities. Let me offer two examples. It is trite that companies can pollute the environment, but the Guiding Principles conceive no independent responsibility for companies in terms of environmental rights or towards the goal of sustainable development under Agenda 21.[313] Another significant omission concerns the rights of vulnerable groups such as women, children and the tribal or indigenous community,[314] despite the fact that in the revised mandate of 2008, the Human Rights Council had specifically requested the SRSG to

---

311 Guiding Principles, above n. 100, Commentary on Principle 12.
312 M. Goodhart, 'Human Rights and Non-State Actors: Theoretical Puzzles' in G. Andreopoulos, Z. F. K. Arat and P. Juviler (eds.), *Non-State Actors in the Human Rights Universe*, Bloomfield: Kumarian Press, 2006, p. 23, at 34–5.
313 'Agenda 21, Chapter 30: Strengthening the Role of Business and Industry'. Available at: www.un-documents.net/a21-30.htm (accessed 2 June 2011).
314 O'Konek, for instance, highlights adverse impact on the human rights of women working in the garment industry. T. O'Konek, 'Corporations and Human Rights Law: The Emerging Consensus and Its Effects on Women's Employment Rights', *Cardozo Journal of Law and Gender*, 2011, vol. 17, 261.

'integrate a gender perspective throughout his work and to give special attention to persons belonging to vulnerable groups, in particular children.'[315] The baseline or minimum responsibility under the term 'internationally recognized human rights' does not encompass international instruments that outline special protective measures for children (e.g. Convention on the Rights of the Child), women (e.g. Convention on the Elimination of All Forms of Discrimination against Women) or indigenous people (e.g. Convention concerning Indigenous and Tribal Peoples in Independent Countries). It is highly inadequate for the Commentary on Principle 12 to pay lip service to this issue and say that companies may need to consider additional standards. Nor is gender-based and sexual violence an issue that demands special attention only in conflict-affected areas, as Principle 7 reminds states.

Another problem with the Guiding Principles is their conscious choice of a terminology that has the potential to undermine human rights in the long run. It is trite that companies can and do violate human rights. However the term 'violation' is used only twice in the 27-page document containing the Guiding Principles; on both occasions with reference to states and not companies. 'Impact' is the term preferred by the SRSG. However, 'impact' is a neutral term, which is not even included in *Black's Law Dictionary* as a legal term. It is really doubtful if 'impact' can carry the weight of gross human rights violations committed by companies. The introduction of the 'risk assessment' tool to the human rights discourse provides another example. Principle 18 provides: 'In order to gauge human rights risks, business enterprises should identify and assess any actual or potential adverse human rights impacts with which they may be involved either through their own activities or as a result of their business relationships'. There are two problems with this innocuous-looking formulation. First, seeing human rights as risk implies that human rights are to be considered relevant and respected, only if they pose a risk to the business. Second, risk assessment necessarily involves a cost–benefit analysis. So, if the *potential* cost of violating human rights is less than the *actual* benefits gained, a company might treat certain violations as part of the business operational cost. If this was the price paid for garnering the support of the business community for the framework and the Guiding Principles, this was definitely a heavy price.

Companies all over the world have routinely employed the principle of separate legal personality and the doctrine of *forum non conveniens* to insulate themselves from legal liability for human rights violations. The Guiding Principles acknowledge these to be 'legal barriers',[316] but do not propose anything to overcome these barriers. This is manifestly inadequate, for the Guiding Principles should have at least outlined some possible options or approaches that states could have invoked to overcome these barriers.

---

315 Human Rights Council, above n. 279, para. 4(d).
316 Guiding Principles, above n. 100, Commentary on Principle 26.

On the face of it, the Guiding Principles give the impression of taking the corporate observation of human rights responsibilities seriously, because both states and companies are expected to take a number of measures, including establishing varied types of grievance mechanisms. However, in practice, the monitoring mechanism is non-existent or deficient to deal with specific instances of abuse, especially if concerned states are unwilling or unable to act against certain companies. For instance, what would happen if a state does not reduce legal barriers resulting in denial of access to remedy (Principle 26)? Similarly, no adverse legal consequences or sanctions may follow if a company does not adopt a human rights policy commitment (Principle 16), conduct the recommended due diligence steps (Principles 17 to 21), provide for remediation for indulging in human rights abuses (Principle 22), or establish an effective grievance mechanism at the institutional level (Principle 29). If victims of corporate human rights abuses cannot approach a designated body to redress breach of the Guiding Principles, then the Guiding Principles do not even match the low threshold of the OECD Guidelines to raise a matter before the NCPs. As a follow-up to the SRSG's mandate, on 16 June 2011 the Human Rights Council decided to constitute a five-member Working Group for three years and establish an annual forum on business and human rights to discuss the trends and challenges in the implementation of the Guiding Principles.[317] It is doubtful if these proposals will really help to bridge the implementation deficits highlighted here.

Last but not least, although the Guiding Principles emphasize the importance of access to remedies and outline a range of redress mechanisms, they conceive 'access to remedy' more as a *duty* relating to states' duty to protect and corporate responsibility to respect human rights. While there is nothing wrong with this formulation, the Guiding Principles seem to sideline access to an effective remedy as a human *right*, recognized in all major international and regional human rights instruments. One negative effect of this sidelining is that no Guiding Principle explicitly recognizes the victims' right to seek adequate reparation in the form of compensation, restitution and rehabilitation – the status of this vital right is rather demoted to the Commentary on Principle 25.

In short, it is argued that the SRSG's framework and the Guiding Principles offer both promises and perils. Consensus itself is neither always good nor a sign of progress. The consensus built around the Guiding Principles masks several hidden hazards in adopting the regulatory ideas floated there. Even if the Guiding Principles are implemented by states and embraced by the business community, they might not make a significant difference in preventing

---

317 Human Rights Council, 'Council Establishes Working Group on Human Rights and Transnational Corporations and Other Business Enterprises' (16 June 2011), www.ohchr.org/en/NewsEvents/Pages/DisplayNews.aspx?NewsID=11165&LangID=E (accessed 17 June 2011).

and remedying corporate human rights abuses, especially in situations where there are governance gaps or companies are reluctant to be guided by the Guiding Principles.

The three-fold inadequacy of the existing regulatory initiatives

I have highlighted the specific limitations of seven representative regulatory initiatives in making companies accountable for human rights violations. Based upon that analysis, some general conclusions about the inadequacy of the existing regulatory framework can be drawn. It is argued that the general deficiencies of the current regulatory framework relate to, and could be classified under, three broad categories: insufficient or contestable rationales for compliance with human rights norms; lack of precise, measurable human rights standards; and deficient or undeveloped implementation and enforcement mechanisms.

Considering that corporations are generally geared to maximize shareholders' profits and they supposedly conduct their business in a rational manner, it is critical that concrete rationales are advanced to back the imposition of legally binding human rights obligations on companies. Such rationales, in order to be logically sustainable, should also take a position *vis-à-vis* the profit maximization motive of corporations. The existing regulatory regimes, however, do not address this important aspect at all, offer general and vague reasons, or worse provide highly contestable and unsound rationales.

The ATCA, as well as the case law generated under it, is silent on why companies should be bound by human rights norms. Corporate codes of conduct, as noted before, provide diverse justifications for companies taking into account human rights norms while doing business. These pious statements directly or indirectly link compliance with human rights to business profit, a rationale that should be avoided for the reasons discussed in the next chapter. Both the ILO Declaration and the OECD Guidelines offer, in almost identical terms, aspirational rationales for complying with human rights or other obligations: it is urged that by observing these standards corporations can make a positive contribution to economic, social and environmental progress and also resolve the difficulties to which their various operations may give rise.[318] Whereas the Global Compact is underpinned by both the business case and the need for creating a public-private partnership to overcome global challenges, the Guiding Principles base corporate responsibility to respect human rights on societal expectation. I find these rationales

---

318 ILO Declaration, above n. 174, p. 188 (para. 2); OECD Guidelines of 2000, above n. 103, p. 238 (para. 10). The OECD Guidelines, in addition, also offer a glimpse of invoking the business case for human rights. OECD Guidelines of 2000, above n. 103, p. 238 (para. 6).

unconvincing and argue in Chapter 5 that corporations ought to respect human rights because of their *relation to* and *position in* society.

Although the presence of precise and measurable human rights standards should be a precondition to any regulatory regime relating to companies, it is doubtful if the existing regulatory initiatives satisfy this basic precondition. Whereas some of the existing mechanisms are very limited in scope, many of them prescribe vague and general human rights standards, do not resolve MNCs' dilemma of applying different standards at 'home' and in 'Rome' and suffer from the problem of over-referencing to state-centric human rights treaties. In the absence of precise, measurable human rights standards that could be applied by and enforced against companies, the existing regulatory framework essentially becomes unworkable. Even if a given company is keen to respect and follow human rights, its executives are likely to struggle to find generally agreeable concrete standards out of an ocean of instruments and standards.

At the end of the day, human rights have no meaning if they cannot be translated into action.[319] Various mechanisms to implement and enforce human rights norms help foster their translation into action. However, the existing regulatory initiatives provide deficient or undeveloped implementation and enforcement mechanisms in view of at least four reasons. First, there is an overdose of dialogue and cooperation. With some possible exceptions, the existing initiatives rely excessively on the strategies of 'dialogue' with, and 'cooperation' of, companies to make the realization of human rights an integral part of their business. Although this approach is not harmful *per se* and in fact is ideal if the dialogue results in companies internalizing human rights norms in their operations, the excessive reliance of these initiatives on this strategy creates the impression that human rights are *not* rights any longer, because their realization seems dependent upon the cooperation (or the lack of it) of companies.[320] The 'dialogue-cooperation strategy' commits a fatal mistake by surrendering human rights to the power of global business and implicitly signalling that human rights are *still* the subject matter of negotiation and bargaining when it comes to their applicability to corporations.

The second problem is the lack of sanctions to enforce corporate human rights obligations. The existing mechanisms are primarily voluntary: non-compliance with human rights obligations is not followed by any civil, criminal or social sanctions. The Guiding Principles envisage a range of

---

319 F. Tulkens, 'Human Rights, Rhetoric or Reality?' *European Review*, 2001, vol. 9, 125, at 128.
320 Donnelly, for example, argues that '... right-holders are authorized to make special claims that ordinarily "trump" utility, social policy, and other moral or political grounds for action ... Claiming a right can "make things happen".' J. Donnelly, *Universal Human Rights: In Theory and Practice*, 2nd edn, Ithaca: Cornell University Press, 2003, p. 8.

mechanisms as part of the access to effective remedy, but it is too early to predict the extent to which states and companies would follow this guidance. So, at this point of time, barring the specific instance mechanism under the OECD Guidelines and the Global Compact's recently introduced procedure to deal with egregious human rights abuses, there are not even institutional processes to complain about breach of regulatory initiatives. To make the situation worse, the existing regulatory initiatives – even if voluntary – have not made full use of the unconventional non-state-based enforcement techniques that rely on market forces and stakeholders.

Third, the current regulatory initiatives that seek to hold companies to account for human rights abuses are manifestly state-focal when it comes to the implementation and the enforcement of obligations. Almost all the existing international regulatory initiatives adopt an indirect approach in that they expect states to enforce human rights obligations against companies. This is problematic because any approach which excessively or exclusively relies upon states to enforce human rights obligations against MNCs is bound to offer limited value.[321] At best, states could only be one of the bearers of this enforcement responsibility and not the sole bearer. Other supra-state mechanisms would have to be put in place to fill in gaps in state-based mechanisms.

Fourth, the existing regulatory initiatives miserably fail to respond to key conceptual (the principle of separate legal personality) and procedural (the doctrine of *forum non conveniens*) hurdles faced by victims in holding companies accountable for human rights abuses. As far as the first issue is concerned, it is critical that a parent company is held liable for human rights violations committed by its subsidiaries as a matter of principle, unless it can show that the violations took place despite due diligence exercised by the parent company. Similarly, it is critical that the corporate misuse of the doctrine of *forum non conveniens* does not leave victims without an adequate judicial forum.[322]

Summary

The objective of this chapter was to demonstrate that the existing regulatory initiatives dealing with corporate human rights violations are inadequate. On the basis of a critical evaluation of seven representative initiatives, I argued that the existing regulatory framework is inadequate to hold companies accountable

---

321 S. Ratner, 'Corporations and Human Rights: A Theory of Legal Responsibility', *Yale Law Journal*, 2001, vol. 111, 443, at 461–3; S. Deva, 'Human Rights Violations by Multinational Corporations and International Law: Where from Here?' *Connecticut Journal of International Law*, 2003, vol. 19, 1, at 48–9.
322 See E. F. Smith, 'Right to Remedies and the Inconvenience of Forum Non Conveniens: Opening US Courts to Victims of Corporate Human Rights Abuses', *Columbia Journal of Law and Social Problems*, 2010, vol. 44, 145. See also *Owusu* v. *Jackson* [2005] 2 WLR 942.

for human rights violations. This inadequacy of the regulatory framework, which is judged in terms of two levels of efficacy, is the result of a three-fold deficiency. The existing framework offers insufficient or contestable rationales for compliance, does not prescribe precise human rights standards and is supported by a deficient or undeveloped implementation-cum-enforcement mechanism.

Since the prevailing regulatory framework is inadequate and has been unable to ensure effective accountability of companies for human rights violations, a search for an alternative model that does not suffer from these infirmities is necessary. I argue that the integrated theory of regulation, which I advance and defend as an alternative in the following chapters of this book, could rectify the deficits that engulf the existing regulatory initiatives. I begin in the next chapter by overcoming the 'why' challenge to humanizing business.

5 Just profit or *just* profit

Why should corporations have human rights obligations?

Why should corporations have human rights obligations? This chapter deals with this question in three stages. It begins with a critical evaluation of a view that rejects the idea of corporations having any human rights responsibilities. Milton Friedman was perhaps the best-known scholar who articulated and defended the position that in a free market economy the only social responsibility of business is to increase shareholders' profits, for a corporation is 'an instrument of the stockholders who own it'.[1] An influential support for Friedman's thesis came from Elaine Sternberg who, in *Just Business: Business Ethics in Action*, argued that the purpose of business 'is maximising owner value over the long term by selling goods or services'.[2] I critique the position taken by both Friedman and Sternberg and try to show why their stand is unsound and should be rejected, in part because many corporations themselves are refusing to follow the course suggested by them.

The chapter then examines a popular economic rationale behind why corporations should respect human rights obligations. This rationale is generally known as the 'business case' for human rights, that is, corporations could not only earn more profit but also gain an economic advantage over their competitors by fulfilling their human rights responsibilities.[3] As the business case is rooted in the economics of goodwill, I label it 'goodwill-nomics' and challenge the usefulness of relying too much on this rationale for promoting corporate human rights responsibilities. Not only is the goodwill-nomics hypothesis based on a series of fragile and unpredictable market assumptions, it tries to resolve a central problem by bypassing it. The key issue is: should corporations comply with human rights obligations even if doing so reduces

---

1 M. Friedman, *Capitalism and Freedom*, 40th anniversary edition, Chicago: University of Chicago Press, 2002, p. 133, and generally pp. 133–6 (emphasis added).
2 E. Sternberg, *Just Business: Business Ethics in Action*, 2nd edn, Oxford: Oxford University Press, 2000, p. 32.
3 See, e.g. M. Porter and M. Kramer, 'The Link between Competitive Advantage and Corporate Social Responsibility', *Harvard Business Review*, 2006, vol. 84:12, 78; S. Greathead, 'The Multinational and the "New Stakeholder": Examining the Business Case for Human Rights', *Vanderbilt Journal of Transnational Law*, 2002, vol. 35, 719.

their profits and/or competitive advantage, and if yes, then why? Instead of taking a stand on this critical issue, goodwill-nomics begs the question by suggesting a positive link between corporate compliance with human rights and corporate profits. It is also pointed out that the business case for human rights is further undermined by the 'prisoner's dilemma', which might discourage some corporations from taking on board human rights obligations.

Finally, this chapter canvasses an alternative justification for 'why' corporations should observe human rights norms while doing business. It is argued that all corporations should be subjected to human rights obligations because of their *relation to* and *position in* society.

Just business or *just* business? Critiquing the thesis of Friedman and Sternberg

There has been a long and inconclusive debate about what *is* or *ought* to be the role and place of corporations within society.[4] Broadly speaking, the debate has unfolded within the stockholder versus stakeholder framework. As early as the 1930s, the Berle–Dodd debate revolved around this question. Berle argued that the powers granted to a corporation or its management 'are necessarily and at all times exercisable *only* for the rateable benefit of all the shareholders as their interest appears'.[5] Dodd countered this position by contending that shareholders 'are not strictly *cestuis que trust*'[6] and that by virtue of both law and public opinion, directors should serve the interests of non-shareholders as well.[7] Berle replied by asserting that Dodd's argument reflected only 'theory, not practice'.[8] Among others, Berle's position was informed by the fear that extending responsibilities beyond shareholders might result in conferring an unguided, uncontrolled discretion on the directors of a corporation.[9]

The most visible and influential spokesperson for the stockholder theory was, however, Milton Friedman, who consistently maintained and expressed

---

4 See, e.g. A. Berle, Jr., 'Corporate Powers as Powers in Trust', *Harvard Law Review*, 1931, vol. 44, 1049; E. Dodd, Jr., 'For Whom are Corporate Managers Trustees?', *Harvard Law Review*, 1932, vol. 45, 1145; A. Berle, Jr., 'For Whom Corporate Managers *are* Trustees: A Note', *Harvard Law Review*, 1932, vol. 45, 1365 (hereinafter Berle, 'A Note'); R. Freeman, *Strategic Management: A Stakeholder Approach*, Boston: Pitman, 1984; F. Easterbrook and D. Fischel, *The Economic Structure of Corporate Law*, Cambridge, Mass.: Harvard University Press, 1991; D. Henderson, *Misguided Virtue: False Notions of Corporate Social Responsibility*, London: Institute of Economic Affairs, 2001; J. Bakan, *The Corporation: The Pathological Pursuit of Profit and Power*, New York: Free Press, 2004.
5 Berle, above n. 4, p. 1049 (emphasis added).
6 Dodd, above n. 4, p. 1146.
7 Ibid., p. 1162.
8 Berle, 'A Note', above n. 4, p. 1367.
9 'When the fiduciary obligation of the corporate management and "control" to stockholders is weakened or eliminated, the management and "control" become for all purposes absolute.' Ibid., p. 1367.

his opinions on this issue for over half a century.[10] Although Friedman's views did not receive support from all corners, he has continued to inspire a new breed of scholars who debunk any notion of corporations having social or human rights responsibilities. Elaine Sternberg is one such scholar, who admittedly defends and extends Friedman's thesis.[11]

Before I proceed to critique the thesis of Friedman and Sternberg, let me provide a signpost here. There is no single stockholder theory, a caveat that equally applies to stakeholder theory.[12] The justifications for why corporations (or directors) owe sole or primary responsibility to their shareholders vary largely. The justifications range from the claim that shareholders are the owners of corporations and are thus entitled to priority, to the fear of directors having unguided and uncontrolled discretion, and to the suggestion that shareholders' primacy is a precondition for the free market. However, the central plank of the stockholder theory has been its insistence on corporations being profit maximizing economic entities.

Friedman's rebuke for corporations having social responsibilities

In his celebrated book *Capitalism and Freedom* (first published in 1962) Friedman briefly dealt with the question of corporate social responsibility (CSR) in a chapter on 'Monopoly and the Social Responsibility of Business and Labour'.[13] Friedman elaborated on his views on CSR in 1970 in an essay published in *The New York Times Magazine*.[14] It is necessary to quote Friedman at length:

> The view has been gaining widespread acceptance that corporate officials and labour leaders have a "social responsibility" that goes beyond serving the interests of their stockholders or their members. This view shows a fundamental misconception of the character and nature of a free market economy. In such an economy, *there is one and only one social responsibility of business – to use its resources and engage in activities designed to increase its profits so long as it stays within the rules of the game*, which is to say, engage in open and free competition, without deception or fraud.
>
> Few trends could so thoroughly undermine the very foundations of our free society as the acceptance by corporate officials of a social

---

10 Friedman, above n. 1; M. Friedman, 'The Social Responsibility of Business Is to Increase Its Profits', *The New York Times Magazine*, 13 September 1970, p. 33, as reproduced in M. Snoeyenbos, R. Almeder and J. Humber (eds.), *Business Ethics*, revised edn, Buffalo: Prometheus Books, 1992, p. 72.
11 Sternberg, above n. 2, pp. 41–2.
12 A. Friedman and S. Miles, *Stakeholders: Theory and Practice*, Oxford: Oxford University Press, 2006, p. 38, and generally pp. 36–82.
13 About three pages are devoted to this discussion in a book of over 200 pages. Friedman, above n. 1, pp. 133–6.
14 Friedman, above n. 10.

responsibility other than making as much money for their stockholders as possible. *This is a fundamentally subversive doctrine*. If businessmen do have a social responsibility, how are they to know what it is? Can self-selected private individuals decide what the social interest is? Can they decide how great a burden they are justified in placing on themselves or their stockholders to serve that social interest?[15]

Responding to the specific instance of corporate donations to support charitable activities, Friedman further noted that '[s]uch giving by corporations is an inappropriate use of corporate funds in a free-enterprise society' because the 'corporation is an instrument of the stockholders who own it'.[16] Nevertheless, Friedman conceded that the 'doctrine of social responsibility is frequently a cloak for actions that are justified on other grounds rather than a real reason for those actions'.[17] For example, corporations may be tempted to rationalize charitable donations or their support for community projects on the ground of social responsibility, rather than as a means to 'generate good will' – a means 'entirely justified in its own self-interest'.[18] In this reasoning, one discerns the roots of the current 'business case' for CSR.

Friedman's attack on CSR was three-pronged:

(i) CSR undermines the free market ideology
(ii) shareholders own the corporation and
(iii) corporations are neither meant nor are suitable to assume social responsibilities.

I assess the merit of these objections one by one.

CSR undermines free markets and capitalism

Friedman saw CSR as undermining both free markets and capitalism, because those who argued for corporations having social responsibilities were 'preaching pure and unadulterated socialism'.[19] CSR, for Friedman, smacked of socialism and was, therefore, incompatible with a free market economy and capitalism.[20] The context and the time in which Friedman was writing (the Cold War era) suggest that his views on CSR were probably informed by how

---

15 Friedman, above n. 1, pp. 133–4 (emphasis added).
16 Ibid., p. 135.
17 Friedman, above n. 10, p.76, and generally pp. 76–7.
18 Ibid., p. 76.
19 Ibid., p. 72.
20 '[T]he doctrine of "social responsibility" *involves the acceptance of the socialist view* that political mechanisms, not market mechanisms, are the appropriate way to determine the allocation of scarce resources to alternative uses.' Ibid., p. 74 (emphasis added).

he regarded it as a Marxist or socialist tool to attack capitalism and the free market economy.[21] It then became natural for Friedman to point his gun at the notion of business having any social responsibilities.

Several objections could be made to this argument which is both theoretically and factually untenable at this point in time.[22] CSR does not seek to substitute, as Friedman supposed, political mechanisms with market mechanisms as a means 'to determine the allocation of scarce resources to alternative uses'.[23] Friedman gave examples of three social objectives – preventing inflation, improving the environment, and reducing poverty – the pursuit of which by corporations under the label of CSR would result in such substitution of mechanisms.[24] Apart from the fact that doubts could be raised about the appropriateness of these examples,[25] it is no one's case that under the CSR discourse the whole responsibility of accomplishing social objectives is transferred from governments to corporations.[26] Corporations, as members of society, are only expected to play their part by taking appropriate measures within their respective areas of operation: for example, ensuring that effluents from their factories are not discharged into rivers so as to preserve the environment, or paying reasonable wages to workers resulting in the reduction of poverty of some people. In fact, if companies fulfilled their legitimate responsibilities, there would be fewer demands for intervention and regulation on the part of states.

Friedman's thesis seems to propose an inverse linkage between CSR and capitalism-cum-free markets: because CSR undermines capitalism and free market ideology, the more emphasis is placed on CSR, the less free markets would become. But this proposition is untrue as a *fact*. Free markets do not mean total absence of rules or regulation. The need for intervention in the field of CSR only arises when companies behave in an irresponsible manner. There is also evidence suggesting a positive relationship between corporations taking on board social or human rights responsibilities and the sustainability

---

21 Ibid., p. 72.
22 See, for example, T. Mulligan, 'A Critique of Milton Friedman's Essay "The Social Responsibility of Business Is to Increase Its Profits"', *Journal of Business Ethics*, 1986, vol. 5, 265, at 268–9.
23 Friedman, above n. 10, p. 74.
24 Ibid., p. 73.
25 For example, hardly anyone expects corporations to prevent inflation as such, unless of course when the pricing of certain essential products (such as life-saving medicines) may directly impinge on the realization of human rights.
26 Parkinson writes that CSR aims to 'constrain' profit making, rather than 'to replace profit seeking with an open-ended goal of maximising the welfare of affected groups'. J. Parkinson, 'The Socially Responsible Company' in M. Addo (ed.), *Human Rights Standards and the Responsibility of Transnational Corporations*, The Hague: Kluwer Law International, 1999, p. 49, at 58.

of capitalism and free markets.[27] Corporations may, therefore, use CSR to counter the legitimacy crisis that they are facing.[28] Conversely, Friedman's thesis tends to posit compatibility between CSR and socialism, which is again based on an inaccurate assumption. As (private) corporations do not have a prominent role to play under socialism, the relevance of CSR in such a system is quite limited. CSR has a legitimate place not so much in socialism as in a capitalist economy based on free market principles, because public expectations grow in proportion to the role played by corporations much more under the latter.

Orlando also counters Friedman's argument – that the free market system is harmed if corporations are asked to take on social obligations – by contending that corporations 'are best thought of as entities permitted to exist by the state because they serve the public good, not because individuals have a right to enrich themselves through them'.[29] Furthermore, capitalism or free markets are not unqualified virtues or sacred frameworks (as the argument that CSR policies will undermine them indirectly suggests) which must be preserved at all costs.[30] Although Friedman himself admitted the limitations of the free market and conceived a role for government,[31] he neglected to acknowledge other infirmities in the working of markets. Markets often fail to provide basic essential services such as access to water, education, health facilities, or transport facilities to *all*[32] and there is nothing wrong with the government offering such services alone or in conjunction with corporations. Sen highlights other pitfalls of the market, observing that market 'efficiency results do not say anything about the equity of outcomes, or about the equity in the distribution of freedoms'[33] and that markets may not be effective in fostering 'public goods' such as environmental preservation, public health care and a malaria-free environment.[34]

Stockholders own the corporation

The idea of CSR runs counter to how Friedman perceived the relation between a corporation, its shareholders and corporate executives. Friedman argued that

---

27 Ibid., p. 50.
28 See, for example, G. Lodge and C. Wilson, *A Corporate Solution to Global Poverty: How Multinationals can Help the Poor and Invigorate their Own Legitimacy*, Princeton: Princeton University Press, 2006.
29 J. Orlando, 'The Ethics of Corporate Downsizing' in William Shaw (ed.), *Ethics at Work: Basic Readings in Business Ethics*, Oxford: Oxford University Press, 2003, p. 31, at 39.
30 See A. Sen, 'The Moral Standing of the Market', *Social Philosophy and Policy*, 1985, vol. 2, 1.
31 Friedman, above n 1, pp. 25–32.
32 United Nations Development Programme, 'Privatising Basic Utilities in Sub-Saharan Africa: The MDG Impact', January 2007. Available at: www.undp-povertycentre.org/pub/IPCPolicyResearchBrief003.pdf> (accessed 20 February 2011).
33 A. Sen, *Development as Freedom*, 1st paperback edn, Oxford: Oxford University Press, 2001, p. 119.
34 Ibid., 127–9. See also C. Stone, *Where the Law Ends: The Social Control of Corporate Behavior*, New York: Harper & Row, 1975, p. 88.

corporate executives as employees or agents of their shareholders have a primary responsibility to their employers to make as much money as possible.[35] Ireland rightly points out that 'a natural corollary' of the assumption that stockholders own the corporation is 'that the interests of shareholders should take priority, if not complete precedence, over all others.'[36] In other words, corporate executives, Friedman thought, could act in a socially responsible manner only by acting against the interests of shareholders.[37] I contest this position on three grounds: first, the assertion that stockholders own corporations is a myth; second, that even if stockholders, *arguendo*, own corporations, they could still be under certain social responsibilities; and third, that corporate executives could earn profits for stockholders even while observing their social responsibilities, at least in some cases.

Although the notion that shareholders own corporations has long, pervasive and influential roots,[38] it has gradually decayed to the extent of being labelled as a 'myth',[39] a 'serious misconception',[40] or something that bears 'an ever-decreasing resemblance to reality'.[41] Had shareholders owned the corporation, they would not have been standing 'last in line to receive the economic benefits of the company's activities'.[42] The conception of 'shareholders as owners' also runs counter to the corporation being regarded as a separate legal person.[43] For these and other reasons, Hill, after analyzing several changing visions of shareholders *vis-à-vis* corporations, concludes that 'a one-dimensional model of the past, such as the "shareholder as owner," is inadequate today and can result in a disjunction between law and reality'.[44]

Even if it is accepted that shareholders are owners of the corporation, this does not negate the responsibilities of owners (shareholders) or their agents (corporate managers and directors) towards other members of the society.

---

35 Friedman, above n. 10, p. 73.
36 P. Ireland, 'Company Law and the Myth of Shareholder Ownership', *Modern Law Review*, 1999, vol. 62, 32, at 33.
37 'What does it mean to say that the corporate executive has a "social responsibility" in his capacity as businessman? If this statement is not pure rhetoric, it must mean that he is to act in some way that is not in the interest of his employers.' Friedman, above n.10, p. 73.
38 J. Hill, 'Visions and Revisions of the Shareholder', *American Journal of Comparative Law*, 2000, vol. 48, 39, at 42–3; Ireland, above n. 36, pp. 32–3.
39 J. Dine, *Companies, International Trade and Human Rights*, Cambridge: Cambridge University Press, 2005, p. 263.
40 Parkinson, above n. 26, p. 52.
41 Hill, above n. 38, p. 43. See also L. A. Stout, 'Bad and Not-so-Bad Arguments for Shareholder Primacy', *Southern California Law Review*, 2002, vol. 75, 1189, at 1190–5.
42 P. Davies, *Gower and Davies's Principles of Modern Company Law*, 7th edn, London: Sweet & Maxwell, 2003, p. 372.
43 Ireland, above n. 36, p. 48; Dine, above n. 39, p. 263.
44 Hill, above n. 38, p. 78.

'Ownership rights are not absolute'[45] and ownership of property does not come without responsibilities.[46] Scholars have advanced a strong case that ownership rights ought to be exercised subject not only to legal but also to moral and ethical responsibilities.[47] Orlando, for instance, forcefully contends that 'it must be understood that one cannot justify the position that shareholder concerns take precedence over all other groups simply by appeal to the fact that the shareholders are the legal owners of the corporation'.[48] Shareholders definitely enjoy 'certain rights, but as their liabilities are limited, so their rights are limited too'.[49] Therefore, while exercising their rights, shareholders are not entitled to violate the rights of others.

In fact, even Friedman conceded the existence of some responsibilities when he said that business should be conducted subject to 'rules of the game', by which he meant that the business 'engages in open and free competition, without deception or fraud'.[50] The real disagreement concerns, therefore, not whether shareholders and corporations should have responsibilities but the extent of such responsibilities. The views of those – such as Friedman and Sternberg – who construe corporate responsibilities and limitations on profit maximization narrowly are contestable. Parkinson aptly argues that Friedman's notion of 'rules of the game' encompasses 'some ill-defined but narrow ethical principles' and 'rests on a very impoverished understanding of what morality entails'.[51]

The 'shareholders as owners' premise, at best, is useful to suggest that shareholders have a legitimate expectation in protecting their investment and also benefiting from it. However, this premise is inadequate to assert that profit has to be maximized at all costs,[52] to suggest that corporations could not have social responsibilities, or to contend that shareholders' interests have an absolute primacy over the interests of other stakeholders.[53] Of course shareholders' investment is often crucial to maintain the economic viability and profitability of corporations. However, shareholders are not the sole contributors or risk takers behind the success of corporations.[54] For example, employees

---

45 'Ownership rights are not absolute (ownership of a knife does not entitle the owner to stab people with it). *That shareholders might own companies does not mean that they may insist that directors attempt to maximise profits in any way at all.*' Parkinson, above n. 26, p. 51 (emphasis added).
46 Dine, above n. 39, p. 257. See also Sen, above n. 30, p. 6.
47 Parkinson, above n. 26, p. 51; Dine, above n. 39, p. 257.
48 Orlando, above n. 29, p. 33.
49 J. Lucas, 'The Responsibilities of a Businessman' in Shaw (ed.), above n. 29, p. 15, at 21.
50 Friedman, above n. 1, p. 133.
51 Parkinson, above n. 26, pp. 49 and 51.
52 Stone, above n. 34, p. 82.
53 Parkinson, above n. 26, p. 52.
54 B. Sheehy, 'Scrooge – The Reluctant Stakeholder: Theoretical Problems in the Shareholder-Stakeholder Debate', *University of Miami Business Law Review*, 2005, vol. 14, 193, at 216–17; S. Kiarie, 'At Crossroads: Shareholder Value, Stakeholder Value and Enlightened Shareholder Value: Which Road should the United Kingdom Take?' *International Company and Commercial Law Review*, 2006, vol. 17, 329, at 332–3.

contribute by putting in labour, supply chains contribute by making available necessary materials and other inputs, consumers contribute by buying goods or services, and governments contribute by maintaining law and order and by creating a business-favourable regulatory environment.[55] All these stakeholders contribute to the working and success of corporations, and take *different kinds of risks* while making their respective contributions.[56] One should not over-play the risk taken by shareholders as that risk-assumption is not unique by any means.[57]

It also seems that Friedman assumed an inherent, permanent and irreconcilable divergence between the interests of shareholders and those of other stakeholders. However, there might not always be a conflict between the interests of stockholders and other stakeholders, at least in the longer run. Friedman himself gave an illustration: a situation, which could be justified in terms of corporate 'self-interest', may be cloaked as an 'exercise of "social responsibility" '.[58] It is not too difficult to conceive of other situations where generally conflicting interests might converge, especially in view of the growing numbers of ethical investors who do not insist merely on maximization of profit.[59] An overlap between the interests of shareholders and other stakeholders is bound to occur because shareholders also act in other capacities such as consumers and/or employees.[60] Similarly, although a corporate decision to adopt an environment-friendly technology may entail more expenditure, this may also reduce operating costs. Therefore, in situations in which there is a convergence in the interests of shareholders and stakeholders, corporate executives could perform their social responsibilities without violating their responsibility to maximize shareholders' profit.

Corporations are not meant, or suitable, to assume social responsibilities

Friedman conceived that CSR would result in corporations doing what states or civil servants should be doing, such as 'imposing taxes' and 'deciding how the tax proceeds shall be spent'.[61] If corporations were to assume social responsibilities, corporate executives would be behaving more like unaccountable, unguided civil servants.[62] This line of argument against CSR also invokes the public–private division of functions, the incapacity of corporate executives to

---

55 J. Post, A. Lawrence, and J. Weber, *Business and Society: Corporate Strategy, Public Policy, Ethics*, 9th edn, Boston: Irwin/Mcgraw-Hill, 1999, p. 9.
56 Kiarie, above n. 54, p. 332.
57 P. Atiyah, *The Rise and Fall of Freedom of Contract*, Oxford: Clarendon Press, 1979, p. 130.
58 Friedman, above n. 10, p. 76.
59 Addo, 'An Introduction', above n. 26, p. 15; Orlando, above n. 29, p. 38.
60 J. Boatright, *Ethics and the Conduct of Business*, 5th edn, Upper Saddle River, New Jersey: Prentice Hall, 2007, p. 376; Kiarie, above n. 54, pp. 333–4.
61 Friedman, above n. 10, p. 74.
62 Ibid., pp. 74–5.

take and implement appropriate decisions and the prisoner's dilemma.[63] Again, it is possible to rebut these objections.

It is difficult to understand, as Mulligan demonstrates, how corporations would in effect be imposing a 'tax' on stockholders while pursuing CSR policies.[64] Friedman was right in asserting that corporations lack any authority whatsoever to impose a tax on shareholders, but he somehow believed that corporations will impose a tax if they assume social responsibilities.[65] There are both conceptual and substantive fallacies in this argument. At the conceptual level, if corporations lack the authority to do 'X', they cannot *legally* do 'X'; they can only do something other than 'X', or risk acting *ultra vires* and thereby losing the benefit of the corporate veil. Tax is a compulsory, coercive exaction of money by a state (or other authority that possesses political power) for common benefit.[66] Corporations cannot impose tax *in this sense* because they lack the required authority and political legitimacy. So even if the assumption of social responsibilities by corporations reduces the profit of shareholders, this could not be because of the imposition of tax. This would amount to a tax only if states decide to levy tax on corporations (and not on shareholders as such) and then spend the collected money to fulfil social responsibilities of corporations. I doubt whether Friedman would have preferred that course.

The substantive fallacy in the argument of Friedman lies in ignoring that shareholders only have an *expectation* of some profits from their investment, but not a *right* to earn a certain amount of profits. Shareholders' profits can fall below the expected level not only because of taxation, but also for several other reasons such as bad investment decision making on the part of management. Would that amount to corporations taxing shareholders? If not, why should one regard as a tax any diminishment in shareholder profits that results from corporations spending their resources to fulfil their legitimate social responsibilities by, for example, paying adequate salaries to employees?

Friedman also pointed out that corporate executives are not experts in handling CSR issues and that they cannot judge the future impact of their actions with a view to achieving given social objectives.[67] The first limb of the argument has some merit,[68] but corporations could overcome this capacity limitation by simply hiring experts. Corporations have the resources to hire experts and there is no reason why they should not do so in the area of social

---

63 Ibid.
64 Mulligan, above n. 22, pp. 266–7. See also Boatright, above n. 60, pp. 375–6.
65 Friedman, above n. 10, pp. 74–5.
66 See B. A. Garner (ed in chief.), *Black's Law Dictionary*, 9th edn, St. Paul, Minn.: West/Thompson Reuters, 2009, p. 1594.
67 Friedman, above n. 10, p. 74.
68 S. Deva, 'Corporate Code of Conduct Bill 2000: Overcoming Hurdles in Enforcing Human Rights Obligations Against Overseas Corporate Hands of Local Corporations', *Newcastle Law Review*, 2004, vol. 8, 87, at 110–11.

responsibility, when they follow this practice in other areas of operation. Regarding the second limb of the argument, it could be said that there is always an element of uncertainty, calculated risk and speculation in almost all business decisions and this is not unique to CSR-related decisions.[69] Therefore, decisions 'about socially responsible actions, no less than decisions about new products or marketing campaigns, can be made using this "business-like" approach'.[70] Besides, Friedman's fear that corporate executives in the course of acting in a socially responsible manner would behave like unaccountable or unguided civil servants disappears to a great extent if the company integrates CSR into its business policy and operations. Parker convincingly argues that by opening up corporations so as to enable stakeholders to participate in corporate deliberations, we can bring more accountability and transparency to corporate functioning.[71]

Friedman's suggestion (based on a private versus public division of functions) that corporations should focus only on efficient wealth creation and that states alone should bear the responsibility of human rights' realization is both obsolete and unsound. Such a position could have been tenable at a time when the welfare state used to play a dominant and pervasive role, including that of protecting and promoting human rights. It is no longer tenable when corporations are performing many public functions and/or providing public services under a free market economy (e.g. providing health services and access to water, managing prisons and detention centres, and ferrying suspected terrorists to outsource torture).[72] It is logical that corporate assumption of public functions and powers ought to be accompanied by corporate acceptance of appropriate social responsibilities. As feminist scholars have shown, the distinction between 'public' and 'private' is also unsound;[73] the distinction is not only difficult to make and maintain but also problematic for several reasons. For example, if we maintain this distinction, then corporations operating in free markets could hardly be subject to human rights norms, nor

---

69 Mulligan, above n. 22, p. 268.
70 Ibid.
71 C. Parker, *The Open Corporation: Effective Self-regulation and Democracy*, Cambridge: Cambridge University Press, 2002.
72 T. O'Neill, 'Water and Freedom: The Privatisation of Water and Its Implications for Democracy and Human Rights in the Developing World', *Colorado Journal of International Environmental Law and Policy*, 2006, vol. 17, 357; N. Rosemann, 'The Privatisation of Human Rights Violations – Business' Impunity or Corporate Responsibility? The Case of Human Rights Abuses and Torture in Iraq', *Non-State Actors and International Law*, 2005, vol. 5, 77; S. Grey, *Ghost Plane: The True Story of the CIA Torture Program*, New York: St Martin's Press, 2006.
73 See, e.g. H. Charlesworth, C. Chinkin and S. Wright, 'Feminist Approaches to International Law', *American Journal of International Law*, 1991, vol. 85, 613; C. Chinkin, 'A Critique of the Public/Private Dimension', *European Journal of International Law*, 1999, vol. 10, 387.

could the question of state responsibility for actions or omissions by corporate agents generally arise.

Such a watertight division of functions also ignores the value of cooperation and the limitations of a 'doing it alone' approach. Cooperation between governments and the private sector is increasingly emphasized to meet contemporary challenges – whether of sustainable development, global warming, or the Millennium Development Goals.[74] The current trend, therefore, is towards establishing 'public–private' partnerships in governance, service delivery and regulation. I explained in the last chapter how the Global Compact envisages such a partnership between governments, international institutions, companies and NGOs to achieve a more inclusive and sustainable global economy.

It seems that the fear of Friedman that CSR would result in corporate executives abusing the trust of shareholders is unfounded as well. Friedman was not the first one to express such fear; Berle also cautioned that CSR might make corporate management 'absolute',[75] as no precise yardsticks would be available to test their conduct. However, we know as a matter of fact how baseless the fear proved. Werner rightly points out: 'Berle's 1932 forecast – that managers would use the opening created by Dodd's thesis to abuse shareholder rights – did not materialize. Shareholders complained for various reasons, but not because managers were sacrificing shareholders for the community's welfare.'[76] The fear is unlikely to materialize in future: first, because many shareholders now insist on corporations behaving as good corporate citizens, and second, because the nature and extent of social responsibilities of corporations – though far from absolutely clear – are getting more and more concrete.

One could point out another paradox in the thesis of Friedman. According to him, *only* 'responsible individuals' could be the bearers of freedom,[77] while corporations, as bearers of freedom to do business and maximize profits, need not be responsible entities so as to have certain social responsibilities. Friedman tries to dispel this contradiction by arguing that corporations are artificial entities unlike individuals and so they could not have responsibilities.[78] But if this is so, how could non-individuals like corporations have and exercise freedoms too? Conversely, if freedoms could be bestowed on corporations, so could responsibilities. Scholars like Goodpaster and Wells have made a strong

---

74 Report of the Secretary General, *In Larger Freedom: Towards Development, Security and Human Rights for All*, A/59/2005 (21 March 2005); Lodge and Wilson, above n. 28.
75 Berle, 'A Note', above n. 4, pp. 1367–8.
76 W. Werner, 'Corporation Law in Search of its Future', *Columbia Law Review*, 1981, vol. 81, 1611, at 1645.
77 Friedman, above n. 1, p. 33 (emphasis added).
78 Friedman, above n. 10, p. 72.

case that corporations in their individual capacities could be made accountable for breach of their responsibilities.[79]

In short, Friedman's views on CSR, though highly influential, are unsound, especially in the current economic climate. More than anything else, his views have been undermined by the conduct of a great number of corporations, which preach and/or practice the CSR mantra, operating in a free market economy.

What is Sternberg's just *business*?

Sternberg in her book *Just Business* not only defends and extends Friedman's thesis but also seeks to 'provide solid arguments for rebutting *trendy, but unethical*, demands for "social responsibility" in business'.[80] Sternberg claims that the Ethical Decision Model presented in the book could be invoked for 'resolving business ethics questions whenever and wherever they arise'.[81] *Just Business* adopts a teleological approach because '[p]urposes are essential for evaluating the goodness' of human conduct.[82] Logically therefore, for Sternberg, 'what constitutes ethical conduct in business depends critically on business's definite purpose'.[83]

How, then, does Sternberg define 'business' and its definite purpose? In a definition carefully worded and meticulously elaborated, she defines 'business' with reference to its purpose: '*The defining purpose of business is maximising owner value over the long term by selling goods or services.*'[84] It is this distinctive purpose that separates, in her view, business from other aggregations like family, club, church, game, and government.[85] Everything that business does should be tested against the criterion of maximizing long-term owner value, something that business should try to achieve only by selling goods or services.[86] But what is this 'value'? What is meant by 'long-term'? Who are the 'owners' of business? What does 'maximization' mean and entail? Sternberg painstakingly explains the meaning of all these phrases.[87]

---

79 K. Goodpaster, 'The Concept of Corporate Responsibility', *Journal of Business Ethics*, 1983, vol. 2, 1, at 9–14; C. Wells, *Corporations and Criminal Responsibility*, 2nd edn, Oxford: Oxford University Press, 2001, pp. 63–105.
80 Sternberg, above n. 2, p. 1 (emphasis added).
81 Ibid., p. 5. The Model involves four steps by a business: clarifying the question; determining the relevance of the question for this business; identifying the circumstantial constraints; and assessing the available options. After this exercise, the right course of action that should be chosen is that which is likely to maximize long-term owner value. Ibid., pp. 113–20.
82 Ibid., p. 4.
83 Ibid.
84 Ibid., p. 32 (emphasis in original).
85 Ibid., pp. 35–40.
86 Ibid., pp. 42–3.
87 Ibid., pp. 42–57.

In her definition of the purpose of business, 'value' – a term that she prefers to use over wealth, asset, revenue, or share price[88] – is nothing but 'financial value'.[89] The owners of businesses are those who own it (i.e. the shareholders of a corporation or partners of a partnership firm).[90] Rather than serving the interests of consumers and employees or stakeholders as such,[91] 'business is automatically accountable . . . [to] its owners . . . simply because it belongs to them: *it is their property*'.[92] Although Sternberg considers the use of the phrase 'long-term' to be strictly speaking 'superfluous', she uses it to highlight two aspects: first, that businesses should 'take into account the future effects of their current actions' because actions generally have 'long-term consequences', and second, that business by nature is not a temporary but a 'sustained activity'.[93] Finally, the objective of business, Sternberg explains, has to be maximizing owner value and 'not just to increase or promote, secure or sustain it' because any '[l]ess stringent objectives than maximising fail to differentiate business from other activities'.[94] Sternberg concedes that the definition of business that she proposes and defends is narrow, but considers this narrowness 'not an ideological requirement, but a logical one'.[95] If business is asked to perform social responsibilities and take on board the interests of all stakeholders, it may fail to serve anyone.

Elaine Sternberg's conception of business as outlined above might create the impression that business could pursue the objective of maximizing long-term owner value without any moral, ethical or legal limits. However, this is not the case. Similar to Friedman's 'rules of the game', she considers that ethics is 'essential for business'.[96] Sternberg offers another *business* reason for why business should take ethics into account: 'A business that ignores the demand of business ethics, or gets them wrong, is unlikely to maximise long-term owner value'.[97] She, in fact, thinks that 'being unethical can cost a business its very life'.[98]

Of course Sternberg does not stop at providing the business case for business ethics. She also outlines the contours of such ethical principles. A 'business will be ethical if it seeks maximum long-term owner value in ethical ways'.[99] What are these ethical ways? Sternberg argues that there are two

---

88 Ibid., pp. 45–8.
89 Ibid., p. 44.
90 Ibid., p. 49.
91 Ibid., pp. 49–53.
92 Ibid., p. 51 (emphasis added).
93 Ibid., pp. 53–4.
94 Ibid., p. 54.
95 Ibid., p. 33, and generally pp. 32–5.
96 Ibid., pp. 15–17.
97 Ibid., p. 19.
98 Ibid.
99 Ibid., p. 58.

fundamental principles of business ethics – 'distributive justice' and 'ordinary decency' – 'without which business as an activity would be impossible' to conduct.[100] Taken together these two principles should ordinarily enhance long-term owner value because 'being ethical is good for business'.[101]

The principle of distributive justice mandates that 'organisational rewards should be proportional to contributions made to organisational ends'.[102] The principle, which explains both *why* and *how* benefits should be allocated, is considered essential for business because it 'encourages contribution' to the defined business purpose (i.e. maximizing long-term owner value by selling goods or services).[103] However, the principle of ordinary decency 'consists of fairness and honesty and refraining from coercion and physical violence, typically within the confines of the law'.[104] Although ordinary decency will imply other values like courage, responsibility and integrity, Sternberg maintains that there is no need to extend the list beyond the four components (i.e. honesty, fairness, refraining from coercion and violence, and respecting the law) which will 'act as constraints on business's legitimate activities'.[105] Sternberg reasons that these components are part of ordinary decency because maximizing long-term owner value would require values such as confidence, trust and respect for property rights. Her flow chart reads like this: 'maximising *long-term owner value* views require considering the long term. But long-term views require *confidence*, which in turn requires *trust*. Moreover, owner value necessarily presupposes ownership, and so requires *respect for property rights*.'[106]

Although the narrowness of Sternberg's twin fundamental ethical principles is critiqued in more detail below, it may be noted at this stage that she does not directly or specifically consider whether these principles will include adherence to human rights. *Prima facie* it seems difficult to imagine how her conception of business ethics could encompass issues related to human rights, beyond perhaps those concerns that could be encompassed by fairness and refraining from coercion and physical violence as part of ordinary decency.[107] Similarly, the performance of social responsibilities by business is also generally foreign, probably contrary, to how Sternberg visualizes business ethics.[108]

---

100 Ibid., p. 79.
101 Ibid., p. 87.
102 Ibid., p. 80, and generally pp. 80–2.
103 Ibid., p. 80.
104 Ibid., p. 82, and generally pp. 82–7.
105 Ibid., pp. 82–3.
106 Ibid., p. 79 (emphasis added).
107 Ibid., pp. 79, 82, 84.
108 'Business ethics can therefore save the business from wasting its resources on objectives, notably those called "social responsibilities", that are by their very nature *wrong* for business.' Ibid., pp. 18–19 (emphasis in original).

To sum up, in order to be ethical as per Sternberg's yardstick, a business action must aim at 'maximising long-term owner value *while* respecting distributive justice and ordinary decency'.[109] Sternberg not only defends but also extends the thesis of Friedman in that she finds Friedman's terminology (e.g. corporate social responsibility as 'socialism' and unauthorized 'taxation') 'too polite'.[110] She strongly believes that '[u]sing business resources for non-business purposes [i.e. social responsibility] is tantamount to *theft*: an unjustified appropriation of the owners' property'.[111] Sternberg argues that '[m]anagers who employ business funds for anything other than the legitimate business objective are simply embezzling'.[112] Such corporate managers are also guilty of the offence of, what Sternberg calls, the 'logical offence of teleopathy': 'Just as prostitution occurs when sex is proffered for money rather than love, so it exists when business pursues love – or "social responsibility" – rather than money.'[113] Therefore, corporations must refrain from performing their social responsibilities unless doing so helps in maximizing owner value.[114] If shareholders as corporate owners decide to 'pursue something other than maximum long-term owner value . . . they are simply not engaging in business'.[115]

How just *is Sternberg's thesis of 'just business'?*

I will try to show why Sternberg's thesis of doing just business subject only to her notions of distributive justice and ordinary decency could not be regarded as *just*. Some of the arguments advanced by Sternberg are similar to those raised by Friedman and have already been rebutted before. For example, we have seen earlier why her assertion that 'shareholders of a corporation are, collectively, its owners',[116] is unsound. The position taken by Sternberg could be assailed on several other grounds as well.

Although Sternberg devotes several pages of her book to carefully defining and distinguishing the key terms used in her thesis, she does not bother to explain what she means by the 'social responsibility' of business. It is nonsensical to ask businesses not to 'waste' their resources on social responsibilities without telling them what these responsibilities are. Not only does Sternberg fail to offer a definition of social responsibility, her analysis, in fact, demonstrates a poor understanding of this term. Let us consider one example.

---

109 Ibid., p. 120 (emphasis in original).
110 Ibid., p. 41.
111 Ibid.
112 Ibid.
113 Ibid., p. 42.
114 Ibid., pp. 56–7, 113–22.
115 Ibid., p. 45.
116 Ibid., p. 200.

Castigating the 'oxymoronic approach' to business ethics (expressed by terms such as social responsibility and stakeholding), she writes: 'that being ethical in business means *replacing* the pursuit of owner value with the pursuit of some other end – social welfare, environmental protection or stakeholder interests, for example.'[117] Hardly anyone – even a stakeholder theorist – expects corporations to substitute their primary goal of wealth maximization with a concern for social services.[118] The CSR discourse makes only a limited claim: that corporations should not maximize shareholder's wealth at the cost of, say, violating labour and human rights or polluting the environment.[119]

Sternberg's lack of clarity surrounding the concept of CSR or stakeholder theory is further demonstrated by the fact that she critiques something that the stakeholder theory does not posit. While pointing out one of the 'four fundamental errors' of stakeholder theory, Sternberg writes: 'in maintaining that all stakeholders are of *equal importance* to a business, and that the business ought to be *answerable equally* to them all, stakeholder theory confounds business with government.'[120] But the stakeholder theory does not make a claim of equality amongst stakeholders:[121] it is the responsibility of directors to balance the interests – none of which are 'primary or over-riding' – of a range of stakeholders.[122]

The *Just Business* thesis of Sternberg is 'Aristotelian in specifying the definition of business in terms of its purpose, and in then determining the proper conduct of business by reference to that definitive purpose'.[123] Megone demonstrates that an alternative approach derived from Aristotle (virtue theory) challenges Sternberg's view that 'the proper purpose of business is to *maximise* long-term owner value by selling goods and services'.[124] In view of varied motivations, Aristotle draws a distinction between two types of commercial activities: 'There are two sorts of wealth getting, as I have said; one is a part of household management, the other is retail trade: the former is necessary and honourable, while that which consists in exchange is justly censured: for it is unnatural.'[125] The pursuit of limitless wealth maximisation by business becomes unnatural for Aristotle because 'it is contrary to what is needed for

---

117 Ibid., pp. x–xi (emphasis added).
118 See M. Hemraj, 'Corporate Governance: Rationalising Stakeholder Doctrine in Corporate Accountability', *Company Lawyer*, 2005, vol. 26:7, 211.
119 Post *et al.*., above n. 55, p. 58; Stone, above n. 34, pp. 230–2.
120 Sternberg, above n. 2, p. 50 (emphasis added).
121 Hemraj, above n. 118, p. 214. Sheehy, above n. 54, p. 207.
122 M. Fogarty, *Company and Corporation – One Law?* London: Geoffrey Chapman, 1965, pp. 8–9.
123 C. Megone, 'Two Aristotelian Approaches to Business Ethics' in C. Megone and S. Robinson (eds.), *Case Histories in Business Ethics*, London: Routledge, 2002, pp. 23, p. 39.
124 Ibid., 50 (emphasis in original).
125 Aristotle, *Politics I*, 10 1258 a39–b3, as quoted by Megone, ibid., p. 50.

the proper development of human nature'.[126] Wealth is only a means and not an end in itself, and in fact, the objective of maximization might result in the means overtaking or overshadowing the ends. In other words, the very purpose of business proposed by Sternberg – maximization of long-term owner value – is contestable.[127] Any doubt about the appropriateness of the purpose of business is fatal for her approach. Leaving aside this doubt, the ends do not always justify the means.[128]

The narrowness with which Sternberg defines two fundamental principles of her business ethics presents another serious difficulty. 'Distributive justice', or merely justice, is a powerful construct with wide-ranging applications. She primarily confines the application of this principle to the allocation of rewards and achievements within business, because this will encourage contribution to the success of business.[129] There is no sound reason, however, why the principle of distributive justice should not be applied to the allocation of, say, business responsibilities. If applied to the identification and allocation of responsibilities, the principle would place responsibility on businesses for those consequences which their activities cause, or to which they contribute. One could see the evolution of the 'polluter pays' principle in the area of environmental law in this light.[130] By Sternberg's own logic, the application of the distributive justice principle to the allocation of responsibilities should necessarily encourage responsible behaviour on the part of business.

Her construction of 'ordinary decency' is similarly problematic. Sternberg deduces four values (outlined above) that are part of ordinary decency because *maximizing long-term owner value* requires confidence, trust and respect for property rights. It is not, however, clear why ordinary decency could, or should, exclude respect for human rights which are based upon respect for individual worth and dignity. If the test for including values within the bracket of ordinary decency is that they help in maximizing long-term owner value, then either human rights also satisfy this test, or none of the included values could. If 'business would be impossible' without what she considers ordinary decency,[131] it would be very difficult, if not impossible, without human rights too. For example, consider whether businesses would like to

---

126 Megone, above n. 123, p. 50.
127 Sir Geoffrey Chandler, 'Keynote Address: Crafting a Human Rights Agenda for Business' in Addo (ed.), above n. 26, p. 39, at 44.
128 Mahatma Gandhi, for example, firmly believed that ends could not justify means: '*I have never believed and I do not now believe that the end justifies the means*. On the contrary it is my firm conviction that there is an intimate connection between the end and the means so much so that *you cannot achieve a good end by bad means*.' Ministry of Information and Broadcasting, Government of India, *The Collected Works of Mahatma Gandhi*, 22 July 1921–25 October 1921, vol. 24, p. 74 (emphasis added).
129 Sternberg, above n. 2, pp. 80–1.
130 See *Indian Council for Enviro-Legal Action* v. *Union of India* (1996) 3 SCC 212.
131 Sternberg, above n. 2, p. 80.

do business without the protection of human rights such as the right to equality, protection of property (including intellectual property) rights, freedom of trade and commerce, freedom of commercial speech, and the right to movement.

Since the business ethics model proposed by Sternberg is universal, it applies equally to international or transnational business. She rightly recognizes the problem posed by 'cross-border, cross-cultural business' and asks the relevant question: 'Is it, for example, ethical to sell elsewhere, products that fail to meet the standards of the sophisticated home markets?'[132] To overcome this ethical dilemma, Sternberg offers the following test for the business:

> If the danger [in selling abroad the products that are regarded unsafe at home] is small, then it is a matter of trade offs. . . . And the lives of starving people can still be saved by food that is wholesome past its "sell by" date. If the products are seriously unsafe, however, then it would be wrong, and counterproductive, to sell them in *any* market. Selling a kettle that is prone to electrocute its user not only violates ordinary decency, but it is more likely to attract costly prosecutions and distrust than profitable repeat business.[133]

The suggested distinction between *small* and *serious* dangers could be contested on ethical grounds itself. Subjecting people to known risks – especially against the background of unequal bargaining positions and a lack of informed consent – might be legal but it is not morally correct, because this will, in effect, result in assigning different values to the life and worth of human beings. It may also be difficult for business people to make and sustain such a distinction during actual decisions taken under the duress of profit maximization. What is the guarantee that the sale of food in developing countries after the 'sell-by' date is likely to save lives rather than cause food poisoning? Moreover, how is the seriousness of the danger to be judged – by the probability or magnitude of harm, or both? Sternberg explicitly offers no concrete guidance in this regard. If her advice to business is to weigh short-term profits that may be gained by selling dangerous products against both the present and future consequences, then this is not an ethical but an economic yardstick, as elaborated further below.

One might also ask if there is much 'ethics' in those decisions of business which are driven solely by the purpose of maximizing long-term owner value. It is no secret that Sternberg wants business to follow ethical principles not because it is the right thing to do (irrespective of the impact on owner value),

---

132 Ibid., p. 89.
133 Ibid., 89 (emphasis in original), and generally pp. 89–90. Boatright also makes similar arguments, which are dealt with in detail in Chapter 6. Boatright, above n. 60, pp. 406–8.

but because 'business ethics actually provide essential support for maximizing long-term owner value'.[134] Despite the fact that business decisions are motivated by the consequence of such decisions (say profit) rather than ethical motives, Sternberg labels the conduct of business to be ethical. She reasons that 'the act that is actually achieved or accomplished, can usually be abstracted away from the doer's motive and evaluated separately'.[135]

To illustrate her argument, she gives the example of a man saving a drowning child for varied motivations.[136] Let me consider the same example with a little variation in the scenario. Can the act of a person who saves a drowning child be considered ethical in the proper sense if it is motivated *only* by a prize? Sternberg is likely to reply in the affirmative: 'Whatever the motive, however, a good act – that of saving a child's life – has been performed.'[137] Sternberg is right when she says that a good motive does not convert a bad or unethical act into a good or ethical act.[138] Nevertheless, motive should be relevant in determining the moral quality of the *act* – the act of a person who saves the child without any motive of prize-getting is much more ethical than that of a person who does the same act for money, or to hold the child for ransom, for that matter.[139] Sternberg tries to overcome this difficulty by making a distinction between 'ethical acts' and 'acting ethically'.[140] Motive, she explains, should be relevant in judging not the *nature of the act* but the *character of the actor*.[141] However, the nature of act and the motive of actor are often interlinked. For example, in criminal law motive is invoked in judging the true colour of a given act.[142] The distinction between the 'act' and 'actor' seems fallacious and indefensible in the context of business by corporations. If a corporation agrees to an out-of-court settlement due to the fear of a heavy penalty that may result from legal proceedings, it is unlikely that stakeholders will treat the act (of giving compensation) as ethical and at the same time consider the actor (the corporation) to have acted unethically, or *vice versa*.

It seems that Sternberg consciously gives a small, selective dose of ethics to business decision-making and hopes that this will allow business to reap the

---

134 Sternberg, above n. 2, p. 15, and generally pp. 15–20, 79–90.
135 Ibid., p. 94.
136 Ibid., pp. 94–5.
137 Ibid., p. 94.
138 'Wrongdoing is not annulled by worthy motives.' Ibid., p. 41.
139 '[The] nature of that which induces the actor to behave in a virtuous way is relevant: *it makes quite a difference whether it is because of fear of legal or social sanction or because it arises from intrinsic motivations.*' S. Zamagni, 'Keynote Address – Religious Values and Corporate Decision Making: An Economist's Perspective', *Fordham Journal of Corporate and Financial Law*, 2006, vol. 11, 573, at 583 (emphasis added).
140 Sternberg, above n. 2, p. 95.
141 Ibid., p. 95.
142 D. Ormerod, *Smith and Hogan Criminal Law*, 11th edn, Oxford: Oxford University Press, 2005, p. 119.

benefits of both the shareholder model and the stakeholder model. This brings incoherence to her thesis as she constantly struggles, rather unsuccessfully, to maintain harmony between the two ideas. Out of several examples of this contradictory posture that one could find (sometimes within a single paragraph) in *Just Business*, one should suffice here: 'Stakeholders . . . have no right to expect the business to be seeking anything but long-term owner value. . . . Nevertheless, given the importance of well-disposed stakeholders to maximising long-term owner value, only a seriously short-sighted business will ignore stakeholder interests.'[143]

Finally, a common point about the position taken by both Friedman and Sternberg *vis-à-vis* CSR may be made. It seems that over the years some scholars, in order to pre-empt any other legitimate claims that could be made against corporations, may have consistently (over)emphasized that the only responsibility that corporations have is to maximize shareholders' profit.[144] For example, way back in 1932, Berle expressed the fear that corporations might be asked to serve the interests of, and share the wealth with, non-shareholders.[145] Such a fear probably explains the extreme stand adopted by certain theorists who wish to accord complete primacy to the interests of stockholders.

Examining the 'business case' for human rights[146]

If Sternberg considers that it is fashionable to talk about the social responsibilities of business, equally fashionable is the use of the 'business case' for human rights (or CSR generally). I critically examine the business case for human rights, which posits that corporate compliance with human rights is necessary for none other than the 'bottom line' reasons. The argument works in both positive and negative ways.[147] Adherence to human rights norms increases profit, goodwill and competitive advantage, while failure to comply with human rights norms results in loss of profit, goodwill, and competitive advantage.

The limited purpose of the inquiry undertaken here is to investigate if the current *over-reliance* on the business case for human rights in scholarly as well as corporate literature is useful and/or theoretically sound. In addition to evaluating the foundation of the business case rooted in the 'goodwill-nomics', it

---

143 Sternberg, above n. 2, p. 121.
144 Lucas, above n. 49, pp. 22–3.
145 Berle, 'A Note', above n. 4, p. 1371.
146 This section draws on my previously published article: S. Deva, 'Sustainable Good Governance and Corporations: An Analysis of Asymmetries', *Georgetown International Environmental Law Review*, 2006, vol. 18, 707, at 741–7.
147 Zadek divides the business case into four interrelated categories: defence (pain alleviation); traditional (cost–benefit); strategic; and new economy (learning, innovation and risk management). S. Zadek, *The Civil Corporation*, London: Earthscan, 2001, pp. 65–8.

is examined if the 'prisoner's dilemma' might discourage some corporations from assuming human rights responsibilities because of the fear of losing competitive advantage in actual market situations.

'Goodwill-nomics': How sound is the business case for human rights?

Several theoretical and empirical studies have tried to investigate the relationship – positive or negative – between CSR (which essentially includes human rights issues) and the financial performance of corporations.[148] Although the results coming from this research so far have not been conclusive or one-sided,[149] it is increasingly suggested that there is a measurable, positive relation between CSR and the ensuing economic benefits. The central economic rationale of this hypothesis revolves around the goodwill, or ill-will, that a corporation might generate because of taking a given stand towards human rights issues. In my view, the business case for human rights is based on the following four interconnected assumptions:

(i) that corporation X adopts policies and takes actions consistent with human rights norms whereas its competing corporation Y does not
(ii) that stakeholders such as consumers, investors, employees, media and NGOs are *aware* of the fact that X is contributing to human rights realization but not Y
(iii) that stakeholders *value* human rights and therefore would be *willing*, as well as *able*, to punish Y and/or reward X for their respective stands *vis-à-vis* human rights issues and
(iv) that the reward and punishment meted out by stakeholders would result in a positive or adverse effect on market share for and goodwill towards X and Y, respectively, thus giving a competitive advantage to the former.

There is nothing fundamentally wrong with the above series of assumptions because several past instances indicate the possibility of this trend materializing.[150] Nevertheless, these assumptions are questionable on several

---

148 See, e.g. M. Pava and J. Krausz, *Corporate Responsibility and Financial Performance*, Westport: Quorum Books, 1995; A. Henriques and J. Richardson (eds.), *The Triple Bottom Line, Does It All Add Up?: Assessing the Sustainability of Business and CSR*, London: Earthscan Publications Ltd., 2004; J. Margolis and J. Walsh, *People and Profits?: The Search for a Link Between a Company's Social and Financial Performance*, Mahwah, NJ: Lawrence Erlbaum Associates Publishers, 2001; U. Steger (ed.), *The Business of Sustainability: Building Industry Cases for Corporate Sustainability*, New York: Palgrave Macmillan, 2004.
149 Porter and Kramer, above n. 3, p. 81–83; Zadek, above n. 147, pp. 93–5.
150 J. Anderson, 'Respecting Human Rights: Multinational Corporations Strike Out', *University of Pennsylvania Journal of Labour and Employment Law*, 2000, vol. 2, 463, at 473–4; Parker, above n. 71, pp. 157–64.

grounds.[151] The very first assumption implicitly permits some corporations to ignore their responsibility to respect human rights, for where is the competitive advantage if all corporations comply with human rights norms? Rather than attempting to reduce the effect of the prisoner's dilemma – which, as I will show below, might discourage corporations like X from taking on board human rights responsibilities – goodwill-nomics treats human rights abuses by certain corporations as a fundamental premise or necessary precondition. This is undoubtedly an unsound and unsatisfactory premise for any theory that seeks to humanize business.

Human rights scholars should find the business case for human rights problematic for another reason. The business case introduces 'cost and benefit' analysis to human rights discourse by connecting corporate compliance with human rights obligations to corporate profits. However, any approach that requires assigning human rights and life itself a calculable value[152] and encourages a trade off between human rights and other goals is questionable for obvious reasons.[153] Corporations should be subject to human rights obligations irrespective of the impact on their profits and competitiveness. Numerous case studies also support human rights discourse's normative abhorrence to the cost–benefit analysis. As we will see in the next chapter, safety standards in Bhopal were lowered because of cost-saving measures, resulting in the loss of thousands of lives. A more recent example is the BP oil spill in the Gulf of Mexico. The National Commission on the BP Deepwater Horizon Oil Spill and Offshore Drilling concluded that various time- and cost-saving decisions taken by BP, Halliburton, and Transocean enhanced risks,[154] again leading to loss of lives and an environmental disaster.

Moreover, the business case hypothesis simply assumes too much; all of these assumptions may not come true in a given case. As Parkinson points out, information flow among various stakeholders is fundamental to the success of this hypothesis: 'For market mechanisms to "punish" a company that behaves

---

151 Stone, above n. 34, pp. 89–92.
152 D. Dalton and R. Cosier, 'An Issue in Corporate Social Responsibility: An Experimental Approach to Establish the Value of Human Life', *Journal of Business Ethics*, 1991, vol. 10, 311.
153 'A right is not something that can be assigned on "efficiency" grounds; a right is precisely an individual's "trump" against the claims of efficiency . . .' R. Langlois, 'Cost–Benefit Analysis, Environmentalism and Rights', *Cato Journal*, 1982, vol. 2, 279, at 283. See also R. Paul Malloy, 'Equating Human Rights and Property Rights – The Need for Moral Judgment in an Economic Analysis of Law and Social Policy', *Ohio State Law Journal*, 1986, vol. 47, 163, at 171–7; R. Cooter, 'The Best Right Laws: Value Foundations of the Economic Analysis of Law' *Notre Dame Law Review*, 1989, vol. 64, 817, at 835–7.
154 National Commission on the BP Deepwater Horizon Oil Spill and Offshore Drilling (US), *Deep Water: The Gulf Oil Disaster and the Future of Offshore Drilling*, 2011, pp. 125–6. Available at: www.oilspillcommission.gov/final-report (accessed 20 June 2011).

irresponsibly it is necessary for those with whom it does business to be *fully informed* about its activities and their impact and to know how its performance compares with that of other companies.'[155] But the flow of information is not always that smooth or forthcoming in markets, particularly because corporations do not normally release self-disparaging data. Nor is the task of comparing the conduct of different corporations an easy one (e.g. the same contractor might be supplying a given product to two competing companies, or a product might be an assembled one comprising several parts manufactured across the globe in diverse conditions).

Even if we assume that consumers and investors are well-informed of the opposing stands of X and Y *vis-à-vis* human rights,[156] there is no guarantee that they would always reward X and/or punish Y. If certain stakeholders do not have a global human rights conscience, they may not respond to human rights violations taking place far from their home. Not every consumer based in Europe is bothered by footballs manufactured in Pakistan employing child labour or chemical pollution caused by a toy manufacturing plant in China. In addition, stakeholders may not fully understand the complex ethical dimensions involved in a given product or service.[157] For example, even environmentally-conscious consumers may find it difficult to compare and then choose the product which is most environment-friendly. Besides, one does not usually boycott each and every product or service. Stakeholders may also think that their conduct will not change the behaviour of a targeted corporation, may not know 'where to apply pressure',[158] or worse may be bewildered by corporate acquisitions (such as of Body Shop by L'Oreal)[159] whereby the distinction between ethical and unethical conduct is lost. Thus a boycott, bad public exposure or 'naming and shaming' will not damage the reputation of concerned corporations in all cases.[160]

It should also be considered that although consumers or investors might want to support human rights, they may balk at the cost of doing so. The more the variance in price between the products and services of X and Y, the less the chances that rewards and sanctions will flow from consumers and investors.[161] The economic capacity of stakeholders, the amount of value they

---

155 Parkinson, above n. 26, 50 (emphasis added).
156 In the age of the internet, stakeholders can know the policies and actions of different corporations in a short span of time.
157 P. Auger et al., 'What will Consumers Pay for Social Product Features?' *Journal of Business Ethics*, 2003, vol. 42, 281, at 296, 299.
158 Stone, above n. 34, pp. 89–90.
159 Editorial, 'Body Shop Sale has the Whiff of Hypocrisy', *South China Morning Post*, 19 March 2006, A10.
160 P. Muchlinski, 'Human Rights and Multinationals: Is There a Problem?' *International Affairs*, 2001, vol. 77, 31, at 39.
161 R. Liubicic, 'Corporate Codes of Conduct and Product Labelling Schemes: The Limits and Possibilities of Promoting International Labour Rights through Private Initiatives', *Law and Policy in International Business*, 1998, vol. 39, 111, at 117–19.

accord to human rights and the affordability of products made in a socially responsible manner will determine to a great extent whether the third assumption turns out to be valid.

Another factor that might work against the business case hypothesis is that consumers and investors may be too hooked on a particular brand name or designer label for the divergence in X's and Y's actions to affect their choice. As Stone points out, consumers might not be in a 'position' to change their market preferences, especially because no viable alternative is available.[162] One could also not ignore the impact of a given product becoming a 'symbol of status or coolness' (e.g. Apple's iPhone), for if that happens, consumers are likely to persist with the product even if they knew that it was manufactured under harsh labour conditions, say, in Foxconn factories in China.[163]

In short, there is no universal or absolute business case for human rights that applies to all kinds of corporations operating in any sector. It will not hold true, for instance, in cases of companies which have no image to protect or which cannot afford to suffer short-term economic loss under the expectation of long-term profits or value enhancement. Similarly, there might (or ought) not to be a business case for certain industries (e.g. tobacco, drug trafficking, and child prostitution). Therefore, the business case for human rights should be treated with caution.[164] Although adherence to human rights norms may bring financial benefits to corporations, this assertion is subject to several uncertain, fluctuating and contestable conditions. There are also several variables linked to the financial performance of a corporation; thus, dissecting one variable and attributing a certain percentage of profits to its influence may not be that convincing. Nor is it always easy to quantify goodwill (generated through acting responsibly) in monetary terms.[165]

The effect of the 'prisoner's dilemma' on corporate behaviour

There may be various reasons why some corporations may not adopt policies or take action to comply with their human rights responsibilities. In view of the fact that corporations are considered economic actors which act rationally,[166] it should be useful to evaluate the economic rationale behind several

---

162 Stone, above n. 34, pp. 90–1.
163 Students and Scholars Against Corporate Misbehaviour (SACOM), *Workers as Machines: Military Management in Foxconn*, Hong Kong: SACOM, 2010. Available at: http://sacom.hk/wp-content/uploads/2010/10/report-on-foxconn-workers-as-machines_sacom3.pdf (accessed 20 June 2011).
164 F. Wettstein, *Multinational Corporations and Global Justice: Human Rights Obligations of a Quasi-Governmental Institution*, Stanford: Stanford Business Books, 2009, pp. 276–80.
165 Porter and Kramer, above n. 3, p. 82–3.
166 R. Posner, *Economic Analysis of Law*, 5th edn, New York: Aspen Publishers, 1998, pp. 3–4.

corporations hesitating to take a walk on the road of human rights.[167] With the help of the prisoner's dilemma, it is argued that some corporations may hesitate to embrace human rights policies because of uncertainty about the stance of their competitors.

If corporations assume responsibility for the protection and promotion of human rights, they have to conduct their business differently. This acting differently – formulating policies, taking actions, monitoring conduct, etc. – will invariably involve some extra expenditure on their part.[168] This brings to the fore the issue of corporations comparing the *costs* of acting differently with the potential *benefits* that may ensue. Unless corporations see ascertainable (rather than speculative) benefits in adopting pro-human rights policies, they are likely to face a business dilemma because costs are generally more certain and easily identifiable than 'potential' and perhaps 'long-term' benefits. Should corporations, then, accept human rights responsibilities or not? This corporate quandary can be understood with the help of the prisoner's dilemma.

The prisoner's dilemma is a situation in which two (or more) persons have to decide on a given issue. Each person has an option to 'co-operate' or 'defect', but each of them may decide to defect in order to maximize their own advantage, even if that harms the other party or hinders the production of common good.[169] Let us assume that two corporations, X and Y, have to decide whether or not to assume human rights responsibilities. Both X and Y have two choices: either to assume responsibilities or not. If both X and Y decide to assume human rights responsibilities, neither will have a competitive (dis)advantage over the other. Similarly, if both decide *not* to assume responsibilities, neither of them will have a competitive (dis)advantage over the other. Whether they have competitive (dis)advantage *vis-à-vis* other corporations in the market, and how assuming responsibilities translates into economic gain under market settings, is an altogether different question. If X decides to assume human rights responsibilities but not Y, X will have a competitive disadvantage *vis-à-vis* Y in terms of the resultant expenditure. Conversely, if X decides not to assume responsibilities whereas Y decides otherwise (i.e. assumes responsibilities), Y will have a competitive disadvantage *vis-à-vis* X.

---

167 Sethi identifies the economics of 'free rider' as one of the rationales. S. Sethi, 'Globalisation and the Good Corporation: A Need for Proactive Co-existence', *Journal of Business Ethics*, 2003, vol. 43, 21, at 27. See also Muchlinski, above n. 160, pp. 35–6.

168 Corporations, for example, would have to outlay extra resources to pay better wages, not employ child labour, invest in the development of environmentally-friendly technology, or abandon a project altogether if it turns out to be harmful for the local community, etc. See K. Herrmann, 'Corporate Social Responsibility and Sustainable Development: The European Union Initiative as a Case Study', *Indiana Journal of Global Legal Studies*, 2004, vol. 11, 205, at 219.

169 S. Scalet, 'Prisoner's Dilemma, Cooperative Norms, and Codes of Business Ethics', *Journal of Business Ethics*, 2006, vol. 65, 309, at 310.

Despite the initial competitive disadvantage that X or Y may have due to one of them assuming human rights responsibilities, this might convert into economic gain in a market setting because of a certain amount of goodwill that will arise from the assumption of these responsibilities. As we have seen above, the gain, if any, and the extent of it will depend on several unpredictable assumptions. This uncertainty triggers the prisoner's dilemma and in turn undercuts the business case for human rights. On the basis of an analysis of the possible consequences of one's conduct, it is likely that rational corporations like X and Y would like to play safe.[170] Given the uncertainty about the behaviour of the other party, the safest (not necessarily the best) course will be to not assume human rights responsibilities, as doing so might place a corporation at a competitive disadvantage *vis-à-vis* other corporations that are not wedded to the agenda of human rights.

The above propositions should be read, however, subject to certain riders. The results are likely to vary if X and Y are allowed to communicate before making a decision, if they knew beforehand how the other is going to act, or if they play this game not just once but repeatedly.[171] For example, if they are able to communicate beforehand, there is transparency in their decision-making process and if the game is played more than once, both X and Y may decide to co-operate (i.e. assume responsibility towards human rights and gain optimal economic dividends).[172] There is also a possibility, as noted by Zamagni, that the conduct of virtuous corporations, which obtain 'optimal results', might influence the behaviour of not-so-virtuous and sceptical corporations.[173]

One should also not ignore the limitations of using the prisoner's dilemma model to understand and explain complex corporate behaviour. Critics point out that it is too simplistic to predict the behaviour of corporations in market settings on the basis of the prisoner's dilemma game played in a controlled environment.[174] Nevertheless, the prisoner's dilemma framework still serves an important purpose. It demonstrates that at least some corporations may hesitate to embrace human rights responsibilities because they are unsure about the behaviour of their competitors. In a situation of uncertainty, the

---

170 M. Velasquez, 'International Business, Morality, and the Common Good', *Business Ethics Quarterly*, 1992, vol. 2, 27, at 34–5.
171 Notes, 'Finding Strategic Corporate Citizenship: A New Game Theoretic View', *Harvard Law Review*, 2004, vol. 117, 1957, at 1964–65; Velasquez, above n. 170, pp. 35–6.
172 Axelrod develops a variation of prisoner's dilemma (iterated prisoner's dilemma) in which actors who have frequent encounters may start co-operating with each other rather than defecting. R. Axelrod, *The Evolution of Cooperation*, London: Penguin Books, 1990.
173 Zamagni, above n. 139, p. 584.
174 Notes, above n. 171, pp. 1961–62. See also R. Solomon, 'Game Theory as a Model for Business and Business Ethics', *Business Ethics Quarterly*, 1999, vol. 9, 11.

safest position, at least for some corporations, will be not to commit to the project of human rights' realization. The weaker the positive link between corporate citizenship and financial performance, the more opportunities there will be for the prisoner's dilemma to dissuade corporations from the task of promoting human rights.

Why should corporations have human rights responsibilities?

After showing why the position taken by Friedman and Sternberg is untenable and why the business case for human rights does not provide a sound basis to ground the human rights responsibilities of companies, I now make positive arguments to demonstrate why companies should have such responsibilities. These arguments seek to augment several alternative principles advanced by scholars to justify the imposition of human rights responsibilities on corporations.[175] It is argued that all corporations ought to be subjected to human rights obligations because of their *relation to* and *position in* society. I explore two strands of this rationale.

The duty of corporations as social organs

Corporations should comply with human rights norms simply because they are social organs.[176] Both the limbs of this claim – that corporations are social organs and that human rights embody such moral-cum-legal norms which every organ of society should follow – can be supported.[177] Despite suggestions that corporations are purely wealth maximizing economic entities, it is undeniable at this point of time that corporations are social organs too. Corporations consist of the people, operated by the people and exist for the people. Bratspies writes that companies are important 'organs of society' by any definition: 'They own property; pay taxes; consume raw materials; generate goods, services, and wastes; and play a central role in the lives of their workers and customers.'[178] The *unpacking* of the corporation reveals that it is an aggregation of individuals glued together by a common purpose. These individuals,

---

175 Dodd, above n. 4; Dine, above n. 39; Sheehy, above n. 54, 230; Wettstein, above n. 164; S. Ratner, 'Corporation and Human Rights: A Theory of Legal Responsibility', *Yale Law Journal*, 2001, vol. 111, 443.
176 J. Zerk, *Multinational and Corporate Social Responsibility: Limitations and Opportunities in International Law*, Cambridge: Cambridge University Press, 2006, p. 32.
177 K. Davis and R. Blomstrom, *Business and Society: Environment and Responsibility*, 3rd edn, New York: McGraw-Hill, 1975, pp. 44–5.
178 R. Bratspies, '"Organs of Society": A Plea for Human Rights Accountability for Transnational Enterprises and Other Business Entities', *Michigan State Journal of International Law*, 2005, vol. 13, 9, at 15.

while acting alone and as natural persons, are integral organs of society and their social status should not cease to exist merely because they decide to act collectively and in an artificial form.

If it is accepted that corporations are social organs, then they ought to comply with basic moral and legal norms of society in which they operate, for not doing so will lead to chaos and instability. Corporations, as moral agents,[179] should observe human rights, which reflect such basic rules of the society. The idea that corporations should have human rights responsibilities is grounded not only in national and international laws, but also in rules of ethical custom and social morality.[180] To illustrate, the right against slavery could be deduced from an implied *moral* rule that certain things are not to be put in the market place for sale, even if such a rule reduces profits or efficiency. It is this rule which underpins the abolition of slavery in that the sale of human beings in open markets was considered repugnant to the moral minimum. Therefore, human rights – which are based upon the worth and dignity of human beings and are non-negotiable – should bind those actors who do business either individually or collectively. Bowie argues that if corporations do not observe certain moral minimum rules (which various human rights embody) of society, their conduct would become 'unjust':

> ... multinational corporations are obligated to follow these [minimum] moral rules. *Because the multinational is practicing business in the society and because these moral norms are necessary for the existence of the society, the multinational has an obligation to support those norms.* Otherwise, multinationals would be in the position of benefiting from doing business with the society while at the same time engaging in activity that undermines the society. *Such conduct would be unjust.*[181]

It is vital to emphasize that corporations are under such a duty not merely for their survival (i.e. the business case for human rights), but because they have a moral and/or legal obligation to do so.

One could also apply the neighbour principle developed by Lord Atkin in *Donoghue* v. *Stevenson*[182] to ground social or human rights responsibilities of corporations. In the instant case, the question before that court was whether

---

179 T. Donaldson, *Corporations and Morality*, Englewood Cliffs, New Jersey: Prentice-Hall Inc., 1982, pp. 18–32; P. French, *Corporate Ethics*, Fort Worth: Harcourt Brace College Publishers, 1995, pp. 9–33.
180 T. Donaldson, 'Moral Minimum for Multinationals', *Ethics and International Affairs*, 1989, vol. 3, 163, at 167; J. Donnelly, *Universal Human Rights: In Theory and Practice*, Ithaca: Cornell University Press, 1989, p. 17.
181 N. Bowie, 'The Moral Obligations of Multinational Corporations' in T. Donaldson and T. W. Dunfee (eds.), *Ethics in Business and Economics*, vol. 1, Aldershot: Dartmouth Publishing, 1997, p. 249 (emphasis added).
182 *Donoghue* v. *Stevenson* [1932] AC 562 (HL).

the manufacturer of a product was under any legal duty to the ultimate purchaser or consumer to take reasonable care that the article is free from defect when the product is not sold directly to the consumer.[183] Moving on from 'a general public sentiment of moral wrongdoing' to a rule of law, Lord Atkin formulated the famous neighbour principle as follows: 'The rule that you are to love your neighbour becomes in law, you must not injure your neighbour; . . . You *must take reasonable care to avoid acts or omissions which you can reasonably foresee would be likely to injure your neighbour.*'[184]

Therefore, every corporation (like any other social being) should take reasonable care that its policies and actions do not violate the interests of its neighbours (i.e. those stakeholders who are affected by the conduct of a given corporation).[185] This idea of exercising care so as not to harm the interest of one's neighbours is arguably based on a mixture of self-interest, cooperation and reciprocity. Such a duty on corporations is justified on the ground that they are in a better position to know the consequences of their conduct and take remedial action.

The position *to both violate and promote human rights*

One main 'overarching objective' of international human rights law is to protect human rights.[186] How could human rights be protected? Human rights are protected by imposing and enforcing duties. The next question is who should be subject to such duties? In order to fulfil this objective fully, obligations should arguably be imposed on *all* those entities, rather than being limited to state actors, which are in a position to violate human rights.

Although the idea of rights or human rights may not have been 'tied' to states jurisprudentially or historically,[187] human rights generally came to be regarded as a protective shield against the powers of an all-pervasive state.[188] Human rights secured a field for individuals in which they could enjoy

---

183 Ibid., pp. 578–9.
184 Ibid., p. 580 (emphasis added).
185 The following test laid down by Wood is useful to ascertain who the neighbours of a given corporation are: 'Businesses are not responsible for solving all social problems. They are, however, responsible *for solving* problems that they have caused, and they are responsible *for helping to solve* problems and social issues related to their business operations and interests.' D. Wood, 'Corporate Social Performance Revisited', *Academy of Management Review*, 1991, vol. 16, 691, at 697 (emphasis added).
186 D. Kinley and J. Tadaki, 'From Talk to Walk: The Emergence of Human Rights Responsibilities for Corporations at International Law', *Virginia Journal of International Law*, 2004, vol. 44, 931, at 962–3.
187 Ratner, above n. 175, pp. 468–9.
188 A. Reinisch, 'The Changing International Legal Framework for Dealing with Non-State Actors' in P. Alston (ed.), *Non-State Actors and Human Rights*, New York: Oxford University Press, 2005, p. 37, at 37–8.

freedoms and liberties without any unjustified state interference. The state had such power because it enjoyed a special *position vis-à-vis* individuals, by virtue of social contract or otherwise. But power alone was not sufficient to violate or promote human rights; there must also be opportunities to do so. The state had these opportunities because it regulated the lives of people and also provided many services to them.[189] These opportunities were again provided by the position that the state had in relation to its people. 'Position', therefore, led to two things: power as well as opportunity to both violate and promote human rights.

Over the years, this position of the state (the principal status as human rights violator and promoter) loosened as non-state actors such as corporations acquired a similar position, because of the delegation or outsourcing of powers and functions by states in a globalized and free market economy.[190] In such a scenario, if the objective is to realize human rights to the fullest extent, then logically corporations, which enjoy a position – both power and opportunity – to violate as well as promote human rights, should be subjected to human rights obligations. Corporations are now performing some of the state's functions and if the loop of human rights obligations is not extended to cover them, it would mean that states can bypass their human rights obligations by privatization and outsourcing of their activities to companies.[191]

As pointed out in Chapter 1, there are no serious theoretical or practical impediments to expanding human rights obligations to companies.[192] Of course, the obligations of corporations cannot be similar to that of states, but this is different from saying that corporations cannot have human rights obligations at all. Some recent developments (e.g. the horizontal application of human rights[193] and the introduction of express constitutional provisions for the private application of human rights)[194] also suggest that the extension of human rights obligations to corporations is not only desirable but also

---

189 International Council on Human Rights Policy (ICHRP), *Beyond Voluntarism: Human Rights and the Developing International Legal Obligations of Companies*, Versoix: ICHRP, 2002, p. 9.
190 Reinisch, above n. 188, pp. 74–7.
191 M.P. Singh, 'Fundamental Rights, State Action and Cricket in India', *Asia Pacific Law Review*, 2005, vol. 13, 203, at 205.
192 Ratner, above n. 175, pp. 496–524; A. Clapham, *Human Rights Obligations of Non-State Actors*, Oxford: Oxford University Press, 2006, pp. 33–58.
193 The 'horizontal' application of human rights refers to a scenario in which the protection of human rights is invoked by an individual against the conduct of a non-state actor. See, for example, *Guerra* v. *Italy* (1998) 26 EHRR 357; *Visakha* v. *State of Rajasthan* AIR 1997 SC 3011. See generally M. Hunt, 'The "Horizontal Effect" of the Human Rights Act', *Public Law*, 1998, 423.
194 Article 8(2) of the Constitution of the Republic of South Africa 1996, for instance, provides: 'A provision of the Bill of Rights binds a natural or a juristic person if, and to the extent that, it is applicable, taking into account the nature of the right and the nature of any duty imposed by the right.'

practicable to implement. One may also refer to a relatively old example to buttress this point. As early as 1950, the Indian Constitution consciously made available the protection of certain fundamental rights (such as the prohibition of untouchability and forced labour) against private individuals,[195] simply because such non-state actors could infringe these human rights.[196]

In short, corporations should be subject to human rights responsibilities because of their current position in society. They possess not only enormous power and opportunity to violate a range of human rights in diverse settings but also have the potential to promote human rights due to their economic, operational, technological and human resource capabilities.

Summary

This chapter made three interrelated claims concerning the 'why' challenge. First, it tried to show that the thesis propounded by scholars like Friedman and Sternberg – that the only responsibility of business is to maximize shareholders' profit or value – is narrow, unsound and outdated in the current economic climate. Second, I pointed out why it is problematic to rely too much on the business case for human rights. Although there is some merit in the business case hypothesis, this merit should not be blown out of proportion in view of the effect of the prisoner's dilemma and the unpredictable nature of the business case assumptions. Third, this chapter advanced a positive argument to justify the imposition of human rights obligations on companies. I argued that all corporations should observe human rights norms while doing business because of their *relation to* and *position in* society. This contention does not seek to reject or undermine the role of corporations in wealth maximization in society. The only limited claim advanced here is that the right to maximize profit should not be at the cost of the rights of other members of the society and that corporations should not be left outside the net of human rights law merely because they are predominantly economic entities.[197]

Berle was not wrong when he submitted almost 80 years ago that 'you cannot abandon emphasis on "the view that business corporations exist for the sole purpose of making profits for their stockholders" *until* such time as you are prepared to offer a clear and reasonably enforceable scheme of responsibilities to someone else'.[198] Now the time has come when an over-emphasis on

---

195 G. Austin, *The Indian Constitution: Cornerstone of a Nation*, Oxford: Clarendon Press, 1966, p. 51.
196 Singh, above n. 191, p. 205.
197 Arrow examines various scenarios in which profit maximization should not be allowed. K. Arrow, 'Social Responsibility and Economic Efficiency', *Public Policy*, 1973, vol. 21, 303.
198 Berle, 'A Note', above n. 4, p. 1367.

the profit maximization thesis should be abandoned in favour of a more balanced view of the role of corporations in society, a view that is capable of meeting the conditions laid down by Berle. Human rights law provides a framework that can be applied to deduce the social responsibilities that corporations have towards their stakeholders. Whereas this chapter developed a justification for why corporations should have such responsibilities, the next chapter examines the principle with reference to which human rights responsibilities of corporations that operate in many countries could be ascertained.

6 How to behave in 'Rome'?

Determining standards applicable to MNCs

This chapter seeks to investigate one issue related to the *what* challenge: what standards of human rights should an MNC apply while operating in different countries with vastly diverse political, social, economic, religious and cultural circumstances? Certain human rights have acquired the *jus cogens* character and regarding these, there will be no or minimal divergence between the standards applicable across the world.[1] MNCs across the globe should not generally face any difficulty in implementing the universal mandate prohibiting, for example, slavery, forced labour, torture, or genocide. However, the precise contour of many other universal human rights is likely to vary from one state to another.[2] For instance, the exact scope of the right to freedom of expression, the right to privacy, the right to a fair trial, the right to fair wages, the right to health, the right to strike or the right to a clean environment is not universally fixed. Amidst the presence of varying standards of human rights, the *localization of universality* becomes a key issue.[3]

In case more than one set of standards regarding a given human rights obligation exists, should MNCs apply the standards of the country of operation (host standards), the standards of the country where the parent corporation is incorporated (home standards), or adopt the same standards throughout the operations of a corporate group (international standards)? This situation will invariably present a formidable challenge to MNCs, especially in those cases where the host state lacks commitment to protect and promote human rights or boasts an oppressive regime. How do, or should, MNCs overcome

---

1 M. Jungk, 'A Practical Guide to Addressing Human Rights Concerns for Companies Operating Abroad' in M. Addo (ed.), *Human Rights Standards and the Responsibility of Transnational Corporations*, The Hague: Kluwer Law International, 1999, p. 171, at 176.
2 For example, '[t]here are no absolute standards of what constitutes low wages or, on the other end of the spectrum, good wages.' E. Mihaly, 'Multinational Companies and Wages in Low-Income Countries', *Journal of Small and Emerging Business Law*, 1999, vol. 3, 1, at 2.
3 The controversy surrounding the involvement of corporations in internet censorship in China demonstrates that there are no universal or common standards as to what constitutes the freedom of speech.

this challenge? This issue has not received adequate attention in human rights literature. Even the existing regulatory regimes hardly offer any help to MNCs in resolving this day-to-day dilemma or the solution that they offer is worse than the problem. For example, although the ILO Declaration provides a yardstick, it paves the way for MNCs, in effect, to comply with the standards of a host country. Paragraph 38 of the ILO Declaration illustrates this. It stipulates that 'multinational enterprises should maintain the highest standards of safety and health, in conformity with national requirements' and the experience of special hazards that an MNC might have.[4] Qualifying 'highest' standards with 'national requirements' will often result in merely complying with no or minimal safety and health standards when MNCs operate in developing or under-developed countries. This is precisely what happened in Bhopal – UCC-UCIL perhaps operated in compliance with the non-existent or lax Indian standards, but not in accordance with the 'highest standards of safety and health,' say, as then prevailing in the US.

This chapter, therefore, tries to throw some light on this business dilemma. It begins with exploring the dilemma that MNCs face with regard to choosing one out of three separate standards of human rights applicable in a given case (assuming inconsistency among them). Then it moves on to explain the two approaches – the *business approach* and the *human approach* – which, I argue, do or should influence MNCs' choice regarding applicable human rights standards. How these two approaches could and should guide MNCs' decisions is further illustrated with the help of Bhopal. It is contended that MNCs should discard the business approach in favour of the human approach, for reliance on the former will often result in human rights violations. In other words, humanizing business demands adherence to the human approach.

How to behave in 'Rome': Three potential options

The proposition that MNCs will normally have an opportunity of choosing one out of three options (*host, home,* or *international* standards) is based on two assumptions. First of all, it is assumed that there is a disparity between the three sets of standards. As noted above, such disparity is very much possible regarding many human rights. The second assumption is that the human rights standards that apply in a host country are lower than the international as well as the home standards. This assumption about the general superiority of home (or even international) standards is valid because the 'home' of a majority of MNCs is *still* in the developed world.[5] On many occasions, developed countries are the host states or developing countries are the home states.

---

4 ILO Tripartite Declaration of Principles Concerning Multinational Enterprises and Social Policy 2000, reprinted in *ILM*, 2002, vol. 41,186, at 193 (para. 38).
5 United Nations Conference on Trade and Development, *World Investment Report 2010: Investing in a Low-Carbon Economy*, New York: UN, 2010, p. 17.

However, in these scenarios MNCs do not face the kind of business dilemmas explored here. This chapter deals with those situations when MNCs based in developed countries operate – through subsidiaries, joint ventures or contractors – in developing countries to lower their operating costs.

Sometimes it is erroneously assumed that there are merely two sets of standards: home and host. Boatright, for instance, writes that there are two extreme options:

> In answer to the question "When in Rome, do what?" there are two extremes. The absolutist position is that business ought to be conducted in the same way the world over with no double standards. . . . This view might be expressed as "When in Rome or anywhere else, do as you would do at home." The opposite extreme is relativism, which may be expressed in the familiar adage, "When in Rome do as the Romans do."[6]

It is unwarranted, and to some extent fallacious, to assume that 'home' standards match 'international' standards, or that 'home' standards would *always* be higher than 'host' standards. There could be situations where the standards applicable even in developed countries (the home states of MNCs) may fall short of international standards. The advice that 'when in Rome or anywhere else, do as you would do at home' will not work when the home standards are lower than the host standards. For instance, a Chinese or an Indian MNC operating in Europe could not hope to maintain Chinese and Indian labour standards or wage levels with impunity. It is, therefore, more plausible to construct MNCs' choices as to available standards in terms of three potential options: host standards, home standards and international standards.

Against this background, let me explore more closely the three options regarding the human rights standards available to MNCs and also suggest advantages as well as limitations associated with choosing one option over the other.

'Host' standards

The 'host' country of an MNC is the country where it operates through its subsidiaries or otherwise. Following the standards adopted by the country of operation is perhaps the easiest option available to MNCs. MNCs that decide to apply host standards will, by implication, bypass – as a matter of policy – international standards and the standards that they might be applying at home or in other operating countries. A standard explanation for such practice is that in order to do business in different countries there is no option but to follow the local applicable laws. Yahoo!, Microsoft and Google, for instance,

---

6 J. Boatright, *Ethics and the Conduct of Business*, 4th edn, Upper Saddle River: Prentice Hall, 2003, p. 414.

used this argument to explain why they agreed to internet censorship in China.[7] Another potential justification for adopting host standards might be that 'when in Rome, do as Romans do', because otherwise MNCs will have a competitive disadvantage *vis-à-vis* local corporations which are normally bound only by the 'local' standards.

Some MNCs may, however, adopt a slightly different policy than to apply the host standards in a routine manner. Some MNCs will generally apply host standards, but occasionally they may choose to apply the *host-plus* standards. Instead of adopting a standard formula, these MNCs might adopt a more flexible 'pick and choose' policy and decide on a case-by-case basis if applying standards higher than the host standards will make business sense. The higher standards in a given scenario may be adopted if doing so has the potential to earn more profits, generate goodwill, attract and retain better staff, or help in occupying a high moral ground *vis-à-vis* competitors. These measures in business management literature are often regarded as part of 'strategic' corporate citizenship.[8] The flexible 'pick and choose' policy nonetheless remains a variation of the application of host standards, for there is no consistent and principled departure from observing the host standards. The higher standards are essentially applied (if at all and often temporarily) merely as a sheer business tactic.

What are the pros and cons of MNCs applying the human rights standards of their host countries? It will usually be easier for MNCs to observe host country standards. However, this option may not be the most efficient, or the safest course available. To implement varying standards, MNCs would have to draft separate codes of conduct for each country of operation and also adopt varied implementation strategies, including training programs for staff. Further, in view of the fact that host standards (i.e. the standards prevailing in many developing countries) may not always offer adequate human rights protection, MNCs may be accused of violating human rights by adopting double standards.

'Home' standards

The second option that an MNC has is to apply in host countries the standards of its home country. The 'home' of an MNC is regarded as the country where the parent corporation is incorporated, though a plea is made to re-conceptualize the concept of the 'home' of MNCs which have become stateless or de-nationalized entities.[9] The adoption of this policy, in effect, means

---

7 S. Deva, 'Corporate Complicity in Internet Censorship in China: Who Cares for the Global Compact or the Global Online Freedom Act?' *George Washington International Law Review*, 2007, vol. 39, 255, at 287–9.
8 M. Porter and M. Kramer, 'The Link between Competitive Advantage and Corporate Social Responsibility', *Harvard Business Review*, 2006, vol. 84:12, 78, at 88–91.
9 J. Dine, 'Multinational Enterprises: International Codes and the Challenge for "Sustainable Development"', *Non-State Actors and International Law*, 2001, vol. 1, 81, at 84–9; J. Zerk, *Multinational and Corporate Social Responsibility: Limitations and Opportunities in International Law*, Cambridge: Cambridge University Press, 2006, pp. 146–50.

choosing the higher of the home and host standards. A corporate policy to apply higher home standards in host countries will face several challenges.[10] The implementation of higher standards will undoubtedly demand additional expenditure, resulting in a possible competitive disadvantage to the concerned MNCs *vis-à-vis* other local corporations operating in the host state. This may also raise concerns in the host country about the erosion of, or disregard for, national sovereignty. Moreover, this approach could lead to situations of conflict between the standards applicable at two places. For example, whereas the home country of an MNC may recognize the freedom of association and the right to collective bargaining, the host country may prohibit the formation of independent trade unions and/or the right to strike.

Some of these challenges are similar to those that are raised to cast doubt on the desirability of home state extraterritorial laws seeking to impose home standards on corporations operating abroad.[11] However, the differences between host and home standards should not necessarily or always result in conflict.[12] There is no real conflict where compliance with both home and host standards is by and large possible. Rather, conflicts ordinarily only arise when the host standards prescribe what the home standards proscribe, or *vice versa*. For instance, laws of host states would hardly prescribe employment of child or forced labour, require the manufacture of potentially harmful substances, or demand the payment of less-than-living wages or pollution of the environment – something which the laws of the home state may expressly prohibit.

In terms of advantages, the adoption of home standards above, or in addition to, host standards should result in a better protection of human rights. This might also bring benefits to the concerned MNCs. Besides attracting and retaining the most talented personnel, this policy may help such MNCs gain a competitive edge over other MNCs and local corporations that continue to apply lower standards. It is also likely that MNCs that adopt higher standards will avoid potential litigation for indulging in human rights abuses.

'International' standards

In cases where the relevant international standards are higher than the home standards, it is possible for an MNC to adopt the former for the whole

---

10 T. McGarity, 'Bhopal and the Export of Hazardous Technologies', *Texas International Law Journal*, 1985, vol. 20, 333, at 335–6.
11 S. Deva, 'Acting Extraterritorially to Tame Multinational Corporations for Human Rights Violations: Who Should "Bell the Cat?"' *Melbourne Journal of International Law*, 2004, vol. 5, 37, at 57–63.
12 M. Gibney and R. Emerick, 'The Extraterritorial Application of United States Law and the Protection of Human Rights: Holding Multinational Corporations to Domestic and International Standards', *Temple International and Comparative Law Journal*, 1996, vol. 10, 123, at 143–4.

corporate group.[13] Complying with international standards, however, does not mean that an MNC would be following the 'same' standards everywhere. I will show below with the help of Bhopal that international standards (or the home standards for that matter) could be adjusted in view of those local differences which help in promoting the realization of human rights in the country of operation.

But why should an MNC adopt international standards? The following example may help in understanding one of the rationales. If the environmental standards in Europe are more stringent than those that prevail in the US, even the application of the US (home) standards in a host country like China may not be the best thing to do when most of the goods manufactured therein are sold in Europe. In view of this, some MNCs may find it desirable to adopt the highest possible international standards as a risk management strategy.[14]

The adoption of international standards for human rights is likely to result in the evolution of comparable standards in all countries where a given MNC operates.[15] This should also cut down the business dilemma that MNCs face in terms of applicable standards in different countries, because MNCs adopting international standards would not have to deliberate upon this question afresh every time they start operations in a new place. However, it will not always be easy to formulate international standards, even regarding those issues which enjoy universal acceptance. Furthermore, as with the application of home standards, the adoption of international standards may also create a problem of conflict with the standards prevailing in a host country.

Resolving the dilemma of varying standards: two approaches

Several guiding principles have been posited to help corporations in resolving the dilemma of varying human rights standards. Such principles often try to tackle the business dilemma within an ethical, moral or human rights framework.[16] For example, Boatright argues that though neither an absolutist nor a relativist position is satisfactory,[17] home standards need not be applied

---

13 Applying the 'consistent best practice' principle, Kerr *et al.* argue that companies must apply the highest standards throughout their business operations. M. Kerr, R. Janda and C. Pitts, *Corporate Social Responsibility: A Legal Analysis*, Markham, Ont.: LexisNexis, 2009, p. 290.
14 N. Hertz, 'New Ethics: Just Do it Right – Smart Firms Know Acting Socially Helps the Bottom Line'. Available at: http://articles.sfgate.com/2005-05-15/opinion/17371943_1_ethical-tobacco-control-framework-convention (accessed 17 June 2011).
15 M. Addo, 'Human Rights and Transnational Corporations – An Introduction' in Addo (ed.), above n. 1, p. 31.
16 Boatright, 4th edn, above n. 6, pp. 411–45; T. Donaldson, *Corporations and Morality*, Englewood Cliffs: Prentice Hall, 1982, pp. 32–4.
17 Boatright, 4th edn, above n. 6, p. 439.

everywhere in view of 'morally relevant' or cultural differences.[18] Donaldson, on the other hand, proposes an 'ethical algorithm' which MNCs could use to find out if the adoption of lower standards in the host country could be justified.[19]

Although ethical, moral or human rights frameworks do provide useful guidance on resolving this business dilemma, these principles do not examine the issue from the *internal* standpoint of corporations. It may be more useful to explore potential guiding principles by placing oneself in the shoes of corporate executives who might be operating with a particular vision of their business enterprises. Based on this understanding, I suggest two approaches – the 'business approach' and the 'human approach' – that do (descriptive) or should (prescriptive) guide MNCs' decisions as to the standards that they apply in a given case. As the titles itself indicate, *business* and *human* respectively are central to these two approaches, which represent contrasting positions as to the place and role of corporations in society. It is suggested that one of these two approaches invariably underpins decisions taken by MNCs as to which human rights standards they should apply out of the three options canvassed above.

No standard standards: The business *approach*

The business approach perceives corporations primarily as economic entities and logically puts profit as reflected in the financial statements first and foremost. This approach is grounded in the well-known assertion that the only social responsibility of business is to increase the profits for its shareholders. As stockholders' profit maximization guides the business approach, the protection and promotion of stakeholders' human rights is not, in itself, considered a part of 'profits' quantified in dollars. For this reason, the business approach does not take a principled stand *vis-à-vis* human rights: it is profits that will determine whether human rights are to be respected and if so, then which standards are to be followed. The 'business case' for human rights (discussed in Chapter 5) is also a variation of this approach in that corporations are counselled to respect human rights in order to gain and maintain an economic advantage, or as a sound risk management exercise.

MNCs that consciously or otherwise adopt the business approach do not have a consistent policy towards the standards that they should apply in a given scenario. Instead, varying standards of human rights may be applied as per infinite local differences. By citing local difficulties in applying the home or uniform standards, the MNCs subscribing to this approach typically settle for host standards, which may be inferior and inadequate. Apart from savings on operational costs, MNCs' choice to adopt the business approach is

---

18 Ibid., pp. 414–17.
19 Donaldson, above n. 16, pp. 95–108.

influenced by legal principles that govern liability for human rights abuses within a corporate group. If parent corporations could be held liable for human rights violations committed by their subsidiaries, they might be more willing to adopt international standards for the whole corporate group instead of outsourcing their human rights responsibilities to their offshore subsidiaries. However, as a general rule across civil and common law jurisdictions, all corporations of a group are treated as separate legal entities and are protected by a veil that could be pierced or lifted only in limited circumstances, which are not always easy to prove.[20] It is arguable, therefore, that the existing legal principles relating to the issue of liability within a corporate group *indirectly* encourage MNCs to adopt varying human rights standards applicable in different host countries.[21]

The adoption of a business approach by MNCs could be challenged on several grounds. To begin with, this approach fails miserably to protect the human rights of people living in developing or under-developed countries where MNCs operate, and should be rejected simply on this ground. This argument is elaborated in greater detail below with the help of the Bhopal case. I have already shown in Chapter 5 why the classical view – which underpins the business approach – about the role of corporations in society is simply indefensible at this point in time on account of a fundamental shift in the position of both states and corporations.

The underlying assumption that the sole (or even predominant) obligation of corporations is to increase shareholders' profit is also shaky. People, of course, invest in corporations in order to maximize their economic gains and there is perhaps nothing wrong with this activity. But this is different from saying that *all* shareholders of an MNC might like it to maximize profits *at all costs*. Shareholders are human beings too and as part of society those people have multiple interests acting in different capacities. Shareholders as consumers or parents might expect to have access to safe products, or to products that are not manufactured using child labour or in a manner harmful to the environment. The business approach, however, fails to respond to such multiple interests of even its shareholders by simply treating all shareholders as one-dimensional, profit-driven persons or organizations.

The business approach is unsound on ethical and moral grounds too. Donaldson makes a strong case for corporations losing their 'moral right to exist' if they fail to perform 'minimal' duties to protect certain fundamental (human) rights.[22] The adoption of double standards by MNCs might result in

---

20 S. Deva, 'Corporate Code of Conduct Bill 2000: Overcoming Hurdles in Enforcing Human Rights Obligations Against Overseas Corporate Hands of Local Corporations', *Newcastle Law Review*, 2004, vol. 8, 87, at 101–3.
21 See R. Meeran, 'The Unveiling of Transnational Corporations: A Direct Approach' in Addo (ed.), above n. 1, p. 161.
22 Donaldson, above n. 16, pp. 62, 81.

breach of these minimal obligations. Therefore, it is arguable that 'any attempt by a multinational to take advantage of discrepancies between the home country and the host country in order to pursue profit . . . without considering the interests of all the stakeholders is immoral.'[23]

In short, it is contended that the business approach, which results in MNCs' applying varying standards of human rights as per local differences with a view only to economic gain, excessively supports the pursuit of profit maximization at the cost of undermining the human rights of stakeholders.

Realization of stakeholders' human rights: The human *approach*

In comparison to the business approach, the human approach would require MNCs to resolve their dilemma as to varying standards with reference to the impact of their decisions, actions or omissions on the realization of human rights of their stakeholders. The human approach takes a more holistic view of the role of corporations in society. It considers corporations an integral part of society; the role of corporations, according to this view, is multi-faceted rather than being limited to efficient wealth creation.[24] The goal of profit maximization is not to be pursued at the expense of other equally important social objectives such as the realization of human rights. Therefore, corporations should not undermine the human rights of their stakeholders while pursuing the task of wealth creation. The human approach would require that MNCs do not always stick to host standards as a rule, but explore if the application of home or international standards is likely to promote better protection and realization of stakeholders' human rights.

The human approach regards human rights above the profit principle and trade considerations. The *humanity* of this approach lies in the fact that it treats each 'human' as an end in itself. Since the existence of human beings is a prerequisite for anything else (including for the existence of corporations) and human rights embody the core interests of human beings,[25] these interests ought not to be subordinated to any other principle which is inferior in status, such as profit maximization or wealth creation.

Although the human approach demands 'a reinterpretation of the role of corporations, of their purpose and legitimacy beyond the profit margin',[26] it

---

23 N. Bowie, 'The Moral Obligations of Multinational Corporations' in T. Donaldson and T. Dunfee (eds.), *Ethics in Business and Economics*, vol. 1, Aldershot: Dartmouth Publishing, 1997, p. 241, at 243.
24 M. Fogarty, *Company and Corporation – One Law?*, London: Geoffrey Chapman, 1965, p. 9.
25 M. Czerny, 'Liberation Theology and Human Rights' in K. Mahoney and P. Mahoney (eds.), *Human Rights in the Twenty-first Century*, Dordrecht: Martinus Nijhoff Publishers, 1993, p. 36.
26 O. Wiggen and L. Bomann-Larsen, 'Addressing Side-Effect Harm in the Business Context: Conceptual and Practical Challenges' in L. Bomann-Larsen and O. Wiggen (eds.), *Responsibility in World Business: Managing Harmful Side-Effects of Corporate Activity*, Tokyo: United Nations University Press, 2004, p. 3.

neither undermines the wealth creation role of corporations, nor demands an application of uniform or universal standards by MNCs regarding all human rights. This approach acknowledges the important role that corporations play in creating wealth efficiently while staying within certain 'rules of the game'. It merely asserts that the protection and promotion of human rights should be an integral part of such rules of the game – not only because human rights are arguably the only universally acceptable aspirational currency,[27] but also because corporations themselves invoke human rights to protect their business interests.[28] In other words, the corporate contribution towards the realization of human rights and other developmental goals should be considered as part of the 'profits' or 'wealth' generated by corporations in both tangible and intangible ways.

Apart from a limited number of human rights that have acquired the status of *jus cogens* and/or *erga omnes* norms, the human approach does not advocate the application of uniform or universal standards by MNCs, as such uniformity might not be desirable or even workable regarding several human rights. MNCs are rather required to adopt a 'context-sensitive approach'[29] by keeping in mind morally relevant local differences.[30] As explained later in this chapter, only those local differences which facilitate the realization of human rights are to be treated as 'morally relevant'.

One might wonder if MNCs could adopt different standards even while guided by the human approach, how is it different from the business approach? Although MNCs could apply variable human rights standards under both the business and human approaches, there is a critical distinction in the reason for adopting different standards in each case. Whereas under the business approach *profit* dictates MNCs' choice to adopt variable (often inferior) host standards, the better *protection of human rights* is the driving force behind choosing different (not necessarily lower) standards under the human approach.

The human approach mooted in this book is based on a modified version of the stakeholder theory. 'The central claim of the stakeholder approach is that corporations are operated or ought to be operated for the benefit of all those who have a *stake* in the enterprise, including employees, customers, suppliers, and the local community'.[31] What is this 'stake', who are the 'holders' of this

---

27 L. Henkin, *The Age of Rights*, New York: Columbia University Press, 1990, p. ix.
28 M. Addo, 'The Corporation as a Victim of Human Rights Violations' in Addo (ed.), above n. 1, p. 190.
29 Wiggen and Bomann-Larsen terms this context-sensitive approach 'casuistic' in that it allows particularities to determine how moral decisions are made. Wiggen and Bomann-Larsen, above n. 26, pp. 6–7.
30 Bowie, above n. 23, p. 243. Bowie draws a prescriptive chart to find out when MNCs should (and should not) do in Rome as Romans do. Ibid., pp. 244–5.
31 J. Boatright, *Ethics and the Conduct of Business*, 5th edn, Upper Saddle River, New Jersey: Prentice Hall, 2007, p. 385 (emphasis in original). See also R. Freeman, *Strategic Management: A Stakeholder Approach*, Boston: Pitman, 1984, pp. 24–5.

stake, and how could the 'benefit of all' stakeholders be served? The stake implies some kind of interest — from employees' expectation of decent wages and working conditions to the community's desire for a clean environment.[32] The holders of this stake are all those who affect, or are affected by, the actions and performance of corporations.[33] The theory proposes a balancing exercise to ensure that the conflicting interests of different stakeholders are simultaneously served to the maximum extent possible.

This version of the stakeholder theory has been modified here by introducing a 'human rights' element into it. This is primarily done to redress some of the 'compelling criticisms' that the stakeholder theory has received.[34] For example, it is argued that the theory prescribes no method to balance stockholders' interests with stakeholders' interests.[35] One could counter this by pleading that human rights could provide a framework for achieving this balance: stockholders and stakeholders might disagree, but they are not likely to dismiss the human rights discourse altogether. Human rights norms set common standards of behaviour which corporations should adhere to while doing business. Moreover, merely because it is difficult to negotiate a balance between conflicting interests does not mean that such a balance cannot be achieved.[36] To illustrate, attempts have been made at national as well as international level to strike a balance between the intellectual property rights of pharmaceutical corporations and the availability of affordable life-saving drugs (as part of the right to health) to people.[37]

It is also contended that the stakeholder theory 'lacks any explicit theoretical moral grounding',[38] that it 'may result in abuse of . . . directors' discretion',[39] and that 'no stakeholder theorist has offered a detailed proposal for changes in corporate governance that would result in a stakeholder corporation'.[40] Bringing human rights within the framework of the stakeholder theory should also redress the first two concerns: human rights could not only

---

32 See A. Corfield, 'The Stakeholder Theory and its Future in Australian Corporate Governance: A Preliminary Analysis', *Bond Law Review*, 1998, vol. 10, 213, at 214.
33 J. Daniels *et al., Globalization and Business*, 1st edn, Upper Saddle River, New Jersey: Prentice Hall, 2002, p. 126; Freeman, above n. 31, p. 46.
34 Dine, above n. 9, pp. 223–5; M. Friedman, *Capitalism and Freedom*, 40th anniversary edition, Chicago: University of Chicago Press, 2002, pp. 133–4; Donaldson, above n. 16, pp. 45–7; E. Sternberg, *Just Business: Business Ethics in Action*, 2nd edn, Oxford: Oxford University Press, 2000, pp. 49–52.
35 Boatright, 5th edn, above n. 31, p. 387; Donaldson, above n. 16, p. 45.
36 J. Lucas, 'The Responsibilities of a Businessman' in W. Shaw (ed.), *Ethics at Work: Basic Readings in Business Ethics*, Oxford: Oxford University Press, 2003, p. 29.
37 See, e.g. S. Joseph, 'Pharmaceutical Corporations and Access to Drugs: The "Fourth Wave" of Corporate Human Rights Scrutiny', *Human Rights Quarterly*, 2003, vol. 25, 425; S. Vachani and N. Smith, 'Socially Responsible Pricing: Lessons from the Pricing of AIDS Drugs in Developing Countries', *California Management Review*, 2004, vol. 47, 117.
38 Donaldson, above n. 16, p. 46.
39 Corfield, above n. 32, p. 227.
40 Boatright, 5th edn, above n. 31, p. 388.

provide a firm grounding for the stakeholder theory, but could also afford guidelines for directors' decisions. Regarding the last concern, it could be said that appropriate structural changes could be made in the corporate governance model so as to give adequate representation to stakeholders.[41] Stone has canvassed a wide range of reforms in corporate structure (such as the appointment of general and special public directors) to make corporations more responsive to the interests of their stakeholders.[42]

'Bhopal' and the two dilemma-resolving approaches

Now let us see how the three potential options and two approaches relate to the dilemma of varying human rights standards in the Bhopal case. Bhopal illustrates why MNCs like UCC tend to be guided by the business approach rather than the human approach. The analysis below will also demonstrate why it is important for the realization of human rights that MNCs reject the business approach in favour of the human approach, because the adoption of the former approach will often result in the violation of human rights.

The business approach: How did UCC resolve the dilemma in Bhopal?

The business approach is clearly manifested in the case of Bhopal. Bhopal signifies how the corporate dilemma of varying standards is resolved rather easily and how the business approach fails to protect even *basic* human rights such as the right to life and the right to health.[43] Which standards of safety and technology should UCC, a company incorporated in the US, have applied in a chemical plant run by its subsidiary at Bhopal, a city in a developing country? As UCC had a similar plant in West Virginia, it could have applied the same (home) standards, lower (host) standards, or even superior standards that might have evolved as its US plant had been established several years prior to the construction of its Bhopal plant. But UCC apparently chose to apply different, inferior technology and safety standards in the Bhopal plant as compared to its West Virginia plant.[44] This factor, in conjunction with

---

41 See Corfield, above n. 32, pp. 232–6.
42 C. Stone, *Where the Law Ends: The Social Control of Corporate Behavior*, New York: Harper & Row, 1975, pp. 134–83.
43 Shue argues that 'rights are basic . . . only if enjoyment of them is essential to the enjoyment of all other rights. This is what is distinctive about a basic right.' H. Shue, *Basic Rights: Subsistence, Affluence, and US Foreign Policy*, 2nd edn, Princeton, New Jersey: Princeton University Press, 1996, p. 19.
44 P. Shrivastava, *Bhopal: Anatomy of a Crisis*, Massachusetts: Ballinger Publishing Co., 1987, pp. 42–57; J. Cassels, *The Uncertain Promise of Law: Lessons from Bhopal*, Toronto: University of Toronto Press, 1993, pp. 18–25; K. Fortun, *Advocacy after Bhopal: Environmentalism, Disaster, New Global Orders*, Chicago: University of Chicago Press, 2001, pp. 121–31.

other variables, contributed to the gas leak.[45] Below is a brief account of those causal factors which demonstrate that UCC applied inferior and largely untested technology and safety standards in the Bhopal plant.[46] Such factors could be divided into three broad parts: technology, training and maintenance, and emergency response.

Although UCC consistently maintained that there was no disparity between the technology and safety standards adopted in its two plants (one in West Virginia and the other in Bhopal),[47] the available evidence and studies support a different conclusion.[48] There was no computerized monitoring at the Bhopal plant, nor was the cooling system based on chloroform – a substance that does not react with MIC gas.[49] There was also a mismatch between the production and storage of MIC on the one hand, and the formulation and processing of Sevin pesticide on the other. Unlike the West Virginia plant where around the clock manufacturing of Sevin required production and storage of a considerable amount of MIC, the storage of a large quantity of MIC for a long period of time at the Bhopal plant was not justified.[50]

In terms of the training of workers and maintenance of the plant, UCC and/or its subsidiary UCIL adopted inferior standards at the Bhopal plant in comparison to the West Virginia plant.[51] The manpower at the Bhopal plant in each shift was cut by half, skilled trained workers were replaced with workers who were unskilled and inexperienced, specialist personnel were pooled together to work as floating generalists, damaged equipment was replaced with sub-standard equipment, and a proper record of the maintenance of the safety valve and other critical parts of the plant was not kept.[52] All these factors directly compromised the safe running of the Bhopal plant,

---

45 Shrivastava, above n. 44, pp. 42, 48–54; Cassels, above n. 44, pp. 12–25.
46 UCC's internal papers admitted that the technology was not adequately tested. 'Union Carbide Corporation's Factory in Bhopal: A Brief and Deadly History', 3. Available at: http://bhopal.net/document_library/Bhopal-BriefAndDeadlyHistory.pdf (accessed 28 May 2011). See also Amnesty International, *Clouds of Injustice: Bhopal Disaster 20 Years On*, London: Amnesty International, 2004, pp. 42–3.
47 T. Jones, *Corporate Killing: Bhopals will Happen*, London: Free Association Books, 1988, p. 17.
48 Amnesty International, above n. 46, p. 42; Cassels, above n. 44, pp. 14, 18–19; L. Shastri, *Bhopal Disaster: An Eye Witness Account*, New Delhi: Criterion Publications, 1985, pp. 26–7, 79.
49 Amnesty International, above n. 46, p. 42.
50 Ibid., p. 41; D. Lapierre and J. Moro, *It Was Five Past Midnight in Bhopal*, New Delhi: Full Circle Publishing, 2001, pp. 86–88; T. Kletz, *Learning from Accidents*, 2nd edn., Oxford: Butterworth-Heinemann, 1994, p. 96.
51 Amnesty International, above n. 46, pp. 42–3.
52 Lapierre and Moro, above n. 50, pp. 200–1; Shrivastava, above n. 44, pp. 48–51; D. Kurzman, *A Killing Wind: Inside Union Carbide and the Bhopal Catastrophe*, New York: McGraw-Hill, 1987, pp. 40–3, 167.

but the story of Bhopal goes beyond the application of double standards, as even those double (inferior) standards were not complied with.[53]

One main reason behind a continuous decline in safety measures as well as the morale and training of employees at the Bhopal plant was cost-cutting measures.[54] These were supervised and implemented by a financial controller whose brief was not safety but improving the 'bottom line' of the company.[55] In view of the ongoing deterioration of safety measures, Bhopal was inevitable.[56] UCC's technicians did, in fact, anticipate some of the operational and maintenance hazards in a report produced in May 1982, but whereas the safety lapses pointed out in this report were not rectified in full, a second report prepared in September 1984 was not communicated to the management of the Bhopal plant.[57]

Unlike the West Virginia plant, there was no robust emergency plan at the Bhopal plant to caution the public in case of any accidental escape of toxic gases.[58] An elaborate public alert system and evacuation procedure was in place at the West Virginia plant, but similar measures were almost missing, or at least had not been shared with the public authorities or general public in Bhopal.[59] With the exception of a loud siren, the Bhopal plant was not equipped with any system to warn the public of a gas leak or advise them what to do in such a situation. Therefore, most of the victims were caught totally unaware by the gas leak; they also had no clue about the wind direction, or the importance of taking simple precautions such as covering one's mouth with a wet towel.[60]

Thus, the application of inferior technology-cum-standards on three counts directly contributed to the gas leak and the consequent violation of the victims' human rights such as the right to life, the right to health, the right to information, and the right to a clean environment. UCC applied inferior technology and implemented cost-cutting measures – which directly compromised safety standards – in the Bhopal plant, knowing very well the hazards

---

53 None of the five major methods of neutralizing MIC leak worked on the night. Kurzman, above n. 52, pp. 50–4. See also J. Cassels, 'Outlaws: Multinational Corporations and Catastrophic Law', *Cumberland Law Review*, 2000–2001, vol. 31, 311, at 317; Kletz, above n. 50, pp. 99–101.
54 R. Trotter, S. Day and A. Love, 'Bhopal, India and Union Carbide: The Second Tragedy', *Journal of Business Ethics*, 1989, vol. 8, 439, at 442.
55 Lapierre and Moro, above n. 50, pp. 195–204.
56 A local journalist, Rajkumar Keswani, had been writing in local newspapers that a disaster at the plant was imminent, but no one took his warnings seriously. Lapierre and Moro, above n. 50, pp. 178–81; Kurzman, above n. 52, pp. 32–5.
57 Cassels, above n. 44, pp. 20–1; Shrivastava, above n. 44, p. 53; Amnesty International, above n. 46, pp. 44–5; Kurzman, above n. 52, pp. 90–1.
58 Kurzman, above n. 52, pp. 26–7.
59 Amnesty International, above n. 46, p. 43; Shastri, above n. 48, p. 26.
60 Cassels, above n. 44, p. 16.

involved in dealing with or storing MIC. MIC being an in-house invention of UCC,[61] the company was very much aware of its chemical composition, reactive nature and health risks associated with human contact with it. UCC's *Reactive and Hazardous Chemicals Manual* had stated clearly that MIC is 'a hazardous material by all means of contact' and 'a recognised poison by inhalation'.[62]

Why did UCC apply different, inferior safety standards while operating away from home? One major justification of any MNC like UCC might run like this: it makes business sense to establish and operate a plant in a developing country like India *only if* lower standards of the host country are applied, otherwise the MNC loses any possible economic advantage to be gained from the developing country's location.[63] This inferiority in overall standards was driven by economic considerations not only in the beginning of UCC's Bhopal operations, but also throughout the life of the plant; there was a direct link between UCIL's losses and the lowering of, or non-compliance with, safety standards.[64]

MNCs are not, however, alone in justifying the adoption of different, inferior standards. Scholars too have rationalized the adoption of inferior standards on a range of grounds – from different local conditions to varying stages of development, acceptable level of risk within the cost–benefit analysis, cultural relativism, and voluntary acceptance of different standards by a host country. I will critically examine the rationale advanced by Boatright, who justifies the disparity in standards in the Bhopal plant as compared to the West Virginia plant in the following words:

> If Rome is a significantly different place, then standards that are appropriate at home do not necessarily apply there. Consumer and worker safety standards in the developed world, for example, are very stringent, reflecting greater affluence and a greater willingness to pay for more safety. The standards of these countries are not always appropriate in poorer, less developed countries with fewer resources and more pressing needs. It may be rational for a government like that of India to prefer a plant design that increases jobs and reduces the price of goods at the expense of safety. The United States government made different trade offs between safety and other values at earlier stages of the country's economic development. On the other hand, the marketing of hazardous consumer

---

61 Lapierre and Moro, above n. 50, pp. 32–3, 43.
62 UCC, *Bhopal Methyl Isocyanate incident Investigation Team Report*, Danbury, March 1985, as quoted in Amnesty International, above n. 46, p. 11.
63 J. Boatright, *Ethics and the Conduct of Business*, 3rd edn, Upper Saddle River, New Jersey: Prentice Hall, 2000, p. 386.
64 Shrivastava, above n. 44, pp. 49–52.

products abroad or the exposure of workers to easily prevented workplace hazards may be considered a violation of basic human rights.[65]

Boatright admits that UCC as a parent company must bear a 'heavy responsibility' for Bhopal.[66] Nevertheless, he seems to justify the conduct of UCC in applying inferior safety standards.[67] Broadly speaking, four arguments are central to Boatright's thesis. UCC, Boatright suggests, was morally justified in adopting inferior standards in the Bhopal plant because:

(i) morally relevant local differences existed between 'home' (the US) and 'Rome' (Bhopal)
(ii) it was not easy for UCC to assess risk in a developing country like India
(iii) the Indian government accepted a higher level of risk because of its unique local developmental needs and
(iv) in comparison to consumers of developed countries, the Bhopal victims did not have the capacity and willingness to pay for higher safety standards.

I will try to demonstrate that none of these justifications holds much water on closer scrutiny. Conversely, even if we concede, for the sake of argument, that the justifications advanced by Boatright have merit, it seems that UCC violated the human rights of the Bhopal victims even by his yardstick. Boatright admits that 'the marketing of hazardous consumer products abroad or the exposure of workers to easily prevented workplace hazards may be considered a violation of basic human rights'.[68] It is worth remembering that the product which proved hazardous (MIC gas) in Bhopal was initially exported from the US, and that the hazards created in the Bhopal chemical plant were easily preventable had there been a willingness on the part of UCC. Moreover, it defies logic as well as any moral compass that Boatright considers the marketing of hazardous consumer products abroad a violation of basic human rights, but finds no such violation if the same products are manufactured locally using a hazardous technology.

Were the differences between Bhopal and West Virginia 'morally relevant'?

Let us try to find out, first, how Bhopal (Rome) was different from West Virginia (home) and second, whether those differences were morally relevant

---

65 Boatright, 3rd edn, above n. 63, p. 379. In subsequent editions of the book, Boatright has substituted the example of Bhopal with another scenario regarding double standards practiced by pharmaceutical companies. Boatright, 4th edn, above n. 6, p. 414; Boatright, 5th edn, above n. 31, p. 407.
66 Boatright, 3rd edn, above n. 63, p. 385.
67 Ibid., pp. 385–8.
68 Ibid., p. 379.

so as to justify the application of inferior safety standards. Bhopal was significantly different from West Virginia in many ways. It was (and is) a small city in the heart of India, striving for industrial development. The infrastructure of transport, safety, health and communication at Bhopal was not comparable with West Virginia. In terms of employment opportunities, wages and working conditions, the people of *Rome* (Bhopal) stood nowhere near to the populace of *home* (West Virginia). In Bhopal, for instance, near the plant site there were many slum dwellers, with no bargaining power, who had migrated from different parts of the country in search of jobs. These people, who constituted much of the workforce in the plant, were generally poor and illiterate and probably unlike the people employed at the West Virginia plant, the 'training, habits, and attitudes of Indian employees were lax and naïve'.[69] The Indian regulatory framework relating to the use of hazardous technology, working conditions, health and safety of workers, and the environment was either non-existent or non-workable.[70]

Boatright is, therefore, right when he observes that in terms of local conditions Bhopal was significantly different from West Virginia. But were these differences, even if material, *morally relevant* to determine which standards UCC-UCIL should apply at the Bhopal plant? What should be the test to judge the 'moral relevance' of local differences so as to justify the adoption of different, inferior standards? Boatright does not elaborate what he means by 'morally relevant differences'. I suggest that one way to judge whether or not a local difference is morally relevant could be to determine whether or not the said difference promotes the realization of human rights.[71] Despite accepting the universality of human rights, I do believe that local (including cultural) differences play an important role in contextualizing, operationalizing and realizing human rights.[72] Nevertheless, a distinction needs to be made between two types of local differences. If local differences require adjustment in standards to such an extent that their accommodation is likely to abridge

---

69 Donaldson, above n. 16, p. 111.
70 India enacted its comprehensive environmental legislation – the Environment Protection Act – only in 1986 (i.e. after Bhopal). There were some laws dealing with industrial safety (the Factories Act 1948), air pollution (the Air (Prevention and Control of Pollution) Act 1981) and insecticides (the Insecticides Act 1968), but these were either outdated or lacked implementation. See C. Abraham and A. Rosencranz, 'An Evaluation of Pollution Control Legislation in India', *Columbia Journal of Environmental Law*, 1986, vol. 11, 101.
71 Fuller defines 'morality of duty' as 'the basic rules without which an ordered society is impossible, or without which an ordered society directed toward certain specific goals must fail of its mark.' L. Fuller, *The Morality of Law*, 2nd Indian reprint, New Delhi: Universal Law Publishing Co. Pvt. Ltd, 2000, pp. 5–6. Human rights are such basic moral rules without which it is impossible to build an orderly society.
72 S. Wright, *International Human Rights, Decolonisation and Globalisation: Becoming Human*, London: Routledge, 2001, pp. 88–93, 111, 213–14.

human rights, then, howsoever material they might be for the place in question, they should be treated as irrelevant. However, if human rights are promoted by the application of different – which need not be inferior – standards in view of some local differences, then such local differences should be considered as relevant.

Let me use some examples to illustrate this distinction further. In order to redress the religious concerns of Hindus, McDonald's in India stopped using beef flavour and/or beef oil for preparing its French fries.[73] As the application of different (but not inferior) standards in this case promoted rather than violated human rights, the religious belief of Hindus, a local difference, could be considered a morally relevant difference. This could not be said of the situation when MNCs exploit illiteracy and a higher level of unemployment to pay unreasonably low or unjust wages, release toxic effluents in view of the undeveloped environmental regime of a country, or insist on their right to continue advertising and marketing some cigarettes as 'light' or less harmful in those countries where tobacco regulations are not stringent.

The differences between Bhopal and West Virginia highlighted in the beginning should have been irrelevant to the question of applicable safety standards in the Bhopal plant, because any dilution in safety standards in the chemical plant directly risked several important human rights.[74] The risk at the Bhopal plant was generated and imposed not by an ignorant and incapable entity, but by UCC which was both aware of the risks and capable of averting them. Different considerations may arguably apply when one cannot reasonably foresee the risk generated by one's action or one does not have the technical and/or economic resources to avoid it.[75] In the Bhopal case, none of these two factors were applicable. UCC was not naïve as to the composition and toxic nature of MIC. It also had the economic capacity to potentially adopt the home (US) or superior standards at the Bhopal plant.[76]

Boatright is, therefore, right when he argues that home standards might not be appropriate everywhere, because MNCs might need to adjust standards to local differences. However, not all differences are relevant to resolving MNCs' dilemma as to varying standards. The differences could hardly be morally relevant, as Boatright seems to suggest, when their accommodation

---

73 See 'No Beef in McDonald's Fries', *BBC News* (4 May 2001). Available at: http://news.bbc.co.uk/1/hi/world/south_asia/1312774.stm (accessed 31 May 2011).
74 Amnesty International, above n. 46, pp. 28–34.
75 For example, to attract responsibility under the principle of double effect (PDE), it is necessary that agents either 'foresee' or '*should* have foreseen' that harmful side effects will occur. Under this principle, actors are blamed 'only for those things that lie within power to do something about'. Wiggen and Bomann-Larsen, above n. 26, pp. 5–6 (emphasis in original).
76 UCC was the seventh largest chemical company in the US, with both assets and annual sales approaching $10 billion. It owned and operated business in 40 countries. Shrivastava, above n. 44, p. 35.

leads to violation of human rights. Local differences should not be used as a pretext to apply different, inferior standards; they should rather be invoked to promote the realization of human rights.

Could UCC really not assess the risks in Bhopal?

Boatright argues that in view of several factors, the task of UCC to assess risks for its Bhopal plant was 'complicated', implying thereby that whatever safety standards it applied should be accepted as appropriate. The risk assessment task was complicated because UCC, for example, could not have known 'the relative weight that other people [say, people of Bhopal] place on the various benefits and harms'.[77] However, it is plausible to argue that risk assessment was neither necessary nor morally desirable in view of the obvious value disparity between the potential benefits (e.g. employment or better wages) and harms (e.g. high likelihood of death or permanent disability).[78] Any suggestion of risk assessment necessarily requires putting a monetary value on human lives and perhaps also to human rights. As I have already pointed out in Chapter 5, such a cost–benefit analysis, which would make human rights a subject of trade-offs, is not suitable for the protection of human rights which ought to enjoy an absolute quality in terms of inviolability.

Conversely, if it is agreed that risk assessment was necessary as part of the normal business decision-making process, UCC was capable of making an appropriate risk assessment, but failed to do so. Had UCC been serious about assessing the relative weight that Indian people attributed to 'access to employment' *vis-à-vis* 'life itself', it could have gleaned this by making relatively little effort, as UCC employed numerous Indian workers and was not a new entrant to the Indian market.

Boatright, however, does not stop at the difficulty in evaluating the potential risks in India. He also points out that risks were increased by local conditions beyond the control of UCC – apparently referring to the illegal slums that the state government had allowed to develop near the Bhopal chemical plant.[79] This reminder, however, fails to note that the gas leak affected about two-thirds of the entire population of Bhopal, not just the people living in the immediate vicinity of the plant. Even if one accepts that there was some contributory negligence on the part of the government, this does not exonerate UCC from exercising reasonable care, as a matter of law as well as morality, under the circumstances.

---

77 Boatright, 3rd edn, above n. 63, p. 386.
78 Risk assessment is also problematic if it gives too much attention to the overall, cumulative welfare. Donaldson, above n. 16, pp. 113–14.
79 Boatright, 3rd edn, above n. 63, p. 386.

So, what if the Indian government agreed to a higher level of risk?

Another argument rooted in local conditions is that such conditions reflect different needs of countries and that MNCs should respect the choices made by governments of those countries in which they operate. UCC was justified, Boatright argues, in applying inferior safety standards at the Bhopal plant because India had accepted a higher level of risk in view of her local development needs.[80] The Indian government could have been interested in the production of pesticides at a low cost and in the creation of the maximum possible number of jobs (which country would not wish for that?), but these expectations of a host country do not justify the almost total relinquishment of safety standards. As explained below, UCC was under a legal obligation to adopt safety standards commensurate to the nature of its activity and this obligation was not negated merely because the government consented to a higher degree of risk.

The argument made by Boatright is based on the 'trade off' hypothesis – that the government of a country could agree to subject its citizens to a higher but avoidable risk in order to meet certain objectives. Bowie, for example, argues that a country could impose lax safety standards regarding drug trials in order to save lives, and that under this scenario it will be 'morally permissible to sell a drug abroad that could not yet be sold' in the home country of an MNC.[81] So, in view of a trade-off (say, between safety and employment) by the Indian government, the conduct of UCC was justified. However, Bowie might not approve the conduct of UCC if India had 'no safety standards at all'.[82] This distinction made by Bowie between lax and no standards is *prima facie* problematic and, in fact, fails to satisfy even his criterion 'that we cannot impose avoidable harm on an innocent third party'.[83] Nonetheless, even if we assume the 'trade off' hypothesis to be valid, at least two conditions should be met to grant it a moral legitimacy: first, there is a flow of information between the concerned MNC, the government and the people, and second, people have a right to participate in the relevant decision-making processes. None of these two conditions were satisfied in the Bhopal case.

Should the protection of human rights depend on 'greater affluence and a greater willingness to pay for more safety'?

Boatright connects the prevalence of higher safety standards in developed countries to 'greater affluence and a greater willingness' of consumers and workers to pay for better safety. In other words, the poor people of Bhopal – who could

---

80 Donaldson makes a similar argument in that his 'ethical algorithm' will permit an MNC to follow inferior standards in the host country if this is due 'to the host country's relative level of economic development'. Donaldson, above n. 16, p. 102.
81 Bowie, above n. 23, pp. 243–4.
82 Ibid., p. 244.
83 Ibid., p. 243.

not afford or were unwilling to pay a premium for higher safety standards – should not have aspired to a better level of human rights protection. This connection between safety standards and economic capability is contestable. It is undeniable that there is a positive relation between economic development and an improvement in lifestyle and general standards (not merely safety standards). However, there are different levels of safety standards. The breach of some safety standards might cause only discomfort, inconvenience or minor injuries, while the abridgement of others might directly challenge the very survival of humans. In Bhopal, as the level of safety standards had a direct relation to the enjoyment of the right to life, the applicability of life-preserving standards should not have been dependent upon the affluence and the paying capacity of stakeholders. The above linkage proposed by Boatright is also immoral because it, in essence, makes a distinction between the value of life in developed and developing countries. It is doubtful if the human rights discourse could tolerate such a discriminatory differentiation in the value of human lives.

In this context, it is worth considering if UCC could employ, for analogical purposes, Article 2(1) of the International Covenant on Economic, Social and Cultural Rights (ICESCR) to justify the application of inferior safety standards in Bhopal.[84] Article 2(1) stipulates that each state party undertakes to take steps 'to the maximum of its available resources, with a view to achieving progressively the full realisation of the rights recognised in the present Covenant'. It is possible to counter any potential corporate reliance on this provision. As safety standards in the Bhopal chemical plant directly concerned the right to life (a right which can be derogated only in emergencies), Article 2(1) could not lend any support to UCC's case. Even if the above yardstick of the ICESCR was applicable in relation to certain rights (e.g. the right to health), UCC was under an obligation to ensure the satisfaction of 'minimum essential levels' of such rights.[85] It is doubtful if UCC – which apparently did not face any resource constraints – fulfilled its 'minimum core' obligation to maintain *essential* safety standards in the Bhopal plant.

The human *approach: How could, and should, UCC have resolved the dilemma in Bhopal?*

What does the human approach counsel MNCs like UCC to do when they face a business dilemma of varying safety standards regarding their operations in different countries? The approach posits that when there is a high probability that the adoption of lower standards will result in a violation of human rights

---

84 International Covenant on Economic, Social and Cultural Rights, GA Res. 2200A (XXI), UN Doc. A/6316 (1966).
85 Committee on Economic, Social and Cultural Rights, 'General Comment No. 3: The Nature of States Parties Obligations (Article 2(1) of the ICESCR)', para. 10. Available at: http://www.unhchr.ch/tbs/doc.nsf/(symbol)/CESCR+General+comment+3. En?OpenDocument (accessed 2 June 2011).

(especially those which Shue characterises as 'basic' rights),[86] MNCs must not apply lower standards. It should not be an adequate moral or legal justification for the concerned MNC that it complied with lower, non-existent, or unimplemented local standards applicable in the host country.[87]

It is safe to argue that UCC was *aware* of the risks associated with MIC gas and had the technical as well as the financial *capability* to handle these risks. UCC could and should have also *foreseen* that if proper precautions were not taken, MIC could react violently and leak out of the tanks, and that such leakage would cause serious harm to, *inter alia*, the life and health of people living in the surrounding areas. This mixture of risk awareness, capacity to avert risks and foreseeability of impinging upon human rights should have compelled UCC to decide that the adoption of lax or lower standards was not an appropriate option. Instead of being influenced by the business approach, UCC could and should have been guided by the human approach and applied the highest possible safety standards in the Bhopal plant.[88] It failed to do so, presumably because the Bhopal plant no longer had any financial importance for UCC and therefore, the safety, viability and successful running of the plant were no longer high on its agenda.

The adoption of a human approach would have required UCC to take at least two measures. First, as an exporter of a potentially hazardous technology, UCC was under a moral duty to caution not only the importing country but also other stakeholders who might be directly affected adversely by the proposed transfer of technology. Applying, with a slight modification, McGarity's 'low road approach',[89] UCC should have properly warned the Indian government about the dangers involved in MIC-based production of pesticides so that the government could have made an informed decision whether, or on what terms, to grant permission to the plant. On the basis of available evidence, it is doubtful if UCC ever *specifically* communicated adequate warnings about the risks involved in the Bhopal plant to the Indian government.[90] On the contrary,

---

86 Shue, above n. 43, p. 19.
87 W. Morehouse and M. Subramaniam, *The Bhopal Tragedy: What Really Happened and What it Means for American Workers and Communities at Risk*, New York: Council for International & Public Affairs, 1986, p. 136.
88 Chopra proposes that a transnational hazardous business activity 'must satisfy the highest standards of environmental protection' and 'human rights'. S. Chopra, 'Multinational Corporations in the Aftermath of Bhopal: The Need for a New Comprehensive Global Regime for Transnational Corporate Activity', *Valparaiso University Law Review*, 1994, vol. 29, 235, at 280.
89 Under the 'low road' approach proposed by McGarity, the exporting country will warn the recipient country about the dangers of a particular technology and then let that country decide for itself. McGarity, above n. 10, pp. 334–5.
90 Merely stating – as UCC claimed to have done – that MIC is a lethal, toxic or hazardous gas does not fully discharge the burden of giving an adequate warning. Hazardous substances are a necessary evil and people consciously deal with them all the time. The real question, therefore, is about the level of risk as well as probability of harm in dealing with a particular potentially hazardous substance, and the capability to minimize such risk or harm.

UCIL represented that it was in 'a particularly advantageous position to implement this project as a result of its close association' with UCC,[91] which claimed to have an expertise in this technology. In addition to cautioning the Indian government, an MNC like UCC should have also shared the information about the hazards involved in the proposed technology with other stakeholders, because governments of developing countries may not always be willing or able to act in the best interests of their people.

Second, the responsibility of UCC does not end at merely communicating the risks of its operations to the stakeholders; it was still under a legal obligation to exercise ordinary care expected in the given circumstances.[92] Even if the Indian government might have given consent to UCC-UCIL to establish and operate a hazardous activity at Bhopal, UCC should have at least applied the home, if not higher, standards relating to technology and safety at the Bhopal chemical plant. One reason is that the consent might not be informed or free, given the disparity between the bargaining positions of MNCs and developing countries. Moreover, the knowledge of risk and consent to such risk is arguably not a good defence to *negligent* conduct;[93] consent by 'neighbours' to a risky activity is not a license to operate in total disregard for their safety. Rather, the consent given by the Indian government must have been based on the premise that despite the risks involved, UCC-UCIL would still adopt a safe technology and implement reasonable safety measures, given the magnitude of risk.

UCC also suggested that variations, if any, in technology or safety standards between its West Virginia plant and the Bhopal plant were attributable to the laws, regulations and policies of the Indian government.[94] This does not seem to be the case.[95] However, even if it is assumed for the sake of argument that the rules and policies of the Indian government had compelled UCC to adopt lower standards, UCC could have still insisted that it would not operate unless the said rules or policies which compromised the plant's safety were modified, or that it would supplement those rules and policies with internal measures to ensure adequate safety. There is no reason to believe that UCC, if it had wished, could not have prevailed over the Indian government in this

---

91 'Written Statement of UCC in the Court of the District Judge, Bhopal', as reproduced in U. Baxi and A. Dhanda (eds.), *Valiant Victims and Lethal Litigation: The Bhopal Case*, Bombay: N M Tripathi Pvt. Ltd., 1990, p. 38.
92 'A man is not bound at his peril to fly from a risk from which it is another's duty to protect him, merely because the risk is known.' Sir F. Pollock, *The Law of Torts: A Treatise on the Principles of Obligations Arising from Civil Wrongs in the Common Law*, 13th edn, London: Stevens & Sons Ltd., 1929, p. 173.
93 Pollock writes that 'the whole law of negligence assumes the principle of *volenti non fit injuria* not to be applicable.' Ibid., p. 172. See also *Wooldridge v Sumner* [1963] 2 QB 43, at 69; *Dann* v. *Hamilton* [1939] 1 KB 509, at 516–17.
94 'Written Statement of UCC in the Court of the District Judge, Bhopal', as reproduced in Baxi and Dhanda (eds.), above n. 91, pp. 51–5, 72.
95 'Reply of Union of India' in Baxi and Dhanda (eds.), ibid, pp. 124–7, 137–8.

respect, as it did in persuading the Indian government to grant an exemption from a law that did not allow a foreigner to hold more than 40 per cent shares in an Indian company. The difference between the two scenarios is apparent: UCC accorded more importance to the control that it must have over UCIL than to the safe running of the Bhopal plant. Of course, such control could have also been used to enhance the safety of the plant, but apparently this did not happen; the control was used to impose cost-cutting measures that directly undermined the safety mechanisms in place.

Summary

This chapter has highlighted the dilemma that MNCs face while operating in different countries which differ drastically from each other in terms of social, economic, political and cultural factors. MNCs usually have a choice between three sets of standards: host standards, home standards, and international standards. The chapter addressed the question of how MNCs should deal with this dilemma, especially because any decision taken in this regard is likely to have a direct bearing on the protection of human rights. From an 'internal' point of view (by placing oneself in the shoes of corporate executives), two approaches were proposed which do or should help MNCs in overcoming this complex dilemma: the *business* approach and the *human* approach. These two approaches represent two contrasting visions of the role and place of corporations in society. Whereas the business approach is wedded to Friedman's classic view, the human approach is grounded in a modified version of the stakeholder theory.

With the help of Bhopal, I have tried to demonstrate that the business approach will often fail to protect the human rights of people in developing countries, as this approach encourages MNCs to always adopt host standards which are inadequate. For this reason, MNCs' decisions should instead be guided by the human approach: to apply in host countries the home or international standards modified in view of morally relevant local differences. Local differences are, according to this approach, morally relevant *only if* they facilitate a better realization of human rights.

7 The integrated theory of regulation

A critical response to 'responsive regulation'

This chapter and the next chapter deal with the final challenge to humanizing business: *how* can companies be made accountable for human rights violations in an effective manner? I demonstrated in Chapter 4 that the existing regulatory framework dealing with human rights violations by companies is inadequate. There is, therefore, an evident need to explore a regulatory framework that could redress the current situation of corporate impunity for human rights violations. This explorative exercise should ideally address two specific issues: identify an appropriate theory for regulating the conduct of companies and apply the identified theory in order to develop a regulatory framework. This chapter deals with the question of a suitable theory. Chapter 8 will then try to outline how a regulatory framework based on such a theory could be developed.

Over the years, various regulatory theories, strategies and models have been mooted on how the behaviour of targeted subjects can be regulated and how optimal results as to the internalization, implementation and enforcement of given rules can be achieved. Scholars have canvassed regulatory tools such as command and control, voluntarism, self-regulation, enforced self-regulation, responsive regulation, reflexive regulation, information-based regulation, economism, and market mechanisms.[1]

In this chapter, I critically examine the theory of responsive regulation put forth by Ian Ayres and John Braithwaite.[2] The theory of responsive regulation, which could be seen as part of a wider critique that the 'command and control' model has attracted in recent times,[3] has proved highly influential

---

1 R. Baldwin and M. Cave, *Understanding Regulation: Theory, Strategy, and Practice*, Oxford: Oxford University Press, 1999, pp. 34–57; N. Gunningham and D. Sinclair, 'Instruments for Environmental Protection' in N. Gunningham, P. Grabosky and D. Sinclair, *Smart Regulation: Designing Environmental Policy*, Oxford: Clarendon Press, 1998, p. 37, at 38–88; E. Orts, 'Reflexive Environmental Law', *Northwestern University Law Review*, 1995, vol. 89, 1227.
2 I. Ayres and J. Braithwaite, *Responsive Regulation: Transcending the Deregulation Debate*, New York: Oxford University Press, 1992.
3 See, e.g. C. Parker, *The Open Corporation: Effective Self-regulation and Democracy*, Cambridge: Cambridge University Press, 2002, pp. 8–12.

both generally and in the specific context of corporate regulation.[4] The efficacy of responsive regulation is specifically tested in the context of the problem investigated in this book: how to ensure that companies respect their human rights obligations? It is contended that although a synergy between persuasion and punishment is desirable for successful regulation, the usefulness of the *progressive* 'enforcement pyramid' in controlling and redressing human rights violations by corporations is suspect and limited.

As an alternative, the 'integrated theory' of regulation is proposed. The theory seeks to achieve *integration* in the following three respects:

(i) between human rights issues and business issues
(ii) between the WWH challenges to humanizing business and
(iii) between different available levels of regulation, strategies of implementation, and types of sanctions.

Whereas the last part of this chapter explains how the integration on the first count could be achieved, the integration on the remaining two counts has been dealt with in different chapters of this book.

Understanding responsive regulation

Ayres and Braithwaite elaborated in detail the idea of 'responsive regulation' in their book, *Responsive Regulation: Transcending the Deregulation Debate*, published in 1992. This book arises from the perceived need to transcend the debate between 'state regulation' of business and 'deregulation'.[5] The essence of responsive regulation is that regulation is 'responsive to industry structure in that different structures will be conducive to different degrees and forms of regulation'.[6] According to this theory, regulatory agencies should keep in mind, among other factors, varying 'motivations' and 'objectives' of targeted firms.[7] Regulators should also be 'responsive to how effectively citizens or corporations are regulating themselves before deciding whether to escalate intervention.'[8]

I first explain key ideas of the theory of responsive regulation and then critically assess its suitability to guide a regulatory framework dealing with corporate human rights responsibilities.

---

4 F. Haines, *Corporate Regulation: Beyond 'Punish' or 'Persuade'*, Oxford: Clarendon Press, 1997, p. 218; N. Gunningham, 'Introduction' in Gunningham *et al.*, above n. 1, p. 3, at 11.
5 Ayres and Braithwaite, above n. 2, p. 3.
6 Ibid., p. 4.
7 Ibid.
8 J. Braithwaite, 'Responsive Regulation and Developing Economies', *World Development*, 2006, vol. 34, 884, at 886.

Progressive enforcement pyramid

The enforcement pyramid (see Figure 7.1) is the central aspect of responsive regulation because 'the achievement of regulatory objectives is more likely when agencies display both a *hierarchy of sanctions* and a *hierarchy of regulatory strategies* of varying degrees of interventionism'.[9] Instead of choosing either persuasion or punishment, the responsive regulatory model invokes a combination of both in a hierarchical order in which one starts with persuasion and then moves on, in an ascending order, from light to severe punishment at the top.[10] Ayres and Braithwaite argue that regulatory sanctions and strategies should be aligned to the mixed motives or objectives of corporate actors in order to ensure an effective and efficient regulatory framework.[11] For example,

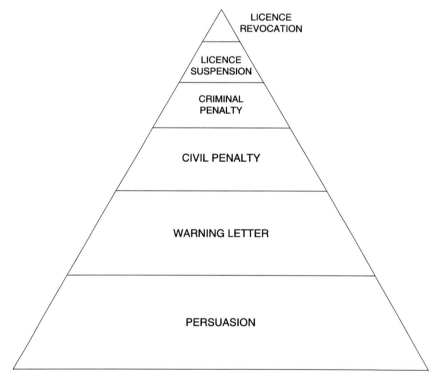

Figure 7.1 Example of an enforcement pyramid of sanctions

(Source: I. Ayres and J. Braithwaite, *Responsive Regulation: Transcending the Deregulation Debate*, New York: Oxford University Press, 1992, p. 35.)

---

9 Ayres and Braithwaite, above n. 2, pp. 5–6 (emphasis added).
10 See J. Braithwaite, 'Convergence in Models of Regulatory Strategy', *Current Issues in Criminal Justice*, 1990, vol. 2, 59.
11 Ayres and Braithwaite, above n. 2, p. 29.

whereas a 'strategy based mostly on persuasion and self-regulation will be exploited when actors are motivated by economic rationality', a 'strategy based mostly on punishment will undermine the good will of actors when they are motivated by a sense of responsibility'.[12] In addition, an all-out punishment strategy tends to prove inefficient because punishment is more expensive to administer than persuasion.[13] In short, regulators will do well if they carry 'big sticks (and crucially, a hierarchy of lesser sanctions)', but speak softly, at least in the beginning.[14]

As the 'trick of successful regulation is to establish a synergy between punishment and persuasion',[15] responsive regulation is designed to help regulators in deciding '[w]hen to punish; when to persuade'.[16] Ayres and Braithwaite invoke the prisoner's dilemma and a tit-for-tat (TFT) enforcement strategy to provide an answer to these questions. Ayres and Braithwaite describe the rationale behind the TFT strategy as follows:

> TFT means that the regulator refrains from a deterrent response as long as the firm is cooperating; but when the firm yields to the temptation to exploit the cooperative posture of the regulator and cheats out on compliance, then the regulator shifts from a cooperative to a deterrent posture. Confronted with the matrix of payoffs typical in the enforcement dilemma, the optimal strategy is for both the firm and the regulator to cooperate until the other defects from cooperation. Then the rational player should retaliate (the state to deterrence regulation; the firm to a law evasion strategy).[17]

This rationale also explains why it is important to start with persuasion rather than punishment – not because 'business people are cooperative in nature', but because the TFT policy requires regulators to try cooperation first as 'the payoffs in the regulation game make cooperation rational until the other defects from cooperation'.[18] Another important reason is that 'punishment as a strategy of first choice is counterproductive in a number of ways'.[19] Ayres and Braithwaite sum up, 'we should be cooperative at first to give others a chance to put their cooperative self forward; we should be tough with cheaters to give them reason to favour their cooperative selves; and we should extend forgiveness to those who show sign of abandoning cheating in favour of cooperation'.[20]

12 Ibid., p. 19.
13 Ibid.
14 Ibid.
15 Ibid., p. 25.
16 Ibid., p. 21.
17 Ibid.
18 Ibid., pp. 21–2.
19 Ibid., p. 26, and generally pp. 25–7, 47–9.
20 Ibid., p. 33.

Corporations, Ayres and Braithwaite argue, are not monolithic and like regulatory actors, they too have multiple selves.[21] Since 'at different moments, in different contexts, the different selves prevail', the 'corporation that the regulator feels should be dealt with as an unscrupulous profit maker this month will be dealt with as a socially responsible corporate citizen the next month.'[22] Moreover, Ayres and Braithwaite envisage that regulators may 'need' to both aggregate and disaggregate corporations: if needed, regulators could deal with a corporate group or an industry association as an aggregation of actors, or disaggregate a corporation into units. Depending upon this aggregation or disaggregation, '[c]ooperative, tough, and forgiving regulatory routines might, therefore, be played *simultaneously* with different audiences in mind as much as *sequentially* as the TFT account implies'.[23]

The progressive punitive scale of the pyramid ensures that 'every escalation of noncompliance by the firm can be matched with a corresponding escalation in punitiveness by the state'.[24] Although persuasion is the preliminary and a dominant regulatory strategy of the pyramid, it may not deliver expected results in all cases, because businesses, as rational actors, might perceive more gains in breaking the law than in complying with it. It is then, Braithwaite reasons, appropriate to move up in the pyramid to make compliance with the law a rational choice: 'Escalation through progressively more deterrent penalties will often take the rational calculator up to the point where it will become rational to comply.'[25]

Since the pyramid depicted in Figure 7.1 was designed with one firm in mind, Ayres and Braithwaite also outline a pyramid of regulatory *strategies* that could be 'pitched at the entire industry'.[26] This more general pyramid starts with self-regulation, moves on to enforced self-regulation, then to command regulation with discretionary punishment, and finally to command regulation with non-discretionary punishment.[27] The visible escalation of sanctions 'gives the state greater capacity to enforce compliance but at the cost of increasingly inflexible and adversarial regulation'.[28] This escalation also ensures that most of the regulatory action takes place at the base of the pyramid (i.e. through persuasion and self-regulation).[29] The pyramid allows the regulators of Ayres and Braithwaite to become *benign big guns*:[30] 'the

---

21 Ibid., p. 31.
22 Ibid.
23 Ibid., p. 34 (emphasis in original).
24 Ibid., p. 37.
25 Braithwaite, above n. 8, p. 887.
26 Ayres and Braithwaite, above n. 2, p. 38.
27 Ibid., pp. 38–9.
28 Ibid., p. 38.
29 Ibid., p. 39.
30 'The benign big guns were agencies that spoke softly while carrying very big sticks.' Ibid., p. 40.

greater the heights of punitiveness to which an agency can escalate, the greater its capacity to push regulation down to the cooperative base of the pyramid'.[31] Since there will not be many opportunities for regulatory agencies to use punitive sanctions of the highest level, the agencies as well as sanctions will be more or less 'benign'.

One might ask, however, if the big guns at the apex of this pyramid are admittedly 'benign' and are to be used sparingly as a last resort, how effective will they be in regulating the conduct of powerful corporations? Ayres and Braithwaite express confidence in the success of regulators, in part, because regulators could 'project an *image of invincibility* to industries that may be more powerful than themselves'.[32]

Tripartism

Ayres and Braithwaite acknowledge that cooperation between regulators and firms also encourages the evolution of capture and corruption of regulators.[33] In order to counter such capture and corruption of regulatory agencies, they introduce the idea of 'tripartism' into their theory of responsive regulation.[34] Tripartism basically involves introducing a third player – a public interest group (PIG) – into the game, along with the regulatory agency and the firm. PIGs are not envisaged to become 'equal partners with industry and government' but only 'credible watchdogs'.[35] The policy of tripartism fosters the participation of PIGs in the regulatory process in the following three ways: granting the PIG 'access to all the information that is available to the regulator'; giving the PIG 'a seat at the negotiating table with the firm and agency when deals are done'; and granting the PIG 'the same standing to sue or prosecute under the regulatory statute as the regulator'.[36]

The presence of PIGs in the game will serve as a powerful deterrent to the capture of regulators, because 'in the presence of empowered PIGs the firm must capture PIGs as well as the agency to be effective'.[37] But what if PIGs, the guardians, are also captured and corrupted? Ayres and Braithwaite rely on the notion of 'contestable guardianship' to limit this possibility.[38] In the context of PIGs, the notion of contestable guardianship implies that different PIGs will compete for 'the privilege of acting as the third player in

---

31 Ibid.
32 Ibid., pp. 44–5 (emphasis added).
33 Ibid., pp. 54–5.
34 Ibid., pp. 54–100.
35 Ibid., p. 100.
36 Ibid., pp. 57–8.
37 Ibid., p. 71. Another reason is that tripartism will 'dramatically' increase the cost of capture, e.g. payment of bribes. Ibid., pp. 70, 73.
38 Ibid., p. 57.

the regulatory negotiation'.[39] Ayres and Braithwaite conclude that the idea of tripartism – which could be applied to any level of the enforcement pyramid – 'might foster the evolution of cooperation while preventing the evolution of inefficient capture and corruption'.[40]

In addition to anticipating this positive outcome, Ayres and Braithwaite also defend tripartism as a process, because through PIGs it provides an 'opportunity for participation by stakeholders in decisions over matters that affect their lives'.[41] One may notice that this vision of tripartism also resembles, at least in its outcome, the public law doctrine of 'checks and balances' as both seek to ensure that no one player could exercise unchecked power.

Enforced self-regulation

Enforced self-regulation is a response not only to the delay, red tape, and costs that can result from imposing detailed government regulations on business,[42] but also 'to the naiveté of trusting companies to regulate themselves'.[43] This model envisages regulation as the result of negotiations between the state and individual firms.[44] The *selfness* of regulation lies in the fact that '[e]ach firm in an industry is required to propose its own regulatory standards if it is to avoid harsher (and less tailored) standards imposed by the state'.[45] The self-regulation is *enforced* because it is mandated by the state and because 'the privately written rules can be publicly enforced'.[46]

Enforced self-regulation is perceived by Ayres and Braithwaite 'as a form of subcontracting regulatory functions to private actors'.[47] Under this model, the regulated firms will perform some or all of the legislative, executive and judicial regulatory functions that were traditionally assigned to the government: 'As self-regulating legislators, firms would devise their own regulatory rules; as self-regulating executives, firms would monitor themselves for noncompliance; and as self-regulating judges, firms would punish and correct episodes of noncompliance.'[48]

Ayres and Braithwaite explain the essential components of the model of enforced self-regulation as follows:

---

39 Ibid., p. 58.
40 Ibid., p. 97.
41 Ibid., p. 82.
42 See K. Arrow, 'Social Responsibility and Economic Efficiency' *Public Policy*, 1973, vol. 21, 303, at 310–11; T. Donaldson, *Corporations and Morality*, Englewood Cliffs, New Jersey: Prentice Hall, 1982, pp. 163–6; M. Clarke, *Regulation: The Social Control of Business between Law and Politics*, London: Macmillan Press, 2000, pp. 111–16.
43 Ayres and Braithwaite, above n. 2, p. 106.
44 Ibid., pp. 101–2.
45 Ibid., p. 101.
46 Ibid.
47 Ibid., p. 103.
48 Ibid.

Under enforced self-regulation, the government would *compel* each company to write a set of rules tailored to the unique set of contingencies facing that firm. *A regulatory agency would either approve these rules* or send them back for revision if they were insufficiently stringent. At this stage in the process, *PIGs would be encouraged to comment on the proposed rule.* Rather than having governmental inspectors enforce the rules, most enforcement duties and costs would be internalised by the company, which would be required to establish its own independent inspectorial group. *Where feasible, PIGs would be represented on this inspection group* . . . The primary function of governmental inspectors would be to ensure the independence of this internal compliance group and to audit its efficiency and toughness. . . .

State involvement would not stop at monitoring. *Violations of the privately written and publicly ratified rules would be punishable by law.* . . . Regulatory agencies would not ratify private rules unless the regulations were consonant with legislatively enacted minimum standards.[49]

From the above passage, one could see that the model of enforced self-regulation appears more like a 'shuttling' exercise, rather than a partnership, between the government agency (state) and the firm (private body) with stop-overs via PIGs (public interest representatives). Such shuttling takes place at all stages – from the formulation of rules to their implementation and enforcement. For example, the government would first compel each corporation to write rules for its operations and then approve such rules once they have been written, including by taking into account the comments of PIGs. Similarly, although corporations will supervise the implementation of rules, this would be monitored by the state and, if feasible, also by PIGs. In this shuttling exercise too, one could notice the doctrine of 'checks and balances' at work in that all three regulatory players provide inputs and exercise a degree of leverage on the working of each other.

Dispelling any fears that the presence of individualized standards might arouse, Ayres and Braithwaite argue that enforced self-regulation 'makes possible nonuniform optimal standards that would give greater protection than any (stricter or more lenient) uniform standard'.[50] The two authors give numerous reasons for the superior protective strengths of the enforced self-regulation model.[51] For instance, tailored rules could be simpler and more specific as well as being more comprehensive; particularistic rules could also be adjusted quickly to changing business environments. It is also suggested that corporations would be more committed to the rules that they wrote and

---

49 Ibid., pp. 106–7 (emphasis added).
50 Ibid., p. 107.
51 Ibid., pp. 110–16. See also J. Braithwaite, 'Enforced Self-Regulation: A New Strategy for Corporate Crime Control', *Michigan Law Review*, 1982, vol. 80, 1466, at 1474–83.

that this would reduce the confusion and costs associated with corporations being subjected to two sets of rules (i.e. applicable government rules and internal corporate rules). Moreover, enforced self-regulation would bring both efficiency and efficacy in the enforcement mechanism.

This is not to say, however, that the model of enforced self-regulation is free from difficulties. Ayres and Braithwaite themselves considered (and by and large dismissed) some of the major weaknesses of this model.[52] The potential weaknesses range from the costs of a government's ratification of private rules to fears of 'industrial absolutism' and moral relativism, and the public scepticism about the independence of corporate inspection groups. An apprehension is also expressed that corporations might end up writing rules in ways that would assist them in evading the spirit of the law. I take up some of these drawbacks of enforced self-regulation in more detail below.

Responsive regulation and corporate human rights abuses: A critique

The theory of responsive regulation – including its constituent ideas of the TFT strategy, the progressive enforcement pyramid, tripartism and enforced self-regulation – advances useful regulatory tools. Nevertheless, apart from raising some general objections to this theory, I contend that any regulatory framework that is solely informed by the theory of responsive regulation will prove ineffective in making companies accountable for human right abuses. One should then look beyond responsive regulation to explore other regulatory options. The integrated theory of regulation, I suggest, could be one such option.

The TFT strategy's over-reliance on the motive of regulatees

Under the model proposed by Ayres and Braithwaite, more or less punitive strategies and sanctions will be adopted in accordance with the motive and previous response of individual actors. From the perspective of regulators, the main difficulty, however, will be to identify the *real* motive of *each* of the corporations. Regulators, being outsiders to corporate decision making, are not placed in an ideal situation to ascertain the motive of corporations. Not to be underestimated is the fact that the task of determining the motive of corporations will be time-consuming. In addition, corporations may also bluff the regulators – the public projection of a given motive may differ from, and in fact mask, the real motive. For instance, a company running mining operations in tribal areas is likely to express its motive in the language of bringing employment and development to the region rather than profit-making even at the risk of displacing tribal people or disrupting their traditional social and cultural life.

---

52 Ayres and Braithwaite, above n. 2, pp. 120–8.

While ascertaining the motive of MNCs – a group of interrelated artificial entities – regulators are likely to face additional challenges. Whose motive will count in the case of MNCs? Will it be the motive of the whole corporate group, a particular subsidiary or its sub-unit, or the motive of management-cum-shareholders? Further, which view should prevail if there is a divergence among the respective motives of a corporation and its managers as well as shareholders?

Additional inherent limitations of the TFT strategy stem from the fact that it is essentially a 'reactive' rather than an active or proactive strategy. Ayres and Braithwaite concede that the 'persuasion first' dimension of the TFT strategy has two limitations. The strategy will fail, first, when faced with regulating the behaviour of a 'pathological[ly] *irrational* organisation' and, second, when faced with a 'determinedly profit-maximising actor' where the actor and the regulator have a one-off encounter.[53] Both these limitations expose the hardship that the TFT strategy would face in dealing with cases of human rights abuses by MNCs. Bakan in *The Corporation* shows us how corporations have a pathological tendency to pursue power and profits.[54] It is also arguable that at least some corporations may acquire this pathological character because they operate rationally, rather than irrationally as Ayres and Braithwaite suggest. If some corporations decide to maximize profits by flouting human rights and environmental laws, it is likely that they are acting rationally because the gains from violating these laws might be more than complying with them.

Similarly, the possibility of companies and regulators having 'one-off encounters' cannot be ruled out in view of how MNCs operate and move their operations from one state to another. For instance, an MNC selling Christmas products could award the contract to a new manufacturer in a different developing country each year. There is also the possibility of a corporation abusing labour rights (such as compulsory overtime with no or minimal payment) not regularly but occasionally as and when needed to meet the supply deadlines.

Ayres and Braithwaite contend that if a corporation 'is *motivated* by social responsibility goals ... then persuasion rather than punishment is the best strategy to further cultivate that motivation'.[55] They further suggest that this 'will be true irrespective of whether the *caring motivation* is itself motivated by profit seeking' or for other benevolent reasons.[56] Apparently, here Ayres and Braithwaite are referring to two types or levels of motivations – the motive to behave in a socially responsible manner and various underlying motives

---

53 Ibid., pp. 29–30 (emphasis added).
54 'The corporation's legally defined mandate is to pursue, relentlessly and without exception, its own self-interest, regardless of the often harmful consequences it might cause to others.' J. Bakan, *The Corporation: The Pathological Pursuit of Profit and Power*, New York: Free Press, 2004, pp. 1–2.
55 Ayres and Braithwaite, above n. 2, p. 29 (emphasis added).
56 Ibid. (emphasis added).

behind this motive – but without acknowledging the fundamental distinction that exists between the two. While critiquing Sternberg's thesis in Chapter 5, I have argued that the difference between these two levels of motive is critical and should not be ignored. If a corporation behaves as a good corporate citizen *merely* because this will enhance its profits, such a corporation can hardly be trusted to have a consistent policy towards human rights. Human rights norms are likely to be shown the door when they start affecting the bottom line adversely. In my view, the persuasion-first TFT strategy is a good option, but only for those corporations which generally accept and show a commitment to human rights though occasionally deviate from this path.[57]

Flaws lurking in the progressively punitive enforcement pyramid

Several flaws in the enforcement pyramid proposed by Ayres and Braithwaite are worth noting. Flexibility in regulation is a central tenet of responsive regulation and the progressively punitive pyramid is designed to accommodate this by ensuring the deployment of appropriate regulatory techniques and sanctions. However, the pyramid that is meant to offer flexibility also constrains this flexibility. For example, regulators always have to begin with persuasion, even if they are convinced of its futility. Conversely, punishment always has to be kept in the background even if bringing it to the foreground might permit regulators to handle certain deviant companies better. Furthermore, as the empirical research of Haines shows, even the escalation and de-escalation of sanctions may not be as easy as the pyramid 'deceptively' suggests.[58]

An *almost irrevocable* presumption that regulators always have to start with persuasion, another facet of the lack of flexibility in the enforcement pyramid, is problematic and also illogical. Braithwaite explains: 'Even with the most serious matters – flouting legal obligations to operate a nuclear power plant safely that risks thousands of lives – we stick with the presumption that it is better to start with dialogue at the base of the pyramid.'[59] This presumption could be overridden if there are 'compelling reasons for doing so'.[60] But if the breach of safety regulations that endangers the lives of thousands of people does not provide a 'compelling' case for overturning the persuasion presumption, it is difficult to conceive what else could.

It is logical for regulators to invoke multiple strategies and sanctions in tune with varying motives of regulated subjects. However, in some situations, insistence on persuasion first defies logic. Why should regulators waste time,

---

57 Black argues that enforced self-regulation will only be effective 'where the regulated are not only *well-intentioned* and well-informed but also well resourced'. J. Black, *Rules and Regulators*, Oxford: Clarendon Press, 1997, p. 40 (emphasis added).
58 Haines, above n. 4, pp. 219–21.
59 Braithwaite, above n. 8, p. 886.
60 Ibid., p. 887.

effort and resources in persuading irrational actors, or those actors which are known defaulters? Gunningham and Sinclair aptly point out that the progressive pyramid will be inappropriate in situations 'which involve a serious risk of irreversible loss or catastrophic damage' or 'where there is only one chance to influence the behaviour in question'.[61] Conversely, it is not clear if the enforcement pyramid would allow for the payment of compensation to victims as well as punishing companies at the top of the pyramid. If such a mixture of diverse remedies is not permitted at any given stage, the pyramid would fail to deliver complete justice in instances involving human rights abuses.

Here it may not be out of place to mention that Professor Braithwaite does not seem to be a consistent advocate of the persuasion-first presumption. In an article published in the *Law and Society Review* in 1981, which critiqued the model of economism, he wrote: 'In domains where the interests threatened are great, we must seize every opportunity to foster deterrence by punishing evil deeds, even when such deeds do not produce harmful consequences.'[62] Thus, Braithwaite at one time was ready to inflict punishment on corporate officials even in those cases where serious harm was a possibility that did not actually materialize.[63] Although what led to this complete turnaround is outside the scope of this book, it suffices to say that Braithwaite himself has recognized in the past that it will not always be prudent to invoke persuasion as a first regulatory strategy in every situation.

The progression to more punitive sanctions under the regulatory pyramid is based on an assumption which is not very sound. Ayres and Braithwaite seem to assume that firms or their units either co-operate or defect and, based on the TFT policy, their conduct should be met with a range of persuasive and coercive strategies arranged in a pyramidal order. But corporations do not always function within this 'either A or B' typology – rather they often wear many hats *at the same time*. In other words, contrary to the suggestion of Ayres and Braithwaite,[64] a corporate actor can have multiple selves not at different points in time, but at any one given point in time. To illustrate, a company accused of violating certain human rights may, at any one time, be refuting such allegations, negotiating an out-of-court settlement with victims' groups, fighting the cases in court, projecting a good image through the media, and influencing government policy on the given issue. All these business strategies are usually employed simultaneously, not sequentially. As the way

---

61 Gunningham and Sinclair, above n. 1, p. 404.
62 J. Braithwaite, 'The Limits of Economism in Controlling Harmful Corporate Conduct', *Law and Society Review*, 1981, vol. 16, 481, at 489.
63 'Just as we wish to punish attempted murders in which no one is hurt, it is important to punish drug company scientists who cover up the fact that rats die from exposure to a drug when it luckily turns out that humans do not react to the product in the same adverse fashion as rats.' Ibid., p. 489.
64 'Business executives have profit-maximising selves and law-abiding selves; *at different moments, in different contexts, the different selves prevail*.' Ayres and Braithwaite, above n. 2, p. 31 (emphasis added).

corporations do business in actual market settings is much more complex than may be expressed in simple 'either A or B' terms, the progressively punitive nature of the pyramid is based on a shaky premise.

Although the progressively punitive regulatory pyramid looks impressive on paper, putting this into practice will not be that easy, especially when dealing with instances of human rights violations by MNCs. Let us consider how the pyramid proposed by Ayres and Braithwaite – which they think might be suitable for 'occupational health and safety, environment . . . regulation'[65] – would work in controlling the conduct of MNCs in these areas. Initial attempts are to be made 'to coax compliance by persuasion'.[66] Persuasion (speaking softly) will be effective only when regulators possess the capacity to inflict a series of escalating punishments (i.e. when they carry a big stick).[67] But big sticks that could be used against MNCs hardly exist in the areas of health, safety and the environment.[68] So, even by the yardstick of Ayres and Braithwaite, it will be difficult to persuade MNCs to comply with their human rights responsibilities in this illustrated area.

There is yet another related difficulty. The critical question is: who is to be persuaded to comply with health and safety standards or environmental regulations? The regulators and the government of a developing country, for instance, could conceivably persuade only a subsidiary located within their territorial jurisdiction, but not the immediate or ultimate parent corporation of the subsidiary which is typically located abroad. Even if regulatory agencies have a big stick, they could hardly use it against parent corporations registered in foreign jurisdictions; consequently, their ability to 'persuade' such corporations will be seriously limited. The end result would be that parent corporations, which control key safety and environmental policy decisions of their subsidiaries, will remain outside the persuasion loop of the pyramid in all but the jurisdiction of their incorporation. However, countries where parent corporations are incorporated or have their headquarters are usually reluctant to exercise the power of persuasion extraterritorially – that is, requiring parent corporations to ensure that even their overseas subsidiaries abide by health and safety standards or environmental regulations.

This limitation will equally extend to other stages of the regulatory pyramid. For example, if a warning letter has to be written, to whom should such a letter be addressed – to a given subsidiary, its parent corporation or both? Similarly, even if a civil or criminal penalty is imposed *only* on the subsidiary, this may not adequately address the situation of human rights violations in a given case. It is precisely for this reason that the liability of a parent corporation for human rights abuses by its subsidiaries is considered

---

65 Ibid., p. 36.
66 Ibid., p. 35.
67 Ibid., pp. 19, 40.
68 S. Picciotto, 'Introduction: Reconceptualising Regulation in an Era of Globalisation', *Journal of Law and Society*, 2002, vol. 29, 1, at 4.

vital. The persuasion logic of Ayres and Braithwaite, therefore, might not work in the case of MNCs because of one of the two reasons. Regulators will either have no effective leverage for persuasion (because they lack a big stick) or their persuasive efforts will not be able to reach those who need to be persuaded (a parent corporation situated abroad) to make any real difference in corporate conduct.

The work of Gunningham, Grabosky and Sinclair highlights another important lacuna in the enforcement pyramid designed by Ayres and Braithwaite. They point out that the 'pyramid is concerned with the behaviour of, and interaction between, *only two parties*: state and business, with only the former acting as regulator and enforcer, and the latter solely in the role of regulatee'.[69] But there is considerable scope for third parties to act as quasi-regulators,[70] or regulation taking the form of a partnership between multiple public and private actors. No doubt, Ayres and Braithwaite introduce the concept of 'tripartism' into their regulatory model, but, as I highlighted previously, the role of PIGs under their framework is quite limited and one-dimensional, that is, only to counter possibilities of corruption and capture of regulators.

Ayres and Braithwaite might respond that these criticisms could be taken care of by appropriately adjusting the 'content' of the pyramid to the particular needs of a given regulatory arena.[71] But even then several aspects of the regulatory pyramid remain problematic. The 'ranking' of strategies/sanctions, for example, offers little guidance to regulators in market settings as to when and where to enter the enforcement pyramid.[72] Even if they enter the pyramid at the right time and level, the responsive regulation model does not tell regulators how long they should try one regulatory technique before moving up or down to the next level. In short, the enforcement pyramid leaves many questions about its workability unresolved. These questions and concerns are not satisfactorily addressed by saying that the theory of responsive regulation is merely about the *form* (and not the content) of the pyramid, because the claims made by Ayres and Braithwaite about the utility of their model are not limited to its formal appeal.

Limitations of the model of enforced self-regulation

The sheer number of MNCs and their subsidiaries presents the first challenge to the model of enforced self-regulation. Black notes that for such 'a system of individualized application of general rules' to work, it may be necessary that regulatees are 'relatively few in number'.[73] One could easily imagine the chaos

---

69 Gunningham and Sinclair, above n. 1, p. 397 (emphasis added).
70 Ibid., pp. 397–400.
71 Ayres and Braithwaite, above n. 2, p. 36.
72 Haines, above n. 4, p. 221.
73 Black, above n. 57, p. 40.

and disorder that is likely to be created if all corporations working in the same sector and in the same country are allowed to have their own rules concerning human rights responsibilities. Individual rule-writing will not only be unnecessary regarding certain fundamental human rights, but will also open the door for corporations to adopt an avoidable *business approach* to define their human rights standards in a given jurisdiction (see the discussion in Chapter 6). In addition, this scenario will also seriously limit the extent to which stakeholders such as green consumers and ethical investors could encourage corporations to behave as responsible corporate citizens, as stakeholders would find it extremely difficult to compare and contrast the conduct of different corporations. Infinite versions of individual rules regarding any given human rights norm is, therefore, bound to undermine the protection of human rights as well as the efficacy of regulation.

Second, since under the enforced self-regulation model, privately written rules are to be ratified by the regulatory agency, this naturally raises the issue of costs involved in the whole process. While defending their model against this criticism, Ayres and Braithwaite suggest that the ratification process might in fact prove cost-effective.[74] One of the reasons for this optimism is that much of the ratification would be 'routine' because corporations are likely to 'adopt large blocks of rules from other companies' or from the model rules proposed by the regulatory agency.[75] However, this explanation goes against their central thesis that individually tailored rules are desirable for several reasons.[76] If individual corporations, despite an opportunity to write their own rules, are likely to copy rules written by other corporations or the model rules drafted by regulators, then this indicates that there is no strong need for individually tailored rules.

Perhaps it is this anticipation of mass borrowing or copying of rules by corporations that allows Ayres and Braithwaite to suggest that the requirement of writing private rules 'should not impose new costs' on corporations beyond delay and paperwork. Otherwise it is hard to believe how the process of writing private rules in millions of instances should not entail significant extra costs for regulators as well as corporations. Ayres and Braithwaite also point out that corporations must already be writing and enforcing their own rules.[77] However, this assumption, even if true, misses an important point. Enforced self-regulation requires self-compliance, not with any kind of private rules, but rather with 'publicly approved' private rules. Therefore, if the existing private rules in a given area do not conform with broad parameters laid down by the regulatory agency or government, which is quite likely, then the rules would have to be written afresh. This should, in turn, result in corporations incurring extra costs, which not many corporations will want to bear. Basically, the proposal of private rule-writing and rule-monitoring

---

74 Ayres and Braithwaite, above n. 2, pp. 120–1.
75 Ibid., p. 121.
76 Ibid., pp. 110–16.
77 Ibid., p. 122.

merely transfers the cost from governments to corporations. But this in itself may not be an improvement on the prevailing situation in terms of cost-savings for end-users, because, in either case, costs are likely to be passed on to taxpayers and consumers, respectively.

Third, it should not be overlooked that the two key attributes of the model of enforced self-regulation – private rule-writing and private monitoring of such rules – do not apply to small business enterprises.[78] This is a serious limitation, making this model unsuitable to deal with corporate human rights abuses. Even if we set aside this limitation for the sake of argument, private writing-cum-monitoring of rules will create challenges when applied to big enterprises like MNCs. Who should be writing rules for an MNC regarding human rights standards? Will it be the ultimate parent corporation, the immediate parent corporation, or individual subsidiaries of a corporate group? Ayres and Braithwaite do not deal squarely with this issue, but their analysis indicates that rule writing-cum-monitoring is likely to be done by each of the subsidiaries of an MNC.[79] This conclusion, however, is impractical because given the way corporations are structured in a group, the parent corporations are bound to exercise some degree of control over how subsidiaries frame rules for themselves.

Fourth, another criticism levied against private rule-writing by corporations is that this will allow them to evade the spirit of the law more easily.[80] Ayres and Braithwaite respond to this criticism by saying that this problem is not uniquely faced, or aggravated, by the model of enforced self-regulation: 'the business community's resourcefulness at law evasion will be cause for weakness in any system of control'.[81] I think it is important to understand fully the validity and implications of this criticism, as well as the assumption on which it is based,[82] considering the ever-increasing power and influence of MNCs. More than ever, MNCs (as well as their organizations)[83] now influence

---

78 Ibid., pp. 106, 121, 128–9. See also R. Fairman and C. Yapp, 'Enforced Self-Regulation, Prescription, and Conceptions of Compliance within Small Businesses: The Impact of Enforcement', *Law and Policy*, 2005, vol. 27, 491.
79 'Under enforced self-regulation, *the* government would compel *each* company to write a set of rules *tailored to the unique set of contingencies facing that firm*.' Ayres and Braithwaite, above n. 2, p. 106 (emphasis added).
80 See B. Hutter, 'Is Enforced Self-regulation a Form of Risk Taking?: The Case of Railway Health and Safety', *International Journal of the Sociology of Law*, 2001, vol. 29, 379.
81 Ayres and Braithwaite, above n. 2, p. 125.
82 One could draw on Waldron's partisan model of law and views taken by the Marxist legal scholars to contend that rules/laws may reflect the interests of rule-makers. J. Waldron, *The Law*, London: Routledge, 1990, pp. 12–13, 19–21.
83 American Chambers of Commerce in Shanghai and US-China Business Council, for example, opposed the Draft Labour Contract Law released by the Chinese government. T. Costello, B. Smith and J. Brecher, 'Labour Rights in China', 19 December 2006. Available at: www.fpif.org/articles/labor_rights_in_china (accessed 8 June 2011). Earlier, the International Chamber of Commerce (ICC) and the International Organisation of Employers (IOE) had opposed the UN Norms. D. Weissbrodt, 'Business and Human Rights', *University of Cincinnati Law Review*, 2005, vol. 74, 55, at 69–70.

law-making and policy formulation in unprecedented ways in developing and developed countries alike.[84] If MNCs are inclined to go the extra mile to ensure that rules made by governments do not inhibit the achievement of their business objectives, one could imagine how easy it will be for them to do so when the task of rule-making – even if subject to approval by the regulatory agency – is assigned to them.

Fifth, doubts could be raised about the independence of internal compliance groups that corporations are expected to establish to monitor the implementation of rules. Ayres and Braithwaite try to dispel such fears, because the independence of compliance groups is 'essential to the success of an enforced self-regulation scheme'.[85] Apart from pointing out the possibility of invoking tripartism, they suggest changes in the organizational structure of corporations to encourage the independence of compliance groups.[86] However, some of these changes are ambitious, unrealistic, or even futile. Consider, for example, the following proposal: 'In multiple-division corporations, compliance heads within each division or subsidiary, in turn, should have only a dotted-line reporting relationship with the chief executive officer of their subsidiary and a firm line to their immediate supervisor within the compliance group'.[87] It is not clear how this organizational change would ensure independence because the supervisor of the compliance group would in any case be answerable to the chief executive officer. Moreover, the tug of the 'dotted line' between division or subsidiary staff and a subsidiary's chief executive officer is invariably made stronger by the fact that the chief executive officer will ultimately be responsible for compensating the compliance supervisor in question.

Such a proposal also wrongly conceives units within a corporation as watertight compartments which could be insulated from the influence of, or interference by, other units.[88] For instance, cost-cutting measures proposed by the finance and accounting department might seriously undermine the extent to which a safety unit in a plant dealing with hazardous substances implements the applicable safety regulations. Bhopal provides a good example of this scenario materializing.[89]

---

84 P. Muchlinski, ' "Global Bukowina" Examined: Viewing the Multinational Enterprise as a Transnational Law-making Community' in G. Teubner (ed.), *Global Law Without a State*, Aldershot: Dartmouth, 1997, pp. 79, 85–101. See generally S. Beder, *Global Spin: The Corporate Assault on Environmentalism*, revised edn, Foxhole, Dartington, Devon: Green Books Ltd., 2002.
85 Ayres and Braithwaite, above n. 2, p. 125.
86 Ibid., pp. 126–7.
87 Ibid., p. 126.
88 Vagts argues that 'all the units [of an MNC] do tend to respond to a common maximising strategy directed from a single "nerve centre".' D. Vagts, *Transnational Business Problems*, 2nd edn., New York: Foundation Press, 1998, p. 114.
89 R. Trotter, S. Day and A. Love, 'Bhopal, India and Union Carbide: The Second Tragedy', *Journal of Business Ethics*, 1989, vol. 8, 439, at 442; D. Lapierre and J. Moro, *It Was Five Past Midnight in Bhopal*, New Delhi: Full Circle Publishing, 2001, pp. 195–204.

Another external coercive measure that Ayres and Braithwaite propose to secure the independence of internal compliance groups deserves critical attention. They write: 'The best guarantee of compliance group independence is external: making the failure to report unrectified violations a crime. Regulatory agencies would continuously audit to determine whether the group was discovering and reporting violations as it should.'[90] One might wonder if *continuous auditing* and *coercive force* of the government is necessary to ensure the independence of internal compliance groups, in the absence of which they will be redundant, then not much is gained by insisting on private monitoring of the enforcement of rules. Perhaps the better alternative could have been to rely on an extended version of tripartism under which NGOs, trade unions, the media, social activists and independent auditors ensure that corporations implement the rules that they have written. Among others, such third parties might also be empowered to approach the courts if they find that a given corporation is acting in breach of its adopted rules or code of conduct.

Integrated theory of regulation

In view of the above drawbacks in the theory of responsive regulation generally and in the model of enforced self-regulation in particular, their usefulness in underpinning a regulatory framework dealing with human rights abuses by corporations is suspect. As an alternative, the integrated theory of regulation is mooted here to underpin a framework which could make companies accountable for human rights abuses. The integrated theory of regulation attempts to fill the gaps in responsive regulation and also seeks to extend the scope of integration.

The integrated theory accepts the initial premises of responsive regulation that regulation should be responsive to the conduct of regulatees and that a synergy between *persuasion* and *punishment* is desirable for successful regulation. However, it questions the usefulness of the enforcement pyramid in which the progressive ranking of various regulatory strategies totally excludes the possibility of using sanctions in the first place. An approach which moves progressively towards more punitive sanctions or regulatory techniques, upon the failure of softer techniques adopted earlier, may prove inadequate in making companies accountable for human rights violations. It is argued, instead, that regulatory techniques should be integrated, that is, employed in 'tandem, to complement one another'[91] rather than being invoked only when the techniques situated lower on the regulatory pyramid fail to deliver. This integration rationale applies equally to the levels at which regulatory initiatives should be put in place and the types of sanctions to be invoked in case of non-compliance.

---

90 Ayres and Braithwaite, above n. 2, p. 127.
91 Haines, above n. 4, p. 221.

The basic distinction between the integrated theory of regulation and the theory of responsive regulation lies in the 'nature' and 'scope' of regulatory integration achieved. Whereas responsive regulation encompasses *progressive* integration, the theory of integrated regulation seeks to achieve *cumulative* and *coordinated* integration. In the former, the integration is vertically ordered in that strategies or sanctions lower in the pyramid must fail first before one may move up to more punitive options. However, the integration is horizontal and simultaneous in the latter – depending upon the need and nature as well as the conduct of a regulated actor, all or some of the available strategies and sanctions may be invoked at the same time, if needed.

The benefit of cumulative integration over progressive integration arises from the fact that the simultaneous availability of strategies and sanctions will enable them to complement each other better. Instead of entering the scene of regulation at a given stage at the demise of strategies and sanctions lower in the pyramid, various strategies and sanctions may offer a helping hand to each other to remedy their respective limitations. Gunningham who, along with Grabosky and Sinclair, seeks to develop an optimal mix of regulatory instruments and parties in the book *Smart Regulation*, sums up – though without using the term 'integrated' – what the integrated theory of regulation aspires to achieve:

> We will argue that such "single instrument" or "single strategy" approaches are misguided, because all instruments have strengths and weaknesses; and because none are sufficiently flexible and resilient to be able to successfully address all environmental problems in all contexts. Accordingly, we maintain that *a better strategy will seek to harness the strengths of individual mechanisms while compensating for their weakness by the use of additional and complementary instruments*.[92]

Another important difference between responsive regulation and integrated regulation relates to the scope of integration. In the former theory, integration is limited to regulatory strategies and sanctions, while in the latter, integration is envisaged in other areas as well. The integrated theory of regulation is, thus, wider in that it also seeks to achieve integration between human rights and business, and between the WWH challenges to the goal of humanizing business.

In fact, the integration under the proposed regulatory theory could be achieved in several arenas. However, as outlined in Chapter 1, this book explores integration only in three areas. The first integration is required between human rights issues and business issues. How this can be achieved is explored below. The second integration is needed between the WWH challenges. I have already explained in Chapter 1 why this integration is vital in

---

92 N. Gunningham, above n. 4, pp. 14–15 (emphasis added).

view of a dynamic relationship that exists between these three challenges. This three-fold integration has been dealt with in different chapters: Chapter 5 confronts the 'why' challenge, Chapter 6 responds to the 'what' challenge, and Chapters 7 and 8 deal with the 'how' challenge. The third integration envisaged by the integrated theory is between the different available levels of regulation, strategies of implementation, and types of sanctions. What this integration entails and how this might be accomplished is explained in detail in the next chapter. It should suffice to reiterate the central assumption behind the proposed integration: as no one single level of regulation, strategy or sanction is adequate to deal effectively with human rights violations by companies, an attempt should be made to combine their potential through integration.

The integrated theory of regulation asserts that it is fundamental that balance and integration are established at a deeper level between human rights issues and business issues at various levels. The interface between business and human rights involves different stakeholders which often have competing and/or conflicting interests.[93] These interests might converge on certain occasions. However, such 'win-win' situations do not always occur and consequently, it is not often easy or even possible for human rights advocates and business representatives to reach agreement on contentious issues. This outcome though should not surprise us too much. The aloofness, if not blatant antagonism, between the structure and content of human rights law and its institutions on the one hand and business-corporate-trade-investment laws and their institutions on the other, is indicative more of frictions rather than synergy between business and human rights.[94] The integrated theory pleads that the success of the project of humanizing business depends (to a great extent) on resolution of this normative tension at a fundamental level, since society needs both human rights and business.[95] Rather than substituting the wealth creation and profit maximization goals of corporations, we could bring in other equally important goals such as the realization of human rights,[96] because '[c]orporations in unprincipled pursuit of profits can do great social harm.'[97]

The process to achieve this integration between human rights and business should take place in several arenas of law such as human rights law, constitutional law, corporate law, trade law, investment law, and intellectual property

---

93 J. Post, A. Lawrence and J. Weber, *Business and Society: Corporate Strategy, Public Policy, Ethics*, 9th edn, Boston: Irwin/Mcgraw-Hill, 1999, p. 11.
94 R. Steinhardt, 'Corporate Responsibility and the International Law of Human Rights: The New *Lex Mercatoria*' in P. Alston (ed.), *Non-State Actors and Human Rights*, New York: Oxford University Press, 2005, p. 177; S. Deva, 'Human Rights Violations by Multinational Corporations and International Law: Where from Here?' *Connecticut Journal of International Law*, 2003, vol. 19, 1, at 32–3.
95 Post *et al.*, above n. 93, p. 17.
96 Donaldson, above n. 42, p. 168 (emphasis in original).
97 Braithwaite, above n. 62, 481.

law.[98] For instance, although corporations can employ constitutional rights to protect their business interests, such rights cannot generally be availed against them. Similarly, while companies can invoke (albeit through states) the dispute settlement mechanism of the WTO to safeguard their interests, victims of corporate human rights violations cannot approach the WTO to seek redress against an infringement of their interests. It is critical that these asymmetries between rights and responsibilities of corporations are rectified.

In recent times, scholars have argued for abandoning this compartmentalized aloofness and achieving integration between human rights and business concerns as well as institutions at several levels.[99] More importantly, corporate laws in several countries have been amended so as to broaden their scope to encompass the interests of stakeholders, apparently to fix the problem of linking corporate irresponsibility to the structure of corporate law.[100] Various approaches are visible to locate interests of non-shareholders within corporate law – from imposing specific duties on directors to consider the interests of stakeholders to mandating disclosure of information related to the environment, and providing for the constitution of stakeholders' committees.[101] It would be useful to refer to a few illustrative examples here.

Section 172(1) of the Companies Act 2006 (UK) imposes a specific duty on company directors to have regard to 'the interests of the company's employees' and 'the impact of the company's operations on the community and the environment' while promoting the success of the company. Section 417(5)(b) further prescribes that the business review in the directors' report should contain information about the company's policies on environmental matters, employees, and other social and community issues. In June 2006, a Joint Committee of the Australian Parliament rejected the need for introducing a similar amendment to the Corporations Act 2001. Nevertheless, the Committee concluded that the existing law did not constrain directors from taking into account the interests of stakeholders and that the 'enlightened

---

98 Ghouri, for example, stresses the need for balancing human rights and the rights of foreign investors under bilateral investment treaties. A. A. Ghouri, 'Positing for Balancing: Investment Treaty Rights and the Rights of Citizens', *Contemporary Asia Arbitration Journal*, 2011, vol. 4:1, 95.

99 E. Petersmann, 'Time for a United Nations "Global Compact" for Integrating Human Rights into the Law of Worldwide Organisations: Lessons from European Integration', *European Journal of International Law*, 2002, vol. 13, 621; R. Wai, 'Countering, Branding, Dealing: Using Economic and Social Rights in and Around the International Trade Regime', *European Journal of International Law*, 2003, vol. 14, 35. But see P. Alston, 'Resisting the Merger and Acquisition of Human Rights by Trade Law: A Reply to Petersmann', *European Journal of International Law*, 2002, vol. 13, 815.

100 R. Hinkley, 'Developing Corporate Conscience' in S. Rees and S. Wright (eds.), *Human Rights and Corporate Responsibility – A Dialogue*, Sydney: Pluto Press, 2000, p. 287, at 288–90.

101 S. Deva, 'Sustainable Development: What Role for the Company Law?' *International and Comparative Corporate Law Journal*, 2011, vol. 8, 76, at 85–8.

shareholders' interest' was the best way forward for Australian corporations.[102] One may thus note that while the UK adopted an *obligatory* approach in terms of placing a duty on directors to take into account the interests of non-shareholders, Australia went for a more conservative *permissive* approach. Section 299(1)(f) of the Corporations Act also deserves a mention here. It provides that if a company's operations are subject to any particular and significant environmental regulation under a Commonwealth or State law, the directors' report for a financial year must provide details of the company's performance in relation to those environmental regulations.

Indonesia is another country that seems to be trying to humanize business through its corporate law. Section 74(1) of the Limited Liability Companies Law 2007 provides that 'companies doing business in the field of and/or in relation to natural resources must put into practice environmental and social responsibility'. Furthermore, Section 66(2)(c) contains a more general provision requiring that the annual reports submitted by the board of directors should contain a report on the implementation of environmental and social responsibility. Section 7(d) of the South African Companies Act 2008 reaffirms, as one of its purposes, 'the concept of the company as a means of achieving ... social benefits'. Clause 158(12)/(13) of India's Companies Bill 2009 proposes that companies above a certain size must constitute a 'stakeholders relationship committee', which must 'consider and resolve the grievances of stakeholders'.

Research by a group of scholars confirms this trend of corporate laws slowly but surely embracing the idea of companies not being exclusively profit maximizing entities:

> Our examination of corporate law in various jurisdictions from around the world (both civil and common law) indicates that the emerging global corporate law consensus is now leaning not towards shareholder primacy but in favour of an approach to corporate decision making that permits and, in some cases, requires the considerations of environmental and social interests in addition to the financial interests of shareholders.[103]

Initiatives to achieve integration between human rights issues and business need not be limited to laws. Educational institutions, for example, could play

---

102 Parliament of Australia Joint Committee on Corporations and Financial Services, *Corporate Responsibility: Managing Risk and Creating Value*, Canberra: Australian Parliament, 2006, p. 63.
103 M. Kerr, R. Janda and C. Pitts, *Corporate Social Responsibility: A Legal Analysis*, Markham, Ont.: LexisNexis, 2009, p. 115. See also the decisions of the Supreme Courts of Canada in *Peoples Department Stores Inc. (Trustee of) v. Wise* [2004] 3 SCR 461, and *BCE Inc. v. 1976 Debentureholders* [2008] 3 SCR 560.

198 *The integrated theory of regulation*

a key role in this process.¹⁰⁴ Business, law and management schools could do more to humanize their curriculum to make future business managers aware of and sensitive to the social responsibilities of companies.¹⁰⁵ Such courses may not *ipso facto* make future business managers virtuous, but they would at least train them to take business decisions that are consistent with human rights law and policy.¹⁰⁶

Similarly, the business-human rights integration may be embedded in strategies of implementation and types of sanctions. To illustrate, balancing between human rights and business considerations is likely to yield a conclusion that states should offer incentives to those corporations which choose to comply with their human rights responsibilities (perhaps even at the cost of possible economic disadvantage) and punish irresponsible corporate citizens. For the same reason, consumers should share the burden of subjecting corporations to human rights responsibilities by, say, being willing to pay more for the products or services offered by corporations that comply with human rights norms. Labelling schemes or certification processes could be quite useful in this context.

Summary

Scholars generally agree that there is a need both to encourage corporations to respect their human rights responsibilities and robustly deal with those corporations who are not so encouraged. However, there is still no consensus as to how this could be achieved and the jury is still out on the question of finding optimal regulatory strategies and sanctions to promote responsible corporate citizenship. Out of many theories, one theory that stands out and has proved highly influential is the theory of responsive regulation advanced by Ayres and Braithwaite. This chapter critically assessed the suitability of this theory to underpin a regulatory regime that could effectively make companies accountable for human rights violations. It is concluded that although this theory provides a useful starting point, the usefulness of the progressive enforcement pyramid as well as enforced self-regulation in controlling and redressing human rights violations by corporations is both suspect and limited.

As an alternative, the integrated theory of regulation is proposed, which builds upon and extends responsive regulation. The point of departure for the integrated theory is that integration between different available strategies of

---

104 See generally R. Levin, 'Global Climate Change: Taking the Battle to the Campus', *Yale Global Online*, 26 February 2007. Available at: http://yaleglobal.yale.edu/content/global-climate-change-taking-battle-campus (accessed 28 May 2011).
105 R. De George, 'Business as a Humanity: A Contradiction in Terms?' in T. Donaldson and R. Freeman (eds.), *Business as a Humanity*, New York: Oxford University Press, 1994, p. 11, at 17.
106 Ibid., p. 18.

implementation and types of sanctions should be *cumulative* and *co-ordinated* rather than being progressive and hierarchically ordered. In order to maximize efficacy, I argue that regulatory techniques and sanctions should be employed simultaneously to complement one another rather than being invoked only when the techniques situated lower on the regulatory pyramid fail to deliver. The integrated theory also emphasizes the need for an integrated treatment of the WWH challenges to humanizing business and integration between human rights and business issues.

Different regulatory initiatives try to attain certain pre-determined objectives.[107] The integrated theory of regulation is also driven by an objective: it seeks to provide a foundation for a regulatory regime that could effectively deal with instances of human rights violations by corporations. Keeping this objective in mind, the theory proposes to maximize the chances of effective regulation by introducing regulatory regimes which utilize integrated strategies of implementation and types of sanctions at institutional, national and international levels. The next chapter explains how this integration could be achieved at various levels.

---

107 Clarke, above n. 42, pp. 7–8.

8 Vision of an integrated framework of corporate regulation

This chapter outlines how the integrated theory of regulation could be employed to assemble various regulatory tools to develop an effective regulatory framework to deal with corporate human rights abuses. In particular, it elaborates the process of integrating different available levels of regulation, strategies of implementation, and types of sanctions. It is proposed that the conduct of companies should be regulated at three levels: at the institutional level through voluntary codes; at the national level by laws enacted by governments of both the home and the host countries of MNCs; and at international level by an instrument stipulating corporate human rights responsibilities. Regulatory initiatives at all three levels should invoke two types of implementation strategies – (dis)incentives and sanctions – and three kinds of sanctions – civil, criminal and social – in an integrated manner.

Two themes underpin the regulatory framework drawn here: *co-ordinated multiplicity* and *informality*. The first of these themes has already been noted in the previous chapter: since no single regulatory theory, strategy, or sanction is flawless, more so when dealing with difficult regulatory targets such as MNCs, we need to invoke more than one strategy or sanction in an integrated fashion. The enforcement pyramid proposed by Ayres and Braithwaite provides one way of achieving this integration. It was, however, contended that this progressive integration would have limited success in relation to companies, especially MNCs. As an alternative, I proposed a 'simultaneous' and 'co-ordinated' integration.

The second theme that underpins the vision of an integrated regulatory framework outlined in this chapter is the reliance on informal, non-legal tools and non-state institutions to ensure that companies comply with their human rights responsibilities. The integrated theory thus underscores the point that 'regulation' should not be seen and linked *exclusively* to formal law, state and legal institutions,[1] because regulatory objectives could be achieved even

---

1 P. Grabosky, N. Gunningham and D. Sinclair, 'Parties, Roles, and Interactions' in N. Gunningham, P. Grabosky and D. Sinclair, *Smart Regulation: Designing Environmental Policy*, Oxford: Clarendon Press, 1998, p. 93; F. Haines, *Corporate Regulation: Beyond 'Punish' or 'Persuade'*, Oxford: Clarendon Press, 1997, pp. 229–33.

outside formal legal processes. The law suffers from inherent limitations in regulating the conduct of corporations,[2] and it is doubtful if law alone could bring about the required change in the behaviour of corporations.[3] It is slow to react to changing corporate structures and behaviours, does not provide enough flexibility to respond effectively to those changes and the process of adjudication is time-consuming and expensive.[4]

Similarly, the limitations of the state as a force for regulating the conduct of MNCs are well-known. Some of these limitations of municipal law arise directly from the nature, power, structure and *modus operandi* of MNCs. Furthermore, in some instances states might be 'unwilling' to regulate or are 'incapable' of regulating MNCs effectively. In the era of globalization, privatization and liberalization of trade, there has also been a significant change in the position and role of states *vis-à-vis* law-making, governance and regulation. Increasingly, more and more issues are being regulated and governed by regional and international treaties, agreements or conventions.[5] States are also under constant pressure from MNCs and international organizations such as the International Monetary Fund (IMF), the World Bank and the WTO to either deregulate as far as possible or entrust the task of regulation to the private sector. Finally, as Gunther Teubner argues, 'globalisation of law creates a multitude of *decentred law-making* processes in various sectors of civil society, *independently of nation states*'.[6] The cumulative effect of all these developments is that the capacity of states to regulate the activities of MNCs has been further weakened.

Therefore, alongside the state-centric institutions, the integrated theory relies on informal and non-state *institutions* (e.g. educational institutions and families), *forums* (from public parks to markets, universities, cyber space including social media and board meetings), *actors* (e.g. employees, consumers, investors, NGOs, trade unions, the media and other social activists), and *means* (e.g. protests, naming and shaming, and boycotts) to enforce human rights responsibilities against companies.

---

2 C. Parker, *The Open Corporation: Effective Self-regulation and Democracy*, Cambridge: Cambridge University Press, 2002, p. viii. See also P. Yeager, *The Limits of Law: The Public Regulation of Private Pollution*, Cambridge: Cambridge University Press, 1991, pp. 29–47.
3 J. Parkinson, 'The Socially Responsible Company' in M. Addo (ed.), *Human Rights Standards and the Responsibility of Transnational Corporations*, The Hague: Kluwer Law International, 1999, p. 49, at 56–7.
4 K. Arrow, 'Social Responsibility and Economic Efficiency', *Public Policy*, 1973, vol. 21, 303, at 310–11; T. Donaldson, *Corporations and Morality*, Englewood Cliffs, New Jersey: Prentice Hall, 1982, pp. 163–6; C. Stone, *Where the Law Ends: The Social Control of Corporate Behaviour*, Prospect Heights, Illinois: Waveland Press, 1991, pp. 93–110.
5 C. Grossman and D. Bradlow, 'Are We Being Propelled towards a People-Centered Transnational Legal Order?' *American University Journal of International Law and Policy*, 1993, vol. 9, 1, at 6.
6 G. Teubner, 'Foreword: Legal Regimes of Global Non-state Actors' in G. Teubner (ed.), *Global Law Without a State*, Aldershot: Dartmouth, 1997, p. xiii (emphasis added).

Levels of regulation

I argue that regulatory measures should be put in place, in an integrated manner, at the institutional, national and international levels to ensure that companies respect their human rights responsibilities. It is the adoption of an integrated approach in both the formulation and the implementation of corporate human rights responsibilities that distinguishes the model proposed here from the current regulatory initiatives operating at various levels. Let me explain how this integration is achievable.

There is a broad consensus that it is important to agree on the human rights responsibilities of companies at an international level; the regulatory initiatives at the UN, ILO and OECD levels attest to this. At the same time, one size cannot fit all types of companies doing business across the globe. MNCs must make any necessary adaptations in view of local differences, an exercise which has its own hazards. To overcome this dilemma, it is suggested that regulatory initiatives at both institutional and national levels should permit necessary modifications in human rights standards by following the 'human approach' elaborated in Chapter 6 with reference to the Bhopal case. MNCs would then be applying in host countries the home or international human rights standards modified in view of *morally relevant* local differences. In this process of integration, a 'top down' approach is visible in that international human rights standards will influence the content of standards at national and institutional levels. However, a 'bottom up' approach will also be at work simultaneously: the standards adopted by companies at an institutional level and the standards formulated by governments at a national level will form the basis for an agreement on standards at international level.[7] The crucial aspect of this integration process is a *continuous upward-downward cycle of dialogue and evolution* between regulatory initiatives at three levels in that they will be informed by the experiences and outcomes of each other. To illustrate, if the government of a state is contemplating enacting a law to impose human rights responsibilities on companies, an integrated regulatory framework would require that the government looks at, and learns lessons from, regulatory initiatives in place at both institutional and international levels to develop its own national standards.

The main benefit of the evolution of corporate human rights responsibilities through this integrated process is that the process could continue even if one of the links in this chain is missing. Let us consider one example. If we have international human rights norms for corporations, then companies could straightaway adopt appropriate business practices based on these standards, irrespective of whether these international norms have been transplanted

---

7 See J. Johnson, 'Public-Private Convergence: How the Private Actor can Shape Public International Labour Standards', *Brooklyn Journal of International Law*, 1998, vol. 24, 291.

to the national level. A combined reading of my arguments in Chapters 5 and 6 provides a normative grounding for this view: corporations, as social organs, are duty bound to observe human rights obligations, and in order to discharge that duty, MNCs should adopt the human approach and look beyond standards applicable in their host countries. In other words, the presence of weak human rights standards (or the total lack of any such standards) in states facing conflict, corruption, or weak governance structures should be no justification for companies operating in such states to violate human rights. Conversely, if no human rights standards are agreed at international level, companies should look for standards applied at a national level – not merely in the country of operation but also in other countries, including their home countries.

In order for the system sketched here to remain effective, there has to be integration between regulatory regimes at three levels in that each should complement the other in enforcing human rights responsibilities against companies. So, if a company does not implement its adopted code of conduct and the enforcement mechanism at the national level is weak or non-existent, then the international regime should step in to avoid any situation of corporate impunity for human rights violations. If there is a situation in which neither the relevant international regime nor the national regime in the host country offer any hope for justice, then extraterritorial law enacted by the home country of a given MNC could provide an avenue. Finally, if no state-based institutions at national and/or international levels are in a position to enforce human rights norms against companies, then civil society organizations should exert pressure on companies in market contexts by relying on social sanctions. The central idea of integrated implementation, thus, is that corporate human rights responsibilities should be enforceable by multiple actors in multiple venues by invoking multiple compliance strategies and sanctions.

The above vision of integration does not imply over-regulation of corporate activities or suggest that more regulations will *ipso facto* result in more effective compliance. Rather the idea is to streamline existing multifarious regulatory initiatives by developing co-ordination amongst them. It is critical to have the option of introducing regulatory initiatives at more than one level because it is highly unlikely that expected initiatives will be put in place or enforced at all levels, or that all regulatory actors will behave in an expected manner. This co-ordinated multiplicity, it is hoped, will offer, in most instances, at least one avenue for justice to victims of corporate human rights abuses.

In order to ensure that corporations uphold their human rights responsibilities, regulatory regimes at all three levels should employ two strategies (incentives and sanctions) and three types of sanctions (civil, criminal, and social). These strategies and sanctions need to be utilized not one after another but simultaneously so as to cover effectively the limitations of each other. I elaborate on this aspect later in this chapter.

Regulation at an institutional level

The corporation is an important institution of society and any attempt to regulate its activities effectively should ideally involve putting in place some regulatory initiatives at the institutional level. The term 'institutional level' is given a wide and varied meaning here in that one single-state-based corporation, an MNC, and each business enterprise of any given industry are treated as an institution for the purposes of this discussion. The regulatory initiatives at the institutional level may take the shape of codes of conduct, guidelines, principles, charters, declarations, citizenship commitments, and/or policy statements. A significant push for putting in place such initiatives will come from external regulatory initiatives in force at national, regional and international levels as well as from expectations, demands or pressures emanating from corporate stakeholders.

The regulatory design proposed here at the institutional level is based on a modified version of 'self-regulation',[8] which is considered to be an integral component of any successful regulatory regime.[9] Two key aspects embody this modification. First, although individual institutions (companies or industry associations for that matter) will design regulatory initiatives themselves, they would be guided by the content of regulatory initiatives at national and international levels as well as by input from their stakeholders. A preformulation consultation with stakeholders is crucial, an aspect that is missing from the proposal advanced by the Guiding Principles that companies should adopt a 'statement of policy' to express their commitment to respect human rights.[10] Second, stakeholders of these institutions will try to ensure, through a range of strategies and sanctions, that the initiatives adopted are implemented in their letter and spirit by the concerned company. This would be in addition to any internal enforcement and compliance mechanism set up by the company in question. In short, the autonomy – the *selfness* – that companies enjoy in both the formulation and implementation of human rights obligations at an institutional level would not be absolute.

This version of self-regulation, advanced here as part of the integrated theory of regulation, is different from the model of enforced self-regulation propounded by Ayres and Braithwaite. The basic difference lies in the fact that unlike enforced self-regulation,[11] the model mooted here does not entail

---

8 'Self-regulation is not a precise concept but ... may be defined as a process whereby an organised group regulates the behaviour of its members.' N. Gunningham and D. Sinclair, 'Instruments for Environmental Protection' in Gunningham *et al.*, above n. 1, p. 37, at 50.
9 M. Clarke, *Regulation: The Social Control of Business between Law and Politics*, London: Macmillan Press Ltd., 2000, p. 3.
10 Human Rights Council, 'Guiding Principles on Business and Human Rights: Implementing the United Nations "Protect, Respect and Remedy" Framework', A/HRC/17/31 (21 March 2011), Principle 14.
11 I. Ayres and J. Braithwaite, *Responsive Regulation: Transcending the Deregulation Debate*, New York: Oxford University Press, 1992, pp. 106–7.

a formal involvement of government agencies either in the writing of rules or their enforcement by corporations. It rather relies on stakeholders to ensure that companies not only adopt appropriate human rights responsibilities but also adhere to such responsibilities. Stakeholders could, nevertheless, rely on government machinery (including the judicial system and/or parliamentary committee processes) to compel corporations to respect their human rights responsibilities.[12] However, this indirect, or background, reliance on government institutions is entirely different from the role of government agencies that Ayres and Braithwaite envisage in enforced self-regulation.

Designing a regulatory initiative at the institutional level

How, according to this scheme, should a company go about designing self-regulatory initiatives at the institutional level? I examine this issue in relation to an MNC, but this can apply to any business enterprise with some modifications. It is proposed that the ultimate parent corporation should draft a code that elaborates broad human rights policies and responsibilities for the whole corporate group. To be in accordance with the integrated framework outlined in this book, it would be essential that the draft code is informed by existing regulatory initiatives of corporate human rights responsibilities at both national and international levels (the parent company may also look horizontally at the codes adopted by other similarly placed MNCs). Furthermore, the draft should be widely publicized so that relevant stakeholders have an opportunity to provide input on the content of the proposed regulatory initiative to be introduced at the institutional level. The code should be adopted only after considering and incorporating, wherever necessary or possible, the suggestions made by stakeholders. This process of benchmarking against national-international norms and consultation with stakeholders should significantly reduce the chances of companies adopting what Murphy terms a 'sham' code.[13]

It is anticipated that MNCs and their stakeholders (or even various stakeholders) might have divergent views about the content of such codes. If no consensus on human rights responsibilities is reached after this deliberative exercise, an MNC should still adopt a code reflective of its position. However, in order to explain reasons behind the contested inclusions and exclusions in a human rights code, I propose that each MNC should issue an *explanatory note* along with its adopted code. Such a note – the production of which is a standard practice followed by legislatures in several countries when enacting new laws – could be used, among others, to explain any special circumstances that required deviations or reservations *vis-à-vis* existing

---

12 This will require relaxing the *locus standi* requirements as elaborated later in this chapter.
13 S. Murphy, 'Taking Multinational Corporate Codes of Conduct to the Next Level', *Columbia Journal of Transnational Law*, 2005, vol. 43, 389, at 400–1, 426.

national or international regulatory initiatives, or why certain suggestions of stakeholders were not included in the code. The requirement of an explanatory note should not only bring fairness, openness and transparency to the decision-making process, but would also bring the norm-setting exercise into the public domain permitting dialogue among stakeholders. Other MNCs as well as regulators at national and international levels could learn lessons from the resultant discussion on the contents of the code and the accompanying explanatory note.

Since the code contemplated above would not be country-specific, but would rather apply across the whole corporate group, the subsidiaries of any one group would potentially need to make some adjustments to the parent code. This adaptation may also be desirable because the subsidiaries of a given MNC may be doing business in diverse sectors and therefore, may feel the need to align their human rights responsibilities with their specific needs. As long as subsidiaries of an MNC follow the *human approach* (developed in Chapter 6) in making such adjustments, this process should present no threat to the realization of human rights. It is, however, critical that all the steps that I have outlined above with reference to the parent code are followed in relation to any subsidiary code.

Apart from detailing human rights responsibilities for the whole corporate group or a given subsidiary as the case may be, the regulatory initiative in the form of a code should also elaborate how the corporation in question plans to implement and integrate its human rights responsibilities into day-to-day business decisions. The human rights issues may, for instance, be integrated into the 'risk assessment procedures'[14] or the due diligence processes of the concerned companies. If the assumption of human rights responsibilities would require any changes in the corporate structure or organization,[15] or the creation of new units or departments, that should also be specified in the code. Jungk, for example, proposes the establishment of a 'human rights policy-unit' in corporations so that 'the humanitarian considerations . . . are interjected into the decision-making process' with consistency.[16] In short, the regulatory initiatives at an institutional level should do everything necessary to 'institutionalize responsibility' despite inherent challenges in doing so.[17]

---

14 Business Leaders Initiative on Human Rights (BLIHR), *Report 3: Towards a 'Common Framework' on Business and Human Rights: Identifying Components*, London: BLIHR, 2006, p. 21.
15 M. Porter and M. Kramer, 'The Link Between Competitive Advantage and Corporate Social Responsibility', *Harvard Business Review*, 2006, vol. 84:12, 78, at 91; J. Dine, *Companies, International Trade and Human Rights*, Cambridge: Cambridge University Press, 2005, p. 222.
16 M. Jungk, 'A Practical Guide to Addressing Human Rights Concerns for Companies Operating Abroad' in Addo (ed.), above n. 3, p. 171, at 183.
17 Parker, above n. 2, p. 61.

Overcoming limitations of institutional codes

Voluntary self-regulation by companies at the institutional level has several inherent weaknesses, some of which I have already discussed in Chapter 4.[18] Although it is not possible to completely overcome all the limitations of self-regulation, two remedial responses are offered. First, external regulatory measures at national and international levels should ameliorate a few shortcomings of corporate self-regulation. That is the very essence of the theory of integrated regulation: complementing the weaknesses of one regime with the strengths of other regimes.

Second, it is hoped that the involvement of stakeholders in the formulation and implementation of corporate human rights responsibilities will counter some of the weaknesses. The appearance of regulatory codes at institutional level may give an impression of being completely voluntary, but this would not be true in reality. Of course, the regulatory initiatives adopted at the institutional level would be voluntary in the sense that governments themselves could not enforce them. Nevertheless, these initiatives would not be altogether without teeth. Apart from the institutional compliance mechanism that an MNC or a business sector should put in place, stakeholders could use the initiatives in a variety of ways to impugn the conduct of a given MNC in the event of deviation from its declared human rights commitments. Civil society organizations could use regulatory codes at the institutional level, for example, to impeach the conduct of corporations in court (assuming that they have the required standing),[19] to run a 'naming and shaming' campaign, or to mobilize support for a boycott of corporate products and services because a particular MNC has not lived up to its commitments. Shareholders could use the same codes to introduce resolutions and demand explanations from management.[20]

Regulation at the institutional level is premised on the belief that regulators have to bestow a *degree* of trust on corporations, which are not only rationally thinking economic animals but are also moral agents who bear

---

18 See also P. Simons, 'Corporate Voluntarism and Human Rights: The Adequacy and Effectiveness of Voluntary Self-Regulation Regimes', *Relations Industrielles*, 2004, vol. 59, 101.

19 See, for example, *Kasky v. Nike, Inc.* 79 Cal. App. 4th 165 (2000); *Kasky v. Nike, Inc.* 27 Cal. 4th 939 (2002); *Nike, Inc. v. Kasky* 539 U.S. 654 (2003). See also M. Sutton, 'Between a Rock and a Judicial Hard Place: Corporate Social Responsibility Reporting and Potential Legal Liability under Kasky v. Nike', *University of Missouri at Kansas City Law Review*, 2004, vol. 72, 1159; M. Kielsgard, 'Unocal and the Demise of Corporate Neutrality', *California Western International Law Journal*, 2005, vol. 36, 185.

20 A. Simaika, 'The Value of Information: Alternatives to Liability in Influencing Corporate Behavior Overseas', *Columbia Journal of Law and Social Problems*, 2005, vol. 38, 321, at 350–1. See also A. Dhir, 'Realigning the Corporate Building Blocks: Shareholder Proposals as a Vehicle for Achieving Corporate Social and Human Rights Accountability', *American Business Law Journal*, 2006, vol. 43, 365; E. Engle, 'What You Don't Know Can Hurt You: Human Rights, Shareholder Activism and Sec Reporting Requirements', *Syracuse Law Review*, 2006, vol. 57, 63.

responsibility for their conduct.²¹ A regulatory environment which is based on complete distrust and lack of cooperation is not conducive to effective regulation. Rather than suffocating corporate moral initiatives, the regulatory regime should provide space for 'the exercise of moral responsibility'.²² However, as we cannot rely too much on the promise of corporations behaving as moral agents and institutionalizing responsibility, regulatory initiatives at the national and international levels are imperative.

Regulation at the national level

Despite all the limitations of law and states in regulating the activities of companies (especially MNCs), laws enacted by states at the national level are still an indispensable medium to control and redress corporate human rights abuses. Hence, state regulation is also an integral part of the integrated theory of regulation. There is one difference though: municipal regulation is considered not as a stand-alone regulatory regime, but as an integral part of a regulatory framework that combines initiatives at both institutional and international levels.

Regulatory regimes at the national level should aim to influence the conduct of companies both from the *outside* and the *inside*.²³ Whereas the former focuses on the 'outcomes' of corporate decision-making, the latter looks to the 'processes' of a decision: the difference lies in whether the concern of the law is *what was the decision*, or also *who took the decision and how*. Under the external influence model, law either specifies an outcome to be achieved (e.g. employ no child labour), or waits for the outcome (i.e. positive or negative impact of a corporate decision on the realization of human rights) on a given issue and then responds accordingly with either incentives or sanctions, as the case may be. Most laws that try to regulate corporate conduct in the area of human rights fall into this category. This approach, though necessary, is not sufficient. It could not, for example, change a company's corporate culture or institutional conscience towards human rights. The law should, then, also try to influence not merely corporate decisions but also decision-making processes by changing the internal structure of corporations,²⁴ so as to discourage companies from externalizing costs and taking decisions which might potentially abridge human rights. Without clearly articulating this crucial distinction between 'decisions' and 'processes' of companies, the Guiding Principles

---

21 Donaldson, above n. 4, pp. 18–32; P. French, *Corporate Ethics*, Fort Worth: Harcourt Brace College Publishers, 1995, pp. 9–33.
22 K. Goodpaster, 'The Concept of Corporate Responsibility', *Journal of Business Ethics*, 1983, vol. 2, 1, at 20–1.
23 See Donaldson, above n. 4, pp. 166–7, 179–209.
24 Stone argues that 'the proponents of corporate responsibility do wrong to put so much emphasis on *what* corporations are deciding rather than on *how* they are deciding – the corporate decision process itself.' Stone, above n. 4, p. 217 (emphasis in original).

rightly remind states to ensure that 'laws and policies governing the creation and ongoing operations of business enterprises, such as corporate law, do not constrain but enable business respect for human rights'.[25]

Influencing corporate conduct from the 'outside'

Let me begin by stating the obvious. Robust regulatory measures must be put in place at the national level to ensure that companies comply with their human rights responsibilities. National regulatory regimes should specify the human rights obligations of corporate actors and also provide for their implementation through multiple enforcement strategies, backed up by a range of sanctions. Currently, hardly any law exists at a national level that deals specifically or comprehensively with instances of corporate human rights violations. The corporate human rights responsibilities could be discerned from several areas of law such as labour relations, industrial planning, consumer protection, investment, or the environment. However, these laws generally lack a clear human rights focus, do not deal with issues such as the responsibility for violations occurring within supply chains, and lack appropriate or innovative sanctions that could be employed against companies. Each state should, therefore, either revise these laws or enact a new law that outlines principles governing corporate human rights responsibilities and expressly extends human rights-related statutes to companies. Such legislative revisions should again be done with reference to corporate human rights responsibilities imposed in other states, the standards developed at international level (including the Model Law on Business and Human Rights, proposed below) and regulatory codes adopted by companies at the institutional level.

To ensure the enforcement of corporate human rights responsibilities, states should rely not only on traditional 'command and control' mechanisms and formal judicial systems but also on non-judicial mechanisms. The efficacy of judicial mechanisms should be strengthened by reducing obstacles in access to justice such as high litigation costs, judicial delays and the lack of adequate legal representation.[26] Moreover, states should consider broadening the jurisdiction of the national human rights institutions (NHRIs) so that they can respond to corporate human rights abuses in diverse ways (e.g. by raising awareness about the human rights responsibilities of companies, conducting independent impact assessments of controversial development projects, facilitating dispute settlement and providing legal advice to victims).[27]

---

25 Guiding Principles, above n. 10, Principle 3. See also Human Rights Council, 'Human Rights and Corporate Law: Trends and Observations from a Cross-national Study Conducted by the Special Representative', A/HRC/17/31/Add.2 (23 May 2011).
26 See Commentary on Guiding Principles, above n. 10, Principle 24.
27 S. Deva, 'Corporate Human Rights Abuses: What Role for the National Human Rights Institutions?' in H. Nasu and B. Saul (eds.), *Human Rights in the Asia Pacific Region: Towards Institution Building*, London: Routledge, 2011, p. 234.

Similarly, rather than relying exclusively on government agencies to enforce corporate human rights responsibilities, states should make the effort to involve corporate stakeholders in the enforcement process and invoke innovative strategies and sanctions, including social sanctions. Governments could, for example, 'make adoption of a code more attractive' to companies,[28] limit the effect of the prisoner's dilemma,[29] set human rights preconditions for companies wishing to do business with the government or receive support from it,[30] and promote 'social reporting' by corporations.[31] Drawing an analogy from an evolving principle of administrative law (i.e. the duty to give reasons)[32] regulatory initiatives at the national level could also impose a requirement on corporations to publicly disclose reasons for making decisions that adversely affect stakeholders in a severe or significant manner. For example, a company should be required to explain why it does not allow collective bargaining, or why it decided to provide funding for a pipeline that displaces indigenous people from their ancestral land.

Another regulatory measure that has received attention in recent years and could be utilized at the national level is to enact an extraterritorial law that imposes and enforces human rights obligations in relation to the overseas activities or subsidiaries of corporations incorporated within the territory of a state.[33] Such initiatives are considered controversial, have their own problems and are not an ideal choice.[34] Nevertheless, it is arguable that extraterritorial measures – especially in relation to *jus cogens* or *erga omnes* human rights norms – are defensible in that they seek to promote not only national objectives but also internationally recognized human rights.[35] Taking the right to

28 Murphy, above n. 13, p. 424.
29 Arrow, above n. 4, p. 310.
30 Guiding Principles, above n. 10, Principles 8 and 9.
31 D. Hess, 'Social Reporting: A Reflexive Law Approach to Corporate Social Responsiveness', *Iowa Journal of Corporation Law*, 1999, vol. 25, 41.
32 Sir W. Wade and C. Forsyth, *Administrative Law*, 9th edn, Oxford: Oxford University Press, 2004, pp. 522–27; H. Barnett, *Constitutional and Administrative Law*, 5th edn, London: Cavendish Publishing Ltd., 2004, pp. 775–8.
33 S. Deva, 'Acting Extraterritorially to Tame Multinational Corporations for Human Rights Violations: Who Should "Bell the Cat?" ', *Melbourne Journal of International Law*, 2004, vol. 5, 37; C. Broecker, ' "Better the Devil You Know": Home State Approaches to Transnational Corporate Accountability', *New York University Journal of International Law and Politics*, 2008, vol. 41, 159; Guiding Principles, above n. 10, Principle 2.
34 P. Muchlinski, *Multinational Enterprises and the Law*, 2nd edn, Oxford: Oxford University Press, 2007, pp. 116–17; H. Ward, 'Securing Transnational Corporate Accountability through National Courts: Implications and Policy Options', *Hastings International and Comparative Law Review*, 2001, vol. 24, 451, at 459–60.
35 Higgins argues that extraterritorial jurisdiction is justified for 'the protection of common values'. R. Higgins, *Problems and Process: International Law and How We Use It*, Oxford: Clarendon Press, 1994, p. 77. See also J. Zerk, *Multinational and Corporate Social Responsibility: Limitations and Opportunities in International Law*, Cambridge: Cambridge University Press, 2006, pp. 151–60; A. Reinisch, 'The Changing International Legal Framework for Dealing with Non-State Actors' in P. Alston (ed.), *Non-State Actors and Human Rights*, Oxford: Oxford University Press, 2005, p. 37, at 58–61.

food as an example, Narula asserts that home states should also act extraterritorially to regulate the conduct of MNCs so that their activities do not undermine this important right.[36]

In view of past state practices, it is very likely that only developed and powerful states would venture to enact such extraterritorial laws. This could be a blessing in disguise because it is this home state extraterritoriality – utilized in jurisdictions where a majority of MNCs are incorporated – that offers more hope for success than host state extraterritoriality.[37] Even if only a few states home to MNCs introduce extraterritorial laws, this should have a ripple effect on the current state of corporate impunity from human rights abuses.

Influencing corporate conduct from the 'inside'

Regarding bringing about *changes from the inside* (i.e. in the process of corporate decision making), states again can take several measures. I will focus here only on one recourse that regulatory initiatives at the national level should take: the amendment of corporate laws. Changes in the area of corporate law are required because the premise on which fundamental principles of the corporate law 'of all economically advanced countries'[38] were based has changed drastically.[39] This disjunction between corporate law and business reality makes it very difficult to inject the idea of human rights responsibilities into corporate decision making.[40] It is, therefore, of fundamental importance that those aspects of existing corporate law which hinder the goal of humanizing business are rectified. I highlight two such aspects here.

First, the uni-focal nature of the present corporate law (or practice) conceiving corporations solely or primarily as profit maximizing entities is problematic and should be altered. Werner has argued that the law should remove the 'pressures' that corporate law creates on corporate managers to pursue the goal of profit maximization with total disregard for the interests of stakeholders other than shareholders.[41] Doing so would also nullify any

---

36 S. Narula, 'The Right to Food: Holding Global Actors Accountable under International Law', *Columbia Journal of Transnational Law*, 2006, vol. 44, 691, at 766–71.
37 Deva, above n. 33, pp. 50–1.
38 P. Davies, *Gower and Davies's Principles of Modern Company Law*, 7th edn, London: Sweet & Maxwell, 2003, p. 176.
39 P. Blumberg, 'Asserting Human Rights against Multinational Corporations under United States Law: Conceptual and Procedural Problems', *American Journal of Comparative Law*, 2002, vol. 50, 493, at 494–5; P. Muchlinski, 'Holding Multinationals to Account: Recent Developments in English Litigation and the Company Law Review', *Company Lawyer*, 2002, vol. 23, issue 6, 168, at 177.
40 Dine, above n. 15, p. 223; P. Redmond, 'Transnational Enterprise and Human Rights: Options for Standard Setting and Compliance', *International Lawyer*, 2003, vol. 37, 69, at 73–5.
41 W. Werner, 'Corporation Law in Search of its Future', *Columbia Law Review*, 1981, vol. 81, 1611, at 1645.

attempt made by corporate executives to justify irresponsible conduct on the ground that it is mandated by corporate law.[42] Several approaches are possible (and in fact have already been adopted by several countries, as mentioned in Chapter 7) to locate stakeholders' interests into corporate law.[43] The UK has embraced the 'duty approach' to impose a duty on directors to take into account the interests of non-shareholders.[44] The South African Companies Act 2008 has adopted the 'purpose approach' by making explicit that one of the purposes of the company is to achieve 'social benefits'.[45]

Another approach is to create a channel to convey stakeholders' views to the board of directors – whether by appointing stakeholders' representatives as directors or establishing stakeholder committees – and thus influence the decision-making process. As the focus here is to temper the composition of the decision-making body, this may be labelled as the 'composition approach'.[46] The Indian Companies Bill 2009 proposes this approach by stipulating that companies above a certain size must constitute a 'stakeholders relationship committee', which must 'consider and resolve the grievances of stakeholders'.[47] Finally, there is the 'reporting or disclosure approach', under which companies are obligated to periodically report to stakeholders their performance on social or environmental issues.[48] Apart from enhancing transparency and information flow, the underlying assumption behind this approach is that stakeholders could use that information to reward or punish the concerned companies.

Second, an important area that requires attention is the way in which MNCs misuse the principles of separate legal personality and limited liability to evade their liability for human rights violations. Although these principles

---

42 For example, during the time when James Hardie was castigated for showing apathy towards asbestos victims, Meredith Hellicar, the chairwoman of James Hardie Industries, observed: 'The fact of the matter is we cannot wish away our legal and fiduciary duties as much as we would like to in many respects. *At the end of the day we are custodians on behalf of the shareholders. We have obligations to our shareholders. I think that perhaps that has been forgotten in all of this.*' 'Don't Forget Our Shareholders: James Hardie Chair', *Sydney Morning Herald*, 17 August 2004. Available at: www.smh.com.au/articles/2004/08/17/1092508432452.html?from=storylhs (accessed 1 June 2011) (emphasis added).
43 S. Deva, 'Corporate Law and Socially Responsible Business: Lessons for Hong Kong', *Hong Kong Lawyer*, June 2011, 16, at 20–4.
44 Companies Act 2006 (UK), s 172(1).
45 South African Companies Act 2008, s 7(d).
46 This is in line with the plea to increase the participation of stakeholders in corporate decision-making bodies and to secure the flow of information between corporations and their stakeholders. Parker, above n. 2, pp. 215–33.
47 Companies Bill 2009 (India), cl 158(12)/(13).
48 See, e.g. Limited Liability Companies Law 2007 (Indonesia), s 66(2)(c); Companies Act 2006 (UK), s 417(5); Corporations Act 2001 (Australia), s 299(1)(f). For further discussion and regulatory trends, see M. Kerr, R. Janda and C. Pitts, *Corporate Social Responsibility: A Legal Analysis*, LexisNexis, 2009, pp. 256–78.

serve an important purpose,[49] they should not be allowed to become a standard refuge for corporate irresponsibility.[50] Several remedial responses have been canvassed as to how to prevent the misuse of these twin principles by MNCs.[51] Muchlinski explains that at least three distinct approaches are possible: allowing case-by-case ad hoc exceptions to the twin principles; the enterprise principle; and the network liability approach.[52] Whereas under the enterprise principle the whole group is treated as one enterprise, the network liability approach – which is geared to deal with non-equity corporate groups – entails joint and several liability of corporations of a group that are actually connected with alleged harms.[53] Of these three options, Blumberg, in particular, has made a forceful plea for recognizing the enterprise principle in situations involving human rights violations by subsidiaries.[54] The theory of 'limited eclipsed personality' could provide an alternative solution.[55] The concept of *eclipsed personality* implies that in cases of alleged human rights violations, the separate legal personality of the subsidiaries of a corporate group should be eclipsed in that victims should be free to sue the immediate or ultimate parent corporation of that group as a matter of principle.[56] The theory is 'limited' in its scope because it is applied to determine the question of liability only within a corporate group (and not between a company and its human shareholders) and only in those cases that involve the violation of human rights.[57] Unlike the enterprise theory, the theory of eclipsed personality does not treat the whole group as one legal person. Under the latter, companies of a group continue to retain their separate legal personality, which is overshadowed temporarily by the parent company.

States may adopt any of these or other solutions. What is crucial, however, is that parent companies are held responsible for human rights violations by their subsidiaries as a rule, rather than on a case-by-case basis under the current corporate veil piercing jurisprudence, unless they can establish, for

49 F. Easterbrook and D. Fischel, 'Limited Liability and Corporation', *University of Chicago Law Review*, 1985, vol. 52, 89, at 93–7; P. Blumberg, *The Multinational Challenge to Corporation Law: The Search for a New Corporate Personality*, New York: Oxford University Press, 1993, pp. 125–33.
50 L. Mitchell, *Corporate Irresponsibility: America's Newest Export*, New Haven: Yale University Press, 2001, p. 53.
51 Zerk, above n. 35, pp. 215–34.
52 Muchlinski, above n. 34, pp. 321–5.
53 Ibid., 316, 324–5.
54 Blumberg, above n. 39; P. Blumberg, 'The Increasing Recognition of Enterprise Principles in Determining Parent and Subsidiary Corporation Liabilities', *Connecticut Law Review*, 1996, vol. 28, 295.
55 S. Deva, 'Corporate Code of Conduct Bill 2000: Overcoming Hurdles in Enforcing Human Rights Obligations Against Overseas Corporate Hands of Local Corporations', *Newcastle Law Review*, 2004, vol. 8, 87, at 104–9.
56 Ibid., 106.
57 Ibid., 107.

instance, that violations occurred despite taking due diligence steps. Establishing such a rule would encourage responsible business on the part of companies without unduly undermining the value of the twin principles.

Regulation at international level

Inherent limitations in regulating the activities of MNCs at the municipal level (pointed out in Chapter 3) indicate the necessity of having an international framework that can formulate corporate human rights responsibilities and ensure their implementation by MNCs.[58] Despite an apparent need to have such a framework, an agreement on developing international norms and an international enforcement mechanism is not proving to be an easy one in view of numerous looming challenges. For one, this would require 'adaptations of the traditional formats of both international instruments and institutions'.[59] Then there is strong opposition and intense lobbying from the business sector against a binding international framework. One cannot also discount the divergence that exists among states about the nature and scope of international regulation, including fears of consequential dilution of their sovereignty.[60]

In my view, there are three major challenges:

(i) What should be the exact nature of the international instrument for companies and to what extent is the state-centric human rights framework relevant to the drafting of this instrument?
(ii) Which international institution or body is appropriate to lead the process of drafting human rights responsibilities for companies?
(iii) How and through which institution(s) could the corporate human rights responsibilities be enforced at international level?

Let me outline how these challenges could be overcome.

Nature of instrument and the role of state-focal human rights framework

I suggest that an instrument of corporate human rights responsibilities at international level should serve twin purposes. It should (i) catalogue responsibilities of companies, outline the principles that underpin these

---

58 Anderson advances an ambitious proposal for developing non-state-centric global human rights law to regulate MNCs. R. J. Anderson, 'Reimagining Human Rights Law: Toward Global Regulation of Transnational Corporations', *Denver University Law Review*, 2010, vol. 88, 183.
59 D. Kinley and J. Tadaki, 'From Talk to Walk: The Emergence of Human Rights Responsibilities for Corporations at International Law', *Virginia Journal of International Law*, 2004, vol. 44, 931, at 994.
60 See Clarke, above n. 9, pp. 192–224.

responsibilities and propose an international implementation mechanism; and (ii) serve as a model law for states in the area of business and human rights. The 'cataloguing' function will enable both companies and their stakeholders to understand better the precise human rights responsibilities of the business. Similar to the Guiding Principles, such an instrument (which may begin as a declaration and take the shape of a convention in due course) should elaborate the principles on which the responsibilities of companies are grounded. It should, for instance, outline the normative reason(s) for companies having human rights responsibilities, state why the 'protect' and 'fulfil' duties of companies are limited in comparison to states, and describe the scope of companies' responsibility for human rights abuses by subsidiaries or other business partners.

However, this international instrument should not stop at merely enumerating principles and expect companies to deduce their responsibilities with reference to the state-centric International Bill of Rights and other international human rights instruments. Rather it should specify these responsibilities in one place. The OECD Guidelines, the ILO Declaration and the UN Norms tell us that this task may be difficult and/or contentious, but not impossible to accomplish. I have already pointed out in Chapter 4 why the easier (and perhaps escapist) route adopted by the Guiding Principles, which though resulted in building a broad consensus on issues concerning business and human rights, may not be the best for the realization of human rights in the long run. Once the corporate human rights responsibilities are agreed upon at international level, they would have to be given a more precise meaning at national level.[61] Such an international agreement on responsibilities will also work as, what Murphy labels, a 'code for codes' that are adopted by companies at institutional level.[62] This again emphasizes the necessity for adopting an integrated approach – between regulatory initiatives at the institutional, national and international levels – to ascertain and entrench the human rights responsibilities of companies.

Equally important for such an international instrument would be to lay down a mechanism to implement and enforce corporate human rights responsibilities. This aspect is dealt with in more detail below. It suffices to point out here that such a mechanism should not rely exclusively on states to implement and enforce corporate human rights responsibilities, for the necessity for having an international regulatory regime is precisely felt because of states' inability or unwillingness to enforce these obligations against powerful MNCs.

The 'modelling' function would not only try to harmonize law on business and human rights but also provide guidance to states in enacting a law to deal with the privatization of human rights. Drawing on the highly successful

---

61 See BLIHR, above n. 14, p. 6.
62 Murphy, above n. 13, pp. 425–6.

approach of model laws adopted by the United Nations Commission on International Trade Law (UNCITRAL) in areas such as arbitration, electronic commerce and privately financed infrastructure projects,[63] it is proposed that in addition to an international convention, a Model Law on Business and Human Rights should be drafted. Such a Model Law should not only propose a framework for states to codify the human rights obligations of companies but also outline various judicial and non-judicial enforcement mechanisms. Furthermore, it should suggest legal approaches to overcome obstacles in access to justice posed by the principle of separate legal personality, the doctrine of *forum non conveniens*, the high cost of litigation, the large number of victims, and judicial delay.

One may object to the above proposals on the ground as to why we need to catalogue the human rights responsibilities of companies if their obligations correspond to all internationally recognized human rights. As pointed out in Chapter 4, it is easier said than done to ascertain corporate responsibilities with reference to state-centric human rights treaties. This difficult task should be performed by human rights experts rather than passing the buck to corporate executives and managers who possess different types of skills. Another objection may be that the proposed international instruments would embody an unsuitable 'one-size-fits-all' approach. My simple response is that both the convention and the Model Law will have some room for the flexibility that we generally associate with international instruments. Moreover, if harmonization of standards at international level can take place in areas such as trade, intellectual property rights, arbitration, taxation and accounting, there are stronger reasons for developing 'flexible uniformity' in the area of human rights, which are more universal at the normative level.

Which international body should hold the reins of the drafting process?

Out of the UN, the ILO and the OECD (all of which have a long experience of promoting human rights with special reference to MNCs), the UN is best placed to take the lead to draft the convention and the Model Law proposed above. The UN is, in fact, bound by its Charter '*to employ international machinery* for the promotion of the economic and social advancement of all peoples'.[64]

---

63 UNCITRAL Model Law on International Commercial Arbitration (adopted in 1985, amended in 2006). Available at: www.uncitral.org/pdf/english/texts/arbitration/ml-arb/07–86998_Ebook.pdf> (accessed 19 June 2011). UNCITRAL Model Law on Electronic Commerce with Guide to Enactment (adopted in 1996). Available at: www.uncitral.org/pdf/english/texts/electcom/05–89450_Ebook.pdf> (accessed 19 June 2011). UNCITRAL Model Legislative Provisions on Privately Financed Infrastructure Projects (adopted in 2003) Available at: www.uncitral.org/pdf/english/texts/procurem/pfip/model/03–90621_Ebook.pdf> (accessed 19 June 2011).
64 Charter of the United Nations, Preamble. Available at: www.un.org/en/documents/charter/preamble.shtml (accessed 10 June 2011) (emphasis added).

Within the UN fold, it is desirable to constitute a 'permanent nodal body' – say a Commission on Business and Human Rights – to deal with all issues in this area and liaise with relevant institutions both inside and outside the UN. For this reason, the decision of the Human Rights Council to constitute a five-member Working Group for a period of three years, as a follow-up to the mandate of the SRSG and the Guiding Principles, is unsatisfactory.[65] It is time that the UN and international community stop giving this ad-hoc, narrow and myopic treatment to the challenges posed by the intersection of business and human rights. Humanizing business requires a coherent and long-term response.

The UN nodal body should work closely with the ILO and the OECD when drafting the human rights responsibilities of companies at international level. However, in view of how this issue is intertwined with trade, commerce, economic aid and development, it is desirable that institutions dealing with these aspects at international level (such as the WTO, the World Bank and the IMF) also be involved in the drafting process.[66] This would ensure that these international institutions – which have no direct or specific human rights mandate – take cognizance of the human rights responsibilities of corporations and make appropriate adjustments in their policies as well as their working practices.[67] Moreover, companies, various non-state organs or institutions and NGOs, who have a stake in the evolution of an effective regulatory regime relating to companies at international level, should also be consulted.[68]

The ultimate aim of such participatory deliberations should be to draw a convention that catalogues the human rights responsibilities of companies and draft the Model Law on Business and Human Rights which can be used by states as a framework for legislating at the municipal level. The draft of both these instruments should consider not only international human rights instruments but also the human rights policies adopted by companies and evolving municipal laws. The proposed convention will be a 'hybrid instrument' in the sense of imposing direct obligations on companies but at the same time retaining the role of states in defining and implementing these responsibilities.[69]

---

65 Human Rights Council, 'Council Establishes Working Group on Human Rights and Transnational Corporations and other Business Enterprises' (16 June 2011). Available at: www.ohchr.org/en/NewsEvents/Pages/DisplayNews.aspx?NewsID=11165&LangID=E (accessed 17 June 2011).
66 See R. Steinhardt, 'Corporate Responsibility and the International Law of Human Rights: The New *Lex Mercatoria*' in Alston (ed.), above n. 35, p. 177, at 202–12.
67 See David Kinley, *Civilising Globalisation: Human Rights and the Global Economy*, Cambridge: Cambridge University Press, 2009; S. Skogly, *The Human Rights Obligations of the World Bank and the International Monetary Fund*, London: Cavendish Publishing, 2001; H. Moris, 'The World Bank and Human Rights: Indispensable Partnership or Mismatched Alliance', *ILSA Journal of International and Comparative Law*, 1997, vol. 4, 173.
68 See Grossman and Bradlow, above n. 5, p. 22; Zerk, above n. 35, pp. 93–102.
69 Kinley and Tadaki, above n. 59, p. 994.

How to enforce human rights responsibilities internationally

The weakness of enforcement mechanisms is often identified as a general lacuna of international law, and the enforcement of human rights standards against companies cannot be totally immune from this weakness.[70] One major reason for an enforcement deficit in international law is that the existing enforcement mechanisms are made impotent by lack of cooperation from states. To overcome this limitation in relation to enforcement against companies, two measures could be introduced. First, it is advisable to invoke a 'plurality of enforcement mechanisms' at international level because 'no single body can provide a comprehensive enforcement mechanism'.[71] Second, there is a need to rely on non-state-based enforcement of corporate human rights responsibilities (i.e. through social sanctions mobilized by stakeholders of companies).

Scholars have explored the possibility of invoking various international institutions – from the UN human rights bodies to the ILO, the WTO, the World Bank, the OECD, and the International Criminal Court (ICC) – to enforce corporate human rights responsibilities.[72] At the risk of over-generalization, a common conclusion of such exploratory exercises has been that these institutions do not offer much scope for robust enforcement of corporate human rights responsibilities. This conclusion is hardly surprising because these bodies were not created to deliver what is expected from them now. Although options do exist to harness institutions such as the WTO[73] and the ICC to enforce human rights responsibilities against companies,[74] it would be too ambitious to hope that these institutions could be harnessed to the extent of being able to redress the situation of corporate impunity for human rights violations.

I, therefore, suggest that existing (primarily) state-focal international institutions should be utilized for what they could possibly deliver. They could be mobilized to exert pressure on states to regulate the conduct of companies more vigorously through municipal measures, as well as by forging regulatory

---

70 Zerk, above n. 35, p. 91; Simaika, above n. 20, pp. 331–3.
71 Kinley and Tadaki, above n. 59, pp. 1019–20.
72 N. Jägers, *Corporate Human Rights Obligations: In Search of Accountability*, Antwerpen: Intersentia, 2002, pp. 217–42; Kinley and Tadaki, above n. 59, pp. 997–1019; International Council on Human Rights Policy (ICHRP), *Beyond Voluntarism: Human Rights and the Developing International Legal Obligations of Companies*, Versoix: ICHRP, 2002, pp. 83–120; A. Clapham, 'The Question of Jurisdiction under International Criminal Court over Legal Persons: Lessons from the Rome Conference on an International Criminal Court' in M. Kamminga and S. Zia-Zarifi (eds.), *Liability of Multinational Corporations under International Law*, The Hague: Kluwer Law International, 2000, p. 139, at 139–95.
73 S. Deva, 'Human Rights Violations by Multinational Corporations and International Law: Where from Here?' *Connecticut Journal of International Law*, 2003, vol. 19, 1, at 22–48.
74 C. Chiomenti, 'Corporations and the International Criminal Court' in O. De Schutter (ed.), *Transnational Corporations and Human Rights*, Oxford: Hart Publishing, 2006, p. 287.

partnerships at regional and international levels. They could also work to influence human rights *policies* rather than the specific conduct of companies, for instance, by insisting on risk assessment for obtaining loans and conducting human rights screening before awarding public procurement contracts. However, in order to achieve such objectives more effectively, it may be appropriate for these institutions to increase the participation of civil society organizations in their deliberations and decision-making processes.

The international enforcement mechanism should complement the municipal mechanism. It should be available, and would be especially useful, in two types of cases: to seek redress against egregious violations of human rights such as complicity in genocide, forced labour, extra-judicial killings, sexual violence, and forced removal from land; and to offer a remedy in those instances where the municipal system does not offer a viable option because of weak governance, conflict zone, oppressive regime, corruption or complicity. The proposed Commission on Business and Human Rights may consider referring the first set of cases to the ICC for investigation and potential prosecution of concerned corporate officials under the Rome Statute. However, if the municipal remedies have been exhausted or recourse to them does not offer any reasonable hope of success for victims in relation to the second set of cases, it should itself investigate the allegations and take appropriate measures.

In addition, and more importantly, the Commission may facilitate the creation of an international monitoring body, with branches in each state, consisting only of civil society organizations. Such a body could verify and investigate, both at local and global levels, the human rights practices adopted by companies *suo motu* as well as in response to complaints received from victims of corporate human rights abuses. If on investigation it finds that a given company is disregarding its human rights responsibilities, it should seek an explanation from the company, and then put the matter in the public domain so that it can provide a basis for the imposition of social sanctions by stakeholders. In specific cases, such a 'non-state, non-corporate' body could also issue recommendations to states, companies and stakeholders regarding measures that they could take at their respective levels to promote human rights' realization.

Critics have pointed out several hazards in relying on civil society organizations to enforce corporate human rights responsibilities. For instance, NGOs' dependence on donations and a lack of transparency as well as accountability of their functioning is a matter of concern.[75] In addition, the possibility of one company using certain civil society organizations to settle scores against its competitors cannot be ruled out. These are legitimate apprehensions, but may be addressed, to some degree, by the fact that those civil society organs which

---

75 J. Bhagwati, *In Defense of Globalization*, New York: Oxford University Press, 2004, pp. 43–8; U. Baxi, *The Future of Human Rights*, New Delhi: Oxford University Press, 2002, pp. 121–5.

indulge in such practices would lose the confidence of their stakeholders and are likely to fade away or would not be taken seriously by the public in future campaigns. Another built-in safeguard would be provided by the presence of multiple civil society organizations; so the capture or corruption of one or a few organizations should not undermine the whole process.

Integrating implementation strategies and sanctions

Since it is likely that not all duty-bearing companies will perform their human rights obligations, we need a mechanism that can ensure that duties are performed most, if not all, of the time. For this reason, the regulatory initiatives that are put in place at all three levels should employ suitable implementation strategies and sanctions so as to ensure that companies that fail to respect their human rights responsibilities are made accountable in an effective manner. I propose that regulatory initiatives invoke two implementation strategies and three types of sanctions in tandem and not one after another as envisaged under the enforcement pyramid of Ayres and Braithwaite. The 'in tandem' application of multiple strategies and sanctions does not mean, for example, that a company that is prosecuted for committing serious human rights abuses also gets incentives (say, tax rebates) at the same time. Rather it implies two things. First, incentives need not be offered to 'all' companies but only to those that deserve them, in the opinion of regulatory agencies or other stakeholders, because of their pro-human rights conduct and commitment. Second, there would be no need to exhaust any single strategy or sanction first before moving to more punitive measures.

It should also be noted that the nature of various strategies and sanctions as well as the *modus operandi* of their administration will vary from one level of regulation to another (see Table 8.1) because regulatory initiatives at each of the three levels differ from each other in several aspects. The table is only *illustrative* and it leaves scope for flexibility in the evolution and incorporation of innovative enforcement strategies or sanctions.

Twin implementation strategies

Regulatory initiatives at the institutional, national and international levels should employ, in an integrated fashion, (dis)incentives and sanctions to ensure that companies comply with their human rights responsibilities. The two strategies seek to combine voluntary and mandatory approaches to fostering human rights compliance because both approaches need to be employed in a complementary way. Arguably, it is more appropriate to frame the inquiry not in terms of 'beyond voluntarism',[76] but *besides* voluntarism.

---

76 The title of the report published by ICHRP, *Beyond Voluntarism*, above n. 72. The report though did not discount altogether the usefulness of voluntary codes. Ibid., p. 9.

Table 8.1 Integrated employment of implementation strategies and sanctions at three regulatory levels

	Strategies of implementation		*Types of sanctions*		
	(Dis)incentives	*Sanctions*	*Civil*	*Criminal*	*Social*
Institutional level	Pay rise; promotion of relevant corporate employees	Demotion; termination of relevant corporate employees	Disciplinary action; demotion; disqualification from directorship	Allocation of criminal liability	Shareholders' proposals; protests by employees and/or trade unions
National level	Tax rebates; citizenship awards; labelling schemes; preferential purchasing or contracting	Public censure; license revocation; fine; incarceration	Reparation; public apology; restitution; injunction; blacklisting; winding up	Public censure; fine; forfeiture of property; imprisonment; license cancellation	Naming and shaming; boycott of goods or services
International level	Citizenship awards; labelling schemes; preferential purchasing or contracting	Reparation; fine; blacklisting; public censure; criminal prosecution	Reparation; trade sanctions; blacklisting for aid and contracts; apology and reconciliation	Public censure; prosecution of concerned corporate officials for international crimes	(Cyber) naming and shaming; boycott of goods or services

Under the integrated theory of regulation, the two implementation strategies encompass a mixture of both 'carrots' and 'sticks' not only within state-based mechanisms, but also outside formal state institutions under market settings. For a number of reasons it is critical to involve markets and market forces in implementing corporate human rights responsibilities. Markets, that enable and sometimes encourage companies to indulge in human rights abuses,[77] could also be used as a strategy to counter such abuses.[78] Corporations respond to markets all the time and therefore, *if* markets could be harnessed to accommodate the human rights agenda (i.e. if corporate stakeholders could align their market choices and behaviour in accordance with human rights norms) this could prove an effective strategy to encourage companies to respect their human rights responsibilities. Conversely, unless a market for corporate social responsibility is created, it will not be easy to sustain

---

77 Murphy, above n. 13, p. 400 (emphasis added).
78 I. Bantekas, 'Corporate Social Responsibility in International Law', *Boston University International Law Journal*, 2004, vol. 22, 309, at 340–1; Steinhardt, above n. 66, pp. 181–7.

corporate interest in and engagement with the project of humanizing business. Furthermore, markets also present an important advantage over conventional methods of administering incentives or sanctions: in offering incentives and disincentives, market forces do not rely on formal state mechanisms as much as regulators do in imposing civil and criminal sanctions.

Regulatory initiatives at all three levels should, therefore, exploit the potential of markets as vehicles to implement corporate human rights responsibilities. In order for markets to work as effective incentive providers, it is, however, vital that stakeholders have a *global*, rather than local, *human rights conscience*. Because of the way MNCs do business, it is not sufficient for corporate stakeholders merely to take into account the well-being (including the human rights realization) of the people closest to them. For example, if consumers of products sold in France are not that bothered about the human rights of people who manufactured these products under exploitative conditions, say, in Peru or Vietnam, the role contemplated for market forces in this chapter will be limited. At the same time, because of this and other limitations in invoking market forces to implement and enforce corporate human rights responsibilities (as highlighted in Chapter 5), the market mechanisms are to be used only as one of the compliance strategies.

(Dis)incentives

Incentives and/or disincentives do not yet constitute a major strategy for promoting responsible corporate behaviour. In view of the importance of (dis)incentives, these features of 'economism' – a model in which economic incentives and/or disincentives are offered to encourage a particular type of conduct[79] – should be incorporated into the regulatory framework dealing with corporate human rights responsibilities. Corporations often find a model of incentives, which is concerned only with 'ultimate results', more attractive than an intrusive regulatory design.[80]

The regulatory initiatives at all three levels should, in their own way, offer incentives to companies to encourage them to comply with human rights norms. At the institutional level a company could, for example, link pay rises, promotion and other benefits of executives – who are assigned the responsibility of implementing and integrating human rights norms into business – to how well the company performs socially and not merely financially. Companies can also rely on (dis)incentives to encourage socially responsible business on the part of their suppliers. Regulatory initiatives at both national and international levels could employ a range of incentives such as providing

---

79 Under the model of economism 'responsible conduct is to be encouraged with economic incentives and disincentives.' J. Braithwaite, 'The Limits of Economism in Controlling Harmful Corporate Conduct', *Law and Society Review*, 1981, vol. 16, 481, at 482.
80 Ibid., 482–3. Braithwaite highlights many advantages that economism has over legalism. Ibid., pp. 483–8.

tax rebates, designing preferential purchasing or contracting policies and offering responsible citizenship awards.[81] These incentives can also work indirectly as disincentives: for instance, the exclusion of firms accused of perpetuating human rights violations from public procurement. It is also possible to envisage regulatory agencies formulating specific rules to offer disincentives to corporations who are indulging in human rights abuses (e.g. the China Banking Regulatory Commission has proposed regulations to prohibit banks from lending money to any industry that 'pollutes or degrades the environment').[82]

In addition to offering (dis)incentives to companies with reference to how their activities affect human rights, governments at national level should also consider taking a few other steps that would indirectly ensure that corporations respect their human rights responsibilities. First, states should offer incentives to 'facilitate the engagement' of socially active groups in enforcing corporate human rights responsibilities.[83] Of several measures proposed by Grabosky *et al.*, one deserves particular mention: that governments 'may improve legal standing – the right to bring an action before a court – of public interest groups'.[84] The question of who represents the victims of corporate human rights abuses often becomes critical because, in a majority of cases, victims (usually many in number) come from relatively disadvantaged sections of society and they are pitted in legal proceedings against very well-resourced MNCs. If *locus standi* was conferred on social action groups to pursue cases in national and/or international judicial bodies, this may help to counter this imbalance, at least partially. The success of public interest litigation in India in providing justice to destitute and disempowered sections of society against powerful actors provides a case in point.[85] It is, therefore, arguable that governments should allow such groups to sue companies in appropriate cases, or at least should not exclude their right to represent victims who consent to such representation. In the Bhopal case, it was the decision of the Indian government to assume, without consent, the exclusive right to represent

---

81 Zerk, above n. 35, pp. 38–40, 188–94; C. McCrudden, 'Corporate Social Responsibility and Public Procurement' in D. McBarnet, A. Voiculescu and T. Campbell (eds.), *The New Corporate Accountability: Corporate Social Responsibility and the Law*, Cambridge: Cambridge University Press, 2007, p. 93.
82 C. Liu and B. Ho, 'Environmental Safeguards for Lending in China', *CSR Asia Weekly*, vol. 3, Week 10, 7 March 2007, p. 3.
83 See Grabosky *et al.*, above n. 1, p. 101, and generally pp. 101–4.
84 Ibid., p. 103. They further note that 'the government may empower third parties to undertake enforcement actions on the part of the state'. Ibid., p. 125.
85 S. Sathe, *Judicial Activism in India – Transgressing Borders and Enforcing Limits*, New Delhi: Oxford University Press, 2002; U. Baxi, 'The Avatars of Indian Judicial Activism: Explorations in the Geographies of [In]justice' in S. Verma and K. Kumar (eds.), *Fifty Years of the Supreme Court of India – Its Grasp and Reach*, New Delhi: Oxford University Press, 2000, p. 156.

victims and thereby almost extinguish the right of social action groups to represent victims that backfired for victims.[86]

Second, a smooth and transparent flow of information between corporations and their stakeholders is *sine qua non* for market forces to offer (dis)incentives[87] as well as to strengthen the existing market for ethical corporate conduct.[88] As markets themselves might not ensure such a flow of information, the law has to step in. Governments could enact or strengthen the freedom of information laws and compel corporations to share information, say, about the human rights impact assessment of a given project with relevant stakeholders. Simaika goes one step further and moots the idea of a national legislation based on an 'international right to know' which would also demand disclosure of information about the overseas activities of an MNC.[89] Of course, corporations could disclose information about their affairs even without a legal requirement, or in some cases might go beyond what law requires. There are, however, concerns that such voluntary disclosure could be selective, or part of a larger window-dressing exercise.

Third, it would also be helpful if governments expanded market indicator(s) of corporate performance. This would enable stakeholders to judge the performance of corporations not merely against financial indicators (profits) but also against social indicators (e.g. how a company contributed to the fulfilment of the right to life and health by making available drugs to HIV patients, how it funded primary education for poor children, or by how much it reduced its carbon emissions).[90] Again the law should take the lead in creating an environment in which corporate performance is assessed and reported publicly according to multiple variables. Accounting standards, at both national and international levels, may be modified to reflect the need for 'triple bottom line' reporting. The resolution of the European Parliament adopted on 13 March 2007 and the King III Report on Corporate Governance in South Africa – both of which call for integrating financial reporting with social and environmental reporting by companies – are steps in the right direction.[91]

---

86 See Chapter 2.
87 N. Gunningham and D. Sinclair, 'Designing Environmental Policy' in Gunningham *et al.*, above n. 1, pp. 375, 431; Parkinson, above n. 3, pp. 59–60.
88 J. Newberg, 'Corporate Codes of Ethics, Mandatory Disclosure, and the Market for Ethical Conduct', *Vermont Law Review*, 2005, vol. 29, 253, at 287–94.
89 Simaika, above n. 20, p. 348, and generally pp. 347–60.
90 See S. Zadek, P. Pruzan and R. Evans (eds.), *Building Corporate Accountability: Emerging Practices in Social and Ethical Accounting, Auditing and Reporting*, London: Earthscan Publications Ltd., 1997.
91 European Parliament, 'Corporate Social Responsibility: A New Partnership', para. 27. Available at: www.europarl.europa.eu/sides/getDoc.do?pubRef=-//EP//TEXT+TA+P6-TA-2007-0062+0+DOC+XML+V0//EN&language=EN (accessed 15 June 2011). Institute of Directors in Southern Africa, *King Code of Governance for South Africa* (2009). Available at: www.iodsa.co.za/en-us/productsservices/kingiiireportpapersguidelines/kingreportoncorporategovernanceinsa/kingiii.aspx (accessed 25 September 2011).

Sanctions

One cannot, however, ignore the limitations of (dis)incentives,[92] as not all companies may respond positively to incentives or disincentives. The regulatory initiatives at the institutional, national and international levels should rely on three types of sanctions: civil, criminal, and social. Whereas civil and criminal sanctions are self-explanatory, by 'social' sanctions I mean the pressure and coercion exerted by stakeholders against companies (e.g. naming and shaming, public protest, awareness campaigns, media exposure, and consumer boycotts).[93] The main advantage of employing social sanctions is that as they are operationalized outside the corridors of the judicial system and without direct support from governments, they do not suffer from the same limitations that are faced by states and litigants seeking to impose civil or criminal sanctions.

Triple sanctions

Regulatory initiatives at all three regulatory levels should be capable of invoking, if needed, a range of sanctions. The availability of a range of sanctions – where 'range' refers not only to *severity* but also to *types* of sanctions – offers at least two advantages. First, sanctions of different severity and type may be suitable for different types of deviant corporations which cannot be encouraged or persuaded to respect human rights norms through incentives. Second, if more than one kind of sanction is available, then regulatory initiatives could use multiple sanctions simultaneously so as to exert more pressure on non-compliant corporate actors. Again one may see a contrast between how sanctions are to be used under the model of responsive regulation (i.e. a progressively punitive pyramid of sanctions)[94] and how sanctions are to be employed under the integrated theory (i.e. invoking civil, criminal, and social sanctions simultaneously) to make companies accountable for human rights abuses. As Table 8.1 illustrates, the type and severity of sanctions will vary among regulatory initiatives at institutional, national and international levels.

Civil sanctions

An order to make reparation is considered the most common civil sanction asserted against those corporations that violate human rights. At present legal proceedings for reparation are filed ordinarily before national courts for a breach of national or international laws. However, it is conceivable for victims of corporate human rights abuses to reach an out-of-court settlement with

---

92 Braithwaite, above n. 79, pp. 488–99.
93 S. Jiangtao, 'Website Names and Shames Polluters', *South China Morning Post*, 15 September 2006, A8.
94 See B. Fisse and J. Braithwaite, *Corporations, Crime and Accountability*, Cambridge: Cambridge University Press, 1993, pp. 141–5.

companies, which in some cases might be fallout of litigation in the first instance. Although such non-judicial settlements raise questions about the suitability of private settlement for redressing public wrongs, this approach has its advantages too (e.g. compensation is delivered to victims directly without the intervention of state agencies which, as Bhopal shows, are more prone to corruption and inefficiency than victims' groups). It is worth noting that reparation could not only serve a remedial or restitutionary purpose, but might also work as a deterrent if the court considers the paying capacity of the concerned company while fixing the amount of compensation,[95] or if the terms of an 'out-of-court' settlement are made public.

In addition to reparation, we can conceive of other types of civil sanctions at all three levels. At an institutional level corporations could, for example, institute internal disciplinary proceedings and/or resort to demoting those corporate executives and officials who contributed to human rights violations in a given case. It is similarly possible to put in place a process to disqualify, as a good corporate governance practice, corporate executives found to be responsible for human rights abuses from being appointed directors of a corporation in future. Companies can also insert a provision in their contracts with supply chains to seek damages from, or withhold payment to, suppliers that are found to indulge in violation of human/labour rights or polluting the environment.

Civil sanctions at both national and international levels may also include restitution, injunction, or formal black-listing of companies (for the purpose, say, of awarding contracts, aid or other government benefits) if they are found to be involved in human rights abuses. There is also a possibility of imposing trade sanctions, within the WTO fold or otherwise, against companies that do not respect human rights while conducting trade and business.[96] One other option that could be explored at both these levels is the model of apology and reconciliation, learning from the success of this model elsewhere.[97]

---

95 The Indian Supreme Court in *M C Mehta* v. *Union of India* AIR 1987 SC 1086 observed:

> We would also like to point out that the measure of compensation in [cases in which an enterprise was carrying on hazardous activity] must be *correlated to the magnitude and capacity of the enterprise* because such compensation must have a deterrent effect. *The larger and more prosperous the enterprise, greater must be the amount of compensation payable by it* for the harm caused on account of an accident in the carrying of the hazardous or inherently dangerous activity by the enterprise.

Ibid., para. 32 (emphasis added).

96 Deva, above n. 73, pp. 22–39; F. Garcia, 'The Global Market and Human Rights: Trading Away the Human Rights Principle', *Brooklyn Journal of International Law*, 1999, vol. 25, 51, at 87–90.

97 See, for example, the success of the South African Truth and Reconciliation Commission in dealing with human rights violations during the apartheid regime. S. Garkawe, 'The South African Truth and Reconciliation Commission: A Suitable Model to Enhance the Role and Rights of the Victims of Gross Violations of Human Rights', *Melbourne University Law Review*, 2003, vol. 27, 334.

Criminal sanctions

Although the imposition of criminal sanctions has to be a matter for regulatory initiatives at both national and international levels, it is possible to imagine some role for companies themselves in enforcing criminal law, if not imposing criminal sanctions. For instance, corporate managers can take measures to deter employees from committing crimes.[98] If a fine is imposed on a company, the company may wish to allocate this liability and recover the fine from the executives or employees who acted with criminal intent. If regulatory initiatives at the institutional level could ensure that the imposition of criminal liability on corporations would 'result in due allocation of responsibility as a matter of internal disciplinary control'[99] and do not allow the corporate form to shield individuals who committed the crime, the efficacy of criminal sanctions could increase immensely.[100]

At present, regulatory initiatives at the national level are the most potent source for imposing various types of criminal sanctions on companies who indulge in egregious human rights abuses. The sanctions might include the imposition of fines, imprisonment, license cancellation, an adverse publicity order, or an order for forfeiture of property or community service. After surveying the legal position in sixteen countries, Ramasastry and Thompson conclude that most countries permit prosecution of legal persons for criminal offences and that it is possible to hold companies liable under national laws for international crimes.[101] It is also *legally* possible to impose criminal liability, including through extraterritorial law, on MNCs for their involvement in human rights violations.[102]

Of course, it is not always easy to inflict criminal sanctions on companies. Questions arise about the (un)desirability of imposing criminal liability upon

---

98 J. Arlen, 'Evolution of Corporate Criminal Liability: Implications for Managers' in R. Gandossy and J. Sonnenfeld (eds.), *Leadership and Governance from the Inside Out*, Hoboken, New Jersey: J Wiley, 2004, p. 191.
99 Fisse and Braithwaite, above n. 94, p. 8, and generally pp. 8–14.
100 Wells highlights one of the paradoxes of current corporate criminal liability regimes: 'On the one hand, the courts have been reluctant to make a company liable for the activities of many of its employees. On the other hand, individual managers have been able to hide behind the corporation.' C. Wells, *Corporations and Criminal Responsibility*, 2nd edn, Oxford: Oxford University Press, 2001, p. 161.
101 A. Ramasastry and R. Thompson (FAFO), *Commerce, Crime and Conflict: Legal Remedies for Private Sector Liability for Grave Breaches of International Law – A Survey of Sixteen Countries*, Oslo: FAFO, 2006.
102 J. Clough, 'Not-so-innocents Abroad: Corporate Criminal Liability for Human Rights Abuses', *Australian Journal of Human Rights*, 2005, vol. 11, 1; E. Engle, 'Extraterritorial Corporate Criminal Liability: A Remedy for Human Rights Violations?', *St John's Journal of Legal Commentary*, 2006, vol. 20, 287.

companies,[103] the lack of political will for doing so,[104] or the paucity of 'prosecutorial resources' potentially inhibiting successful prosecution of companies and/or their executives.[105] There are also other technical hurdles like the difficulty in establishing a legal basis for corporate liability and the challenge of attributing wrongs within a corporate structure and of finding appropriate standards of *mens rea*.[106] Even if criminal sanctions are imposed on corporate wrongdoers guilty of human rights violations, they might not prove an effective deterrent. Coffee highlights the problem of a 'deterrence trap' that arises in relation to corporate crimes[107] – it is 'difficult to set a sanction high enough to be both collectable and sufficient for deterrence'.[108] However, as far as the legal or technical hurdles are concerned, there is no theoretical reason why these cannot be overcome.[109]

At international level, although it is desirable to have a judicial body which could administer criminal sanctions against companies, the establishment of such a body is unlikely to happen in the near future for political reasons and because of the powerful corporate lobbying against any such initiative. The ICC is perhaps the only recourse available at this moment. However, here also the scope of imposing criminal sanctions against companies is seriously limited. The Rome Statute does not, in its current form, allow for the prosecution of companies, though there was a provision for prosecuting legal persons in the initial draft.[110] Moreover, liability is limited, at this stage, to the three most serious crimes: genocide, crimes against humanity, and war crimes.[111] Thus, the existing position is far from satisfactory. Nevertheless, the limited window of opportunity offered by the Rome Statute to investigate

---

103 V. Khanna, 'Corporate Criminal Liability: What Purpose Does It Serve?' *Harvard Law Review*, 1995, vol. 109, 1477.
104 As discussed in Chapter 2, in the case of Bhopal, the Indian government did not show a strong political will to extradite and prosecute Warren Anderson, the former Chairman of UCC.
105 Braithwaite, above n. 79, p. 482.
106 T. Kaye, 'Corporate Manslaughter: Who Pays? The Ferryman?' in D. Feldman and F. Meisel, *Corporate and Commercial Law: Modern Developments*, London: Lloyd's of London Press, 1996, p. 354. See also J. Quaid, 'The Assessment of Corporate Criminal Liability on the Basis of Corporate Identity: An Analysis', *McGill Law Journal*, 1998, vol. 43, 67; C. Wells and J. Elias, '"Catching the Conscience of the King": Corporate Players on the International Stage' in Alston (ed.), above n. 35, p. 141.
107 J. Coffee, Jr, '"No Soul to Damn; No Body to Kick": An Unscandalised Inquiry into the Problem of Corporate Punishment', *Michigan Law Review*, 1980, vol. 79, 386, at 389–93.
108 Braithwaite, above n. 79, 491.
109 Kaye, above n. 106, p. 349.
110 Clapham, above n. 72, pp. 143–59.
111 Rome Statute of the International Criminal Court, UN Doc. A/CONF.183/9 (1998), art. 5. By an amendment in June 2010, the 'crime of aggression' has been defined and added to the list of prosecutable offences, but the ICC may exercise jurisdiction over this crime only after 1 January 2017.

and/or prosecute corporate executives should be utilized in appropriate cases. Prospects for prosecution should be explored, for example, in relation to corporate executives' role in funding the conflict in Congo,[112] or those involved in the administration of torture and inhumane treatment of prisoners of war as part of the 'war on terror',[113] or in forcible transfers of population for development projects in contravention of the existing guidelines.[114]

Social sanctions

The prevailing regulatory paradigm does not see states alone as 'central to regulation'[115] and tends to rely also on non-state actors to enforce norms through a range of informal means. The integrated theory of regulation likewise contemplates enforcing corporate human rights responsibilities through the imposition of social sanctions, which operate primarily outside the boundaries of the judicial system and without much government help. Instead of states and their various regulatory agencies imposing sanctions, various constituents of society (i.e. 'social actors') perform the role of regulators in employing social sanctions against corporations in coercing them to comply with human rights norms.[116]

Various social actors – which act individually as well as collectively and which operate from the local to national, regional and international levels – such as employees, consumers, investors, the media, NGOs, social activists, environmentalists, trade unions, and students will play an important role in exerting social sanctions against those companies which violate human rights.[117] Grabosky *et al.* highlight the important contributions that social actors could make in the regulatory process. These include educating the community, providing information to regulators and regulatees, acting as private enforcers, and initiating litigation to seek compensation or preventing an impending harm.[118] In addition to these measures (which are likely to

---

112 S. Kabel, 'Our Business is People (Even If It Kills Them): The Contribution of Multinational Enterprises to the Conflict in the Democratic Republic of Congo', *Tulane Journal of International and Comparative Law*, 2004, vol. 12, 461.
113 See N. Rosemann, 'The Privatization of Human Rights Violations – Business' Impunity or Corporate Responsibility? The Case of Human Rights Abuses and Torture in Iraq', *Non-State Actors and International Law*, 2005, vol. 5, 77.
114 Comprehensive Human Rights Guidelines on Development-Based Displacement, E/CN.4/Sub.2/1997/7 (2 July 1997); Basic Principles and Guidelines on Development-Based Evictions and Displacement, E/CN.4/2006/41 (16 March 2006).
115 Haines, above n. 1, p. 229.
116 Deva, above n. 55, pp. 109–15.
117 See S. Gioseffi, 'Corporate Accountability: Achieving Internal Self-Governance through Sustainability Reports', *Cornell Journal of Law & Public Policy*, 2004, vol. 13, 503.
118 Grabosky *et al.*, above n. 1, pp. 94–8. See also A. Bianchi, 'Globalisation of Human Rights: The Role of Non-state Actors' in Teubner (ed.), above n. 6, pp. 179, at 185–92.

influence the conduct of corporations indirectly), social actors 'may also bring pressure to bear *directly* on companies and industries.'[119]

There are several instances when these social actors have forced companies operating in market settings to change their business practices inconsistent with human rights norms.[120] I cite here two examples which illustrate how social pressures or sanctions, without the intervention of states or international institutions, could encourage companies to contribute to the realization of human rights while doing business. First, in response to a shareholder proposal, The Hershey Company, the largest North American chocolate and snack food company, agreed to create a broad supplier code of conduct that will not only cover the entire supply chain of the company but will also have provisions for implementation and monitoring.[121] Second, in November 2006, Nike 'announced that the company is ceasing orders with its hand-stitched soccer ball supplier, Saga Sports, based in Sialkot, Pakistan, due to the contract factory's failure to correct significant labour compliance violations'.[122] It is clear from these two examples – in which the two MNCs responded to concerns raised by their stakeholders about their business practices – that social actors could affect in many ways how corporations operate, or should operate, in market settings.[123]

The idea of social sanctions tries to exploit the corporate desire to maintain reputation and market goodwill, something which they often try to protect vigorously.[124] Corporations as well as corporate executives care about their reputation, as the research of Fisse and Braithwaite shows, because they think that adverse publicity might have a negative impact on the profitability of corporations.[125] Nothing works better as a sanction against corporate wrongdoing than something which has the potential to reduce their profits. Although the risk of negative publicity might not affect the behaviour of all types of corporations equally,[126] this type of sanction is still worth trying, because a majority of MNCs that have been castigated for egregious human rights violations are well-known and have had high public profiles. Moreover, even if the

---

119 Grabosky *et al.*, above n. 1, p. 99 (emphasis added).
120 Parker, above n. 2, pp. 157–64; Zerk, above n. 35, pp. 23–4.
121 A. Odell, 'Chocolate Giant Commits to Responsible Supplier Code', 8 March 2007. Available at: www.socialfunds.com/news/article.cgi/2245.html (accessed 9 June 2011).
122 Press Release, 'Nike Ends Orders with Soccer Ball Manufacturer', 20 November 2006. Available at: http://phx.corporate-ir.net/phoenix.zhtml?c=100529&p=irol-newsArticle&ID=1062659&highlight=> (accessed 20 June 2011).
123 Smith demonstrates this with special reference to consumers. N. Smith, *Morality and the Market: Consumer Pressure for Corporate Accountability*, London: Routledge, 1990.
124 Zadek label this 'civil regulation' in that the reputation of companies can be damaged by civil actions so as to affect their business performance. S. Zadek, *The Civil Corporation*, London: Earthscan, 2001, pp. 55–7.
125 B. Fisse and J. Braithwaite, *The Impact of Publicity on Corporate Offenders*, Albany: State University of New York Press, 1983.
126 Haines, above n. 1, p. 222.

actual target of social sanctions is a high-profile MNC, the imposition of social sanctions should have some deterrent effect on the conduct of other bystander MNCs (or smaller corporations) which are beyond the radar of the public gaze.

With a likelihood of increasing public participation in regulation in future,[127] the usefulness and significance of social sanctions is also bound to increase. The regulatory value of social sanctions will be highest in those situations in which governments are unwilling to impose or incapable of imposing civil and/or criminal sanctions against companies for human rights abuses – thus ameliorating the limitations of formal state-based enforcement mechanisms.

Summary

Hess notes that '[p]roducing socially responsible corporations is an extremely arduous task for the law'.[128] Nevertheless, regulatory efforts – both within the fold of formal law and through informal means of regulation – could be made to remedy the current situation of corporate impunity for human rights violations. In this chapter I have tried to show how a regulatory framework based on the integrated theory of regulation could be put in place to humanize business. Such a framework should not only be able to encourage companies to comply with their human rights obligations but also make them accountable for human rights violations affecting the usually disadvantaged sections of society.

The integrated theory of regulation is based on two well-founded assumptions. First, as no single regulatory theory, strategy, or sanction is adequate to deal with difficult regulatory targets such as MNCs, we need to invoke more than one strategy or sanction in an integrated fashion. Second, in view of the inherent limitations of law and states in regulating MNCs, it is imperative to employ non-legal regulatory initiatives, techniques and sanctions that do not primarily rely on government agencies, processes, or mechanisms. However, this is not to discount the important role that states and national as well as international law have to play in regulating the activities of MNCs. In view of these assumptions, the integrated theory mooted for regulatory initiatives at institutional, national and international levels to be put in place. Initiatives at all three levels should invoke, not in a progressive but an integrated manner, two implementation strategies (incentives/disincentives, and sanctions) and three types of sanctions (civil, criminal, and social) in order to achieve a robust enforcement mechanism.

Integration is also to be achieved between human rights issues and business issues and between the WWH challenges to humanizing business. This cumulative integration should result in the evolution of a regulatory framework that is able to avoid and handle future Bhopals more effectively.

---

127 Clarke, above n. 9, p. 234.
128 Hess, above n. 31, p. 84.

9   Conclusion

Human rights discourse has proven to be dynamic and ever-evolving. At different points in time, different issues have dominated the debate – from war and peace to the appropriate theory of human rights, the relative importance of different generations of rights, the human right to self-determination and development, universalism versus cultural relativism, Asian values, national sovereignty, enforcement mechanisms, trade-related rights, the special rights of minorities and vulnerable people, terrorism and the consequent 'war on terror', and the current project of spreading freedom and democracy. Human rights discourse has shown tremendous resilience in responding to the diverse kinds of challenges thrown at it by these issues.

One of the dominant themes of the current human rights discourse relates to the nature, extent and enforcement of human rights responsibilities of non-state actors such as corporations. This theme is often explored, as in this book, with a special focus on MNCs, because they are considered more difficult regulatory targets in view of their unique structure, *modus operandi*, power, and trans-border operations. Globalization, increasing liberalization of trade under the WTO, the outsourcing of public services by states to companies, technological revolution, investment-driven development, and the evolution and expanding influence of civil society organizations have provided further impetus and added newer dimensions to the issue of corporate human rights responsibility.[1]

MNCs are uniquely powerful institutions.[2] Day-to-day decisions made by companies affect, directly or indirectly, the interests (including human rights) of the entire community. Although corporations have the potential to make a positive contribution in the promotion of human rights, a gap between their

---

1 See P. Alston, 'The "Not-a-Cat" Syndrome: Can the International Human Rights Regime Accommodate Non-State Actors?' in P. Alston (ed.), *Non-State Actors and Human Rights*, Oxford: Oxford University Press, 2005, p. 3, at 17–19.
2 'By scanning the entire planet for opportunities, by shifting its resources from industry to industry and country to country, and by keeping its overriding goal simple – worldwide profit maximisation – it has become *an institution of unique power*.' R. Barnet and R. Muller, *Global Reach: The Power of the Multinational Corporations*, New York: Simon and Schuster, 1974, p. 363 (emphasis added).

potential and *performance* has often remained, making them the constant target for (excessive) criticism from several corners.³ Instances of companies' involvement in human rights abuses, acting alone or in complicity with states and their private arms, are too well documented to be dismissed as academic fantasy. Many case studies also illustrate how companies have indulged in human rights abuses in the communities in which they operate. Out of these widely discussed case studies, one glaring omission that I noticed was UCC's role in Bhopal, where a massive leakage of toxic gases on the night of 2 December 1984 killed thousands of people, injured several hundred thousand and also caused extensive environmental pollution. Barring a few exceptions, the existing academic literature has primarily analyzed Bhopal as a mass toxic tort or an environmental disaster. However, Bhopal, as I have tried to demonstrate in Chapters 2 and 6, could also be seen as a site where an MNC violated several human rights of the people of a developing country (e.g. the right to life, the right to health, the right to information, and the right to a clean environment). By analyzing Bhopal from a human rights perspective, this book sought to fill a significant gap in existing scholarship.

The choice of Bhopal as a case study was justified because it symbolizes a typical scenario of MNCs' involvement in human rights violations: an MNC from a developed country undermined the human rights of mostly poor and illiterate populace of a developing country by exploiting the loopholes in the regulatory framework. Bhopal remains relevant today, as it has been for more than 27 years since the gas leak in the chemical plant, because the Bhopal victims faced almost all the major legal and practical challenges that are commonly faced by victims of corporate human rights abuses – and to date those challenges by and large remain unanswered. I employed Bhopal not only to show how the roots of corporate human rights abuses could be traced to the circumstances and conditions under which MNCs enter and continue to operate in emerging markets of developing countries, but also to demonstrate how MNCs are often able to enjoy impunity for human rights violations by exploiting the inadequacies of current regulatory initiatives.

The instances of corporate human rights abuse have been met with diverse regulatory responses at various levels – from institutional to national, regional and international levels – flowing from both internal and external sources. There is, therefore, no regulatory vacuum as some commentators have suggested.⁴ What we are witnessing, rather, is a situation where the existing

---

3 J. Bhagwati, *In Defense of Globalization*, New York: Oxford University Press, 2004, p. ix, and generally pp. 22–4, 162–90.
4 See, e.g. J. Siegle, 'Suing US Corporations in Domestic Courts for Environmental Wrongs Committed Abroad through the Extraterritorial Application of Federal Statutes', *University of Miami Business Law Review*, 2002, vol. 10, 393; M. Ellinikos, 'American MNCs Continue to Profit from the Use of Forced and Slave Labour Begging the Question: Should America Take a Cue from Germany?', *Columbia Journal of Law and Social Problems*, 2001, vol. 35, 1, at 32.

regulatory initiatives are proving inadequate to make companies accountable for human rights abuses. This inadequacy arises partly because companies (especially MNCs) are difficult regulatory targets because of five regulatory dilemmas that their regulation poses: *who* should regulate *what* activities of *which* corporation, *where*, and *how*? Furthermore, the law has reacted slowly to transformations in the institution of the corporation generally,[5] something that squarely applies to how it has responded to corporate human rights violations. The law also suffers from several serious limitations that hamper its ability to tame the activities of powerful artificial entities which operate at a transnational level.

Overcoming regulatory hurdles: an integrated theory of regulation

Against this background, this book advanced two claims: one prerequisite and the other central. The prerequisite claim was that existing regulatory initiatives concerning corporate human rights responsibilities are inadequate. The inadequacy was judged with reference to their efficacy at preventive and redressive levels. I argued in Chapter 3 that a regulatory initiative should be considered 'effective' if it can prevent or pre-empt, at least in some cases, human rights violations by companies (the preventive level) *and* could offer adequate relief to victims in cases of violations (the redressive level). In order to choose a representative sample out of numerous regulatory initiatives and evaluate their efficacy, I contended that the existing regulatory initiatives could be differentiated from one another, and also classified into different heads, on the basis of five criteria: the *source* from which they flow; the *content* of human rights obligations; the *targeting approach* adopted by initiatives; their *level of operation*; and their *nature* in terms of compliance strategy.

Applying these five criteria, the provisions, scope and working of the following seven representative regulatory initiatives were examined critically in Chapter 4: the ATCA, corporate codes of conduct, the OECD Guidelines, the ILO Declaration, the Global Compact, the UN Norms and the Guiding Principles. This specific analysis supported a general claim about the inadequacy of the existing regulatory framework, the efficacy of which was judged in relation to the twin test of efficacy described above. I argued that the inadequacy of the current regulatory framework relating to corporate human rights responsibilities is the result of a three-fold deficiency. The existing framework offers insufficient or contestable rationales for compliance, does not prescribe precise human rights standards, and is supported by a deficient or undeveloped implementation-cum-enforcement mechanism.

---

5 L. Sealy, 'Perception and Policy in Company Law Reform' in D. Feldman and F. Meisel, *Corporate and Commercial Law: Modern Developments*, London: Lloyd's of London Press, 1996, p.11, at 28.

The central claim that I have made is that the integrated theory of regulation proposed in this book can redress, to a large extent, the threefold inadequacy of the existing regulatory framework. The theory seeks to achieve *integration* in the following three respects: between human rights issues and business issues; between the WWH challenges to humanizing business; and finally between different available levels of regulation, strategies of implementation, and types of sanctions.

The integration on the last two counts is dealt with in the next section. But let me recapitulate here why integration in the sense of balancing between human rights issues and business issues is essential and how this could be accomplished. The interface between business and human rights involves different stakeholders that often have competing and/or conflicting interests, which is also reflected in the isolated evolution of human rights law and its institutions on the one hand and business-corporate-investment-trade law and their institutions on the other. Since both the effective realization of human rights and the presence of a healthy business environment are important for the development of individuals as well as society as a whole, it is imperative that a balance is established between human rights issues and business issues. Unless this is done, regulatory initiatives that seek to promote corporate human rights responsibilities will continue to struggle in achieving regulatory objectives.

The process to achieve this integration between human rights and business should take place at various avenues, forums and levels. Taking corporate law as an example, I showed how several states have tried to rectify the uni-focal nature of the corporation and corporate law. This is being done, for instance, by requiring directors to take into account the interests of various stakeholders when making business decisions, by imposing an obligation on companies to disclose their social performance, or by requiring companies to provide forums where the interests of stakeholders could be considered.

The 'WWH' challenges to humanizing business

The integrated theory of regulation seeks to overcome the three major challenges that any theory that seeks to humanize business faces: *Why* should corporations have human rights responsibilities? *What* is the nature and extent of these responsibilities, especially for companies operating in different countries? *How* could human rights responsibilities be enforced against companies in an effective manner? An integrated response to the WWH challenges is necessary to understand and benefit from the dynamic relationship that exists between them. The nature and extent of corporate responsibilities (what) depends, among others, on normative rationales for corporations having such responsibilities (why). Similarly, if we know the reasons for why companies tend to comply or ignore their human rights responsibilities, these reasons can help in designing a robust regulatory framework (how).

Why? – The relation *of corporations to,* and position *in, society*

At the outset, the integrated theory of regulation rebutted the thesis of scholars such as Friedman and Sternberg who argued that, subject to certain ill-defined and narrow rules of the game, the only social responsibility or purpose of business is to maximize shareholders' profit. I tried to demonstrate in Chapter 5 why such a view is unsound and simply untenable in the current economic climate. In particular, the views of Friedman that CSR will undermine the free market economy, that stockholders own the corporation, and that corporations are unsuitable to assume social responsibilities were refuted. Similarly, I showed why Sternberg's thesis of just business is not *just*: she not only fails to appreciate the true meaning of the concept of CSR, but also misconstrues two key concepts of her theory (i.e. 'ordinary decency' and 'distributive justice'). One should also not ignore that corporations too are eschewing the model of shareholders' absolute primacy to which Friedman and Sternberg subscribe.[6] Many corporations have started contributing to human rights realization by adopting positive measures in that regard.[7]

I also argued that it is problematic to rely too much on the 'business case' for human rights. Although there is some merit in the business case hypothesis, this should not be overstated in view of the unpredictable nature of the assumptions that underpin the business case. In addition, the prisoner's dilemma might discourage corporations from taking on board their human rights responsibilities. The business case for human rights, by implication, also tends to indicate that corporations need not observe human rights obligations if doing so interferes with their goal of profit maximization. Equally problematic is the attempt of the Guiding Principles to ground corporate responsibilities on societal expectations. Whoever may represent 'society', they are unlikely to have the same or uniform expectations from companies. It would also be difficult to measure the expectations of society. It is, therefore, essential to ground corporate human rights responsibilities on some other, stronger theoretical premises. I contended that all corporations should be subject to human rights obligations because of their *relation to* and *position in* society. Corporations should be bound by human rights norms because they are social organs and they possess the position to both violate and promote human rights.

An assertion that corporations should have human rights responsibilities does not seek to reject or undermine the wealth maximizing role of corporations

---

6 In a survey conducted by McKinsey of 4,238 executives in 116 countries, only 16 per cent of executives agreed with Friedman's position. McKinsey, 'The McKinsey Global Survey of Business Executives: Business and Society', *McKinsey Quarterly*, 2006, vol. 2, pp. 33–9.

7 Business and Human Rights Resource Centre, 'Positive Human Rights Initiatives by Companies Featured in Our Weekly Updates', 10 February 2005 – 24 December 2008. Available at: www.business-humanrights.org/Documents/Chart-Positive.doc (accessed 10 June 2011).

in society. The only limited claim is that the right to maximize profit should not be enjoyed at the cost of the rights of other members of society and that corporations should not be left outside the net of human rights law merely because they are predominantly economic entities. In other words, the plea is only to reconceptualize the place and role of corporations in society in view of the changing interface of corporations and states.[8] At the same time, making available the protection of human rights law against the conduct of non-state actors such as corporations will also demand a paradigmatic shift in traditional human rights law, practice and institutional framework. Such a shift is, however, needed if the human rights discourse has to remain alive to the changing needs of society, otherwise its efficacy and usefulness will be undermined.[9]

What? – Human *approach to overcome MNCs' dilemma of varying standards*

Several aspects concerning the nature and extent of corporate responsibilities remain unresolved. This book dealt with one of such aspects. As MNCs operate in several countries that differ from one another in material terms, which human rights standards should they adopt out of host standards, home standards, and international standards? How this business dilemma is resolved will have a direct bearing on the protection of human rights.

Approaching the dilemma from an 'internal' point of view (placing oneself in the shoes of corporate executives), the following two approaches, which do or could help MNCs in overcoming this complex dilemma, were canvassed in Chapter 6: the *business* approach and the *human* approach. These two approaches represent two contrasting visions of the role and place of corporations in society. The business approach, which is wedded to Friedman's classical view about corporations, does not take a principled stand *vis-à-vis* human rights. It is profit that will determine whether human rights are to be respected and if so, then which standards are to be followed. The human approach, which is grounded in a modified version of stakeholder theory, takes a more holistic view of the role of corporations in society. Under the human approach, MNCs would resolve their dilemma as to varying standards with reference to the impact of their decisions, actions or omissions on the realization of the human rights of their stakeholders.

With reference to Bhopal, I tried to demonstrate that the business approach will often fail to protect the human rights of people in developing countries, for this approach encourages MNCs to invariably adopt host standards which are inadequate most of the time. For this reason, the decisions of MNCs should instead be guided by the human approach: they should apply in host countries

---

8 J. Post, L. Preston and S. Sachs, *Redefining the Corporation: Stakeholder Management and Organisational Wealth*, Stanford: Stanford Business Books, 2002, pp. 10–12.
9 Alston, above n. 1, p. 6.

the relevant home or international standards, modified in view of morally relevant local differences. Local differences, according to this approach, are morally relevant *only if* their recognition facilitates better realization of human rights. The human approach is also consistent with the policy of 'universalism' that MNCs employ in relation to promoting free trade.[10]

How? – Integrating *available levels of regulation, strategies of implementation, and types of sanctions*

It is encouraging to note that more and more companies are adopting human rights codes or policies and have started responding to the concerns raised by various stakeholders about their activities. Nevertheless, the overall picture is still far from perfect and victims of corporate human rights abuses still face an uphill task in bringing to justice companies and their executives. Various existing regulatory initiatives that seek to make corporations accountable for the violations of human rights suffer from serious deficiencies. To remedy this situation, I argued in Chapter 7 that the integrated theory of regulation could be employed to develop an effective regulatory framework.

The integrated theory – which was developed as a critical response to the responsive regulation model proposed by Ayres and Braithwaite – posits that since no single regulatory theory, strategy, or sanction is foolproof, more so when dealing with difficult regulatory targets such as MNCs, we need to invoke more than one strategy or sanction in an integrated fashion. I contended that the integration between different available strategies of implementation and types of sanctions should be *cumulative* and *co-ordinated* rather than being progressive and hierarchically ordered, as the enforcement pyramid proposed by Ayres and Braithwaite suggests. To maximize efficacy, regulatory techniques and sanctions should be employed simultaneously to complement one another rather than being invoked only when the techniques situated lower on the regulatory pyramid fail to deliver.

Based on the integrated theory, a regulatory framework for corporate accountability for human rights violations was outlined in Chapter 8. It was proposed that regulatory initiatives introduced at institutional, national and international levels should define human rights responsibilities and enforce them against companies by employing various types of (dis)incentives and sanctions. Out of various ideas that were canvassed as part of the integrated regulatory framework, a few merit reiteration here. In the formulation of corporate human rights responsibilities, there should be a *continuous cycle of dialogue* between regulatory initiatives at three levels in that they will be informed by the experiences and outcomes of each other. Apart from the formulation of

---

10 S. Rees, 'Omissions in the 20th Century: Priorities for the 21st' in S. Rees and S. Wright (eds.), *Human Rights and Corporate Responsibility – A Dialogue*, Sydney: Pluto Press, 2000, p. 296, at 298.

corporate human rights responsibilities at institutional and national levels, it is fundamental that the responsibilities of companies are catalogued, in a declaration or convention, at international level with reference to the state-centric International Bill of Rights. In addition, I proposed that a Model Law on Business and Human Rights should be drafted to provide a template for states to deal with the challenges arising out of the privatization of human rights. The SRSG may pat his back for the 'so-called' consensus that he built around the 'protect, respect and remedy' framework and for the unanimous approval of the Guiding Principles by the Human Rights Council. However, the fact of the matter is that instead of setting global human rights standards for companies, the Guiding Principles leave it to companies to ascertain their human rights responsibilities on a case-by-case basis. This circular approach (directing companies to international treaties drafted by states for states) is unsatisfactory, because it would neither offer concrete guidance to companies nor let stakeholders conclude easily if a company is in breach of its obligations.

Regulation is all about changing the behaviour of targeted regulatees. Therefore, regulatory initiatives at the national level should try to influence corporate conduct 'from inside' by amending corporate laws. If the project of corporate human rights responsibilities has to succeed in any real sense, it is especially critical to rectify the uni-focal nature of the corporation to maximize profits at will by externalizing costs. Corporate law should ensure that companies do not ignore the interests of their stakeholders. States should also try to overcome the obstacles posed to victims by the principles of limited liability and separate legal personality.

Since implementation of corporate human rights responsibilities is critical, regulatory initiatives at all levels should also rely on informal, non-legal tools and non-state institutions to ensure that companies comply with their human rights responsibilities. The over-reliance placed by the Guiding Principles on states to implement and enforce corporate human rights responsibilities is misplaced. States would continue to have a key role in ensuring that companies comply with their human rights responsibilities. But at the same time, a robust supra-state alternative should be available to deal with those situations where states are unable or unwilling to act against powerful companies, or where egregious violations of human rights become a matter of global concern. It is proposed that the UN should establish a body (e.g. the Commission on Business and Human Rights) to coordinate the task of formulating and implementing corporate human rights responsibilities at international level in a systematic and coherent manner.

Moreover, there is a need to harness and fully utilize the potential of market participants in administering social incentives and social sanctions. One proposal to institutionalize this idea could be to establish an international monitoring body, with branches in each state, consisting only of civil society organizations. Such a 'non-state, non-corporate' body should verify and investigate alleged human rights abuses by companies. If, upon investigation, this body finds that a given company is disregarding human rights responsibilities, it should seek an explanation from the company, make remedial recommendations, and then put the matter in the public domain so that this process could provide a basis for the imposition of social sanctions by stakeholders in appropriate cases.

Moving ahead beyond 'consensus'

If the goal of realizing human rights is to be achieved fully, then we should not merely be asking if this or that state has violated human rights in a given case. Rather than focusing principally on 'who' violated human rights norms, inquiry should be directed more to the *human* 'whose' rights are violated, because human rights are premised on protecting human dignity from whatever source the threat originates. For people whose human rights are violated, it makes little or no difference if the violator is a state or a non-state actor. Of course, the obligations of non-state actors should not, and need not, be similar to those of states. However, this is different from saying that non-state actors such as companies cannot have legally binding human rights obligations. Human rights law, both at national and international levels, is not only capable but is also incrementally moving in the direction of imposing human rights obligations on a range of (public, semi-public and private) actors. There is a need to move decisively to formulate as well as enforce human rights obligations against companies, rather than to be swayed by the rhetoric of consensus floated by the SRSG.

I am under no illusion that the project of extending and enforcing human rights obligations against companies will be easy or that it will have a short gestation period;[11] the history of human rights law and practice suggests otherwise. Nevertheless, this project's goals are achievable. What is, however, vital is that we walk in the right direction and use the appropriate tools. We do not do this when we are reminded that the only social responsibility of companies is to maximize profit, when the human rights responsibilities of companies are grounded on the 'business case' or societal expectations, when we are told about the futility of defining corporate responsibilities at international level, when states' obligations are confined to the 'protect' component of the duty typology, when companies are assured that they have only a *responsibility* to *respect* human rights, when no concrete solutions are offered to overcome obstacles in access to justice, and when no compelling need is felt to put in place an international enforcement mechanism.

As an alternative, this book has suggested the direction and the tools that should be adopted to accomplish the goal of humanizing business. Setting that goal and working towards achieving it is more important than aspiring for a consensus at the cost of undermining human rights.

---

11 'The move away from state actors will be resisted by the many powerful interests that benefit from the relative immunity provided by narrow conceptions of human rights.' C. Jochnick, 'Confronting the Impunity of Non-State Actors: New Fields for the Promotion of Human Rights', *Human Rights Quarterly*, 1999, vol. 21, 56, at 79.

Bibliography

Books, Book chapters and Reports

Addo, M. (ed.), *Human Rights Standards and the Responsibility of Transnational Corporations*, Hague: Kluwer Law International, 1999.

——, 'Human Rights and Transnational Corporations – An Introduction' in M. Addo (ed.), *Human Rights Standards and the Responsibility of Transnational Corporations*, Hague: Kluwer Law International, 1999, p. 31.

——, 'The Corporation as a Victim of Human rights Violations' in M. Addo (ed.), *Human Rights Standards and the Responsibility of Transnational Corporations*, Hague: Kluwer Law International, 1999, p. 190.

Alston, P. (ed.), *Non-State Actors and Human Rights*, New York: Oxford University Press, 2005.

——, 'The "Not-a-Cat" Syndrome: Can the International Human Rights Regime Accommodate Non-State Actors?' in P. Alston (ed.), *Non-State Actors and Human Rights*, Oxford: Oxford University Press, 2005, p. 3.

Amnesty International, *Clouds of Injustice: Bhopal Disaster 20 Years On*, London: Amnesty International, 2004.

——, *Undermining Freedom of Expression in China: The Role of Yahoo, Microsoft and Google*, London: Amnesty International, 2006.

Anderson, M., 'An Overview' in A. Boyle and M. Anderson (eds), *Human Rights Approaches to Environmental Protection*, New York: Oxford University Press, 1996, p. 1.

Arlen, J., 'Evolution of Corporate Criminal Liability: Implications for Managers' in R. Gandossy and J. Sonnenfeld (eds), *Leadership and Governance from the Inside Out*, Hoboken, New Jersey: J Wiley, 2004, p. 191.

Atiyah, P., *The Rise and Fall of Freedom of Contract*, Oxford: Clarendon Press, 1979.

Austin, G., *The Indian Constitution: Cornerstone of a Nation*, Oxford: Clarendon Press, 1966.

Axelrod, R., *The Evolution of Cooperation*, London: Penguin Books, 1990.

Ayres, I. and Braithwaite, J., *Responsive Regulation: Transcending the Deregulation Debate*, New York: Oxford University Press, 1992.

Bakan, J., *The Corporation: The Pathological Pursuit of Profit and Power*, New York: Free Press, 2004.

Baldwin, R. and Cave, M., *Understanding Regulation: Theory, Strategy, and Practice*, Oxford: Oxford University Press, 1999.

Barnet, R. and Muller, R., *Global Reach: The Power of the Multinational Corporations*, New York: Simon and Schuster, 1974.

Barnett, H., *Constitutional and Administrative Law*, 5th edn, London: Cavendish Publishing Ltd., 2004.

Baxi, U., *The Future of Human Rights*, New Delhi: Oxford University Press, 2002.

——, 'An Introduction' in U. Baxi and A. Dhanda (eds), *Valiant Victims and Lethal Litigation: The Bhopal Case*, Bombay: N M Tripathi Pvt. Ltd, 1990, p. i.

——, 'The Avatars of Indian Judicial Activism: Explorations in the Geographies of [In]justice' in S. Verma and K. Kumar (eds), *Fifty Years of the Supreme Court of India – Its Grasp and Reach*, New Delhi: Oxford University Press, 2000, p. 156.

——, 'The "Just War" for Profit and Power?: The Bhopal Catastrophe and the Principle of Double Effect' in L. Bomann-Larsen and O. Wiggen (eds), *Responsibility in World Business: Managing Harmful Side-Effects of Corporate Activity*, Tokyo: United Nations University Press, 2004, p. 4.

Baxi, U. and Dhanda, A. (eds), *Valiant Victims and Lethal Litigation: The Bhopal Case*, Bombay: N M Tripathi Pvt. Ltd, 1990.

Beder, S., *Global Spin: The Corporate Assault on Environmentalism*, revised edn, Foxhole, Dartington, Devon: Green Books Ltd., 2002.

Bhagwati, J., *In Defense of Globalization*, New York: Oxford University Press, 2004.

Bianchi, A., 'Globalisation of Human Rights: The Role of Non-state Actors' in G. Teubner (ed.), *Global Law Without a State*, Aldershot: Dartmouth, 1997, p. 179.

Black, E., *IBM and the Holocaust: The Strategic Alliance between Nazi Germany and America's Most Powerful Corporation*, New York: Crown Publishers, 2001.

Black, J., *Rules and Regulators*, Oxford: Clarendon Press, 1997.

Blumberg, P., *The Multinational Challenge to Corporation Law: The Search for a New Corporate Personality*, New York: Oxford University Press, 1993.

Boatright, J., *Ethics and the Conduct of Business*, 3rd edn, Upper Saddle River, New Jersey: Prentice Hall, 2000.

——, *Ethics and the Conduct of Business*, 4th edn, Upper Saddle River, New Jersey: Prentice Hall, 2003.

——, *Ethics and the Conduct of Business*, 5th edn, Upper Saddle River, New Jersey: Prentice Hall, 2007.

Bogard, W., *The Bhopal Tragedy: Language, Logic, and Politics in the Production of a Hazard*, Boulder, Colorado: Westview Press, 1989.

Bowie, N., 'The Moral Obligations of Multinational Corporations' in T. Donaldson and T. Dunfee (eds), *Ethics in Business and Economics*, vol. 1, Aldershot: Dartmouth Publishing, 1997, p. 249.

Brownlie, I., *Principles of Public International Law*, 6th edn, Oxford: Oxford University Press, 2003.

Business Leaders Initiative on Human Rights (BLIHR), *Report 3: Towards a 'Common Framework' on Business and Human Rights: Identifying Components*, London: BLIHR, 2006.

Cassels, J., *The Uncertain Promise of Law: Lessons from Bhopal*, Toronto: University of Toronto Press, 1993.

Chandler, Sir G., 'Keynote Address: Crafting a Human Rights Agenda for Business' in M. Addo (ed.), *Human Rights Standards and the Responsibility of Transnational Corporations*, The Hague: Kluwer Law International, 1999, p. 39.

Chiomenti, C., 'Corporations and the International Criminal Court' in O. De Schutter (ed.), *Transnational Corporations and Human Rights*, Oxford: Hart Publishing, 2006, p. 287.
Clapham, A., *Human Rights in the Private Sphere*, New York: Oxford University Press, 1993.
——, *Human Rights Obligations of Non-State Actors*, Oxford: Oxford University Press, 2006.
——, 'The Question of Jurisdiction under International Criminal Court over Legal Persons: Lessons from the Rome Conference on an International Criminal Court' in M. Kamminga and S. Zia-Zarifi (eds), *Liability of Multinational Corporations under International Law*, The Hague: Kluwer Law International, 2000, p. 139.
Clarke, M., *Regulation: The Social Control of Business between Law and Politics*, London: Macmillan Press, 2000.
Commission on Human Rights, 'Interim Report of the Special Representative of the Secretary General on the Issue of Human Rights and Transnational Corporations and Other Business Enterprises', E/CN.4/2006/97 (22 February 2006).
Czerny, M., 'Liberation Theology and Human Rights' in K. Mahoney and P. Mahoney (eds), *Human Rights in the Twenty-first Century*, Dordrecht: Martinus Nijhoff Publishers, 1993, p. 36.
Daniels, J., Radebaugh L. H. and Sullivan, D. P., *Globalization and Business*, 1st edn, Upper Saddle River, New Jersey: Prentice Hall, 2002.
Davies, P., *Gower and Davies's Principles of Modern Company Law*, 7th edn, London: Sweet & Maxwell, 2003.
Davis, K. and Blomstrom, R., *Business and Society: Environment and Responsibility*, 3rd edn, New York: McGraw-Hill, 1975.
De George, R., 'Business as a Humanity: A Contradiction in Terms?' in T. Donaldson and R. Freeman (eds), *Business as a Humanity*, New York: Oxford University Press, 1994, p. 11.
Deva, S., 'Corporate Human Rights Abuses: What Role for the National Human Rights Institutions?' in H. Nasu and B. Saul (eds), *Human Rights in the Asia Pacific Region: Towards Institution Building*, London: Routledge, 2011, p. 234.
——,'"Protect, Respect and Remedy": A Critique of the SRSG's Framework for Business and Human Rights' in K. Buhmann, L. Roseberry and M. Morsing (eds), *Corporate Social and Human Rights Responsibilities: Global Legal and Management Perspectives*, Hampshire: Palgrave Macmillan, 2011, p. 108.
Dine, J., *Companies, International Trade and Human Rights*, Cambridge: Cambridge University Press, 2005.
Donaldson, T., *Corporations and Morality*, Englewood Cliffs, New Jersey: Prentice-Hall Inc., 1982.
——, *The Ethics of International Business*, New York: Oxford University Press, 1989.
Donnelly, J., *Universal Human Rights: In Theory and Practice*, Ithaca: Cornell University Press, 1989.
Dworkin, R., *Taking Rights Seriously*, London: Duckworth, 1977.
Easterbrook, F. and Fischel, D., *The Economic Structure of Corporate Law*, Cambridge, Mass.: Harvard University Press, 1991.
Eroglu, M., *Multinational Enterprises and Tort Liabilities: An Interdisciplinary and Comparative Examination*, Gloucester: Edward Elgar Publishing, 2008.
Fisse, B. and Braithwaite, J., *Corporations, Crime and Accountability*, Cambridge: Cambridge University Press, 1993.

———, *The Impact of Publicity on Corporate Offenders*, Albany: State University of New York Press, 1983.
Fogarty, M., *Company and Corporation – One Law?* London: Geoffrey Chapman, 1965.
Fortun, K., *Advocacy after Bhopal: Environmentalism, Disaster, New Global Orders*, Chicago: University of Chicago Press, 2001.
Freeman, R., *Strategic Management: A Stakeholder Approach*, Boston: Pitman, 1984.
French, P., *Corporate Ethics*, Fort Worth: Harcourt Brace College Publishers, 1995.
Friedman, A. and Miles S., *Stakeholders: Theory and Practice*, Oxford: Oxford University Press, 2006.
Friedman, M., *Capitalism and Freedom*, 40th anniversary edition, Chicago: University of Chicago Press, 2002.
Fuller, L., *The Morality of Law*, 2nd Indian reprint, New Delhi: Universal Law Publishing Co. Pvt. Ltd, 2000.
Garner, B. A. (ed.-in-chief.), *Black's Law Dictionary*, 9th edn, St. Paul, Minn.: West/Thompson Reuters, 2009.
Goodhart, M., 'Human Rights and Non-State Actors: Theoretical Puzzles' in G. Andreopoulos, Z. F. K. Arat and P. Juviler (eds.), *Non-State Actors in the Human Rights Universe*, Bloomfield: Kumarian Press, 2006, p. 23.
Grabosky, P., Gunningham, N. and Sinclair, D., 'Parties, Roles, and Interactions' in N. Gunningham, P. Grabosky and D. Sinclair, *Smart Regulation: Designing Environmental Policy*, Oxford: Clarendon Press, 1998, p. 93.
Grey, S., *Ghost Plane: The True Story of the CIA Torture Program*, New York: St Martins Press, 2006.
Gunningham, N., 'Introduction' in N. Gunningham, P. Grabosky and D. Sinclair, *Smart Regulation: Designing Environmental Policy*, Oxford: Clarendon Press, 1998, p. 3.
Gunningham, N. and Sinclair, D., 'Instruments for Environmental Protection' in N. Gunningham, P. Grabosky and D. Sinclair, *Smart Regulation: Designing Environmental Policy*, Oxford: Clarendon Press, 1998, p. 37.
Haines, F., *Corporate Regulation: Beyond 'Punish' or 'Persuade'*, Oxford: Clarendon Press, 1997.
Hamid, U. and Johner, O., 'The United Nations Global Compact Communication on Progress Policy: Origins, Trends and Challenges' in A. Rasche and G. Kell (eds), *The United Nations Global Compact: Achievements, Trends and Challenges*, Cambridge: Cambridge University Press, 2010, p. 265.
Harlow, C., *State Liability: Tort Law and Beyond*, Oxford: Oxford University Press, 2004.
Heap, S. and Varoufakis, Y., *Game Theory: A Critical Text*, 2nd edn, London: Routledge, 2004.
Heenan, D. and Perlmutter, H., *Multinational Organization Development*, Reading, Massachusetts: Addison-Wesley, 1979.
Henderson, D., *Misguided Virtue: False Notions of Corporate Social Responsibility*, London: Institute of Economic Affairs, 2001.
Henkin, L., *The Age of Rights*, New York: Columbia University Press, 1990.
Henriques, A., and Richardson, J. (eds), *The Triple Bottom Line, Does It All Add Up?: Assessing the Sustainability of Business and CSR*, London: Earthscan Publications Ltd., 2004.
Higgins, R., *Problems and Process: International Law and How We Use It*, Oxford: Clarendon Press, 1994.

Hinkley, R., 'Developing Corporate Conscience' in S. Rees and S. Wright (eds), *Human Rights and Corporate Responsibility – A Dialogue*, Sydney: Pluto Press, 2000, p. 287.

Human Rights Council, 'Business and Human Rights in Conflict-Affected Regions: Challenges and Options towards State Response', A/HRC/17/32 (27 May 2011).

——, 'Business and Human Rights: Further Steps toward the Operationalization of the "Protect, Respect and Remedy" Framework', A/HRC/14/27 (9 April 2010).

——, 'Business and Human Rights: Towards Operationalizing the "Protect, Respect and Remedy" Framework', A/HRC/11/13 (22 April 2009).

——, 'Guiding Principles on Business and Human Rights: Implementing the United Nations "Protect, Respect and Remedy" Framework', A/HRC/17/31 (21 March 2011), Principle 31.

——, 'Human Rights and Corporate Law: Trends and Observations from a Cross-national Study Conducted by the Special Representative', A/HRC/17/31/Add.2 (23 May 2011).

——, 'Principles for Responsible Contracts: Integrating the Management of Human Rights Risks into State-Investor Contract Negotiations – Guidance for Negotiators', A/HRC/17/31/Add.3 (25 May 2011).

——, 'Protect, Respect and Remedy: A Framework for Business and Human Rights', A/HRC/8/5 (7 April 2008).

——, 'Report of the SRSG: Business and Human Rights – Mapping International Standards of Responsibility and Accountability for Corporate Acts', A/HRC/4/35 (19 February 2007).

——, 'Report of the SRSG: Corporate Responsibility under International Law and Issues in Extraterritorial Regulation – Summary and Legal Workshops', A/HRC/4/35/Add.2 (15 February 2007).

Human Rights Watch (HRW), *"Race to the Bottom": Corporate Complicity in Chinese Internet Censorship*, New York: HRW, 2006.

Ijalaye, D., *The Extension of Corporate Personality in International Law*, New York: Oceana Publications, 1978.

International Council on Human Rights Policy (ICHRP), *Beyond Voluntarism: Human Rights and the Developing International Legal Obligations of Companies*, Versoix: ICHRP, 2002.

Jägers, N., *Corporate Human Rights Obligations: In Search of Accountability*, Antwerpen: Intersentia, 2002.

Jones, T., *Corporate Killing: Bhopals will Happen*, London: Free Association Books, 1988.

Joseph, S., *Corporations and Transnational Human Rights Litigation*, Oxford: Hart Publishing, 2004.

Jungk, M., 'A Practical Guide to Addressing Human Rights Concerns for Companies Operating Abroad' in M. Addo (ed.), *Human Rights Standards and the Responsibility of Transnational Corporations*, The Hague: Kluwer Law International, 1999, p. 171.

Karl J., 'The OECD Guidelines for Multinational Enterprises' in M. Addo (ed.), *Human Rights Standards and the Responsibility of Transnational Corporations*, Hague: Kluwer Law International, 1999, p. 89.

Kaye, T., 'Corporate Manslaughter: Who Pays? The Ferryman?' in D. Feldman and F. Meisel, *Corporate and Commercial Law: Modern Developments*, London: Lloyd's of London Press, 1996, p. 354.

Keay, J., *The Honourable Company: A History of the English East India Company*, London: Harper Collins Publishers, 1991.
Kerr, M., Janda, R. and Pitts, C., *Corporate Social Responsibility: A Legal Analysis*, Markham, Ont.: LexisNexis, 2009.
Kinley, D., *Civilising Globalisation: Human Rights and the Global Economy*, Cambridge: Cambridge University Press, 2009.
Kletz, T., *Learning from Accidents*, 2nd edn, Oxford: Butterworth-Heinemann, 1994.
Kurzman, D., *A Killing Wind: Inside Union Carbide and the Bhopal Catastrophe*, New York: McGraw-Hill, 1987.
Labunska, I., Stephenson, A., Brigden, K., Stringer, R., Santillo, D. and Johnston, P. A., *The Bhopal Legacy: Toxic Contaminants at the Former Union Carbide Factory Site, Bhopal, India – 15 Years after the Bhopal Accident*, Exeter: Greenpeace Research Laboratories, 1999.
Lapierre, D. and Moro, J., *It Was Five Past Midnight in Bhopal*, New Delhi: Full Circle Publishing, 2001.
Lodge, G. and Wilson, C., *A Corporate Solution to Global Poverty: How Multinationals can Help the Poor and Invigorate their Own Legitimacy*, Princeton: Princeton University Press, 2006.
Lord Bingham of Cornhill, 'Tort and Human Rights' in P. Cane and J. Stapleton (eds), *The Law of Obligations: Essays in Celebration of John Fleming*, Oxford: Clarendon Press, 1998, p. 1.
Lucas, J., 'The Responsibilities of a Businessman' in W. Shaw (ed.), *Ethics at Work: Basic Readings in Business Ethics*, Oxford: Oxford University Press, 2003.
McCrudden, C., 'Corporate Social Responsibility and Public Procurement' in D. McBarnet, A. Voiculescu and T. Campbell (eds), *The New Corporate Accountability: Corporate Social Responsibility and the Law*, Cambridge: Cambridge University Press, 2007, p. 93.
Margolis, J. and Walsh, J., *People and Profits?: The Search for a Link Between a Company's Social and Financial Performance*, Mahwah, NJ: Lawrence Erlbaum Associates Publishers, 2001.
Meeran, R., 'The Unveiling of Transnational Corporations: A Direct Approach' in M. Addo (ed.), *Human Rights Standards and the Responsibility of Transnational Corporations*, Hague: Kluwer Law International, 1999, p. 161.
Megone, C., 'Two Aristotelian Approaches to Business Ethics' in C. Megone and S. Robinson (eds), *Case Histories in Business Ethics*, London: Routledge, 2002, p. 23.
Menon, N.R.M. (ed.), *Documents and Court Opinions on Bhopal Gas Leak Disaster Case*, Bangalore: National Law School of India University, 1991.
Micklethwait, J. and Wooldridge, A., *The Company: A Short History of a Revolutionary Idea*, New York: Modern Library, 2003.
Ministry of Information and Broadcasting, Government of India, *The Collected Works of Mahatma Gandhi*, 22 July 1921 – 25 October 1921, vol. 24, New Delhi.
Mitchell, L., *Corporate Irresponsibility: America's Newest Export*, New Haven: Yale University Press, 2001.
Morehouse, W. and Subramaniam, M., *The Bhopal Tragedy: What Really Happened and What it Means for American Workers and Communities at Risk*, New York: Council for International & Public Affairs, 1986.
Muchlinski, P., '"Global Bukowina" Examined: Viewing the Multinational Enterprise as a Transnational Law-making Community' in G. Teubner (ed.), *Global Law Without a State*, Aldershot: Dartmouth, 1997, p. 79.

——, *Multinational Enterprises and the Law*, 2nd edn, Oxford: Oxford University Press, 2007.

Murphy, J., *Street on Torts*, 1st Indian reprint, New Delhi: Oxford University Press, 2006.

Organisation for Economic Co-operation and Development (OECD), *Codes of Corporate Conduct: An Expanded Review of their Content*, TD/TC/WP(99)56/FINAL, June 2000.

——, *Corporate Responsibility: Private Initiatives and Public Goals*, Paris: OECD, 2001.

OECD Watch, *10 Years On: Assessing the Contribution of the OECD Guidelines for Multinational Enterprises to Responsible Business Conduct*, June 2010.

Orlando, J., 'The Ethics of Corporate Downsizing' in W. Shaw (ed.), *Ethics at Work: Basic Readings in Business Ethics*, Oxford: Oxford University Press, 2003, p. 31.

Ormerod, D., *Smith and Hogan Criminal Law*, 11th edn, Oxford: Oxford University Press, 2005.

Parker, C., *The Open Corporation: Effective Self-regulation and Democracy*, Cambridge: Cambridge University Press, 2002.

Parkinson, J., 'The Socially Responsible Company' in M. Addo (ed.), *Human Rights Standards and the Responsibility of Transnational Corporations*, The Hague: Kluwer Law International, 1999, p. 49.

Parliament of Australia Joint Committee on Corporations and Financial Services, *Corporate Responsibility: Managing Risk and Creating Value*, Canberra: Australian Parliament, 2006.

Pava, M. and Krausz, J., *Corporate Responsibility and Financial Performance*, Westport: Quorum Books, 1995.

Pollock, Sir F., *The Law of Torts: A Treatise on the Principles of Obligations Arising from Civil Wrongs in the Common Law*, 13th edn, London: Stevens & Sons Ltd., 1929.

Posner, R., *Economic Analysis of Law*, 5th edn, New York: Aspen, 1998.

Post, J. E., Lawrence, A. T. and Weber, J., *Business and Society: Corporate Strategy, Public Policy, Ethics*, 9th edn, Boston: Irwin/McGraw-Hill, 1999.

Post, J., Preston, L. and Sachs, S., *Redefining the Corporation: Stakeholder Management and Organisational Wealth*, Stanford: Stanford Business Books, 2002.

Prakash, O., *European Commercial Enterprise in Pre-colonial India*, Cambridge: Cambridge University Press, 1998.

Rajagopal, B., *International Law from Below: Development, Social Movements and Third World Resistance*, Cambridge: Cambridge University Press, 2003.

Ramasastry, A. and Thompson, R. (FAFO), *Commerce, Crime and Conflict: Legal Remedies for Private Sector Liability for Grave Breaches of International Law – A Survey of Sixteen Countries*, Oslo: FAFO, 2006.

Rasche, A. and Kell, G. (eds), *The United Nations Global Compact: Achievements, Trends and Challenges*, Cambridge: Cambridge University Press, 2010.

Raz, J., *The Morality of Freedom*, Oxford: Clarendon Press, 1986.

Rees, S., 'Omissions in the 20th Century: Priorities for the 21st' in S. Rees and S. Wright (eds), *Human Rights and Corporate Responsibility – A Dialogue*, Sydney: Pluto Press, 2000, p. 296.

Rees, S. and Wright, S., 'Human Rights and Business Controversies' in S. Rees and S. Wright (eds), *Human Rights and Corporate Responsibility – A Dialogue*, Sydney: Pluto Press, 2000.

——, (eds), *Human Rights and Corporate Responsibility – A Dialogue*, Sydney: Pluto Press, 2000.

Reinisch, A., 'The Changing International Legal Framework for Dealing with Non-State Actors' in P. Alston (ed.), *Non-State Actors and Human Rights*, New York: Oxford University Press, 2005.

Sathe, S., *Judicial Activism in India – Transgressing Borders and Enforcing Limits*, New Delhi: Oxford University Press, 2002.

Scott, C., (ed.), *Torture as Tort: Comparative Perspectives on the Development of Transnational Human Rights Litigation*, Oxford: Hart Publishing, 2001.

Sealy, L., 'Perception and Policy in Company Law Reform' in D. Feldman and F. Meisel, *Corporate and Commercial Law: Modern Developments*, London: Lloyd's of London Press, 1996.

Secretary-General of the United Nations, *In Larger Freedom: Towards Development, Security and Human Rights for All*, New York: UN, 2005.

Seid, S., *Global Regulation of Foreign Direct Investment*, Aldershot: Ashgate, 2002.

Sen, A., *Development as Freedom*, 1st paperback edn, Oxford: Oxford University Press, 2001.

Shastri, L., *Bhopal Disaster: An Eye Witness Account*, New Delhi: Criterion Publications, 1985.

Shaw, M., *International Law*, 3rd edn, Cambridge: Grotius Publications, 1991.

Shelton, D., 'Protecting Human Rights in a Globalising World' in C. Ku and P. Diehl (eds), *International Law: Classic and Contemporary Readings*, 2nd edn, Boulder, Colorado: Rienner Publishers, 2003.

Shrivastava, P., *Bhopal: Anatomy of a Crisis*, Massachusetts: Ballinger Publishing Co., 1987.

Shue, H., *Basic Rights: Subsistence, Affluence, and US Foreign Policy*, 2nd edn, Princeton: Princeton University Press, 1996.

Singh, G., *Ratanlal and Dhirajlal's The Law of Torts*, 23rd edn, Nagpur: Wadhwa & Co., 1997.

Singh, M.P., *Shukla's Constitution of India*, 11th edn, Lucknow: Eastern Book Co., 2008.

Skogly, S., *The Human Rights Obligations of the World Bank and the International Monetary Fund*, London: Cavendish Publishing, 2001.

Smith, N., *Morality and the Market: Consumer Pressure for Corporate Accountability*, London: Routledge, 1990.

Sneoyenbos, M., Almeder, R. and Humber, J. (eds), *Business Ethics*, revised edn, Buffalo: Prometheus Books, 1992.

Steger, U. (ed.), *The Business of Sustainability: Building Industry Cases for Corporate Sustainability*, New York: Palgrave Macmillan, 2004.

Steinhardt, R., 'Corporate Responsibility and the International Law of Human Rights: The New *Lex Mercatoria*' in P. Alston (ed.), *Non-State Actors and Human Rights*, New York: Oxford University Press, 2005, p. 177.

Sternberg, E., *Just Business: Business Ethics in Action*, 2nd edn, Oxford: Oxford University Press, 2000.

Stone, C., *Where the Law Ends: The Social Control of Corporate Behavior*, New York: Harper & Row, 1975.

——, *Where the Law Ends: The Social Control of Corporate Behavior*, Prospect Heights, Illinois: Waveland Press, 1991.

Stringer, R., Labunska I., Brigden, K. and Santillo, D, *Chemical Stockpiles at Union Carbide India Limited in Bhopal: An Investigation*, Exeter: Greenpeace Research Laboratories, 2002.

Teubner, G., 'Foreword: Legal Regimes of Global Non-state Actors' in G. Teubner (ed.), *Global Law Without a State*, Aldershot: Dartmouth, 1997, p. xiii.

Tyagi, Y., *The UN Human Rights Committee: Practice and Procedure*, Cambridge: Cambridge University Press, 2011.

Union Carbide Corporation (UCC), *Bhopal Methyl Isocyanate Incident Investigation Team Report*, Danbury: UCC, 1985.

United Nations High Commissioner on Human Rights, 'Report of the United Nations High Commissioner on Human Rights on the Responsibilities of Transnational Corporations and Related Business Enterprises with Regard to Human Rights', E/CN.4/2005/91 (15 February 2005).

United Nations Conference on Trade and Development (UNCTAD), *World Investment Report 1999: Foreign Direct Investment and the Challenge of Development*, New York: UN, 1999.

——, *World Investment Report 2010: Investing in a Low-Carbon Economy*, New York: UN, 2010.

Utting, P., 'Regulating Business via Multistakeholder Initiatives: A Preliminary Assessment' in R. Jenkins, P. Utting and R. A. Pino, *Voluntary Approaches to Corporate Responsibility: Readings and a Resource Guide*, Geneva: UN-NGLS, 2002, 61.

Vagts, D., *Transnational Business Problems*, 2nd edn, New York: Foundation Press, 1998.

Wade, Sir W. and Forsyth, C., *Administrative Law*, 9th edn, Oxford: Oxford University Press, 2004.

Waldron, J., *The Law*, London: Routledge, 1990.

Wells, C., *Corporations and Criminal Responsibility*, 2nd edn, Oxford: Oxford University Press, 2001.

Wells, C. and Elias, J., '"Catching the Conscience of the King": Corporate Players on the International Stage' in P. Alston (ed.), *Non-State Actors and Human Rights*, New York: Oxford University Press, 2005, p. 141.

Wettstein F., *Multinational Corporations and Global Justice: Human Rights Obligations of a Quasi-governmental Institution*, Stanford: Stanford Business Books, 2009.

Wiggen, O. and Bomann-Larsen, L., 'Addressing Side-Effect Harm in the Business Context: Conceptual and Practical Challenges' in L. Bomann-Larsen and O. Wiggen (eds), *Responsibility in World Business: Managing Harmful Side-effects of Corporate Activity*, Tokyo: United Nations University Press, 2004, p. 3.

Wright, J., *Tort Law and Human Rights*, Oxford, Portland Oregon: Hart Publishing, 2001.

Wright, R., 'The Standards of Care in Negligence Law' in D. Owen (ed.), *Philosophical Foundations of Tort Law*, Oxford: Clarendon Press, 1995, p. 249.

Wright, S., *International Human Rights, Decolonisation and Globalisation: Becoming Human*, London: Routledge, 2001.

Wynhoven, U. and Stausberg, M., 'The United Nations Global Compact's Governance Framework and Integrity Measures' in A. Rasche and G. Kell (eds), *The United Nations Global Compact: Achievements, Trends and Challenges*, Cambridge: Cambridge University Press, 2010, p. 251.

Yeager, P., *The Limits of Law: The Public Regulation of Private Pollution*, Cambridge: Cambridge University Press, 1991.

Zadek, S., *The Civil Corporation*, London: Earthscan, 2001.

Zadek, S., Pruzan, P. and Evans, R. (eds), *Building Corporate Accountability: Emerging Practices in Social and Ethical Accounting, Auditing and Reporting*, London: Earthscan Publications Ltd., 1997.

Zerk, J., *Multinational and Corporate Social Responsibility: Limitations and Opportunities in International Law*, Cambridge: Cambridge University Press, 2006.

Journal articles

Abraham, C. and Rosencranz, A., 'An Evaluation of Pollution Control Legislation in India', *Columbia Journal of Environmental Law*, 1986, vol. 11, 101.

Alston, P., 'Resisting the Merger and Acquisition of Human Rights by Trade Law: A Reply to Petersmann', *European Journal of International Law*, 2002, vol. 13, 815.

Anderson, J., 'Respecting Human Rights: Multinational Corporations Strike Out', *University of Pennsylvania Journal of Labour and Employment Law*, 2000, vol. 2, 463.

Anderson, R., 'Reimagining Human Rights Law: Toward Global Regulation of Transnational Corporations', *Denver University Law Review*, 2010, vol. 88, 183.

Arrow, K., 'Social Responsibility and Economic Efficiency', *Public Policy*, 1973, vol. 21, 303.

Auger, P., Burke, P., Devinney, T. M. and Louviere, J. J., 'What will Consumers Pay for Social Product Features?', *Journal of Business Ethics*, 2003, vol. 42, 281.

Baez, C., Dearing, M., Delatour, M. and Dixon, C., 'Multinational Enterprises and Human Rights', *University of Miami International and Comparative Law Review*, 1999–2000, vol. 8, 183.

Baker, M., 'Tightening the Toothless Vice: Codes of Conduct and the American Multinational Enterprise', *Wisconsin International Law Journal* 2001, vol. 20, 89.

Bantekas, I., 'Corporate Social Responsibility in International Law', *Boston University International Law Journal*, 2004, vol. 22, 309.

Baue, B., 'Win or Lose in Court: Alien Tort Claims Act Pushes Corporate Respect for Human Rights', *Business Ethics*, Summer 2006, 12.

Baxi, U., 'Market Fundamentalisms: Business Ethics at the Altar of Human Rights', *Human Rights Law Review*, 2005, vol. 5, 1.

Berle, A. Jr., 'Corporate Powers as Powers in Trust', *Harvard Law Review*, 1931, vol. 44, 1049.

——, 'For Whom Corporate Managers *are* Trustees: A Note', *Harvard Law Review*, 1932, vol. 45, 1365.

Bilchitz, D., 'The Ruggie Framework: An Adequate Rubric for Corporate Human Rights Obligations?', *Sur – International Journal of Human Rights*, 2010, vol. 7:12, 199.

Blackett, A., 'Global Governance, Legal Pluralism and the Decentred State: A Labour Law Critique of Codes of Corporate Conduct', *Indiana Journal of Global Legal Studies*, 2001, vol. 8, 401.

Blumberg, P., 'The Increasing Recognition of Enterprise Principles in Determining Parent and Subsidiary Corporation Liabilities', *Connecticut Law Review*, 1996, vol. 28, 295.

——, 'Asserting Human Rights against Multinational Corporations under United States Law: Conceptual and Procedural Problems', *American Journal of Comparative Law*, 2002, vol. 50, 493 (Suppl.).

Boeving, J., 'Half Full ... or Completely Empty?: Environmental Alien Tort Claims Post *Sosa v. Alvarez-Machain*', *Georgetown International Environmental Law Review*, 2005, vol. 18, 109.

Borg, L., 'Sharing the Blame for September Eleventh: The Case for New Law to Regulate the Activities of American Corporations Abroad', *Arizona Journal of International and Comparative Law*, 2003, vol. 20, 607.

Bradley, C., 'Customary International Law and Private Rights of Action', *Chicago Journal of International Law*, 2000, vol. 1, 421.

——, 'The Costs of International Human Rights Litigation', *Chicago Journal of International Law*, 2001, vol. 2, 457.

Bradley, C., Goldsmith, J. and Moore, D., 'Sosa, Customary International Law, and the Continuing Relevance of Erie', *Harvard Law Review*, 2007, vol. 120, 869.

Bradley, C. and Goldsmith, J., 'The Current Illegitimacy of International Human Rights Litigation', *Fordham Law Review*, 1996, vol. 6, 6319.

Braithwaite, J., 'Convergence in Models of Regulatory Strategy', *Current Issues in Criminal Justice*, 1990, vol. 2, 59.

——, 'Enforced Self-Regulation: A New Strategy for Corporate Crime Control', *Michigan Law Review*, 1982, vol. 80, 1466.

——, 'Responsive Regulation and Developing Economies', *World Development*, 2006, vol. 34, 884.

——, 'The Limits of Economism in Controlling Harmful Corporate Conduct', *Law and Society Review*, 1981, vol. 16, 481.

Braithwaite, J. and Drahos, P., 'Zero Tolerance, Naming and Shaming: Is there a Case for it with Crimes of the Powerful?', *The Australian and New Zealand Journal of Criminology*, 2002, vol. 35, 269.

Bratspies, R., '"Organs of Society": A Plea for Human Rights Accountability for Transnational Enterprises and Other Business Entities', *Michigan State Journal of International Law*, 2005, vol. 13, 9.

Broecker, C., '"Better the Devil You Know": Home State Approaches to Transnational Corporate Accountability', *New York University Journal of International Law and Politics*, 2008, vol. 41, 159.

Bunn, I., 'Global Advocacy for Corporate Accountability: Transatlantic Perspectives from the NGO Community', *American University International Law Review*, 2004, vol. 19, 1265.

Carr, C., 'Carbide Escape: Why India's Awkward Strategy Forced the Settlement?', *The American Lawyer*, May 1989, 99.

Cassel, D., 'Corporate Initiatives: A Second Human Rights Revolution?', *Fordham International Law Journal* 1996, vol. 19, 1963.

Cassels, J., 'Outlaws: Multinational Corporations and Catastrophic Law', *Cumberland Law Review* 2000–2001, vol. 31, 311.

Casto, W., 'The Federal Court's Protective Jurisdiction over Torts Committed in Violation of the Law of Nations', *Connecticut Law Review*, 1986, vol. 18, 467.

Charlesworth, H., Chinkin C. and Wright, S., 'Feminist Approaches to International Law', *American Journal of International Law*, 1991, vol. 85, 613.

Chinkin, C., 'A Critique of the Public/Private Dimension', *European Journal of International Law*, 1999, vol. 10, 387.

Chopra, S., 'Multinational Corporations in the Aftermath of Bhopal: The Need for a New Comprehensive Global Regime for Transnational Corporate Activity, *Valparaiso University Law Review*, 1994, vol. 29, 235.

Clapham, A. and Jerbi, S., 'Categories of Corporate Complicity in Human Rights Abuses', *Hastings International and Comparative Law Review* 2001, vol. 24, 339.

Cleveland, S., 'Global Labour Rights and the Alien Tort Claims Act', *Texas Law Review* 1998, vol. 76, 1533.
Clough, J., 'Not-so-innocents Abroad: Corporate Criminal Liability for Human Rights Abuses', *Australian Journal of Human Rights*, 2005, vol. 11, 1.
Coffee, J. Jr, '"No Soul to Damn; No Body to Kick": An Unscandalised Inquiry into the Problem of Corporate Punishment', *Michigan Law Review*, 1980, vol. 79, 386.
Compa, L., 'Exceptions and Conditions: The Multilateral Agreement on Investment and International Labor Rights: A Failed Connection', *Cornell International Law Journal* 1998, vol. 31, 683.
Cooter, R., 'The Best Right Laws: Value Foundations of the Economic Analysis of Law', *Notre Dame Law Review*, 1989, vol. 64, 817.
Corfield, A., 'The Stakeholder Theory and its Future in Australian Corporate Governance: A Preliminary Analysis', *Bond Law Review*, 1998, vol. 10, 213.
D'Amato, A., 'What does Tel-Oren Tell Lawyers? Judge Bork's Concept of the Law of Nations is Seriously Mistaken', *American Journal of International Law*, 1985, vol. 79, 92.
Dalton, D. and Cosier, R., 'An Issue in Corporate Social Responsibility: An Experimental Approach to Establish the Value of Human Life', *Journal of Business Ethics*, 1991, vol. 10, 311.
Deva, S., 'Human Rights Violations by Multinational Corporations and International Law: Where from Here?', *Connecticut Journal of International Law* 2003, vol. 19, 1.
——, 'Acting Extraterritorially to Tame Multinational Corporations for Human Rights Violations: Who Should "Bell the Cat?"', *Melbourne Journal of International Law*, 2004, vol. 5, 37.
——, 'Corporate Code of Conduct Bill 2000: Overcoming Hurdles in Enforcing Human Rights Obligations Against Overseas Corporate Hands of Local Corporations', *Newcastle Law Review*, 2004, vol. 8, 87.
——, 'From 3/12 to 9/11: Future of Human Rights?', *Economic and Political Weekly*, 2004, vol. 39, 5198.
——, 'The *Sangam* of Foreign Investment, Multinational Corporations and Human Rights: An Indian Perspective for a Developing Asia', *Singapore Journal of Legal Studies*, 2004, 305.
——, 'UN's Human Rights Norms for Transnational Corporations and Other Business Enterprises: An Imperfect Step in the Right Direction?', *ILSA Journal of International and Comparative Law*, 2004, vol. 10, 493.
——, 'Corporate Complicity in Internet Censorship in China: Who Cares for the Global Compact or the Global Online Freedom Act?', *George Washington International Law Review*, 2007, vol. 39, 255.
——, 'Global Compact: A Critique of UN's "Public-Private" Partnership for Promoting Corporate Citizenship', *Syracuse Journal of International Law and Commerce*, 2006, vol. 34, 107.
——, 'Human Rights Realisation in an Era of Globalisation: The Indian Experience', *Buffalo Human Rights Law Review*, 2006, vol. 12, 93.
——, 'Corporate Law and Socially Responsible Business: Lessons for Hong Kong', *Hong Kong Lawyer*, June 2011, 16.
——, 'Sustainable Development: What Role for the Company Law?', *International and Comparative Corporate Law Journal*, 2011, vol. 8, 76.
Developments in the Law, 'International Criminal Law: Corporate Liability for Violations of International Human Rights Law', *Harvard Law Review* 2001, vol. 114, 2025.

Dhir, A., 'Realigning the Corporate Building Blocks: Shareholder Proposals as a Vehicle for Achieving Corporate Social and Human Rights Accountability', *American Business Law Journal*, 2006, vol. 43, 365.

Dine, J., 'Multinational Enterprises: International Codes and the Challenge for "Sustainable Development" ', *Non-State Actors and International Law*, 2001, vol. 1, 81.

Dinham, B. and Sarangi, S., 'The Bhopal Gas Tragedy of 1984 to? The Evasion of Corporate Responsibility', *Environment and Urbanization*, 2002, vol. 14, 89.

Dodd, E. Jr., 'For Whom are Corporate Managers Trustees?', *Harvard Law Review*, 1932, vol. 45, 1145.

Dodge, W., 'Which Torts in Violation of the Law of Nations?', *Hastings International and Comparative Law Review*, 2001, vol. 24, 351.

Donaldson, T., 'Moral Minimum for Multinationals', *Ethics and International Affairs*, 1989, vol. 3, 163.

Easterbrook, F. and Fischel, D., 'Limited Liability and Corporation', *University of Chicago Law Review*, 1985, vol. 52, 89.

Ellinikos, M., 'American MNCs Continue to Profit from the Use of Forced and Slave Labour Begging the Question: Should America Take a Cue from Germany?', *Columbia Journal of Law and Social Problems*, 2001, vol. 35, 1.

Engle, E., 'Corporate Social Responsibility: Market-Based Remedies for International Human Rights Violations?', *Willamette Law Review*, 2004, vol. 40, 103.

——, 'Extraterritorial Corporate Criminal Liability: A Remedy for Human Rights Violations?', *St John's Journal of Legal Commentary*, 2006, vol. 20, 287.

——, 'What You Don't Know Can Hurt You: Human Rights, Shareholder Activism and Sec Reporting Requirements', *Syracuse Law Review*, 2006, vol. 57, 63.

Fairman, R. and Yapp, C., 'Enforced Self-Regulation, Prescription, and Conceptions of Compliance within Small Businesses: The Impact of Enforcement', *Law and Policy*, 2005, vol. 27, 491.

Farmer, R., 'Parent Corporation Responsibility for the Environmental Liabilities of the Subsidiary: A Search for the Appropriate Standard', *Iowa Journal of Corporation Law*, 1994, vol. 19, 769.

Fishman, B., 'Binding Corporations to Human Rights Norms through Public Law Settlement', *New York University Law Review*, 2006, vol. 81, 1433.

Fitzgerald, S., 'Corporate Accountability for Human Rights Violations in Australian Domestic Law', *Australian Journal of Human Rights*, 2005, vol. 11, 33.

Fowler, R., 'International Environmental Standards For Transnational Corporations', *Environmental Law*, 1995, vol. 1, 16.

Frey, B., 'The Legal and Ethical Responsibilities of Transnational Corporations in the Protection of International Human Rights', *Minnesota Journal of Global Trade*, 1997, vol. 6, 153.

Friedman, M., 'The Social Responsibility of Business Is to Increase Its Profits', *New York Times Magazine*, 13 September 1970.

Galanter, M., 'Legal Torpor: Why so Little has Happened in India after the Bhopal Tragedy?', *Texas International Law Journal*, 1985, vol. 20, 273.

Garcia, F., 'The Global Market and Human Rights: Trading Away the Human Rights Principle', *Brooklyn Journal of International Law*, 1999, vol. 24, 51.

Garkawe, S., 'The South African Truth and Reconciliation Commission: A Suitable Model to Enhance the Role and Rights of the Victims of Gross Violations of Human Rights', *Melbourne University Law Review*, 2003, vol. 27, 334.

Ghouri, A. A., 'Positing for Balancing: Investment Treaty Rights and the Rights of Citizens', *Contemporary Asia Arbitration Journal*, 2011, vol. 4:1, 95.

Gibney, M. and Emerick, R., 'The Extraterritorial Application of United States Law and the Protection of Human Rights: Holding Multinational Corporations to Domestic and International Standards', *Temple International and Comparative Law Journal*, 1996, vol. 10, 123.

Gioseffi, S., 'Corporate Accountability: Achieving Internal Self-Governance through Sustainability Reports', *Cornell Journal of Law and Public Policy*, 2004, vol. 13, 503.

Gomez, V., 'The Sosa Standard: What Does it Mean for Future ATS Litigation?' *Pepperdine Law Review*, 2006, vol. 33, 469.

Goodpaster, K., 'The Concept of Corporate Responsibility', *Journal of Business Ethics*, 1983, vol. 2, 1.

Greathead, S., 'The Multinational and the "New Stakeholder": Examining the Business Case for Human Rights', *Vanderbilt Journal of Transnational Law*, 2002, vol. 35, 719.

Grossman, C. and Bradlow, D., 'Are We Being Propelled Towards a People-Centered Transnational Legal Order?', *American University Journal of International Law and Policy*, 1993, vol. 9, 1.

Han, X., 'The Wiwa Cases', *Chinese Journal of International Law*, 2010, vol. 9, 433.

Harbour, F., 'Moral Agency and Moral Responsibility in Humanitarian Intervention', *Global Society*, 2004, vol. 18, 61.

Hawkes, L., '*Parens Patriae* and the Union Carbide Case: The Disaster at Bhopal Continues', *Cornell International Law Journal*, 1998, vol. 21, 181.

Hemraj, M., 'Corporate Governance: Rationalising Stakeholder Doctrine in Corporate Accountability', *Company Lawyer*, 2005, vol. 26:7, 211.

Henkin, L., 'The Universal Declaration at 50 and the Challenge of Global Markets', *Brooklyn Journal of International Law*, 1999, vol. 25, 17.

Herrmann, K., 'Corporate Social Responsibility and Sustainable Development: The European Union Initiative as a Case Study', *Indiana Journal of Global Legal Studies*, 2004, vol. 11, 205.

Hess, D. 'Social Reporting: A Reflexive Law Approach to Corporate Social Responsiveness', *Iowa Journal of Corporation Law*, 1999, vol. 25, 41.

Hill, J., 'Visions and Revisions of the Shareholder', *American Journal of Comparative Law*, 2000, vol. 48, 39.

Hillemanns, C., 'UN Norms of the Responsibilities of Transnational Corporations and Other Business Enterprises With Regard to Human Rights', *German Law Journal*, 2003, vol. 4, 1065.

Howland, T., 'Can International Law Prevent Another Bhopal Tragedy?', *Denver Journal of International Law and Policy*, 1987, vol. 15, 301.

Hunt, M., 'The "Horizontal Effect" of the Human Rights Act', *Public Law*, 1998, 423.

Hutter, B., 'Is Enforced Self-regulation a Form of Risk Taking?: The Case of Railway Health and Safety', *International Journal of the Sociology of Law*, 2001, vol. 29, 379.

Ireland, P., 'Company Law and the Myth of Shareholder Ownership', *Modern Law Review*, 1999, vol. 62, 32.

Jaffe, N. and Weiss, J., 'The Self-Regulating Corporation: How Corporate Codes can Save Our Children', *Fordham Journal of Corporate and Financial Law*, 2006, vol. 11, 893.

Jiangtao, S. 'Website Names and Shames Polluters', *South China Morning Post*, 15 September 2006, A8.
Jochnick, C., 'Confronting the Impunity of Non-State Actors: New Fields for the Promotion of Human Rights', *Human Rights Quarterly*, 1999, vol. 21, 56.
Johns, F., 'The Invisibility of the Transnational Corporation: An Analysis of International Law and Legal Theory', *Melbourne University Law Review*, 1994, vol. 19, 893.
Johnson, J., 'Public-Private Convergence: How the Private Actor can Shape Public International Labour Standards', *Brooklyn Journal of International Law*, 1998, vol. 24, 291.
Joseph, S., 'Pharmaceutical Corporations and Access to Drugs: The "Fourth Wave" of Corporate Human Rights Scrutiny', *Human Rights Quarterly*, 2003, vol. 25, 425.
Kabel, S., 'Our Business is People (Even if It Kills Them): The Contribution of Multinational Enterprises to the Conflict in the Democratic Republic of Congo', *Tulane Journal of International and Comparative Law*, 2004, vol. 12, 461.
Kell, G., 'The Global Compact: Origins, Operations, Progress, Challenges', *Journal of Corporate Citizenship*, 2003, vol. 11, 35.
Khanna, V., 'Corporate Criminal Liability: What Purpose Does It Serve?', *Harvard Law Review*, 1995, vol. 109, 1477.
Kiarie, S., 'At Crossroads: Shareholder Value, Stakeholder Value and Enlightened Shareholder Value: Which Road should the United Kingdom Take', *International Company and Commercial Law Review*, 2006, vol. 17, 329.
Kielsgard, M. D., 'Unocal and the Demise of Corporate Neutrality', *California Western International Law Journal*, 2005, vol. 36, 185.
King, B., 'The UN Global Compact: Responsibility for Human Rights, Labour Relations, and the Environment in Developing Nations', *Cornell International Law Journal*, 2001, vol. 34, 481.
Kinley, D. and Chambers, R., 'The UN Human Rights Norms for Corporations: The Private Implications of Public International Law', *Human Rights Law Review*, 2006, vol. 6, 447.
Kinley, D. and Tadaki, J., 'From Talk to Walk: The Emergence of Human Rights Responsibilities for Corporations at International Law', *Virginia Journal of International Law*, 2004, vol. 44, 931.
Kochan, D., 'Constitutional Structure as a Limitation on the Scope of the "Law of Nations" in the Alien Tort Claims Act', *Cornell International Law Journal*, 1998, vol. 31, 153.
Ku, J., 'The Curious Case of Corporate Liability under the Alien Tort Statute: A Flawed System of Judicial Lawmaking', *Virginia Journal of International Law*, 2011, vol. 51, 353.
Lambert, L., 'At the Crossroads of Environmental and Human Rights Standards: *Aguinda* v. *Texaco, Inc.*, Using the Alien Tort Claims Act to Hold Multinational Corporate Violators of International Laws Accountable in US Courts', *Journal of Transnational Law and Policy*, 2000, vol. 10, 109.
Langlois, R., 'Cost–Benefit Analysis, Environmentalism and Rights', *Cato Journal*, 1982, vol. 2, 279.
Liu, C. and Ho, B., 'Environmental Safeguards for Lending in China', *CSR Asia Weekly*, vol. 3, Week 10, 7 March 2007, 3.

Liubicic, R., 'Corporate Codes of Conduct and Product Labelling Schemes: The Limits and Possibilities of Promoting International Labour Rights through Private Initiatives', *Law and Policy in International Business*, 1998, vol. 39, 111.

Lu, S., 'Corporate Codes of Conduct and the FTC: Advancing Human Rights through Deceptive Advertising Law', *Columbia Journal of Transnational Law*, 2000, vol. 38, 603.

McBeth, A., 'A Look at Corporate Code of Conduct Legislation', *Common Law World Review*, 2004, vol. 33, 222.

Macek, E., 'Scratching the Corporate Back: Why Corporations Have No Incentive to Define Human Rights', *Minnesota Journal of Global Trade*, 2002, vol. 11, 101.

McGarity, T., 'Bhopal and the Export of Hazardous Technologies', *Texas International Law Journal*, 1985, vol. 20, 333.

McKinsey, 'The McKinsey Global Survey of Business Executives: Business and Society', *McKinsey Quarterly*, 2006, vol. 2, p. 33.

Malloy, R., 'Equating Human Rights and Property Rights – The Need for Moral Judgment in an Economic Analysis of Law and Social Policy', *Ohio State Law Journal*, 1986, vol. 47, 163.

Mares, R., 'Transnational Corporate Responsibility for the 21st Century: Defining the Limits of Corporate Responsibilities against the Concept of Legal Positive Obligations', *George Washington International Law Review*, 2009, vol. 40, 1157.

Meyer, W. and Stefanova, B., 'Human Rights, the UN Global Compact, and the Global Governance', *Cornell International Law Journal*, 2001, vol. 34, 501.

Mihaly, E., 'Multinational Companies and Wages in Low-Income Countries', *Journal of Small and Emerging Business Law*, 1999, vol. 3, 1, 2.

Monshipouri, M., Welch, C., Jr and Kennedy, E., 'Multinational Corporations and the Ethics of Global Responsibility: Problems and Possibilities', *Human Rights Quarterly* 2003, vol. 25, 965.

Moris, H., 'The World Bank and Human Rights: Indispensable Partnership or Mismatched Alliance', *ILSA Journal of International and Comparative Law*, 1997, vol. 4, 173.

Muchlinski, P., 'The Bhopal Case: Controlling Ultrahazardous Activities Undertaken by Foreign Investors', *Modern Law Review*, 1987, vol. 50, 545.

——, 'Human Rights and Multinationals: Is There a Problem?', *International Affairs*, 2001, vol. 77, 31.

——, 'Holding Multinationals to Account: Recent Developments in English Litigation and the Company Law Review', *Company Lawyer*, 2002, vol. 23, issue 6, 168.

Mulligan, T., 'A Critique of Milton Friedman's Essay "The Social Responsibility of Business Is to Increase Its Profits"', *Journal of Business Ethics*, 1986, vol. 5, 265.

Muralidharan, S., 'Bhopal: Continuing Institutional Crisis', *Economic and Political Weekly*, 2004, vol. 39, 5196.

Murphy, S., 'Taking Multinational Corporate Codes of Conduct to the Next Level', *Columbia Journal of Transnational Law*, 2005, vol. 43, 389.

Murray, O., Kinley, D. and Pitts, C., 'Exaggerated Rumours of the Death of an Alien Tort? Corporations, Human Rights and the Remarkable Case of *Kiobel*', *Melbourne Journal of International Law*, 2011, vol. 12, 57.

Narula, S., 'The Right to Food: Holding Global Actors Accountable under International Law', *Columbia Journal of Transnational Law*, 2006, vol. 44, 691.

Newberg, J., 'Corporate Codes of Ethics, Mandatory Disclosure, and the Market for Ethical Conduct', *Vermont Law Review*, 2005, vol. 29, 253.

Nolan, J., 'The United Nations' Compact With Business: Hindering or Helping the Protection of Human Rights?', *University of Queensland Law Journal*, 2005, vol. 24, 445.

——, 'With Power Comes Responsibility: Human Rights and Corporate Accountability', *University of New South Wales Law Journal*, 2005, vol. 28, 581.

Notes, 'Finding Strategic Corporate Citizenship: A New Game Theoretic View', *Harvard Law Review*, 2004, vol. 117, 1957.

Ohlin, J., 'Is the Concept of the Person Necessary for Human Rights?', *Columbia Law Review*, 2005, vol. 105, 209.

O'Konek, T., 'Corporations and Human Rights Law: The Emerging Consensus and Its Effects on Women's Employment Rights', *Cardozo Journal of Law and Gender*, 2011, vol. 17, 261.

O'Neill, T., 'Water and Freedom: The Privatisation of Water and Its Implications for Democracy and Human Rights in the Developing World', *Colorado Journal of International Environmental Law and Policy*, 2006, vol. 17, 357.

Orts, E., 'Reflexive Environmental Law', *Northwestern University Law Review*, 1995, vol. 89, 1227.

Oshionebo, E., 'The UN Global Compact and Accountability of Transnational Corporations: Separating Myth from Realities', *Florida Journal of International Law*, 2007, vol. 17, 1.

Paust, J., 'Human Rights Responsibilities of Private Corporations', *Vanderbilt Journal of Transnational Law*, 2002, vol. 35, 801.

——, 'Nonstate Actor Participation in International law and the Pretence of Exclusion', *Virginia Journal of International Law*, 2011, vol. 51, 977.

Petersmann, E., 'Time for a United Nations "Global Compact" for Integrating Human Rights into the Law of Worldwide Organisations: Lessons from European Integration', *European Journal of International Law*, 2002, vol. 13, 621.

Picciotto, S., 'Introduction: Reconceptualising Regulation in an Era of Globalisation', *Journal of Law and Society*, 2002, vol. 29, 1.

——, 'Rights, Responsibilities and Regulation of International Business', *Columbia Journal of Transnational Law*, 2003, vol. 42, 131.

Pillay, S., 'Absence of Justice: Lessons from the Bhopal Union Carbide Disaster for Latin America', *Michigan State Journal of International Law*, vol. 14, 2006, 479.

Porter, M. and Kramer, M., 'The Link between Competitive Advantage and Corporate Social Responsibility', *Harvard Business Review*, 2006, vol. 84:12, 78.

Quaid, J., 'The Assessment of Corporate Criminal Liability on the Basis of Corporate Identity: An Analysis', *McGill Law Journal*, 1998, vol. 43, 67.

Ramsey, M., 'Multinational Corporate Liability under the Alien Tort Claims Act: Some Structural Concerns', *Hastings International and Comparative Law Review*, 2001, vol. 24, 361.

Ratner, S., 'Corporations and Human Rights: A Theory of Legal Responsibility', *Yale Law Journal*, 2001, vol. 111, 443.

Redmond, P., 'Transnational Enterprise and Human Rights: Options for Standard Setting and Compliance', *International Lawyer*, 2003, vol. 37, 69.

Rosemann, N., 'The Privatisation of Human Rights Violations – Business' Impunity or Corporate Responsibility? The Case of Human Rights Abuses and Torture in Iraq', *Non-State Actors and International Law*, 2005, vol. 5, 77.

Ruggie, J., ' "Trade, Sustainability and Global Governance": Keynote Address', *Columbia Journal of Environmental Law*, 2002, vol. 27, 297.

Rule, T., 'Using "Norms" to Change International Law: UN Human Rights Laws Sneaking in Through the Back Door?' *Chicago Journal of International Law*, 2004, vol. 5, 326.

Sacharoff, A., 'Multinationals in Host Countries: Can they be Held Liable under the Alien Tort Claims Act for Human Rights Violations?', *Brooklyn Journal of International Law*, 1998, vol. 23, 927.

Scalet, S., 'Prisoner's Dilemma, Cooperative Norms, and Codes of Business Ethics', *Journal of Business Ethics*, 2006, vol. 65, 309.

Sen, A., 'The Moral Standing of the Market', *Social Philosophy and Policy*, 1985, vol. 2, 1.

Sethi, S., 'Globalisation and the Good Corporation: A Need for Proactive Co-existence', *Journal of Business Ethics*, 2003, vol. 43, 21.

Shaughnessy, M., 'The United Nations Global Compact and the Continuing Debate about the Effectiveness of Corporate Voluntary Codes of Conduct', *Colorado Journal of International Law and Policy*, 2000, 159.

Sheehy, B., 'Scrooge – The Reluctant Stakeholder: Theoretical Problems in the Shareholder-Stakeholder Debate', *University of Miami Business Law Review*, 2005, vol. 14, 193.

Shelton, D., 'Challenges to the Future of Civil and Political Rights', *Washington and Lee Law Review*, 1998, vol. 55, 669.

Siegle, J., 'Suing US Corporations in Domestic Courts for Environmental Wrongs Committed Abroad through the Extraterritorial Application of Federal Statutes', *University of Miami Business Law Review*, 2002, vol. 10, 393.

Simaika, A., 'The Value of Information: Alternatives to Liability in Influencing Corporate Behavior Overseas', *Columbia Journal of Law and Social Problems*, 2005, vol. 38, 321.

Simons, P., 'Corporate Voluntarism and Human Rights: The Adequacy and Effectiveness of Voluntary Self-Regulation Regimes', *Relations Industrielles*, 2004, vol. 59, 101.

Singh, M., 'Fundamental Rights, State Action and Cricket in India', *Asia Pacific Law Review*, 2005, vol. 13, 203.

Skolnik, M., 'The *Forum non Conveniens* Doctrine in Alien Tort Claims Act Cases: A Shell of its Former Self after Wiwa', *Emory International Law Review*, 2002, vol. 16, 187.

Slawotsky, J., 'Doing Business Around the World: Corporate Liability under the Alien Tort Claims Act', *Michigan State Law Review*, 2005, vol. 13, 1065.

Smith, E. F., 'Right to Remedies and the Inconvenience of Forum Non Conveniens: Opening US Courts to Victims of Corporate Human Rights Abuses', *Columbia Journal of Law and Social Problems*, 2010, vol. 44, 145.

Solomon, R., 'Game Theory as a Model for Business and Business Ethics', *Business Ethics Quarterly*, 1999, vol. 9, 11.

Stapleton, J., 'The Golden Thread at the Heart of Tort Law: Protection of the Vulnerable', *Australian Bar Review*, 2003, vol. 24, 1.

Stephens, B., 'The Amorality of Profit: Transnational Corporations and Human Rights', *Berkeley Journal of International Law*, 2002, vol. 20, 45.

Stout, L. A., 'Bad and Not-so-Bad Arguments for Shareholder Primacy', *Southern California Law Review*, 2002, vol. 75, 1189.

Sutton, M., 'Between a Rock and a Judicial Hard Place: Corporate Social Responsibility Reporting and Potential Legal Liability Under *Kasky* v. *Nike*', *University of Missouri at Kansas City Law Review*, 2004, vol. 72, 1159.

Taylor A., 'The UN and the Global Compact', *New York Law School Journal of Human Rights*, 2001, vol. 17, 975.

Trotter, R., Day, S. and Love, A., 'Bhopal, India and Union Carbide: The Second Tragedy', *Journal of Business Ethics*, 1989, vol. 8, 439.

Tulkens, F., 'Human Rights, Rhetoric or Reality?', *European Review*, 2001, vol. 9, 125.

Tzeutschler, G., 'Corporate Violator: The Alien Tort Liability of Transnational Corporations for Human Rights Abuses Abroad', *Columbia Human Rights Law Review*, 1999, vol. 30, 359.

Vachani, S. and Smith, N., 'Socially Responsible Pricing: Lessons from the Pricing of AIDS Drugs in Developing Countries', *California Management Review*, 2004, vol. 47, 117.

Velasquez, M., 'International Business, Morality, and the Common Good, *Business Ethics Quarterly*, 1992, vol. 2, 27.

Wai, R., 'Countering, Branding, Dealing: Using Economic and Social Rights in and Around the International Trade Regime', *European Journal of International Law*, 2003, vol. 14, 35.

Ward, H., 'Securing Transnational Corporate Accountability through National Courts: Implications and Policy Options', *Hastings International and Comparative Law Review*, 2001, vol. 24, 451.

Weissbrodt, D. and Kruger, M., 'Norms of the Responsibilities of Transnational Corporations and Other Business Enterprises with Regard to Human Rights', *American Journal of International Law*, 2003, vol. 97, 901.

Weissbrodt, D., 'Business and Human Rights', *University of Cincinnati Law Review*, 2005, vol. 74, 55.

Werner, W., 'Corporation Law in Search of its Future', *Columbia Law Review*, 1981, vol. 81, 1611.

Westfield, E., 'Globalisation, Governance, and Multinational Enterprise Responsibility: Corporate Codes of Conduct in the 21st Century', *Virginia Journal of International Law*, 2002, vol. 42, 1075.

Wood, D., 'Corporate Social Performance Revisited', *Academy of Management Review*, 1991, vol. 16, 691.

Zamagni, S., 'Religious Values and Corporate Decision Making: An Economist's Perspective', *Fordham Journal of Corporate and Financial Law*, 2006, vol. 11, 573.

Electronic resources

Amnesty International, 'Human Rights Principles for Companies', AI Index: ACT 70/01/98. Available at: http://web.amnesty.org/library/Index/engACT700011998 (accessed 10 June 2011).

Apple Supplier Code of Conduct (Version 3.1, 2009). Available at: http://images.apple.com/supplierresponsibility/pdf/Supplier_Code_of_Conduct_V3_1.pdf (accessed 10 June 2011).

Baby Milk Action, 'Nestle, the UN Global Compact and OECD Guidelines'. Available at: http://info.babymilkaction.org/news/policyblog210510 (accessed 9 February 2011).

Baker, M., 'Blackwater Settles Series of Civil Lawsuits', *The Guardian*, 7 January 2010. Available at: www.guardian.co.uk/world/feedarticle/8888224 (accessed 6 June 2011).

Bhopal Gas Tragedy Relief and Rehabilitation Department, Bhopal, State of Madhya Pradesh, 'Profile'. Available at: www.mp.nic.in/bgtrrdmp/profile.htm (accessed 10 June 2011).

Bhopal Net, 'Union Carbide Corporation's Factory in Bhopal: A Brief and Deadly History'. Available at: http://bhopal.net/document_library/Bhopal-BriefAnd-DeadlyHistory.pdf (accessed 28 May 2011).

British Broadcasting Corporation, 'No Beef in McDonald's Fries', *BBC News*, 4 May 2001. Available at: http://news.bbc.co.uk/1/hi/world/south_asia/1312774.stm (accessed 31 May 2011).

——, 'Yahoo Settles Its China Lawsuit', *BBC News*, 13 November 2007. Available at: http://news.bbc.co.uk/2/hi/7093564.stm (accessed 6 June 2011).

Burton, B., 'The Big Ugly at Ok Tedi', *Multinational Monitor*, January/February 2002, vol. 23. Available at: http://multinationalmonitor.org/mm2002/02jan-feb/jan-feb02front.html (accessed 10 June 2011).

Business and Human Rights Resource Centre, 'Positive Human Rights Initiatives by Companies Featured in Our Weekly Updates', 10 February 2005 – 24 December 2008. Available at: www.business-humanrights.org/Documents/Chart-Positive.doc (accessed 10 June 2011).

Campbell, D., 'Energy Giant Agrees Settlement with Burmese Villagers', *The Guardian*, 15 December 2004. Available at: www.guardian.co.uk/world/2004/dec/15/burma.duncancampbell (accessed 6 June 2011).

Christian Aid, Amnesty International and Friends of the Earth, *Flagship or Failure? The UK's Implementation of the OECD Guidelines and Approach to Corporate Accountability* (November 2005). Available at: www.christian-aid.org.uk/indepth/601flag/Final%20OECD%20Report.pdf (accessed 10 June 2011).

Clean Clothes Campaign, 'Code of Labour Practices for the Apparel Industry Including Sportswear' (1998). Available at: www.cleanclothes.org/codes/ccccode.htm (accessed 10 June 2011).

Cohen, E. and Slob, B., 'Letter to Mr Georg Kell, Executive Director of the Global Compact', 15 December 2008. Available at: http://investorsagainstgenocide.net/2008-1215%20UNGC%20complaint%20against%20PetroChina.pdf (accessed 9 February 2011).

Commission of the European Communities, 'Implementing the Partnership for Growth and Jobs: Making Europe a Pole of Excellence on Corporate Social Responsibility', COM(2006) 136 Final. Available at: http://eur-lex.europa.eu/LexUriServ/LexUriServ.do?uri=COM:2006:0136:FIN:en:PDF (accessed 2 June 2011).

Committee on Economic, Social and Cultural Rights, 'General Comment No. 3: The Nature of States Parties Obligations (Article 2(1) of the ICESCR)'. Available at: www.unhchr.ch/tbs/doc.nsf/(symbol)/CESCR+General+comment+3.En?OpenDocument (accessed 2 June 2011).

Costello, T., Smith, B. and Brecher, J., 'Labour Rights in China', 19 December 2006. Available at: www.fpif.org/articles/labor_rights_in_china (accessed 8 June 2011).

Department for Business, Innovation and Skills, 'UK NCP Follow-up Statement: Complaint from Survival International against Vedanta Resources plc' (March 2010). Available at: www.bis.gov.uk/assets/biscore/business-sectors/docs/10-778-survival-international-against-vedanta-resources.pdf (accessed 10 June 2011).

European Commission, 'European Commission's Green Paper on Promoting a European Framework for Corporate Social Responsibility', COM(2001) 366 Final. Available at: http://eur-lex.europa.eu/LexUriServ/site/en/com/2001/com2001_0366en01.pdf (accessed 2 June 2011).

European Parliament, 'Corporate Social Responsibility: A New Partnership'. Available at: www.europarl.europa.eu/sides/getDoc.do?pubRef=-//EP//TEXT+TA+P6-TA-2007-0062+0+DOC+XML+V0//EN&language=EN (accessed 15 June 2011).

Frontline, 'Litigation: Opinion of the Attorney General', *Frontline*, vol. 19:1 (5-18 January 2002), Available at: www.hinduonnet.com/fline/fl1901/19011020.htm (accessed 10 June 2011).

Global Compact Office, 'Note on Integrity Measures'. Available at: www.unglobalcompact.org/AboutTheGC/gc_integrity_mesures.pdf (accessed 10 June 2011).

——, 'Final Report: Inaugural Meeting of the Global Compact Board', 28 June 2006. Available at: www.unglobalcompact.org/docs/about_the_gc/final_rep_board030806.pdf (accessed 20 May 2011).

——, 'Global Compact: Report on Progress and Activities', July 2002 (Draft). Available at: www.iccwbo.org/home/global_compact/ProgressReport%20July%203.pdf (accessed 15 June 2011).

Global Reporting Initiative, 'The 2002 Sustainability Reporting Guidelines'. Available at: www.globalreporting.org/guidelines/2002/gri_companion_lite.pdf (accessed 10 June 2011).

Gupta, S., 'Bhopal Gas Case Verdict: Justice Delayed, Denied', *The Times of India*, 8 June 2010. Available at: http://timesofindia.indiatimes.com/india/Bhopal-gas-case-verdict-Justice-delayed-denied/articleshow/6021821.cms (accessed 28 May 2011).

Hardie, J., 'Asbestos Compensation'. Available at: www.ir.jameshardie.com.au/jh/asbestos_compensation.jsp (accessed 10 June 2011).

Hertz, N., 'New Ethics: Just Do it Right – Smart Firms Know Acting Socially Helps the Bottom Line'. Available at: http://articles.sfgate.com/2005-05-15/opinion/17371943_1_ethical-tobacco-control-framework-convention (accessed 17 June 2011).

Human Rights Council, 'Council Establishes Working Group on Human Rights and Transnational Corporations and other Business Enterprises' (16 June 2011). Available at: www.ohchr.org/en/NewsEvents/Pages/DisplayNews.aspx?NewsID=11165&LangID=E (accessed 17 June 2011).

——, 'New Guiding Principles on Business and Human Rights Endorsed by the UN Human Rights Council' (16 June 2011). Available at: www.ohchr.org/en/NewsEvents/Pages/DisplayNews.aspx?NewsID=11164&LangID=E (accessed 17 June 2011).

Institute of Directors in Southern Africa, *King Code of Governance for South Africa* (2009). Available at: www.iodsa.co.za/en-us/productsservices/kingiiireport-papersguidelines/kingreportoncorporategovernanceinsa/kingiii.aspx (accessed 25 September 2011).

International Labour Organization, 'ILO Declaration on Fundamental Principles and Rights at Work', 86th Session, June 1998. Available at: www.ilo.org/declaration/thedeclaration/textdeclaration/lang-en/index.htm (accessed 26 January 2011).

Leon H. Sullivan Foundation, 'Global Sullivan Principles of Social Responsibility'. Available at: www.thesullivanfoundation.org/about/global_sullivan_principles (accessed 29 June 2011)

Levin, R., 'Global Climate Change: Taking the Battle to the Campus', *Yale Global Online*, 26 February 2007. Available at: http://yaleglobal.yale.edu/content/global-climate-change-taking-battle-campus (accessed 28 May 2011).

Mahapatra, D., 'SC Reopens Bhopal Case, Notices to Accused on Homicide Charge', *The Times of India*, 1 September 2010. Available at: http://articles.timesofindia.indiatimes.com/2010-09-01/india/28217038_1_s-b-majmudar-curative-petition-devadatt-kamat (accessed 28 May 2011).

——, 'SC Dismisses CBI petition, rejects harsher punishment for Bhopal gas tragedy accused', *The Times of India*, 11 May 2011. Available at: http://articles.timesofindia.indiatimes.com/2011-05-11/india/29531515_1_bhopal-gas-tragedy-deadly-methyl-isocyanate-gas-review-petition (accessed 28 May 2011).

Ministry of Environment and Forests, 'Press Release: Bhopal Environmental Remediation Oversight Committee Constituted', 7 July 2010. Available at: http://moef.nic.in/downloads/public-information/PM_Bhopal.pdf (accessed 28 May 2011).

Murlidhar, S., 'Unsettling Truths, Untold Tales: The Bhopal Gas Tragedy Victims' "Twenty Years" of Courtroom Struggles for Justice', *IELRC Working Paper 2004/5*. Available at: www.ielrc.org/content/w0405.pdf (accessed 28 January 2007).

National Commission on the BP Deepwater Horizon Oil Spill and Offshore Drilling (US), *Deep Water: The Gulf Oil Disaster and the Future of Offshore Drilling*, 2011. Available at: www.oilspillcommission.gov/final-report (accessed 20 June 2011).

Nike Inc., 'Nike Ends Orders With Soccer Ball Manufacturer', 20 November 2006. Available at: http://phx.corporate-ir.net/phoenix.zhtml?c=100529&p=irol-newsArticle&ID=1062659&highlight= (accessed 20 June 2011).

Odell, A., 'Chocolate Giant Commits to Responsible Supplier Code', 8 March 2007. Available at: www.socialfunds.com/news/article.cgi/2245.html (accessed 9 June 2011).

Organisation for Economic Co-operation and Development (OECD), 'Consultation on the Guidelines for Multinational Enterprises and the UN "Protect, Respect and Remedy" Framework'. Available at: www.oecd.org/document/36/0,3746,en_2649_34889_46078244_1_1_1_1,00.html (accessed 18 June 2011).

——, 'OECD Guidelines for Multinational Enterprises: 2005 Annual Meeting of the National Contact Points – Report by the Chair', June 2005. Available at: www.oecd.org/dataoecd/ 20/13/35387363.pdf (accessed 10 June 2011).

——, 'Terms of Reference for an Update of the OECD Guidelines for Multinational Enterprises', May 2010. Available at: www.oecd.org/dataoecd/61/41/45124171.pdf (accessed 18 June 2011).

——, OECD Guidelines for Multinational Enterprises: Recommendations for Responsible Business Conduct in a Global Context, 25 May 2011. Available at: www.oecd.org/dataoecd/43/29/48004323.pdf (accessed 10 June 2011).

PriceWaterhouseCoopers, 'The UN Global Compact: Moving to the Business Mainstream, An Interview with Georg Kell', *Corporate Responsibility Report*, Winter 2005, vol. 2. Available at: www.unglobalcompact.org/docs/news_events/9.5/pwc_int_2005.pdf (accessed 10 June 2011).

Social Accountability International, Social Accountability (SA) 8000. Available at: www.sa-intl.org/_data/n_0001/resources/live/2008StdEnglishFinal.pdf (accessed 31 May 2011).

SRSG, 'Opening Statement to United Nations Human Rights Council' (25 September 2006). Available at: http://198.170.85.29/Ruggie-statement-to-UN-Human-Rights-Council-25-Sep-2006.pdf (accessed 11 June 2011).

Statement by the Australian National Contact Point, 'GSL Australia Specific Instance'. Available at: www.ausncp.gov.au/content/reports_newsletters/downloads/reports/GSL_Statement.pdf (accessed 10 June 2011).

Students and Scholars Against Corporate Misbehaviour (SACOM), 'Workers as Machines: Military Management in Foxconn', October 2010. Available at: http://sacom.hk/wp-content/uploads/2010/10/report-on-foxconn-workers-as-machines_sacom3.pdf (accessed 20 June 2011).

Sydney Morning Herald, 'Don't Forget Our Shareholders: James Hardie Chair', *Sydney Morning Herald*, 17 August 2004. Available at: www.smh.com.au/articles/2004/08/17/1092508432452.html?from=storylhs (accessed 1 June 2011).

The Hindu, 'Supreme Court Sore Over Delay in Bhopal Gas Tragedy Case', *The Hindu*, 8 August 2010. Available at: www.hindu.com/2010/08/08/stories/2010080859750400.htm (accessed 28 May 2011).

The Special Commission of Inquiry into Medical Research and Compensation Foundation. Available at: www.dpc.nsw.gov.au/publications/publications/publication_list_-_new#11330 (accessed 31 May 2011).

The Times of India, 'GoM for Hike in Payout, Review of Verdicts', *The Times of India*, 22 June 2010. Available at: http://timesofindia.indiatimes.com/india/GoM-for-hike-in-payout-review-of-verdicts/articleshow/6076562.cms (accessed 28 May 2011).

UN, 'Charter of the United Nations', Preamble. Available at: www.un.org/en/documents/charter/preamble.shtml (accessed 10 June 2011).

UN Documents Cooperation Circles, 'Agenda 21, Chapter 30: Strengthening the Role of Business and Industry'. Available at: www.un-documents.net/a21-30.htm (accessed 2 June 2011).

UN Global Compact. Available at: www.unglobalcompact.org (accessed 2 June 2011).

——, 'Differentiation Programme'. Available at: www.unglobalcompact.org/COP/differentiation_programme.html (accessed 10 June 2011).

——, 'How to Participate: Business Organizations'. Available at: www.unglobalcompact.org/HowToParticipate/How_to_Apply_Business.html (accessed 10 June 2011).

——, 'Human Rights and Business Dilemmas Forum'. Available at: http://human-rights.unglobalcompact.org/ (accessed 10 June 2011).

——, 'Integrity Measures'. Available at: www.unglobalcompact.org/AboutTheGC/IntegrityMeasures/index.html (accessed 10 June 2011).

——, 'Issue Specific Guidance'. Available at: www.unglobalcompact.org/COP/making_progress/issue_specific_guidance.html (accessed 10 June 2011).

——, 'Overview of the UN Global Compact'. Available at: www.unglobalcompact.org/AboutTheGC/index.html (accessed 10 June 2011).

——, 'Policy for the Communication on Progress'. Available at: www.unglobalcompact.org/docs/communication_on_progress/COP_Policy.pdf (accessed 10 June 2011).

——, 'Policy on the Use of the Global Compact Name and Logos'. Available at: www.unglobalcompact.org/AboutTheGC/Global_Compact_Logo/GC_Logo_Policy.html (accessed 10 June 2011).

——, 'Subsidiary Participation and Communication on Progress'. Available at: www.unglobalcompact.org/HowToParticipate/Business_Participation/Subsidiary_Engagement.html (accessed 10 June 2011).

——, 'The Ten Principles'. Available at: www.unglobalcompact.org/AboutTheGC/TheTenPrinciples/index.html (accessed 2 June 2011).

——, 'The UN Global Compact Board'. Available at: www.unglobalcompact.org/AboutTheGC/The_Global_Compact_Board.html (accessed 10 June 2011).

——, 'UN Global Compact Office Responds to NGO Letter (Update: 9 February 2009)'. Available at: www.unglobalcompact.org/NewsAndEvents/news_archives/2009_01_12b.html (accessed 9 February 2011).

United Nations Development Programme, 'Privatising Basic Utilities in Sub-Saharan Africa: The MDG Impact', January 2007. Available at: www.undp-povertycentre.org/pub/IPCPolicyResearchBrief003.pdf (accessed 20 February 2011).

United Nations Commission on International Trade Law (UNCITRAL), UNCITRAL Model Law on International Commercial Arbitration (adopted in 1985, amended in 2006). Available at: www.uncitral.org/pdf/english/texts/arbitration/ml-arb/07-86998_Ebook.pdf (accessed 19 June 2011).

——, UNCITRAL Model Legislative Provisions on Privately Financed Infrastructure Projects (adopted in 2003). Available at: www.uncitral.org/pdf/english/texts/procurem/pfip/model/03-90621_Ebook.pdf (accessed 16 June 2011).

——, UNCITRAL Model Law on Electronic Commerce with Guide to Enactment (adopted in 1996). Available at: www.uncitral.org/pdf/english/texts/electcom/05-89450_Ebook.pdf (accessed 19 June 2011).

Venkatesan, J, 'Court Orders Relief to Bhopal Gas Victims', *The Hindu* (20 July 2004). Available at: www.thehindu.com/2004/07/20/stories/2004072008760100.htm (accessed 14 June 2011).

Vidal, J., 'Shell Settlement With Ogoni People Stops Short of Full Justice', *The Guardian*, 10 June 2009. Available at: www.guardian.co.uk/environment/cif-green/2009/jun/09/saro-wiwa-shell (accessed 6 June 2011).

Index

access to remedies 106, 107–8, 109, 114, 116–17
access to justice obstacles 209, 216, 239–40; *see also* justice
accountability *vs* responsibility 22–3
Alien Tort Claims Act 1789 (ATCA), US 6, 49, 56, 60, 62, 66–7; Bhopal case 42–3; *Kiobel* challenge 72–4; limitations 68–74, 115; meaning of 'law of nations' after *Sosa* 70–2; government opposition 51, 72; positive effects 74
Amnesty International 31, 32–3, 36, 54
Anderson, W. 43, 44
Apple: iPhone 143; 2011 Supplier Responsibility Report 77
Atkin, Lord 147–8
Ayres, I. and Braithwaite, J. 22, 177–89, 190–3, 200, 204–5

Bakan, J. 185
Baxi, U. 40
Berle Jnr, A. 120, 130, 139, 150–1
Bhopal: as representative case study 2, 24, 45, 233; as symbol of corporate impunity 26, 45, 233; as symbol of inhumane business 2; different labels 25–6
Bhopal chemical plant (UCC/UCIL) 2, 13, 24, 24–6; Bhopal Act (1985), India 37–8; business approach 163–72; causes and consequences of gas leak 29–31; context of entry and operations 26–9; human approach 172–5; human rights lens 31–6; Indian courts 39–41, 43–4; litigation phases 36–44; right to information 165–6; right to life and health 32, 36, 163, 165–6, 172; right to representation 37; right to a safe/clean environment 32, 36; risk assessment and safety standards 170–2; settlement/compensation 40–2, 49; US courts 38–9, 41–3; *vs* West Virginia 163–5, 167–70; *see also* Bhopal
Boatright, J. 154, 157–8, 166–7, 169–70, 171–2
Bowie, N. 147
BP oil spill 141
Braithwaite, J. 186, 187; Ayres, I. and 22, 177–89, 190–3, 200, 204–5
Bratspies, R. 146
British East India Company 4–5
business approach to standards 158–60, 163–72
business case: for business ethics 132–3; for CSR 122, 139–40; goodwillnomics 140–6; for human rights 139–46
business dilemma: application to Bhopal 163–75; cost *vs* benefits 144; differences in operating environment 10; forum to discuss 98; three options 153–7; two approaches 157–63; *see also* business approach to standards; human approach to standards; standards

capitalism, CSR undermining of 122–4
charitable donations 122
civil sanctions 225–6; *see also* compensation
civil society organizations *see* non-governmental organizations (NGOs)
class action: in Bhopal case 37; against Wal-Mart 76;
codes of conduct 50, 54, 56, 58–60, 74–5, 115, 155, 204–8; advantages

75–6; applicability to suppliers 77; impeaching corporate conduct 53; limitations 76–9
Companies Act (2006), UK 196, 212
Companies Act (2008), South Africa 197, 212
Companies Bill (2009), India 197, 212
Compensation 48, 50, 63, 70, 114, 138, 187, 226; asbestos victims 49; Bhopal victims 39–42, 43, 49
Complicity: aiding and abetting liability 69; in conflict zones 111; in egregious human rights violations 219; of PetroChina 99; with state agencies 3, 5, 19–20, 233
consumers 55, 61, 78, 127, 132, 140, 142–3, 159, 167, 171, 190–1, 198, 201, 222, 229
corporate accountability (for human rights violations): evasion of 2, 13; determination of standards 11; regulatory framework for 12–14, 25, 115–18, 176, 184, 200, 208, 222, 231, 234–6, 238; obstacles in 12, 25, 76, 239–40; *vs* corporate responsibility 22–3; *see also* responsibilities/obligations
corporate groups *see* multinational corporations (MNCs)
corporate law: duties on directors 196–7, 212, 235; fostering respect for human rights 109, 209; global consensus 197; influencing corporate conduct 'from the inside' 211–14, 239; integrating human rights and business 22, 195–8, 235; limited liability 50, 212–13, 239; recognition of stakeholders' interests 196, 212; role in humanizing business 197, 211; separate legal personality 50, 58, 212–13, 239; uni-focal nature 211, 235, 239
corporate social responsibility (CSR): akin to theft 134; business case for 122, 139–40; Friedman's rebuke 121–2; implication for companies 135; stockholder ownership 124–7; undermines free markets and capitalism 122–4; unsuitability of companies 127–31; *see also* social responsibilities of business
corporate veil: piercing of 40, 50, 57, 159, 213; *see also* parent companies

corporations: duty as social organs 146–8; position to violate and promote human rights 148–50
Corporations Act (2001), Australia 196–7, 212
cost-benefit analysis 35, 113, 141, 144, 166; *see also* BP oil spill
criminal liability: at the institutional level 227; extradition 43–4, 51; for Bhopal 43–4; immunity from 41; of companies, 6; under Rome Statute 228–9
criminal sanctions 227–9

directors: abuse of discretion 162–3; balancing conflicting interests 135; disqualification 226; duties towards stakeholders 196–7, 212, 235; responsible to whom 120–1, 125
disincentives 220–5
Dodd Jnr, E. 120, 130
Donaldson, T. 18, 158, 159
due diligence 20, 57, 86, 106–9, 111, 114, 117, 207, 214,

eclipsed personality concept 213
efficacy ('twin efficacy' test) 47–50
enforced self-regulation *see* self-regulation
enterprise *vs* entity responsibility 57–9
entity principle *vs* enterprise principle 57–8, 64–5, 213
environmental pollution/contamination, Bhopal 42–3
ethical decision model *see* just business
external and internal sources of regulatory initiatives 53–5
extraterritorial regulation 4–5, 51, 57, 62, 65, 106, 109, 156, 188, 203, 210–11, 227

Foreign Exchange Regulation Act (1973), India 27–8
forum non conveniens 12, 25, 38–9, 48, 51, 69–70, 104, 113, 117, 216
free markets, CSR undermining of 122–4
Friedman, M. 10, 14, 119, 120–32, 134, 139, 175, 236–7

Global Compact 8, 17, 49, 56, 58–9, 92–4, 115–16, 117; deficiencies 96–100; evolution 94–6

globalization: impact on the position and role of states 201; influence 3–4; of today and yesterday 2–3
Goodpaster, K. 130–1
goodwill-nomics 119–20, 139–46
Greenpeace 42
Guiding Principles on Business and Human Rights: consensus 16, 105, 114, 215, 239–40; critique 109–15; due diligence 57, 106–7, 109; evolution 8–9, 104–9; grievance mechanisms 59, 62–3, 79, 107–9, 116–17; influence on the 2011 update of the OECD Guidelines 85–6; meaning of 'internationally recognised rights' 16, 56; nature of corporate responsibilities 18–19, 57, 110–11; remediation of adverse impacts 62; responsibility *vs* duty 18, 106; Working Group 218
Gunningham, N. et al. 189, 194; and Sinclair, D. 187

Hill, J. 125
home standards 152, 154, 155–7, 169, 237
host standards 14, 152, 154–6, 158, 160, 161, 163, 237
human approach to standards 160–3, 172–5, 237–8
human rights 16–18; business case for 139–46; corporate position to violate and promote 148–50; duty typology 110; international law 6–9; *jus cogens* 6–7, 69, 152, 161, 210; violation 18–21; *see also* standards
humanizing business: adherence to the human approach 153; goal of 16, 109, 240; long-term response 217; meaning 1, 100; obstacles 2, 25, 211; three challenges to 9–13, 23, 176–7, 195, 235; *see also* integrated theory of regulation

ILO Declaration 8, 17, 31, 33, 56, 58–9, 88–9; limitations 90–2; scope 89–90, 115
incentives 222–4
Industrial Development and Regulation Act (1951), India 27
institutional level regulation 204–8
integrated theory of regulation: basic idea 2, 15, 22, 177, 193–5, 235, 238–40; coordinated multiplicity 63, 200, 203; critique of responsive regulation 184–93; differences with responsive regulation 193–4, 198–9; framework 13, 23, 118; implementation strategies 220–5; informality 15, 200–1; integrating human rights and business issues 195–8, 235; levels of regulation (institutional, national and international) 202–20; triple sanctions 225–31; *see also* WWH (why, what and how) challenges
internal and external sources of regulatory initiatives 53–5
International Bill of Rights 16–17, 65, 101, 107, 112, 215, 239
International Covenant on Economic, Social and Cultural Rights (ICESCR) 112, 172
international human rights law 6–9
International Labour Organization *see* ILO Declaration
international level regulation 214–20
International Monetary Fund (IMF) 201, 217
international standards 156–7
Ireland, P. 125

James Hardie 49, 51, 212
Jones, T. 27–8
Jungk, M. 206
jus cogens 6–7, 69, 152, 161, 210
just business: critique 134–9; Sternberg's conceptualization 131–4
justice: cost of 48, 209, 216; distributive 133–4, 136, 236; for Bhopal victims 24, 36–45; *see also* access to justice obstacles; victims

labour rights 55, 86, 89, 90, 92, 185
legal aid 48
Leval, Justice 73
levels of regulation 59–60, 202–20
Limited Liability Companies Law (2007), Indonesia 197
limited liability principle 36, 50, 212–13, 239

mass tort 24, 233
Megone, C. 135
morally relevant differences 14, 158, 161, 167–70, 175, 202, 238
motives of regulatees 184–6
Mulligan, T. 128

multinational corporations (MNCs): application of inferior standards 13, 26, 30, 158–60, 163–6; definition 21, 57; difficult regulatory targets 2, 46, 50–2, 63, 200, 232; entry to and operations in developing countries 26, 45; evasion of accountability 2, 13, 212; influencing laws and policies 26–9, 191–2; regulation of activities at international level 6–8, 15, 17, 31, 214–20; regulatory dilemmas 50–63, 237–8; states' hesitation to regulate 5, 8, 51, 54, 201; subjects of international law 17; *see also* Bhopal chemical plant (UCC/UCIL); business dilemma; parent companies; regulatory initiatives; standards

'naming and shaming' 23, 61, 92, 142, 201, 207, 221, 225
National Contact Points (NCPs) 81–8, 114
national level regulation 208–14; *see also* extraterritorial regulation
negligence 34, 36, 44; contributory negligence 35, 170; duty of care 34, 62, 65
non-governmental organizations (NGOs)/civil society organizations 5, 54, 55, 78, 217; Amnesty International 31, 32–3, 36; criticisms of 219–20; Global Compact Board 96; Greenpeace 42; NCPs 85, 87; partnership 130; tripartism 193

OECD Guidelines 8, 17, 55–6, 58–9, 80, 96, 102, 112, 114–15, 117, 202, 215; 2011 update 85–8; drawbacks 82–5; positives of the 2000 review 80–2
Orlando, J. 124, 126

parens patriae 37
parent companies: enterprise *vs* entity responsibility 57–9; liability of 50, 57, 213–14; Union Carbide Corporation (UCC) 26–9, 38–9
Parker, C. 129
Parkinson, J. 141–2
preventative and redressive regulatory initiatives 47–50
prisoner's dilemma 10, 78, 120, 140–1, 143–6, 179, 210, 236
profit maximization 10–11, 22, 115, 126, 127, 131, 135–7, 151, 158, 160, 195, 211–12, 236; business approach to standards 158–60, 163–72
progressive enforcement pyramid 178–81; limitations 186–9
'protect, respect and remedy' framework 85, 104–11; 113–14, 239; *see also* Guiding Principles on Business and Human Rights
public interest groups (PIGs) 181–2

'race to the bottom' 81
Raz, J. 17
redressive and preventive regulatory initiatives 47–50
regulatees, motives of 184–6
regulatory dilemmas 50–2, 237–8
regulatory initiatives: analytical framework 46–63; content 55–7; enforcement 60–3; historical development 4–9; inadequacy 115–17; sources 53–5; target approach 57–9; taxonomy 13, 46, 52–63, 64–5; 'twin efficacy' test 47–50; *see also* extraterritorial regulation (and *specific regulatory initiatives*)
responsibilities/obligations: breadth and depth 55–7; of corporations 146–50; *vs* accountability 22–3; *see also* business case; corporate social responsibility (CSR); just business
responsive regulation 14, 22, 176–84, 198; *see also* integrated theory of regulation
Rome Statute 111, 219, 228
Ruggie, J. 105, 108; *see also* SRSG

sanctions: civil 225–6; criminal 227–9; social 229–31; in tandem application 225; types and severity 225; *see also* 'naming and shaming'
Secretary-General's Special Representative on human rights and transnational corporations and other business enterprises (SRSG) 8, 16, 85–86, 100, 103–5, 106, 108–14, 217, 239–40; *see also* Guiding Principles on Business and Human Rights
self-regulation 182–4; limitations 189–93
Sen, A. 124
separate legal personality principle 12, 36, 48, 50, 58, 104, 113, 117, 159, 212–13, 216, 239

settlement: as mercy/charity 48; mediated 84; opaqueness 25; out-of-court 6, 67, 74, 138, 187, 225–6; *see also* compensation
shareholders: as owners 121, 124–7, 132, 134; ethical attitude 130, 159; resolutions 36, 61, 207; taxation of 128; *see also* profit maximization
Shue, H. 91
social responsibilities of business 14, 119, 121–3, 127, 131–4, 139, 158, 236; *see also* corporate social responsibility (CSR)
social sanctions 48, 85, 88, 203, 210, 218–19, 225, 229–31, 239–40
sources of regulatory initiatives 53–5
stakeholder rights 160–3
stakeholder theory 121, 135, 161–3, 237
standards 152–3; business approach 158–60, 163–72; dilemma of variation 157–63; home 155–6; host 154–5; human approach 160–3, 172–5; international 156–7
Sternberg, E. 10, 14, 119, 121, 131–9, 146, 150, 186, 236
stockholder ownership 124–7
stockholder theory 120–1, 138–9
strict liability principle 35, 36
suppliers/supply chains 1, 4, 18, 21, 76–7, 80, 102, 161, 222, 226

target approach of regulatory initiatives 57–9
Teubner, G. 201
tort law 34–7, 60; *see also* Alien Tort Claims Act (ATCA); negligence; strict liability principle
tripartism 181–2
'twin efficacy' test 47–50, 64, 74, 79, 92, 104, 234

twin implementation strategies 220–5

Union Carbide Company/Union Carbide India Ltd (UCC/UCIL) *see* Bhopal chemical plant
United Nations Human Rights Norms 8, 17, 56, 58–9, 62; contributions 100–2; shortcomings 103–4; SRSG 85, 86, 100, 103; *see also* Global Compact; Guiding Principles on Business and Human Rights
Universal Declaration of Human Rights (UDHR) 7, 33, 90, 92, 101,

Victims: adequate relief 47–8, 234; bargaining position 74; *locus standi* 223–4; poor and ignorant 25, 37, 48; quest for justice 36–44; right to participate in proceedings 37, 41; *see also* access to justice obstacles, Bhopal; Bhopal chemical plant (UCC/UCIL); compensation; James Hardie; settlement
voluntary regulation: *vs* mandatory regulation 60–3; *see also* codes of conduct; self-regulation

Werner, W. 130, 211
World Bank 201, 217, 218
World Trade Organization (WTO) 3, 196, 217, 218

WWH (why, what and how) challenges 1–4, 22, 177, 235–40; existing regulatory initiatives 52–63; nature and interrelationship 9–12; *see also* integrated theory of regulation